PENGUIN HANDBOOKS

THE PENGUIN COOKERY BOOK

Bee Nilson was born in New Zealand where she received her professional training. After graduating as Bachelor of Home Science of the University of Otago, she came to England and settled in London where she has been teaching and writing about cookery and nutrition ever since. She is a State Registered Dietitian, a member of the British Dietetic Association, the New Zealand Dietetic Association, and the Nutrition Society. She also holds the Diploma in Education of London University.

During the war she was at the Ministry of Food and compiled the *A.B.C. of Cookery* and other Stationery Office Publications. Her other books include the Penguin Handbook *Cooking for Special Diets*, *The Book of Meat Cookery*, *Pears Family Cookbook*, and *Deep Freeze Cooking*.

· BEE NILSON

THE PENGUIN COOKERY BOOK

THIRD EDITION

PENGUIN BOOKS

Penguin Books Ltd, Harmondsworth, Middlesex, England
Penguin Books Inc., 7110 Ambassador Road, Baltimore, Maryland 21207, U.S.A.
Penguin Books Australia Ltd, Ringwood, Victoria, Australia
Penguin Books Canada Ltd, 41 Steelcase Road West, Markham, Ontario, Canada
Penguin Books (N.Z.) Ltd, 182–190 Wairau Road, Auckland 10, New Zealand

—

First published 1952
Reprinted 1953, 1954, 1955
Second edition 1959
Reprinted 1961, 1963, 1965, 1967, 1969, 1971
Third edition 1972
Reprinted 1973, 1974, 1975

—

Copyright © Bee Nilson, 1952, 1959, 1972

—

Made and printed in Great Britain
by Richard Clay (The Chaucer Press), Ltd,
Bungay, Suffolk
Set in Monotype Baskerville

Contents

Introduction 7

1. How to Use the Recipes 9

2. Glossary of Cooking Terms 18

3. Seasoning and Serving 25

4. Kitchen Equipment 28

5. Stocks and Soups 36

6. Sauces 49

7. Stuffings and Forcemeats 71

8. Fats and Frying 76

9. Milk, Cream, and Cheese 87

10. Eggs 100

11. Fish 119

12. Meat, Poultry, and Game 155

13. Vegetables, Herbs, and Salads 216

14. Fruit and Nuts 269

15. Cereals and Starch Foods 287

16. Sugar, Sweets, Icings, and Cake Fillings 305

17. Jellies and Aspic 320

18. Cakes, Puddings, Pastry, and Batters 329

19. Bread and Sandwiches 399

20. Beverages 414

21. Ice-cream and Frozen Puddings 424

22. Hors-d'œuvre and Savouries 431

CONTENTS

23. Planning and Preparing Meals   445

    Index   458

USING THE INDEX

The easiest and quickest way of finding any information in this book is to look in the Index. Here you will find all the ways of cooking any particular type of food grouped together. For example, under 'C' will be found all recipes using, as a principal ingredient, celery, cheese, chicken, chocolate, cocoa, coffee, and so on.

As the method I have used in this book does not lend itself to a separate section on puddings, you will find all the recipes suitable for puddings given in the Index under 'P'.

Introduction

This new edition has been completely revised and brought up to date. Many of the recipes are new and the others have been modernized. It is still a book for beginners, as well as a useful reference for the more experienced cook. The basic methods of cooking different kinds of foods are illustrated by recipes. These are simple to make, but interesting and varied, including traditional British recipes and recipes from other countries.

All recipes are given in both weights and measures. The use of standard measures as an alternative to weighing has been appreciated by the many cooks in this country who find measuring quicker than weighing, and by many readers overseas in countries where measuring is the traditional method of preparation. This edition makes the recipes useful to even more people by relating the weights and measures to the metric system. All temperatures are given in both Fahrenheit and Centigrade, with the equivalent gas number.

In most recipes I have kept to the method of giving ingredients in detail with a cross-reference to the basic method of preparation to be followed. This enables the book to be comprehensive while at the same time compact. Many readers have commented on this feature and the fact that so small a book covers the cooking of everything likely to be used in the average household.

The use of cross-references also means that the beginner, when in doubt about a cooking process, can turn immediately to the needed information.

Brides have told me that the simplicity of the book has given them confidence, and husbands have written of their appreciation of the results.

Bachelors, too, have taught themselves to cook from it and have liked the simple and precise instructions.

I hope this new edition will prove even more useful.

1971   BEE NILSON

CHAPTER I

How to Use the Recipes

1. Weights and Measures

With all foods normally purchased in known weights (fats, meats, fish, fruit, vegetables), I have given quantities in ounces or pounds followed by grams or kilograms in brackets. I believe this will help the housewife who is already familiar with the British system of weighing to adjust to using quantities of food purchased in metric weights.

These are not exact equivalents, but practical ones for cooking and shopping. For example, if you have been in the habit of using 4 ounces of fat in a recipe, in metric you will need about 125 grams. It can be marked off from a pat of known size sold in grams, in the same way as you have always done with pats sold in ounces.

With items such as flour, sugar, cereals, and so on, where one normally buys a packet and uses small amounts at a time, I have given the alternative to ounces as spoons or cups. The cup and spoon measures used have the following values:

1 cup = ½ pint or 10 fluid ounces. (The metric equivalent is 284 millilitres, so a scant 300-ml. measure will be the alternative in metric.)

1 tablespoon = 15 millilitres and is the size of a medicinal tablespoon (marked on a medicinal glass).

1 teaspoon = 5 millilitres and is the size of the medicinal teaspoon.

The spoons used for testing the original recipes in earlier editions of this book were the old British Standards Institution standard kitchen measuring spoons. Compared with the 15-millilitre tablespoon and 5-millilitre teaspoon the sizes were 17·7 and 5·9 millilitres respectively. It will be seen from the Table of Weights and Measures, No. 5, that the millilitre is a very tiny measure and I find that using a slightly smaller spoon does not noticeably affect the results when one is using level measures.

2. How to Measure

Using level measures is the easiest and most accurate way of measuring. Heaped measures are not reliable, as a heaped spoon can hold anything from three to five times as much as a level one, depending on the way it is heaped. The rounded spoon is used by many cooks, but I have found this method slow and inaccurate when compared with the level measure. In the time taken to measure a rounded spoon (as much above the bowl as below) several level spoons can be measured with greater accuracy.

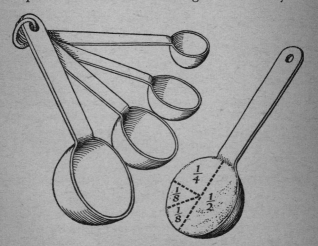

A LEVEL SPOON is one in which the contents are levelled off to the rim of the spoon by running the straight edge of a knife along the top. To measure fractions of spoons use the small measures provided in measuring sets or divide the spoon as shown in the accompanying diagram.

A LEVEL CUP of dry ingredients is measured by spooning the ingredients in lightly to heap it a little, and then levelling off with the straight edge of a knife. If the ingredients are packed by dipping the cup into the bag or tin, or by shaking down, the measure will not be the same as indicated in the recipes. Fats, syrups, and jam should be well packed.

TO MEASURE FATS easily, mark the pat when you buy it, making half, quarter, and smaller markings. You will then be able to see how much to cut off for the various weights needed in the recipes.

3. American Measures

1 USA cup	= 8 fluid ounces = approximately 227 ml.
1 USA tablespoon	= $\frac{1}{2}$ fluid ounce = approximately 14 ml.
1 USA teaspoon	= $\frac{1}{6}$ fluid ounce = approximately 5 ml.
1 USA pint	= 16 fluid ounces.

This means that if American standard measuring cups and spoons are used with these recipes, the spoons can be taken as interchangeable with the British ones, but you will need to use $1\frac{1}{4}$ times the number of British cups.

4. How to Weigh

When using scales with loose weights, place the required weight in the centre of one pan of the scales and the food in the other. When the correct weight is in, the pans should see-saw up and down, and not be down permanently on one side. To weigh sticky things like syrup and fat, sprinkle the pan lightly with a little flour before putting in the food.

5. Table of Weights and Measures

BRITISH

1 pound	= 16 ounces
1 pint	= 20 fluid ounces
1/4 pint	= 1 gill = 10 tablespoons
1/8 pint	= 1/2 gill = 5 tablespoons
1 quart	= 2 pints
1 gallon	= 4 quarts = 8 pints

METRIC

1 kilogram	= 1,000 grams
1 litre	= 1,000 millilitres = 10 decilitres
1 metre	= 100 centimetres = 1,000 millimetres

CONVERSION TABLE

1 ounce	= 28·35 grams
1 pound	= 453·6 grams = approximately 1/2 kilogram
1 fluid ounce	= 28·41 millilitres
1 pint	= 568·2 millilitres = approximately 1/2 litre
1 inch	= 2·54 centimetres = 25·4 millimetres

6. Abbreviations Used in the Recipes

tsp.	= teaspoon	temp.	= temperature
Tbs.	= tablespoon	g.	= gram(s)
c.	= cup	kg.	= kilogram
pt.	= pint	cm.	= centimetre
qt.	= quart	mm.	= millimetre
lb.	= pound	l.	= litre
oz.	= ounce	dl.	= decilitre
S.R.	= self-raising	ml.	= millilitre

7. How to Follow a Recipe

1. Assemble the ingredients you require, checking them carefully with the recipe. Unless you are an experienced

cook, it is not wise to omit ingredients, substitute others, or alter the quantities.

2. Assemble all the mixing and cooking utensils you will need.

3. Do as much preparation as possible before starting the actual cooking – for example, measure out the ingredients, peel and chop vegetables, grease cake-tins, etc.

4. If the oven is to be used, be sure it is heated in time and that the oven-racks are in the correct positions.

5. Most recipes for four can be halved, or the amounts can be increased by half as much again for six, or doubled for eight. It is important to remember that, for sauces and milk puddings which are to be boiled, the amount of evaporation will be proportionately greater with a small amount and the mixture will be thicker. Conversely, with double the recipe a little more thickening or less liquid may be needed. When the quantities of cake mixtures are altered, the size of the tins and the cooking times will need altering too.

8. Shopping Suggestions

Keep a pad and pencil in the kitchen to make a note when any supplies are nearly finished. This, plus a menu plan for at least a week, will help to reduce the number of times you need to shop. If you have the facilities for long storage (a good-sized store cupboard, refrigerator and freezer), you can obviously buy in larger quantities less frequently than with more modest storage facilities.

The following list shows the average safe storage life for foods under different conditions. This enables you to see where you, personally, can safely shop ahead. You will find more information on the storage of foods in each chapter under **General Information**.

Foods suitable for storage in a dry kitchen cupboard:

DRY STORES, e.g. flour, sugar, packet foods, canned and bottled foods, if in airtight containers or unopened packets, will keep for many weeks.

BISCUITS in unopened packets or airtight containers, several weeks.

BREAD, BUNS AND ROLLS in polythene bags or airtight containers, 3–4 days; in the freezer, a month.

CAKES in an airtight wrapper or container, a week or more depending on variety; in freezer, a month or more.

Foods needing cool or cold storage (approx. 40° F. or 5° C.): This means refrigeration, or a cold larder in the winter months.

CHEESE : hard or boxed cheese will keep in a cupboard for up to a week, 2–4 weeks in a polythene wrapper in the refrigerator; soft and cream cheese will keep a week in the refrigerator.

EGGS will keep several days in a cupboard, 2 weeks in a refrigerator.

FATS (butter, margarine, lard, etc.), several weeks in the refrigerator, a month or more in the freezer.

FISH (fresh or smoked), 1–3 days in the refrigerator, several weeks in the freezer.

FRUIT : soft fruit 1–3 days in the refrigerator, a year in the freezer; other fruit a week or more in a cool room, several weeks in the refrigerator, a year in the freezer.

MEAT, GAME AND POULTRY : sausages, 3 days in refrigerator, a month in the freezer; sliced bacon, a week in the refrigerator; cooked meats and pies, 24 hours in the refrigerator, home-cooked, 1–3 days; fresh meat, 2–5 days in the refrigerator, a month or more in the freezer.

MILK AND CREAM, 3–5 days in the refrigerator.

VEGETABLES : green vegetables up to a week in the refrigerator; root vegetables in a cool, dark store, or in the refrigerator, for several weeks.

9. Quantities of Food to Buy for Average Portions

Fish	*Amount per person*
Crabs	1 small
Cutlets	½ lb. (250 g.)
Fillets	6–8 oz. (250 g.)
Fish, whole	½–¾ lb. (250 g.)
Lobster	½–¾ lb. (250 g.)
Mussels	1 pt. (½ l.)
Prawns	½ pt. (¼ l.)

Fruit for cooking	4–8 oz. (125–250 g.)

Meat (see also No. 322)

Cooked	2–3 oz. (50 g.)
With bone	½–¾ lb. (250 g.)
Without bone	4–6 oz. (125 g.)

Vegetables

Artichokes, globe	1
Artichokes, Jerusalem	½ lb. (250 g.)
Asparagus	6–8 pieces
Beans, broad	¾–1 lb. (500 g.)
Beans, dried	2–4 oz. (50–125 g.)
Beans, French or runner	6–8 oz. (250 g.)
Beetroot	6–8 oz. (250 g.)
Brussels Sprouts, Cabbage, Savoy	6–8 oz. (250 g.)
Carrots	6–8 oz. (250 g.)
Celery	½ head
Celeriac	6–8 oz. (250 g.)
Chicory	4 oz. (125 g.)
Kale	½ lb. (250 g.)
Kohl Rabi	6–8 oz. (250 g.)

Vegetables	Amount per person
Leeks	$\frac{1}{2}-\frac{3}{4}$ lb. (250 g.)
Marrow	$\frac{1}{2}-\frac{3}{4}$ lb. (250 g.)
Mushrooms	2–4 oz. (50–125 g.)
Parsnips	6–8 oz. (250 g.)
Peas	$\frac{1}{2}$ lb. (250 g.)
Peas, dried	2–4 oz. (50–125 g.)
Potatoes	$\frac{1}{2}$ lb. (250 g.)
Spinach	$\frac{1}{2}$ lb. (250 g.)
Swedes and Turnips	6–8 oz. (250 g.)
Tomatoes	4–6 oz. (125 g.)
Watercress	1–2 oz. (25–50 g.)

10. Quantities of Cooked Dishes to Allow

	Amount per person
Custards	$\frac{1}{4}$ pt. milk (125 ml.)
Jellies	$\frac{1}{4}-\frac{1}{3}$ pt. (125 ml.)
Milk Puddings	$\frac{1}{4}-\frac{1}{3}$ pt. milk (125 ml.)
Pastry	2 oz. flour (50 g.)
Sauces	$\frac{1}{8}-\frac{1}{4}$ pt. liquid (125 ml.)
Soups	$\frac{1}{3}-\frac{1}{2}$ pt. (250 ml.)
Steamed Puddings	2 oz. flour (50 g.)

11. Temperatures

	°F.	°C.
Freezer storage	0	−18
Refrigerator	40–50	5–10
Freezing water	32	0
Tepid or lukewarm	90–100	30–35
Simmering	185	85
Boiling	212	100

For fat temperatures see No. 149 and for sugar temperatures see No. 660.

OVEN TEMPERATURES vary a great deal and it is always advisable to follow the instructions provided by the makers. You will find temperatures are given with the individual recipes. These are meant as a guide only, and will vary with different ovens.

The following table will be found a useful guide:

	Electric (°F.)	(°C.)	Gas mark
VERY SLOW OVEN	250–275	120–140	$\frac{1}{4}$–$\frac{1}{2}$
SLOW	300–325	150–160	1–2
MODERATE	350–375	180–190	3–5
MODERATELY HOT	375–400	190–200	5–6
HOT	400–425	200–220	6–7
VERY HOT	450–475	230–250	8–9

CHAPTER 2

Glossary of Cooking Terms

12. Terms Used in the Recipes

AU GRATIN. A food is prepared au gratin when it is covered with sauce, then sprinkled with breadcrumbs and dotted with fat, after which it is browned in the oven or under the grill. It is served in the cooking-dish, and may have cheese mixed with either the sauce or the crumbs.

BAKING. Any food cooked in the oven may be called 'baked', but the term is most generally used for cakes, pastry, meat, fish, and vegetables, cooked in the oven without liquid or with a little fat.

When learning how to use a new oven it is always advisable to follow the instructions provided by the maker.

With most ovens best results are obtained if only foods requiring about the same temperature are cooked together. Dishes should not be crowded too close to one another, or the circulation of hot air will be stopped and baking will be uneven. Baking trays should not fill the oven space completely but should leave room for heat to circulate.

BASTING means keeping the surface of food moist by spooning liquid or melted fat over it at frequent intervals.

BEATING is vigorous mixing with a wooden spoon or an egg-whisk to make a mixture smooth and beat air into it.

BLANCHING. One method of blanching is to dip the food in boiling water for a minute and then into cold water. This method is used to remove the skins from fruit, tomatoes, nuts, etc. A second method is used for preparing offal for cooking. The food is put in cold water to cover, brought to the boil, drained, and again put in cold water to cover. In some cases the food is cooked a little before draining.

BLENDING is used to describe the thorough mixing of ingredients, especially mixing flour or starch to a paste with cold liquid. Add liquid gradually, as too much at the beginning causes lumps which are difficult to remove.

BOILING. This means cooking food in boiling liquid, but many foods are called 'boiled' when they are actually cooked below boiling point – that is, 'simmered' or 'poached'. When boiling, use only sufficient heat to keep the liquid bubbling gently. Violent boiling wastes fuel and spoils the appearance of the food. It is used only when a liquid is to be 'reduced' or made thicker by evaporation of water, which takes place more quickly with rapid boiling.

BOUQUET GARNI. This is usually made up of a small sprig of thyme, a small bay leaf, and two sprigs of parsley, tied together with thread; or their equivalent in dried herbs tied in muslin. It is used for flavouring soups, stock, stews, and other savoury dishes.

BRAISING. See No. 404.

BREADCRUMBS. See No. 876.

BRUSH WITH EGG OR MILK. A pastry brush is used to cover the surface of foods such as scones or pastry with a coating of egg or milk before baking. This improves their appearance. See also 'Glaze'.

CASSEROLE. Any heat-resisting baking-dish with a lid may be called a casserole. It is used for cooking all sorts of food in the oven, and the food is usually served in the casserole.

CEREALS. See No. 612.

COAT. To cover with a thin layer.

CONSISTENCY. This is the term used to describe the thickness of a mixture, as with cakes and batters; see No. 726.

CREAMING. This means beating until the mixture is of the consistency of cream. 'Creamed' fat and sugar are beaten until they look like whipped cream. 'Creamed' fat is softened and made smooth by beating.

CROÛTONS. These are small cubes or squares of toasted

or fried bread used for garnishing soup and savoury dishes.

CUT AND FOLD. This method is used for combining two mixtures without beating. One mixture is folded over the other by turning gently with a spoon. The cutting is done by occasionally passing the spoon down through the centre of the mixture. These actions are repeated gently until the ingredients are well mixed.

DICE are small cubes. The easiest way of dicing food is to cut it in thin strips and then cut the strips across to make the dice.

DISSOLVE. Some foods, such as sugar or salt, 'dissolve' when mixed with a liquid.

DOT means to cover with small pieces, generally fat.

DREDGE means to sprinkle lightly. Special containers or 'dredgers' with perforated tops are used for flour or sugar; but a tin the lid of which has been pierced with holes will do.

DRIPPING. Fat from cooked meat, or that rendered down from raw fat, is called dripping. See Nos. 138–9.

DRY INGREDIENTS include flour, sugar, salt, spices, and so on, but not fat, liquid, syrup, jam, etc.

FILLET. When fish is boned, the pieces are called 'fillets', see No. 236.

With meat the word refers to a special cut, without bone, which is used for frying or grilling, see No. 325.

GARNISH. Trimming or decoration.

GLAZE. A food is glazed when it is brushed with liquid to give a shiny surface. Egg and milk glazes are brushed on before cooking; sugar and water is put on 10–15 minutes before cooking is finished. See No. 661. For meat glaze see No. 717.

GRATE. Food is grated when it is shaved into small shreds on a grater. There are many different graters, but for general purposes the kinds required are: fine, for nutmegs and onion juice; medium, for lemon or orange rind, cheese, and breadcrumbs; coarse, for vegetables and suet.

GRILL. Grilled food is cooked by direct red heat. A grill is also useful for browning the tops of savoury dishes and for making toast. For details of grilling consult the index.

KNEAD. To pummel or work a dough lightly with the knuckles to give a smooth texture.

MARINADE. A mixture of vinegar, oil, and seasoning in which meat is sometimes soaked before cooking. See No. 369.

MIXING. Combining ingredients by continuous stirring.

PARBOILING. Boiling for only part of the usual time. Cooking is then finished some other way.

POACHING. Cooking in liquid below boiling point, see Nos. 189–92, 237, 589.

PULSES. Dried peas and beans, lentils, and split peas.

PURÉE. A fine pulp obtained by rubbing cooked food through a sieve, or by pulping in an electric liquidizer or blender.

SCALD. This may mean to heat a liquid to just under boiling point, as with milk, see No. 155, or to pour on boiling water.

SEAR. To brown or form a coating on the surface of meat by using a fierce heat for a short time.

SEASONED FLOUR. Flour mixed with salt and pepper, and used for dusting meat and fish before cooking. Mix 1 level Tbs. salt, ¾ level tsp. pepper, and 1 c. flour. Keep in a dredger ready for use.

SEASONING. Generally salt and pepper, but may include other flavourings.

SIFT. Pass through a sieve or flour sifter to remove lumps and mix the ingredients well, at the same time aerating the mixture.

SIMMER. Cook below boiling point – about 185° F. (85° C.). Only an occasional bubble or agitation appears on the surface of the liquid.

SKEWER. A metal or wooden pin used for fastening food together, as in trussing poultry.

TEPID. Just warm to the finger. A mixture of two parts of cold water and one part of boiling water gives about the right heat, 80° F. (30° C.).

WHIPPING. The same as beating, but generally used for cream and eggs.

13. French Cooking Terms

ANGLAISE, or À L'ANGLAISE, means to cook plainly in water or to coat in egg and breadcrumbs before frying.

AU BEURRE NOIR means with Brown Butter Sauce, see No. 111.

AU FROMAGE means with cheese.

AU GRATIN, see No. 12.

BAIN-MARIE is a container of hot water in which other utensils are stood to keep hot, e.g. sauces.

BEIGNETS are fritters.

BLANQUETTE is a stew of white meat which starts with a roux sauce, and then the meat and vegetables are cooked in it. Cream or egg is added to the sauce before serving.

BOUQUET GARNI, see No. 12.

BROCHETTES are small pieces of meat threaded on skewers and grilled, similar to Lamb Shashlik, see No. 372.

CIVET DE LIÈVRE is similar to jugged hare, see No. 351.

COLBERT, or À LA COLBERT, means served with a sauce similar to Parsley Butter, No. 123.

COMPÔTE, or EN COMPÔTE, means stewed, generally fruit, see No. 589.

CONDÉ, or À LA CONDÉ, means served with sweet rice cooked in milk, see No. 642.

CONSOMMÉ is a clear meat stock.

CÔTELETTE is a cutlet or chop.

COURT-BOUILLON is a mixture of water, vegetables, seasoning, and wine or vinegar, used for boiling fish, see No. 237.

CRÈME DE MENTHE is peppermint flavouring, see No. 705.

CUIT AU BEURRE means cooked with butter.

DORÉ is a special method of cooking fish, see No. 263.

ESCALOPE is a very thin slice of meat, most often a slice of veal from the top of the leg, see No. 384.

FLORENTINE, or À LA FLORENTINE, means cooked or served with spinach.

FRICASSÉE is like a Blanquette, but the meat is fried before being put in the sauce to cook. In English cooking the word is often used for a dish in which cooked meat is reheated in a sauce and then served with bacon rolls, see No. 423.

FRIT is fried, generally in deep fat.

HACHI means minced.

JARDINIÈRE means a garnish of several different kinds of cooked vegetables, arranged in separate heaps, see No. 412, or cooked together, see No. 438.

LYONNAISE means cooked with onions, see No. 466.

MACÉDOINE is a mixture of fruit or vegetables, see No. 437.

MARINADE, see No. 12.

MEUNIÈRE, or À LA MEUNIÈRE, is a special way of cooking fish, see Nos. 263 and 267.

MIREPOIX is a mixture of chopped vegetables with ham or bacon and herbs, used for flavouring meat and poultry during cooking.

MORNAY is with a cheese sauce, see No. 190.

PARMENTIER means cooked with potatoes as part of the dish.

PORTUGAISE, or À LA PORTUGAISE, means cooked or served with tomatoes.

POT AU FEU is boiled beef with vegetables. The stock is used for soup.

PURÉE, or EN PURÉE, means rubbed through a sieve to make a pulp.

RAGOÛT is similar to a stew, but the liquid is first made into a sauce by the roux method, and the other ingredients are then added and cooked in the sauce.

ROBE DE CHAMBRE, or EN ROBE DE CHAMBRE, means in the skin or without peeling.

RÔTI means roasted.

ROUX is a mixture of melted fat and flour which forms the basis of most sauces, see No. 69.

SAUTÉ means fried in shallow fat, see No. 148.

TOURNEDOS is a special piece of steak for frying or grilling, see No. 368.

VINAIGRETTE is a mixture of oil, vinegar, and seasonings, see No. 119.

VOL-AU-VENT is a puff pastry case, see No. 810.

CHAPTER 3

Seasoning and Serving

14. The Use of Seasonings and Flavourings

Good cooking is not necessarily achieved by the preparation of expensive and elaborate dishes, but is built on a foundation of simple dishes perfectly cooked, seasoned, and served. Many cooks either leave flavouring out of all dishes, in which case their cooking is dull and tasteless, or they overdo it and drown the natural flavour of the food. The art of good seasoning is to use enough to improve the flavour of a food, not to mask it. There are some exceptions to this general rule – for example, curries and goulash; but even here the effect is obtained by a clever blending of many different flavourings.

Seasonings have no real food value, but they have an important part to play in good nutrition. They make food more appetizing, causing the digestive juices to flow freely and to digest the food properly, so that the body obtains full value from it.

It is advisable to buy only small amounts of spices and flavourings at a time, as they become stale with keeping. Always store them in air-tight jars. If you have a garden or window-box you will be able to grow fresh herbs of all kinds; but if not, small amounts of dried herbs may be used in most cases in place of the fresh.

The following is a list of flavourings and seasonings mentioned in the recipes. Suggestions for using different herbs will be found in Chapter 13, 'Vegetables'.

Bay leaves   Celery salt and seed
Capers   Chillies
Cayenne pepper   Chives

Cinnamon
Cloves
Curry powder
Flavouring essences,
     various
Garlic
Ginger
Horse-radish
Lemon-rind and juice
Mace
Marjoram
Mint
Mustard

Nutmeg
Onions
Orange rind and juice
Paprika pepper
Parsley
Pepper
Sage
Salt
Sugar
Thyme
Vinegar (wine, cider, or
     malt)

15. Serving and Garnishing

Many otherwise excellent dishes are spoilt by being badly served, the plates cold when they should be hot, food thrown or tipped on to the dishes, instead of being attractively arranged, and so on.

On the other hand, many dishes are spoilt because the cook has devoted time that should have been spent in preparation and cooking to over-decorating and ornamenting the dish. This is one of the most common failings of cooks who persuade themselves that if a dish is well decorated or 'finished', to use the technical term, it must be superior. The first-class cook is one who has learnt to prepare food perfectly, to flavour it with imagination and discretion, and to serve it simply, yet in an eye-appealing and appetizing manner.

16. Suggestions for Serving

For hot food always have well-heated dishes, and make sure the food is hot when it comes to the table. Too much time spent in decorating hot dishes generally means they are cold by the time they are served. Good effects can be obtained by using colour – serving in coloured dishes or with vegetables of contrasting colours. Many a dish can be improved by serving the meat on a big platter with coloured vegetables round it, instead of in their separate vegetable dishes.

Try to avoid serving white or pale foods in plain white dishes. Make white foods attractive by sprinkling on a little paprika pepper, chopped parsley, or other herbs, and for sweet dishes decorate with coloured jam or fruit.

With most of the recipes in this book I have suggested ways of serving the dish to make it attractive, and sauces and other accompaniments to go with it.

CHAPTER 4

Kitchen Equipment

17. Equipment for Preparing Simple Meals

2 small stew pans
2 large stew pans
1 frying pan
1 kettle
1 roasting pan (usually supplied with cooker)
2 pie-dishes
2 casseroles with lids
4 basins, assorted sizes
1 pair kitchen scales and/or kitchen measures
1 set measuring spoons
1 round strainer
1 colander
2 wooden spoons or stirrers
1 perforated spoon
1 fish slice
1 basting spoon
1 ladle

1 chopping knife
1 vegetable knife
1 palette knife
1 knife sharpener
1 cook's fork
1 pair kitchen scissors
1 can opener
1 corkscrew
1 grater
1 chopping board
1 potato masher or ricer
Salt and pepper shakers or grinders
1 saucepan cleaner – nylon or steel wool pads
1 refuse bin with lid
Kitchen cloths, oven cloths, swabs, nylon brushes

18. Equipment for Cake- and Pastry-making and for more Elaborate Cooking

3 round cake tins, assorted sizes
2 sandwich tins
1 flan ring
1 set bun tins

1 oblong or square cake tin
1 loaf tin
1 Swiss roll tin
2 baking trays
1 set piping tubes and bag

1 wire egg whisk
1 pastry brush
1 wire cake cooler
1 set biscuit cutters, fluted
1 set biscuit cutters, plain
1 biscuit forcer
1 rolling pin
1 flour and/or sugar dredger
1 double boiler

1 steamer
1 omelet pan
1 ring or border mould
1 jelly mould
1 pie plate
4–6 individual pudding moulds
1 pie funnel
1 sugar or fat thermometer
1 frying basket

19. Useful Labour-saving Equipment

1 potato peeler
1 grapefruit knife
1 boning knife
1 apple corer
1 garlic press
1 egg slicer
1 lemon squeezer or juice extractor

1 coffee maker
1 electric coffee grinder
1 hand-operated or electric shredder
1 hand-held electric beater
1 electric blender
1 electric mincer

The electric equipment already listed is the most useful to have but there are many others available as individual items or as attachments for a large mixer.

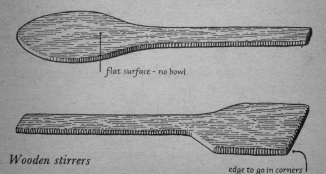

flat surface - no bowl

Wooden stirrers

edge to go in corners

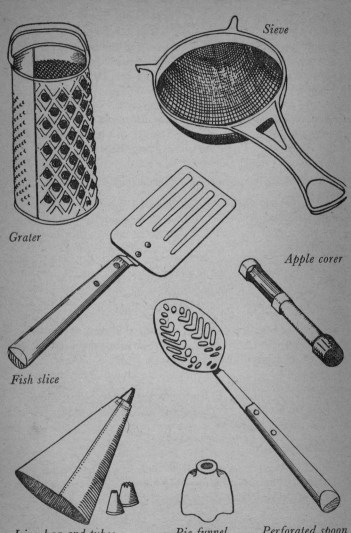

Grater

Sieve

Fish slice

Apple corer

Icing bag and tubes

Pie funnel

Perforated spoon

20. Choice of Kitchen Utensils

Having the right utensil of good quality can make the difference between success or failure, and it most certainly does make a great difference to the amount of time and labour involved. Other craftsmen who handle tools – such as carpenters, builders, engineers, etc. – all know it is difficult to obtain good results with shoddy and inadequate equipment. It is just the same with cooking. When buying new equipment it is, therefore, important to know how to choose wisely, and I hope the following tips will help the inexperienced.

21. Saucepans

No matter what kind of cooker you use, it is important to have good thick pans. Thin pans buckle with the heat, make food stick and burn, and are an endless source of worry and hard work. Aluminium or stainless steel are the most hard-wearing. If enamel pans are preferred, they should be very good quality, as poor enamel soon chips. Good pans have well-fitting lids and insulated handles, so that they do not become too hot. They should also be smooth in all joints, without crevices and dents, which are hard to keep clean. Pans which are specially treated to make them non-stick are ideal for easy washing-up, but it is important to buy ones of good quality and to use them with care.

22. Frying-pans

It is even more important that these should be thick and heavy. Thin frying-pans soon buckle, and food burns in one spot and does not cook in another.

Scales and Measures. See Nos. 1–5.

23. Kitchen Knives and Cutting Tools

Good, sharp knives save endless time, so it is advisable to buy the best you can find and keep them sharp. Cooking with ordinary table knives is very difficult, as well as being hard on the knives. A potato peeler is useful for many vegetables and, once you have the knack of using it, is much faster and better than an ordinary vegetable knife.

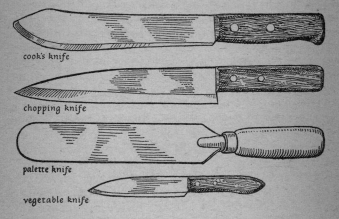

cook's knife

chopping knife

palette knife

vegetable knife

24. Cake tins, Roasting pans, and Baking trays

Aluminium cake tins with a non-stick surface are the best to use. For small cakes use aluminium bun tins, paper cases or foil cases. If there is no roasting pan provided with your cooker buy one of good quality aluminium or steel. Baking trays of aluminium, with turned-up edges, are the best for most ovens and these can also be used for making Swiss rolls.

25. Pie-dishes and Casseroles

These can be of heat-resisting glass or china, enamel, aluminium, or steel. The most useful casseroles are those which can be used on top of the stove as well as in the oven, and which are sufficiently attractive to be sent to the table. The lids should fit well. Sometimes the lids are suitable for using alone as baking-dishes for fish, tomatoes, and other similar foods.

26. Electric Cooking Utensils

These include power-driven beaters, mixers, blenders (or liquidizers), sieves, mincers, potato peelers, juice extractors, shredders, coffee grinders and knife sharpeners. Portable frying pans, stew pans and others are useful for table-cooking and to extend the range of your cooker-top. Which of these utensils will be really useful to you depends on the kind and range of cooking you do.

As a beginning I think a good portable electric beater is the most useful. This does all the beating jobs such as creaming fat and sugar, beating eggs, sauces and batters, and, being portable, it can be used in any mixing bowl and in saucepans on the cooker. It will not mix dough or do heavy jobs like adding flour and fruit to large cakes.

For other jobs there are either separate machines for particular uses or you can buy a basic mixing machine with the attachments you need. Two or three specialist machines can, however, be a better buy than one large one which is never fully used.

27. The Care of Cooking Utensils

1. Always wash and rinse well, as dirty utensils spoil the flavour of food cooked in them. To make cleaning easy put all utensils to soak as soon as they are finished with. Those used for flour mixtures, fish, egg, and milk should be soaked in cold water, as hot tends to make the food stick.

2. If food sticks or burns, soak the dishes well before attempting to clean them. Then use fine steel wool or a nylon pot scraper.

3. Never pour cold liquid into a very hot pan or dish. Either cool the pan or heat the liquid.

4. To obtain a smooth surface on frying-pans, for omelets and pancakes, rub the dry pan with cooking salt and a piece of paper.

ALUMINIUM. Do not use soda or strong washing-powders, as these tend to pit the surface, as does failure to dry the pans properly. Fine steel wool is the best thing to use for cleaning aluminium, or use nylon pads.

GLASS, EARTHENWARE, AND CHINA. If food sticks, soak until it can be removed easily and avoid scratching by scouring. Do not plunge a hot dish into cold water.

ENAMEL. Avoid scouring, as this scratches the enamel. If the pan has burnt, boil salt water in it several times until the burn has softened enough to remove without scratching. Once the surface has been scratched, foods burn more readily. Do not use chipped enamel utensils, as small bits are likely to come off into the food. An empty pan should never be put on a hot stove, or the enamel will chip.

STEEL. Avoid scratching with scourers and always dry well.

TIN. Avoid harsh scouring which scratches the tin and always dry well to prevent rust. Dry with a cloth and then stand in a warm place.

WOOD. Scour well and dry thoroughly. Fine steel wool is good for cleaning wood.

NON-STICK PANS. It is important to follow the maker's instructions for their use and care, otherwise the non-stick coating may be damaged.

28. Pressure Cookers

These are time- and fuel-savers, and can be a great help to the busy housewife. There are many different types, each sold with detailed instructions for use. These should be followed carefully.

Though many people use pressure cookers for cooking

vegetables, the greatest saving in time is made with dishes which usually take $\frac{3}{4}$ hour or longer to cook; for example, making soups and stock, boiling beetroot, stewing, braising, boiling meat, and cooking dried peas, beans, and lentils.

In a number of such recipes I have indicated the times I use for pressure cooking. These are intended as a guide only, and may need adjusting with different cookers. As a general rule the time required in a pressure cooker is $\frac{1}{4}$–$\frac{1}{3}$ of that needed for boiling in a saucepan.

CHAPTER 5

Stocks and Soups

29. Food Value

Soups range from the clear consommé – a well-flavoured stock with various garnishes – to the thick Scotch Broth and American Chowders. In between are the vegetable soups and the very useful cream soups suitable for the first course of a light meal or for a supper dish for the children, being an excellent way of giving them more milk and vegetables.

The food value of soups depends on the ingredients used. A soup made only of stock has very little food value, but does serve to stimulate the appetite. On the other hand, soups containing milk, cheese, meat or fish, and vegetables can be nourishing enough to make a meal in themselves.

30. General Information

The old method of making household stock from meat and bones has been replaced in many modern homes by the use of meat cubes, meat or vegetable extract, bone stock, vegetable stock or canned consommé. A stock which is suitable for most dishes can be made by using meat or vegetable extract mixed with either vegetable or bone stock. It is important, however, to choose a good extract, as some have such a pronounced flavour that they spoil the flavour of the stock, instead of improving it. There are some excellent extracts on the market, and it is worth while spending the extra money to buy one of good quality.

Stocks and soups do not keep well in hot weather, and must be used up quickly or boiled up every day. They will keep for some days in a refrigerator but should be covered to prevent the flavour from mixing with other foods, and to prevent evaporation.

Stock which has been boiled to concentrate it can be frozen in an ice-cube tray and the cubes stored in a polythene bag in the freezer. Soups, too, can be stored in the freezer.

Always taste a soup before serving, to make sure it is well seasoned, and serve it hot. If it is a white soup, such as potato, it can be made more attractive by adding small cubes of fried bread or toast, chopped parsley, paprika pepper, or other garnish.

31. Bone Stock. Cooking time 2–3 hours or $\frac{3}{4}$ hour pressure cooking

Use any kind of bones, cooked or uncooked. Put them in a saucepan with cold water to cover. Bring to the boil and skim. For each pint of water add 1 onion, 1 carrot, and a bouquet garni, see No. 12. Cover the pan and simmer very slowly or pressure cook. Strain and, when cold, remove the fat. Add this to your stock of fat for clarifying.

32. Quickly Made Stock

Dissolve meat or soup cubes or meat or vegetable extract in boiling water or vegetable water. Generally allow 1 cube or 1 level tsp. extract to $\frac{1}{2}$ pt. water (1 c.), but for exact amounts follow the instructions of the maker.

33. Vegetable Stock. Cooking time 20–30 minutes or 5–10 minutes pressure cooking

Use any mixture of vegetables, such as the outside leaves of cabbage, cauliflower stalks, outside celery stalks and leaves, green tops of leeks, watercress stalks, mushroom stalks and peelings, and any other vegetables available. Chop or shred them finely, and add boiling water to come three-quarters of the way up the vegetables. Add a few bacon rinds, a bouquet garni, a few peppercorns, and one or two cloves. Cover and boil or pressure cook. Strain and use.

34. Fish Stock. Cooking time 20 minutes

Use fish bones, heads, skin, and other trimmings. Cover with cold water, and for each ½ lb. (250 g.) of trimmings add 1 small onion, 1 clove, ¼ bay leaf, and a small sprig of parsley. Cover the pan and boil for 20 minutes. Strain and use for fish soups, or sauces to serve with fish.

35. Mushroom Stock. Cooking time 10–15 minutes

Use the stalks and peelings of mushrooms. Wash them well and put in a pan with water to cover. Boil for 10–15 minutes and then strain.

36. Recipe for Mixed Vegetable Soup. Cooking time about ¾ hour or 10 minutes pressure cooking

Quantities for 4–5 helpings:

1 lb. mixed vegetables (500 g.) (e.g. 1 onion, 1 carrot, 2 or 3 cabbage leaves, piece of swede or turnip, 1 stalk of celery, 1 small parsnip)	1 oz. dripping (25 g.) 2 pt. stock (4 c.) 2–3 tsp. salt Pinch of pepper 4 Tbs. grated cheese

Measures level.

1. Prepare and slice the vegetables. Cabbage should be sliced finely and then cut across in two or three places to give short pieces.

2. Melt the dripping in a saucepan and add the vegetables. Put on the lid and cook gently for about 15 minutes without browning. Shake the pan occasionally to prevent sticking.

3. Add the stock and seasoning and boil gently until the vegetables are tender.

4. The soup may be served as it is or with the vegetables rubbed through a sieve or put in a blender. Taste for seasoning, and serve the cheese separately, to be sprinkled on at the table.

37. Minestrone

Make in the same way as Mixed Vegetable Soup, No. 36, adding one or two tomatoes or $\frac{1}{2}$ c. tomato juice or purée, and $\frac{1}{4}$ c. spaghetti or broken macaroni with the stock. Serve with cheese.

38. Artichoke Soup. Cooking time $\frac{1}{2}$–$\frac{3}{4}$ hour or 10 minutes pressure cooking

Quantities for 4–5 helpings:

1$\frac{1}{2}$ lb. Jerusalem artichokes (6 large)	1$\frac{1}{2}$ pt. vegetable stock (3 c.)
	Pinch of pepper
1 onion	$\frac{1}{2}$ pt. milk (1 c.)
1 stalk celery	1–2 tsp. salt
1 oz. fat or dripping (25 g.)	

Measures level. Cook in the same way as Mixed Vegetable Soup, No. 36. When cooked, rub through a sieve or put in a blender, and reheat with the milk and seasoning. Taste for seasoning. Serve with chopped parsley sprinkled on, or with croûtons of fried or toasted bread.

39. Mock Oyster Soup

Make in the same way as Artichoke Soup, No. 38, but use Fish Stock, No. 34, instead of the vegetable stock.

40. Leek Soup. Cooking time 20–30 minutes

Quantities for 4–5 helpings:

8 oz. leeks (4 small or 2 large)	1 tsp. salt
	Pinch of pepper
½ oz. dripping (1 Tbs.)	2 oz. breadcrumbs (1 c.)
2 pt. stock (4 c.)	1 oz. grated cheese (25 g.)

Measures level. Cook as described for Mixed Vegetable Soup, No. 36, adding the breadcrumbs and cheese just before serving. Taste for seasoning.

41. Lentil Soup. Cooking time 2 hours or ½ hour pressure cooking

Quantities for 4–5 helpings:

1 oz. dripping (2 Tbs.)	Pinch of dried thyme or little chopped savory
1 carrot, diced	
1 onion, sliced	1–2 tsp. salt
1 turnip, diced	Pinch of pepper
2 pt. stock (4 c.)	½ pt. milk (1 c.)
3 or 4 bacon rinds	
8 oz. lentils or split peas (1 c.)	

Measures level. Cook in the same way as Mixed Vegetable Soup, No. 36, adding the lentils and flavouring with the stock. Cook gently for 2 hours or until the lentils are tender. Rub through a sieve or put in a blender. Return to the pan and add the milk. Heat, without boiling, and taste for seasoning. Serve with croûtons of fried or toasted bread.

42. Onion Soup. Cooking time ½ hour

Quantities for 4 helpings:

8 oz. onions (4 small)	1–2 tsp. salt
½ oz. fat or dripping (1 Tbs.)	Pinch of pepper
	4 slices thin toast
2 pt. stock (4 c.)	4 Tbs. grated cheese

Measures level. Cook as described for Mixed Vegetable Soup, No. 36, slicing the onions very thinly. Serve the toast and cheese separately, or put a slice of toast sprinkled with cheese in the bottom of the soup plate before pouring in the soup.

43. Potato and Mint Soup. Cooking time $\frac{1}{2}$ hour

Quantities for 4 helpings:

1 lb. potatoes (4 medium) $\frac{1}{2}$ pt. milk (1 c.)
1 oz. margarine (25 g.)   1–2 tsp. salt
1$\frac{1}{2}$ pt. water (3 c.)   Pinch of pepper
3 or 4 sprigs of mint

Measures level. Cook as described for Mixed Vegetable Soup, No. 36, adding the mint with the water. When the potatoes are tender, rub through a sieve or put in a blender. Add the milk and re-heat. Taste for seasoning.

44. Potato and Watercress Soup. Cooking time $\frac{1}{2}$ hour

Quantities for 4 helpings:

1 lb. potatoes (4 medium)   2 oz. chopped watercress
2 oz. leek or onion, sliced   ($\frac{2}{3}$ c.)
   (1 small)   1 pt. water (2 c.)
2 bacon rinds   1–2 tsp. salt
$\frac{1}{2}$ oz. fat or dripping   Pinch of pepper
   (1 Tbs.) $\frac{1}{2}$ pt. milk (1 c.)

Measures level. Cook as described for Mixed Vegetable Soup, No. 36, adding the bacon rinds with the potato, and the watercress with the water. When the potatoes are tender, rub through a sieve or put in a blender and re-heat with the milk. Taste for seasoning.

45. Vichyssoise. Cooking time $\frac{3}{4}$ hour

Quantities for 4–6 helpings:

4 leeks	1 pt. chicken stock (2 c.)
2 oz. butter (50 g.)	$\frac{1}{4}$ pt. double cream ($\frac{1}{2}$ c.)
3 small potatoes, peeled and diced	Chopped chives
Salt and pepper	

Measures level. Use only the white part of the leeks. Cut them in quarters lengthwise and wash well. Drain and chop. Melt the butter in a pan and cook the leeks gently until softened but not brown. Add potatoes, salt and pepper, and water barely to cover. Simmer for 15 minutes. Add the stock and cook until the potatoes are tender. Rub through a sieve or put in the blender.

When the soup is to be served cold, chill it thoroughly, and beat in the cream just before serving. To serve hot, add the cream and re-heat without boiling. Serve sprinkled with chives in season, or other green herbs.

46. Cream of Vegetable Soup. Cooking time $\frac{3}{4}$ hour

Quantities for 4 helpings:

1 pt. thin sauce No. 69, made with milk (2 c.)	Salt and pepper to taste
$\frac{1}{2}$ pt. vegetable purée, see Nos. 46–53 (1 c.)	2 Tbs. chopped parsley or watercress

Measures level. To make the purée, prepare and chop or slice the vegetables and cook them in $\frac{1}{2}$ pt. boiling salted water, or in a pressure cooker, until they are quite tender. Alternatively, use canned vegetables. Then rub through a sieve or put in the blender and, if necessary, make up to $\frac{1}{2}$ pt. (1 c.) with water or vegetable stock. Return to the pan and heat. Add the hot purée gradually to the hot sauce. Taste for seasoning and serve at once. The soup should be the consistency of thin cream. If it is too thick, add some

milk or some vegetable stock. If cream soups are allowed to
stand they tend to curdle, so do not combine purée and
sauce until just before serving. Have the plates well heated.
Sprinkle with the parsley or watercress.

47. Cream of Celery Soup

Use 3 c. celery cut in half-inch lengths and 1 slice of onion,
to make the purée for Recipe No. 46.

48. Cream of Tomato Soup

Use ¾ lb. (375 g.) tomatoes to make the purée for Recipe
No. 46, or use ½ pt. (1 c.) tomato purée from bottled or
canned tomatoes. Add a pinch of paprika for extra flavour
and ½ tsp. sugar.

49. Cream of Pea Soup

Soak 6 oz. dried peas (¾ c.) and cook them to make the
purée for Recipe No. 46. For the way to cook dried peas see
No. 550, or use canned peas.

50. Cream of Spinach Soup

Use ¾ lb. (375 g.) spinach to make the purée for Recipe
No. 46.

51. Cream of Carrot Soup

Use 1 lb. carrots (4 medium) and 1 slice onion to make the
purée for Recipe No. 46, or use canned carrots.

52. Cream of Artichoke Soup

Use 1 lb. artichokes (4 large) and 1 slice onion to make the
purée for Recipe No. 46.

53. Cream of Swede Soup

Use 1 lb. (500 g.) of swedes and 1 slice onion, to make the purée for Recipe No. 46.

54. Creamed Oyster or Mussel Soup (using canned fish)

Measure the fish and liquid and make 1½ times that amount of thin sauce No. 69, using milk, or part milk and part Fish Stock, No. 34. Chop the shell-fish and add to the hot sauce with their liquid. Season with salt and pepper, a pinch of ground mace, and a squeeze of lemon juice. Heat without boiling. Sprinkle with chopped parsley.

55. Chestnut Soup. Cooking time 1 hour or 15–20 minutes pressure cooking

Quantities for 4–5 helpings:

1½ lb. chestnuts (4 doz.)	2 tsp. sugar
1 oz. chopped bacon (25 g.)	1 pt. water (2 c.)
1 large potato	Salt and pepper to taste
1 large carrot	About 1 pt. hot stock (2 c.)
1 bay leaf	Croûtons of fried bread

Measures level. Cut the tops off the chestnuts and bake them in the oven or grill them for 20 minutes. Remove the shells and the skins. Slice the vegetables. Put chestnuts, bacon, vegetables, sugar, and water in a pan and cook gently until tender – about ¾ hour. Rub through a sieve or put in the blender and add sufficient hot stock to make it the right consistency for serving, or like thin cream. Heat for a minute or two longer, and taste for seasoning. Serve with croûtons of fried bread.

56. Tomato Soup (using fresh tomatoes). Cooking time
½–¾ hour

Quantities for 3 helpings:

1 onion, sliced	½ tsp. sugar
1 small carrot, chopped	1 tsp. salt
1 oz. dripping (25 g.)	Bouquet garni
1 pt. stock (2 c.)	Pinch of pepper
1 lb. tomatoes, chopped	1 Tbs. flour
(½ kg.), or 14 oz. canned	2 or 3 Tbs. milk
(2 c.)	

3 or 4 bacon rinds

Measures level. Fry the onion and carrot in the dripping, using a saucepan. Add the stock, tomatoes, and flavourings. Cook gently until the tomatoes are soft, then rub through a sieve. Return to the pan. Mix the flour to a smooth cream with the milk, add some of the hot soup, mix well, and return to the pan. Stir until it boils, and cook for 5 minutes. Taste for seasoning and serve.

57. Mushroom Soup. Cooking time ½ hour

Quantities for 4 helpings:

8 oz. mushrooms (250 g.)	Salt and pepper
1½ pt. water or chicken	4 Tbs. cream
stock (3 c.)	4 Tbs. milk
1 slice onion	Lemon juice
2 oz. butter (50 g.)	Nutmeg
1 oz. flour (3 Tbs.)	

Measures level. Chop the mushrooms, including the stalks. Add to the hot stock or water with the chopped onion. Boil gently for 20 minutes and then sieve or put in the blender. Melt the butter and mix in the flour. Cook for a minute or two and then add the mushroom liquid. Stir until boiling and boil for a few minutes. Season to taste, add the milk and cream, and a little lemon juice and grated nutmeg to taste. Serve at once.

58. Fish Chowder. Cooking time ½–¾ hour

Quantities for 4 helpings:

8 oz. fish fillets (250 g.)	¾ c. diced carrots
½ oz. fat (1 Tbs.)	¾ c. diced potatoes
1 rasher bacon or 2 rinds	1 c. milk
1 small onion, chopped	1 tsp. salt
1½ c. water or Fish Stock,	Pinch of pepper
No. 34	Chopped parsley

Measures level. Cut the fish in small pieces, removing any skin. Chop the bacon, and brown in the fat with the onion, using a saucepan. Add the fish stock or water and bring to the boil. Add the carrots and boil until nearly tender. Then add the potatoes and seasoning and cook until tender. Add the fish and simmer for 10 minutes. Add the milk and reheat. Taste for seasoning. Serve sprinkled with chopped parsley.

59. Mussel Soup. Cooking time 20–30 minutes

Quantities for 4 helpings:

2 doz. mussels (about 2 pt.)	1 clove
1½ pt. water (3 c.)	1 oz. margarine (25 g.)
1 onion, sliced	2 Tbs. flour
2 or 3 peppercorns	½ pt. milk (1 c.)
Sprig parsley	Salt and pepper
1 bay leaf	Chopped parsley

Measures level. Wash the mussels in several waters, taking care to scrub off all the sand. Put in a saucepan with the water, onion, and seasonings. Simmer for 15 minutes, when the mussel shells should be opened. Strain through fine muslin, keeping the stock. Remove the mussels from the shells, taking off the small beard under the black tongue. Melt the margarine and add the flour. Stir in the milk and cook for 5 minutes. Add the mussel stock gradually. Season well and, when boiling, add the mussels and serve at once, sprinkled with chopped parsley.

60. Gaspacho (Spanish cold soup)

Quantities for 4 helpings:

¾ pt. canned tomato juice
  (1½ c.)
½ lb. cucumber (250 g.)
  peeled and grated
  coarsely
Pinch of pepper

Pinch of dried garlic
2 Tbs. olive oil
2 Tbs. wine vinegar
1 Tbs. red wine
Sugar and salt to taste
Chopped parsley

Measures level. Mix all the ingredients together except the parsley. Chill thoroughly in the refrigerator and serve with chopped parsley to garnish.

61. Bortsch. Cooking time ¾ hour

Quantities for 4–6 helpings:

2 medium onions, shredded
8 oz. raw beetroot, peeled
  and shredded (250 g.)
1 Tbs. sugar
1 Tbs. vinegar
2 pt. beef stock (4 c.)

6 oz. shredded cabbage
  (3 c.)
2 Tbs. tomato paste
Salt and pepper
Sour cream or yogurt

Measures level. Put onion, beetroot, sugar, vinegar and stock in a pan and boil gently for 20 minutes. Add the cabbage and boil for a further 20 minutes. Add the tomato paste, season to taste and add more stock or water if needed. Cook until the cabbage is tender. Put a spoonful of cream or yogurt in each plate as the soup is served.

62. Canned Consommé

Quantities for 4 helpings: 1½ pt. (3 c.)

This is suitable for serving in any of the traditional ways for consommé, as well as to replace stock for making soups, sauces, and other recipes requiring beef stock

    When refrigerated for several hours it makes an excellent jellied consommé for summer meals.

63. Consommé Julienne

Quantities as above

To each qt. (4 c.) of consommé add ½ c. mixed cooked vegetables cut in fine strips. Suitable vegetables are carrots, celery, French beans, turnips, or swedes. In addition add 1 Tbs. minced or finely chopped leek or onion.

64. Consommé Parmesan

Quantities as above

Add 2 level Tbs. grated Parmesan cheese to each pint of hot consommé. Stir until melted. If no Parmesan is available, use dry Cheddar instead, but add 3 level Tbs. to a pint.

65. Consommé with Egg and Sherry

Quantities for 4–6 helpings:

1½ pt. consommé (3 c.)   1 Tbs. sherry
4 eggs

Heat consommé to boiling point, remove from the heat, add unbeaten eggs and sherry and beat well, using a rotary or electric beater. Serve at once in soup cups or bowls.

CHAPTER 6

Sauces

66. Food Value

The chief value of sauces is that they improve the flavour and appearance of other foods. Otherwise their usefulness depends on the choice of ingredients. For example, milk, eggs or cheese add protein, minerals and vitamins; fat, flour and sugar add calories; while the use of vegetable stock can add vitamins.

Sauces can be used to turn vegetables and pasta into main dishes suitable for lunch or supper; for example, Cauliflower au Gratin and Macaroni Cheese.

67. General Information

The two main methods of making sauces are the 'roux' method and the 'blending' method. I have given each of these in detail followed by a variety of recipes using the method. Once you have learnt the basic methods all the other sauces can be made easily and quickly.

Most sauces can be made in advance and kept over hot water until required, and so you avoid having to attend to them at the last minute. A small double boiler is ideal for this purpose, but a good alternative is either to stand the pan in another pan of hot water or put the sauce in a basin over hot water.

If the roux has been properly cooked, see No. 69, there should be no danger of a skin forming on top; but stir the sauce occasionally just to make sure it will stay smooth.

To prevent a skin forming on sweet sauces made by the blending method, see No. 95, sprinkle a little sugar over the top.

If you have a blender there is no need to worry about lumpy sauces or skin on top. Simply put the sauce in the blender for a few seconds and it will become fine and smooth. A good alternative is to beat the sauce with a small wire whisk.

Ready prepared canned and packet sauces are useful for emergency stores and for saving time. They can be improved by the addition of a little butter, cream, evaporated milk or wine as well as by additional seasoning and fresh herbs. Concentrated canned soups are suitable for replacing sauces in casseroles, but need to be used with discretion or they may be too salty and strong in flavour for all tastes, and can mask the natural flavour of the other ingredients in the recipe.

Throughout this book, reference numbers of appropriate sauces are given in recipes, but packet or canned sauces will do as time-savers. If you have a freezer, it is worth while making double the amount of sauce you require for one recipe and freezing the remainder. Most recipes, except those of the mayonnaise type, are suitable for freezing.

68. Thickenings Used for Sauces

The most common thickenings are flour, cornflour, custard powder, arrowroot, potato flour, eggs, and vegetable or fruit purées.

To improve their flavour, all sauces thickened with flour or other starchy foods should be very thoroughly cooked. Five minutes is the shortest possible cooking time for flour and cornflour, and longer will improve them. After a sauce has thickened you can put it over boiling water to continue cooking. It will then not need watching and stirring in case it should burn, and can safely have 10 minutes or longer cooking.

Arrowroot and potato flour or fécule are the only starch thickenings which are cooked as soon as they thicken.

The amount of thickening required depends on the kind

of sauce and the way it is to be used. Not all flours thicken to the same extent – for example, 1½ Tbs. wholemeal flour, 1 Tbs. white flour, and ⅔ Tbs. cornflour or arrowroot are about equal in thickening.

A THIN OR POURING SAUCE is used for general purposes.

A THICK OR COATING SAUCE is used when the sauce is intended to coat the food and stay on.

69. The Roux Method of Making a Sauce. Cooking time 10 minutes or longer

Quantities for 4–8 helpings: (When making only half a recipe use a little less than half the thickening or thin as necessary before serving; a small quantity of sauce is always thicker because there is greater evaporation during cooking.)

Ingredients	Thin or Pouring Sauce	Thick or Coating Sauce
Butter, margarine, fat or oil .	1 oz. (25 g.)	2 oz. (50 g.)
Flour	1 oz. (3 Tbs.)	2 oz. (6 Tbs.)
Liquid (milk, stock, or half and half)	1 pt. (2 c.)	1 pt. (2 c.)

Measures level.

1. Melt the fat and stir in the flour. Mix well and cook very gently for 1–2 minutes or until it looks mealy for a white sauce, or until brown for a brown sauce. This mixture of fat and flour is called a 'roux'.

2. Add the cold or warm (not hot) liquid and stir or whisk vigorously until the sauce is smooth and boiling. Boil it gently for 5 minutes or cook for 10–20 minutes over boiling water, stirring occasionally. If the sauce shows any tendency to be lumpy, either beat it hard with a small wire whisk or put it in the blender for a few seconds. Whisking or blending very much improves texture and appearance.

3. If the sauce is to be kept hot for any length of time it

must either be put in a double boiler or the saucepan stood in another pan of simmering water; stir occasionally to prevent a skin from forming or run a thin layer of melted butter or margarine over the top. Stir this in before serving the sauce.

70. The One-Stage Method of Making a Sauce

This is similar to using a packet sauce mix. The method is suitable for any recipe using the roux method, and is specially useful with a blender or liquidizer. Put the flour, liquid and seasoning in the blender and mix. Soft fat or oil may be added too, otherwise melt it in the pan before adding the blended mix. Stir until it boils.

Without a blender, melt the fat and add the other ingredients, beating with a rotary beater or hand electric mixer until the sauce boils.

71. Sauce for Boiled Vegetables

1 oz. fat (25 g.)
1 oz. flour (3 Tbs.)
½ pt. vegetable stock or milk (1 c.)

Salt and pepper to taste
Pinch of nutmeg or mace
Chopped parsley or other green herbs

Measures level. Make according to the Roux Method, No. 69. Optional additions, 2 Tbs. cream or 1 egg yolk.

72. Anchovy Sauce (for fish)

1–2 oz. margarine (25–50 g.)
1–2 oz. flour (3–6 Tbs.)

1 pt. liquid (2 c.)
Pepper to taste
2–3 tsp. anchovy essence

Measures level. For the liquid use fish stock, or the liquid from boiled fish, or milk. Make according to the Roux Method, No. 69, adding the anchovy essence when the sauce is cooked. Add pepper to taste.

73. Brown Sauce (for meat, poultry, fish, vegetables, macaroni)

2 oz. fat (50 g.)
2 onions, sliced
2 small carrots, sliced
1 oz. flour (3 Tbs.)
1 pt. stock (2 c.)

$\frac{1}{4}$ bay leaf
Sprig of parsley
Salt and pepper to taste
Gravy browning if
    necessary

Measures level. Fry the vegetables and fat in the saucepan until they are lightly browned. Add the flour, and cook until light brown. Then add the bay leaf and parsley and finish in the same way as for the Roux Method, No. 69. Strain before using, and add gravy browning if a darker colour is required. Season to taste.

74. Caper Sauce (for mutton, lamb, or herrings)

2 oz. margarine (50 g.)
2 oz. flour (6 Tbs.)
1 pt. liquid (2 c.)
2 Tbs. chopped capers

$1\frac{1}{2}$ Tbs. vinegar from the
    capers
Salt and pepper to taste

Measures level. For the liquid use vegetable stock, fish stock, or the liquid from boiling fish or meat. Make according to the Roux Method, No. 69, adding the capers and the vinegar when the sauce is cooked. Season to taste.

75. Cheese Sauce (for fish, vegetables, macaroni, etc.)

1–2 oz. margarine
    (25–50 g.)
1–2 oz. flour (3–6 Tbs.)
1 pt. liquid (2 c.)

3–4 oz. grated cheese
    (75–125 g.)
Pinch of mace or nutmeg
Salt and pepper to taste

Measures level. For the liquid use vegetable stock, fish stock, or milk. Make according to the Roux Method, No. 69. Add the cheese just before serving, and do not allow the sauce to boil afterwards, or the cheese will become stringy. Stir until the cheese is melted. Season to taste.

76. Curry Sauce (for eggs, fish, vegetables, meat)

2 oz. fat (50 g.)
2 onions, chopped
2 oz. flour (6–7 Tbs.)
2 Tbs. curry powder
1 pt. stock (2 c.)
2 apples, chopped

1 tomato, chopped
1 tsp. brown sugar
1 tsp. salt
Rind and juice ½ lemon
1 bay leaf
1 Tbs. chutney

Measures level. Fry the onion in the fat, and add the curry powder with the flour, finishing as for the Roux Method, No. 69. Add all the other ingredients and cook for 20 minutes. Strain and re-heat before serving.

77. Egg Sauce (for fish and poultry)

1 oz. margarine (25 g.)
1 oz. flour (3 Tbs.)
1 pt. stock or milk (2 c.)

2–3 hard-boiled eggs
Pinch of nutmeg
Salt and pepper to taste

Measures level. Make according to the Roux Method, No. 69. Add the chopped eggs and seasoning when the sauce is cooked.

78. Fennel Sauce (for herrings, mackerel, and boiled mutton)

1 oz. margarine (25 g.)
1 oz. flour (3 Tbs.)
1 pt. stock (2 c.)
1½ Tbs. vinegar

Salt and pepper to taste
4 Tbs. chopped fennel
1 Tbs. sugar
1 egg yolk

Measures level. Make according to the Roux Method, No. 69. Add the chopped fennel, vinegar, sugar, and egg, and heat for another minute. Season well.

79. Gravy (for roast meat)

3 Tbs. dripping
1 oz. flour (3 Tbs.)
1 pt. stock (2 c.)

Salt and pepper
Gravy browning

Measures level. Remove the roast from the pan and pour off all the dripping, except the amount needed for the gravy. Add the flour and proceed as in the Roux Method, No. 69, browning the flour slightly. Add gravy browning if a darker colour is required. Season to taste.

80. Horse-radish Sauce (for beef, herrings, or mackerel)

1 oz. margarine (25 g.)
2 tsp. dry mustard
1 oz. flour (3 Tbs.)
½ pt. stock or milk (1 c.)
1 tsp. salt

1 tsp. sugar
½ c. grated horse-radish or bottled sauce
3 Tbs. vinegar

Measures level. Make by the Roux Method, No. 69, adding the mustard with the flour. When the sauce is cooked stir in the salt, sugar, vinegar, and horse-radish, which should be finely grated – this is easiest to do sideways and not across the end of the root. Serve hot or cold.

81. Lobster or Shrimp Sauce

1–2 oz. margarine (25–50 g.)
½ pt. shelled shrimps or chopped lobster meat (1 c.)

1–2 oz. flour (3–6 Tbs.)
1 pt. fish stock (2 c.)
2 tsp. anchovy essence
Lemon juice
Cayenne pepper

Measures level. Make according to the Roux Method, No. 69. When the sauce is cooked add the fish and seasonings to taste.

82. Mushroom Sauce (for fish, meat, poultry, omelets)

1 pt. Brown Sauce, No. 73 (2 c.), or Espagnole Sauce, No. 93

2 dozen small mushrooms

Chop the mushrooms, and cook them in the sauce for 5 minutes. For extra flavour the mushroom stalks and peelings should be boiled with the brown sauce before it is strained.

83. Mussel or Oyster Sauce (for fish)

2 oz. margarine (50 g.)	Pinch of mace
2 oz. flour (6 Tbs.)	2 dozen mussels or oysters
1 pt. milk or fish stock (2 c.)	1 tsp. anchovy essence
	1 tsp. lemon juice
Salt and pepper to taste	

Measures level. Make the sauce according to the Roux Method, No. 69. Open the mussels as described in No. 301, or open oysters (No. 305). Either canned oysters or mussels may also be used. Add the fish to the sauce with the flavourings. Heat for a minute or two without boiling. Serve hot.

84. Mustard Sauce (for fish)

2 oz. margarine (50 g.)	1 Tbs. dry mustard
2 oz. flour (6 Tbs.)	1 Tbs. vinegar
1 pt. fish stock or milk (2 c.)	Salt and pepper to taste

Measures level. Make the sauce according to the Roux Method, No. 69. Mix the mustard and vinegar together and add to the cooked sauce. Season well.

85. Onion Sauce (for mutton, lamb, tripe, rabbit, chicken, etc.)

8 oz. chopped onions (250 g.)	$\frac{1}{2}$ pt. stock or milk (1 c.)
1 oz. fat (25 g.)	Pinch sugar
1 Tbs. flour	Pinch mace or nutmeg
	Salt and pepper

Measures level. Heat the fat and stew the onions slowly in it until they are soft but not browned. Add the flour and mix well. Add the liquid and stir until it boils and then simmer until the onion is quite tender, 10–15 minutes. Season to taste and either serve as it is, rub through a sieve, or put in the blender to make a smooth sauce. Serve hot.

86. Paprika Sauce (for fish, meat, poultry, potatoes, and sausages)

2 oz. fat (50 g.)   2 tsp. paprika pepper
8 oz. chopped onion   1 pt. stock (2 c.)
   (4 small)   2 Tbs. vinegar
2 oz. flour (6 Tbs.)   Salt to taste

Measures level. Fry the onions in the fat before adding the paprika and flour. Then finish by the Roux Method, No. 69. Add the vinegar with the stock. Add salt to taste.

87. Parsley Sauce (for fish, vegetables, eggs, meat, and poultry)

1–2 oz. margarine   Salt and pepper
   (25–50 g.)   4 Tbs. chopped parsley
1–2 oz. flour (3–6 Tbs.)   For fish add 1 Tbs. lemon
1 pt. stock (2 c.)   juice or vinegar

Measures level. Make according to the Roux Method, No. 69. Add the parsley just before serving and season well.

88. Sour-sweet Onion Sauce (for fish, sausages, rissoles, etc.)

2 oz. fat (50 g.)   Salt and pepper
8 oz. onion, finely sliced   2 tsp. sugar
   (4 small)   2 Tbs. vinegar
1 oz. flour (3 Tbs.)   Gravy browning
1 pt. stock (2 c.)

Measures level. Fry the onions in the fat until brown and then finish by the Roux Method, No. 69. Add the seasonings and vinegar at the end, and gravy browning, if necessary.

89. Tomato Sauce (for fish, meat, vegetables, eggs)

1 oz. fat (25 g.)
1 onion, chopped
2 or 3 bacon rinds
1 oz. flour (3 Tbs.)
½ bay leaf

½ pt. tomato juice or 2 Tbs.
tomato paste made up to
½ pt. with water (1 c.)
½ pt. stock (1 c.)
½ tsp. sugar
Salt and pepper to taste

Measures level. Fry the onion and bacon rinds in the fat, and then add the flour and finish as for the Roux Method, No. 69, adding the bay leaf with the stock and tomato. Boil for ½ hour. Strain before using and add the sugar and seasonings to taste.

90. Béchamel Sauce (French White Sauce)

1 pt. milk (2 c.)
1 shallot or small onion
Piece of carrot
Piece of celery
1 bay leaf
10 peppercorns

1 oz. butter or margarine
(25 g.)
1 oz. cornflour (3 Tbs.)
Salt
4 Tbs. single cream

Measures level. Heat the milk, vegetables, bay leaf and peppercorns to boiling, remove from the heat and leave for 5 minutes to infuse. Strain, allow to cool a little and then finish the sauce by the Roux Method, No. 69, adding the cream just before serving.

91. Velouté Sauce (for poultry and vegetables)

1 oz. butter or margarine
(25 g.)
1 oz. cornflour (3 Tbs.)
1 pt. chicken or veal
stock (2 c.)

Ground nutmeg or mace
to taste
Salt and pepper

Measures level. Make according to the Roux Method, No. 69.

92. Suprême Sauce (for poultry and vegetables)

1 pt. Velouté Sauce, No. 91 ¼ pt. single cream (½ c.)
  (2 c.) 3 egg yolks
Chicken stock Seasoning

Use chicken stock to make the sauce thinner. Mix egg yolks
and cream and add a little of the hot sauce, mix well, return
to the pan and stir until the sauce thickens without boiling.
Taste for seasoning.

93. Espagnole Sauce (for meat and game)

2 oz. butter (50 g.) 1 oz. cornflour (3 Tbs.)
2 oz. chopped ham or 1 pt. brown stock (2 c.)
  bacon (50 g.) 2 Tbs. tomato paste
1 medium onion, chopped ¼ c. sherry or Madeira
1 small carrot, chopped Salt and pepper
4 oz. mushrooms, chopped
  (125 g.)

Measures level. Heat the butter and fry the ham or bacon,
onion, carrot and mushrooms until they begin to brown.
Then finish as with the Roux Method, No. 69, adding the
tomato paste with the stock. Simmer for 1 hour. Strain.
Add the sherry and seasoning just before serving and thin
with stock as necessary.

94. Hollandaise Sauce

3 oz. butter (75 g.) 2 Tbs. boiling water
½ tsp. flour 2 Tbs. lemon juice
2 egg yolks Few grains cayenne pepper

Cream the butter and flour. Beat the egg yolks until thick
and light and add them to the butter. Gradually mix in the
boiling water. Put the sauce over a low heat or in a double
boiler or basin over boiling water and stir until the sauce
thickens. Add lemon juice and seasoning. The sauce may be

made in advance, stored in the refrigerator and re-heated, adding a little hot water if it is too thick. Serve warm.

95. Blending Method for Sauces with Little or No Fat

This is the method used for most sweet sauces. The thickening is usually cornflour, arrowroot, custard powder or potato flour, and sometimes egg as well.
Cooking time about 10 minutes.

Quantities for 4–8 helpings:

Ingredients	Thin or Pouring Sauce	Medium or Coating Sauce
Cornflour, arrowroot, custard powder or potato flour .	1 Tbs.	2 Tbs.
With egg	½ Tbs. cornflour &c. and 1 egg yolk	1 Tbs. cornflour etc. and 1 egg or 2 yolks
Liquid: milk, stock, or fruit juice	1 pint (2 c.)	1 pint (2 c.)
Butter or cream . . .	to taste	to taste

Measures level.

1. Mix the dry ingredients (i.e. thickening, sugar, spices, cocoa, etc.) to a smooth paste with a little of the cold liquid. This is called 'blending'.

2. Bring the remaining liquid to the boil in a small saucepan, and pour it into the blended ingredients. Mix well and return to the pan.

3. Stir until the mixture boils, and boil gently for 5 minutes or longer. If the sauce is put over boiling water it will cook without fear of burning.

4. To add egg, remove the sauce from the heat, beat the egg to mix and either beat in a little of the sauce or mix the egg with cream. Add this to the rest of the sauce and heat gently until it thickens. It is better not to allow it to boil again. Butter or cream added without eggs should go in just before serving.

96. Butterscotch Sauce (for steamed or baked puddings, ices, and moulds)

1–2 Tbs. cornflour	½ oz. butter (1 Tbs.)
¼ tsp. salt	4 oz. brown sugar (½ c.)
1 pt. milk (2 c.)	Vanilla essence to taste

Measures level. Make the sauce by the Blending Method, as in No. 95. Heat the butter and sugar together until liquid. Stir this into the hot sauce and mix until melted. Add vanilla essence to taste and serve hot or cold.

97. Caramel Sauce (for steamed or baked puddings, ices, and moulds)

2 oz. sugar (4 Tbs.)	1–2 Tbs. cornflour
2 Tbs. water	¼ tsp. salt
1 pt. milk (2 c.)	Vanilla essence to taste

Measures level. Caramelize the sugar and water by boiling together in a small heavy pan until toffee-coloured. Dissolve the caramel in the hot milk and make the sauce by the Blending Method, as in No. 95. Add vanilla essence to taste. Serve hot or cold. If necessary, thin with milk or cream.

98. Cinnamon or Nutmeg Sauce (for steamed or baked puddings)

1–2 Tbs. cornflour	½–1 tsp. cinnamon or
¼ tsp. salt	nutmeg
2–4 Tbs. sugar	1 pt. milk or water (2 c.)

Measures level. Make according to the Blending Method, No. 95, adding the spice with the flour. Serve hot.

99. Chocolate Sauce (for steamed or baked puddings, ices, fruit, and moulds)

1–2 Tbs. cornflour	3 Tbs. sugar
¼ tsp. salt	1 pt. milk (2 c.)
2 Tbs. cocoa	Vanilla essence to taste

Measures level. Make according to the Blending Method, No. 95. Add vanilla essence to taste and serve hot or cold.

100. Fruit Sauce (for puddings and ices)

1–2 Tbs. cornflour, arrowroot or potato flour
Sugar to taste

1 pt. fruit juice (2 c.)
1 Tbs. lemon juice

Measures level. The fruit juice can be from bottled, stewed or canned fruit. Make by the Blending Method, No. 95, adding sugar according to the tartness of the fruit juice and lemon juice to bring out the flavour. Serve hot or cold.

101. Jam or Marmalade Sauce (for puddings and ices)

1 Tbs. cornflour
½ pt. water (1 c.)

4 oz. jam or marmalade (4 Tbs.)
2 tsp. lemon juice

Measures level. Make according to the Blending Method, No. 95. Add the lemon juice and the jam or marmalade, which may be sieved or not according to taste. Serve hot or cold.

102. Lemon Sauce (for puddings and ices)

1–2 Tbs. cornflour
4 Tbs. sugar

1 pt. water (2 c.)
2 lemons, rind and juice

Measures level. Make according to the Blending Method, No. 95, adding the grated lemon rind to the water. Add the lemon juice when cooking is finished. Serve hot or cold.

103. Orange Sauce (for puddings and ices)

1–2 Tbs. cornflour
4 Tbs. sugar
1 pt. water (2 c.)

2 oranges, rind and juice
1 Tbs. marmalade

Measures level. Make by the Blending Method, No. 95, adding the orange rind to the water. Add the orange juice and marmalade when cooking is finished. Serve hot or cold.

104. Sherry Sauce (for steamed puddings)

Add 2–4 Tbs. sherry to Custard Sauce, No. 105. Serve hot.

105. Custard Sauce (for puddings and fruit)

Cooking time 10–15 minutes

Quantities for 6–8 helpings:

1 pt. milk (2 c.)	1 Tbs. sugar
2 eggs or 4 yolks	Flavouring to taste

Measures level. Heat the milk to just below boiling. Beat the eggs and sugar together slightly, and pour on the hot milk, stirring well. Cook over boiling water until the custard coats the back of the wooden spoon used for stirring. Stir frequently to keep the custard smooth. Flavour to taste and serve hot or cold.

N.B. Care must be taken to remove from the heat as soon as it is cooked because overcooking causes curdling.

106. Savoury Sauces without Fat

Some people are advised to avoid fatty sauces or use very little fat, but still want to have savoury sauces. Any of the recipes from Nos. 69 to 89 may be made by the Blending Method described in No. 95, except those where vegetables have to be fried in fat at the beginning.

107. Syrup or Honey Sauce (for puddings, fritters, dough-nuts)

Cooking time 1 minute

Quantities for 6–8 helpings:

8 oz. syrup or honey (½ c.)
½ pt. water (1 c.)

Rind and juice of 1 lemon or pinch of ground ginger

Measures level. Heat the syrup or honey and water together in a small saucepan and add the lemon or ginger. Serve hot.

108. Apple Sauce (for pork, game, or sausages)

Cooking time ½ hour

Quantities for 4 helpings:

1 lb. cooking apples (500 g.)

2 oz. sugar (¼ c.)

Peel, core, and slice the apples and cook in a saucepan with just enough water to prevent burning. When cooked to a pulp rub through a sieve, add the sugar and re-heat. Serve hot.

109. Cranberry Sauce (for roast turkey)

Quantities for 4–6 helpings:

8 oz. cranberries (250 g.)
¼ pt. water (½ c.)

4 oz. sugar (½ c.)

Measures level. Boil the cranberries and water in a saucepan, crushing them with a spoon during cooking. When quite tender rub through a sieve. Add the sugar and stir until dissolved. Pour into a small mould and leave 12 hours before using. The contents will then turn out like a jelly.

If a hot sauce is preferred, use enough hot water to make the purée the desired consistency for serving, like hot apple sauce.

110. Melba Sauce (for ices and fruit)

Quantities for 4 helpings:

¾ lb. fresh or frozen
    raspberries (375 g.)
½ Tbs. cornflour or potato
    flour

Sugar
Lemon juice

Measures level. Cook the fruit gently, without water, until it is reduced to a pulp. Sieve. Blend the thickening with a little cold water and add it to the fruit. Stir and heat until it boils, when potato starch will be cooked but cornflour should be simmered for 2–3 minutes. Add sugar and lemon to taste. It may be used hot or chilled.

111. Brown Butter Sauce

Melt the butter in a small saucepan, allowing ½–1 oz. (25 g.) per person. Cook it gently until it turns brown. Then add ½ tsp. chopped parsley and ½ tsp. of vinegar for each ounce of butter and pour quickly over the food.

112. French Mustard

3 Tbs. mustard
½ tsp. sugar
½ tsp. salt
Pinch of pepper

1½ tsp. vinegar, malt or
    tarragon
1½ tsp. oil

Measures level. Mix the mustard to a very stiff paste with a little cold water. Add the other ingredients and mix well.

113. Mayonnaise. Time to make, about 20 minutes

Quantities for about $\frac{3}{4}$ pt. ($1\frac{1}{2}$ c.):

2 egg yolks	Pinch cayenne pepper
1 tsp. salt	$1\frac{1}{2}$ Tbs. vinegar
$\frac{1}{2}$ tsp. mustard	$\frac{1}{2}$ pt. oil (1 c.)

Measures level.

1. Mix the egg yolks with the salt, mustard, pepper, and 1 Tbs. of the vinegar. Beat well with a rotary beater or wire whisk.

2. Be sure the oil is room temperature and not cold, or the mayonnaise will curdle. While beating hard, add the oil $\frac{1}{2}$ tsp. at a time, and make sure it is well blended in before adding more. When a quarter of the oil has been used add 1 Tbs. at a time.

3. When all the oil is in, add the rest of the vinegar.

N.B. Great care must be taken to add the oil very gradually, especially at first. Mayonnaise curdles if the oil is added too quickly or if too much oil is used for the amount of egg; or if the oil is too cold. If it does curdle, beat the curdled mayonnaise gradually into another egg yolk. Cover and keep in a cool place.

114. Economical Salad Dressing. (This uses far less oil than real mayonnaise, and is therefore cheaper to make and more easily digested. It may be used in the same way as mayonnaise.)

Quantities for $\frac{1}{2} - \frac{3}{4}$ pt. ($1 - 1\frac{1}{2}$ c.):

1 oz. flour (3 Tbs.)	1 egg
1 tsp. dry mustard	$\frac{1}{2}$ pt. water (1 c.)
Few grains cayenne pepper	4 Tbs. vinegar
1 tsp. salt	3 Tbs. salad oil
1 Tbs. sugar	

Measures level. Mix the first six ingredients together and stir in the water gradually. Add the vinegar and cook over boiling water until it thickens, and then for 5 minutes more. Cool and beat in the oil.

115. Quick Salad Dressing

Quantities for 4 helpings:

½ tsp. dry mustard
½ tsp. salt
Pinch of pepper
¼ pt. evaporated milk
   (½ c.)

Pinch of sugar
1 Tbs. lemon juice or
   ½ Tbs. vinegar
4 Tbs. olive oil

Measures level. Mix the mustard, salt, sugar, and pepper in a small basin. Add the milk, lemon or vinegar, and the oil. Beat until smooth.

116. Yogurt Salad Dressing

Quantities for 4 helpings:

1½ Tbs. lemon juice
¼ tsp. French mustard
Pinch of pepper
¼ tsp. salt

¼ pt. yogurt (1 small
   carton or ½ c.)
Chopped fresh herbs
   (optional)

Mix lemon juice and seasonings and slowly stir in the yogurt and herbs. Mix thoroughly and chill for ½ hour before using.

117. Tartare Sauce (for fried and grilled fish, meat, and salads)

Quantities for 4 helpings:

½ pt. Mayonnaise, No. 113
   (1 c.)
2 Tbs. chopped gherkins
   or capers

1 tsp. finely chopped onion

Measures level. Mix well.

118. French Dressing (for salads)

Quantities for 1 large bowl (salad for 4–6 helpings):

1½ Tbs. oil   Pinch dry mustard
Pinch pepper   ½ Tbs. malt or wine
¼ tsp. salt   vinegar

Mix the oil and seasoning and add the vinegar. Stir before using, as the ingredients separate out on standing. If preferred, a large amount may be mixed and kept in a covered jar. Shake before using.

119. Vinaigrette Sauce (for calf's head, asparagus, artichokes, etc.)

Time about 5 minutes

Quantities for 4 helpings:

4 Tbs. salad oil   Salt and pepper
2 Tbs. tarragon or malt   ½ tsp. made mustard
   vinegar
1 tsp. each of finely
   chopped gherkin,
   shallot, and parsley

Mix well, and again before serving.

120. Mint Sauce (for roast lamb)

Quantities for 4 helpings:

¼ c. chopped fresh mint   ¼ pt. wine or malt vinegar
1 Tbs. sugar   (½ c.)

Measures level. Mix the ingredients together and allow to stand for 2 hours before using, so that the flavours will be well blended. The mint can often be chopped more easily if the sugar is sprinkled over it first.

121. Bread Sauce (for poultry and sausages)

Cooking time 25 minutes

Quantities for 4 helpings:

1 onion
4 cloves
½ pt. milk (1 c.)
2 oz. breadcrumbs (1 c.)

1 oz. butter or margarine
   (25 g.)
Salt and pepper

Measures level. Slice the onion. Heat the onion, cloves, and milk together for about 10 minutes, or until the milk is well flavoured. Strain. Add the breadcrumbs and cook slowly, without boiling, until the crumbs swell. Add the butter or margarine. Season well and serve hot. The sauce may be kept hot for some time, if put over hot water.

122. Basting Sauces for Grills

These are brushed over food before and during grilling to keep the surface moist and add flavouring. Sometimes the food is steeped or marinaded in the sauce for several hours before grilling. The sauce ingredients are mixed together and left to stand a while before use. Stir and then spoon or brush over the food.

Quantities for 4 helpings:

BASIC SAUCE

1 tsp. dry mustard
2 tsp. Worcester sauce
2 Tbs. vinegar or lemon
   juice

3 Tbs. oil or melted butter
   or margarine

For additional flavour add crushed or dried garlic or garlic salt and chopped or dried herbs.

WINE SAUCE. Use red or white wine, sherry or vermouth. Mix equal quantities of oil and wine with chopped marjoram, thyme or rosemary, garlic, and bay leaf. Leave to infuse for several hours before use.

FOR FISH

2 Tbs. oil or melted butter or margarine	¼ tsp. salt
	Pinch pepper
1–2 tsp. lemon juice	

For flavouring add one of the following: 1 Tbs. minced onion; 1 tsp. made mustard; 1 Tbs. chopped olives; 1–2 Tbs. wine; 1 tsp. anchovy essence.

123. Parsley Butter (for grilled fish and meat)

Quantities for 2–4 helpings:

1 oz. butter (25 g.)	Salt and pepper
2 Tbs. chopped parsley	Few drops lemon juice

Measures level. Work the ingredients well together. Leave to set, and then mould into small pats to put on top of the meat or fish just before serving.

124. Watercress Butter

Make in the same way as Parsley Butter, but use chopped watercress instead of parsley and onion juice in place of the lemon.

125. Hard Sauce (for steamed puddings or cake fillings)

Quantities for 4 helpings:

2 oz. butter (50 g.)	½ tsp. vanilla essence or
4 oz. icing (¾ c.) or caster sugar (½ c.)	1 Tbs. sherry or rum

Measures level. Cream the ingredients together and flavour to taste. This sauce is served separately. When put on the hot pudding it melts and forms a coating.

CUMBERLAND RUM BUTTER is made in the same way, but using light brown sugar instead of the icing sugar, adding nutmeg and cinnamon to taste and flavouring with rum.

CHAPTER 7

Stuffings and Forcemeats

126. Food Value

As most stuffings consist of a basis of either bread, potato,
or chestnuts, with some fat added, they serve the same
purpose as potatoes or bread eaten with the meat, that is,
to provide calories. The addition of egg to bind the ingredients adds protein, but the quantity is generally small.

127. General Information

Although stuffing is often used to add bulk to small joints
of meat, its real purpose is to add flavour, and for this
reason it should always be very well seasoned. Fresh or
dried herbs are used, as well as the various spices. Onion
juice or fried onion is better than raw onion, unless the meat
has very long and thorough cooking. Other ingredients used
are lemon rind, apple, celery, bacon, sausage meat, prunes,
chestnuts, and, with poultry, the cooked chopped giblets.
Stuffed meat and fish should be cooked very thoroughly to
ensure the destruction of any bacteria introduced from the
hands during boning and stuffing.

Packet stuffings are made from dried crumbs, and good
brands form a useful stand-by for an emergency.

The best stuffings are made from fresh breadcrumbs, see
No. 876, although soaked stale bread may be used instead.
The bread is soaked in stock or water until quite soft, then
all surplus moisture squeezed out, and the bread mashed
until smooth. Sometimes it is heated in a pan to drive off
the moisture.

Stuffings should be dry enough to keep their shape but

not enough to be solid and hard when cooked. The amount of moisture needed depends on the method of cooking. If the mixture is to be formed into balls and cooked separately from the joint, it will need to be firmer than when used inside meat or poultry.

If a blender is available the bread and onion, cut in small pieces, and the herbs can be processed together. This saves a great deal of preparation time.

128. Lemon Butter Stuffing (for Poultry and fish)

Quantities for 1 small chicken:

2 oz. melted butter
  (50 g.)
2 oz. breadcrumbs (1 c.)
Grated rind ½ lemon
½ Tbs. lemon juice

2 Tbs. chopped parsley
Pinch dried thyme or
  marjoram
Pinch salt and pepper
1 small egg

Measures level. Mix ingredients thoroughly using enough egg to bind.

129. Chestnut Stuffing (for turkey)

Quantities for a 12–14 lb. (5–6 kg.) turkey:

2 lb. chestnuts (1 kg.)
4 oz. butter or dripping,
  melted (125 g.)
4 oz. breadcrumbs (2 c.)
1 lb. sausage meat (500 g.)

1 Tbs. chopped parsley
2 tsp. salt
Pinch of pepper
Stock to moisten

Measures level. Shell the nuts as for Chestnut Soup, No. 55. Barely cover with stock, and cook slowly until they are tender and almost dry. Rub them through a sieve and mix with the melted fat and other ingredients.

130. Fish Stuffing (for baked fish)

Quantities for a 3–4 lb. (1½–2 kg.) fish:

3 oz. breadcrumbs (1½ c.)   ½ tsp. salt
1 Tbs. chopped parsley   Pinch of pepper
1 tsp. onion juice   ½ tsp. anchovy essence
1 Tbs. chopped capers   Egg or milk to bind
½ oz. melted butter or
  margarine (1 Tbs.)

Measures level. Mix all the ingredients together.

131. Mint or Watercress Stuffing (for lamb or mutton)

Quantities for a shoulder:

8 oz. breadcrumbs (4 c.)   3 Tbs. chopped parsley
½ c. chopped fresh mint or   1 tsp. salt
  1½ c. chopped watercress   Pinch of pepper
4 Tbs. chopped onion   1 Tbs. sugar
3 oz. margarine or dripping
  (75 g.)

Measures level. Fry the onion in a little of the fat and mix
all the ingredients together.

132. Prune and Apple Stuffing (for roast goose)

Quantities for 1 goose:

1 lb. prunes (500 g.)   3 oz. sugar (6 Tbs.)
2 lb. apples (1 kg.)   1 Tbs. water
1 oz. butter or margarine
  (25 g.)

Measures level. Soak the prunes overnight and then remove
the stones. Peel, core, and slice the apples. Place all the
ingredients in a pan and cook very gently for 2–3 hours
until the mixture is the consistency of jam. Stir frequently.
  ALTERNATIVE RECIPE. Use equal quantities of prunes

and dried apple rings. Blanch the prunes by soaking them in boiling water for 5 minutes or by placing them in a moderate oven. Remove the stones. Fill the bird three-quarters full, allowing room for the fruit to swell.

133. Sage and Onion Stuffing (for goose, duck, or pork)

Quantities for 1 goose or 2 ducks:

4 large onions
10 fresh sage leaves or 1
   tsp. dried sage
1 oz. melted butter or
   margarine (25 g.)

4 oz. breadcrumbs (2 c.)
2 tsp. salt
Pinch of pepper

Measures level. Peel the onions and boil them for 5 minutes. Dip the sage in the boiling water for a minute. Chop or mince the onions and sage and mix all the ingredients together.

134. Turkey Stuffing

Quantities for a 14–16 lb. (6–7 kg.) turkey:

2 rashers bacon, chopped
4 oz. melted fat (125 g.)
Liver, heart, and gizzard
¼ small clove garlic,
   chopped
1 lb. hot mashed potatoes
   or canned chestnut
   purée (2 c.)
2 c. breadcrumbs
2 Tbs. chopped parsley

¼ tsp. each of nutmeg,
   thyme, and marjoram
2 tsp. salt
Pinch of pepper
2 or 3 Tbs. wine vinegar
8 oz. prunes, soaked and
   chopped (250 g.)
Stock from the giblets for
   mixing

Measures level. Chop the bacon and fry it for a few minutes in a little of the fat, with the chopped liver and garlic. The other giblets should be cooked according to No. 332. Chop them finely. Mix all the ingredients together with the rest of the dripping and enough stock to moisten. This stuffing is good either hot or cold, and should be a rich plum colour.

135. Veal Forcemeat (for meat, chicken, duckling, or fish)

Quantities for 1 chicken:

2 oz. stale breadcrumbs (1 c.)	½ tsp. grated lemon rind
2 oz. suet (6 Tbs.)	Pinch of mace
1 Tbs. chopped parsley	½ tsp. salt
1 tsp. dried thyme or savory	Pinch of pepper
	1 egg
	Milk to mix

Measures level. Prepare the bread and grate the suet finely. Mix all the ingredients together. If the stuffing is to be used for poultry, add the liver, chopped and fried as in No. 134. Also suitable for forcemeat balls. Roll mixture in floured hands.

CHAPTER 8

Fats and Frying

136. Food Value

Fat is a concentrated source of energy, giving twice as many calories per gram as starches and sugars. It is, therefore, important in the diets of those who lead very active lives as it helps to give energy without bulk. As people become more affluent they tend to eat more fat but there is medical evidence that this is not a wise thing to do and that people leading sedentary lives should be careful not to eat too many fried foods, pastry, puddings, cream, butter or margarine.

Other foods which contain fat are meats, bacon, ham, poultry, game, whole milk, cheese, eggs, nuts and oily fish such as herrings and salmon; but by far the greatest amount of fat consumed comes from that used in cooking and for spreading on bread.

Two very important vitamins are found in some fats – vitamins A and D in butter, margarine, fish-liver oils, and oily fish such as herrings and sardines. The only other good source of vitamin D is sunshine, so in winter it is advisable to have liberal amounts of foods containing vitamin D or take regular doses of cod-liver oil or its equivalent. Vitamin D is essential for building and maintaining strong bones and teeth.

137. Keeping Fats

Fats readily pick up other flavours and are affected by warmth and light. They should always have a protective cover (foil is ideal), and be kept cool. They will keep several weeks in a cold larder or refrigerator, longer in a freezer. Oil keeps better when it is in either a tin or a coloured bottle and should be kept cool, but not refrigerated. Dripping should be kept in a covered jar and, if it is to last any length of time, should be clarified (see No. 139), as pieces of food and gravy soon become mouldy and spoil the fat.

138. Rendering Fat

A good supply of clean dripping suitable for all cooking purposes can be obtained by rendering down suet and pieces of fat cut from raw or cooked meat. Rendering is merely heating in some way to melt the fat from the surrounding tissues. Care must be taken to see that it is not overheated in the process, or the fat will be spoiled.

Method 1. Cut the fat in small pieces or mince it, put it in a pan in a slow to moderate oven, and cook until the fat has melted and only pieces of brown tissue are left. Strain into a clean basin.

Method 2. Prepare the fat as before and place in a pan without a lid, and with a very little water. Boil until the water has been driven off, and then heat very gently until the fat has melted. Strain as before. A safer way of heating is to put the fat in a double boiler. In this case the initial water will not be needed.

139. Clarifying Dripping

Used dripping is generally full of pieces of food and gravy, and this makes it unsuitable for frying or for most cooking purposes. It can be cleaned, or clarified, quite easily. It is a good idea to keep one jar for used dripping and another for clarified dripping. When the used dripping jar is full, clarify it, and you can go on using the same fat a number of times.

1. Put the dripping in a pan without the lid, and cover

with cold water. If two or three pieces of raw potato are added they will absorb flavours. Bring to the boil and boil gently for 2 to 3 minutes.

2. Strain into a clean basin and leave until cold.

3. Lift the fat off the top of the water and scrape any particles off the bottom of the fat.

4. This fat is now ready for cakes, pastry, and spreads, but if it is wanted for keeping or for frying, all the water must be evaporated by melting the fat in a pan and heating until it stops bubbling. Pour into a clean, dry jar.

140. Fats for Spreading

Butter and margarine are most people's choice, with good beef dripping to spread on hot toast. Goose dripping can be used for the same purpose, and in some countries pork fat or lard is used.

For economical spreading a fat should be soft, so warm it slightly if it is very cold, and beat well. Butter may be made to go much farther by beating in warm milk or water, 4 oz. (125 g.) butter taking 2–3 Tbs. of liquid.

141. Fats for Pastry, Cakes, and Puddings

BUTTER. Because of the excellent flavour of all goods baked with butter, it is still considered the ideal fat to use for cakes, pastry, and puddings.

MARGARINE. Suitable for all purposes. A soft margarine (spreading when cold) creams more readily and makes shorter pastry than a firm one. A firm margarine is better for puff pastry.

LARD. This is the 'shortest' of all fats, and in pastry-making less need be used than with other fats. It is excellent mixed with butter or margarine. It may be used in cakes, but less is required than when butter or margarine is used and, because lard has a pronounced flavour, it should be used alone only in cakes which have flavouring or spices added.

DRIPPING. Clarified beef dripping is excellent for cakes and pastry, but mutton dripping is not satisfactory, as it is too hard. A mixture of the two fats is very good. Warm the mutton fat and beat in the beef dripping.

COOKING FATS. These are usually soft fats which cream readily and make good short pastry. They are suitable for cakes, puddings and pastry, but are usually flavourless and lack the vitamins A and D found in butter and margarine.

SUET. When rendering down, suet can be used in the same way as dripping, but in its natural state it is suitable only for suet pastry and certain types of steamed puddings. To prepare suet for pastry remove any skin, and grate or chop finely. Dredge with flour to prevent the flakes from sticking together. Packet suets have already been grated and mixed with a starchy substance to keep the flakes separate.

OIL. This is suitable for mixing cakes, pastry, and similar foods. 1 oz. (2 Tbs.) oil will replace 2 oz. (50 g.) of other fat. The oil is used to mix the dry ingredients, together with any additional liquid needed to make the cake the right consistency. Hard dripping is very much improved if beaten with a fork to soften it and 2 tsp. of oil to each 4 oz. ($\frac{1}{2}$ c.) fat is then beaten in thoroughly.

142. Fats for Frying

The best fats to use for frying are those which have what is known as a high 'smoking temperature' – that means they can be heated to a very high temperature without burning. Oils have the highest smoking temperature, and are by far the best for deep-fat frying. Butter is often used for shallow frying because of the flavour it gives the food, and clean dripping or cooking fat is suitable for browning meat or vegetables as the preliminary stage in cooking.

143. How to Fry

Fried foods are probably responsible for more indigestion than any others. The reason for this is that unless the food is very carefully fried it soaks up a lot of fat. Fat forms a coating round the starch and protein in the food and hinders its proper digestion. In addition, fat which has been allowed to smoke contains a substance irritating to the intestine.

There are two ways of avoiding this danger: first, see that the food is properly coated before frying, and second, see that the fat used is very hot, and do not try to fry too much at once.

Of the two methods of frying given, Nos. 148 and 149, deep-fat frying is the best to use, but this needs plenty of fat. If deep-fat frying is out of the question, grilling or baking is recommended as being better than the more usual shallow frying, especially for foods which tend to soak up fat.

144. Coating Food for Frying

The only foods which can be fried satisfactorily without a coating of some kind are raw meat, raw potatoes, mushrooms, tomatoes, bacon, eggs, fish, sausages, doughnuts, pancakes, and fritters.

The coating must be something which will set hard as soon as it comes in contact with the hot fat, thus preventing fat from soaking through to the food inside. Incidentally, it also saves fat, for less is used up in frying well-coated food.

145. Flour and Milk Coating (suitable for shallow frying)

Dry the food well and dip it in seasoned flour (see No. 12), then in milk, and then coat well in flour for a second time.

146. Egg and Breadcrumb Coating (suitable for deep or shallow frying)

Dry the food well, and dust it with seasoned flour (see No. 12). Then dip it in beaten egg and make sure the whole surface is evenly covered. A pastry brush is a great help with this. The egg should be beaten up lightly and mixed with 2 Tbs. cold water to each egg. One egg coats eight or more rissoles.

After coating with egg, dip the food in fine fresh or dried breadcrumbs (see No. 876) and pat well to make the crumbs stick. Coarse crumbs should not be used, as they fall off during frying and make the fat dirty. Fresh breadcrumbs give a better colour and flavour to fried foods than the dried. Put the crumbs on a piece of greaseproof paper, place the food in the crumbs, and lift and shake until well coated.

147. Batter Coating (suitable for deep frying)

Use the Fritter Batter, No. 865. Dip the food in seasoned flour. Use a skewer or a fork to hold it, and dip it in the batter, which should be thick enough to coat the food evenly. Drain for a moment, and then lower into the hot fat.

148. Shallow or Dry Frying (or to sauté)

1. It is difficult to fry well with a cheap, thin pan. Buy the thickest and heaviest you can find. It will be a good investment.

2. Use clean or clarified fat or oil (see No. 139), and it should be free from moisture, as water in fat makes it splutter when heated, and you will have a greasy mess all over the stove. If the fat has water in it, heat the pan and fat very, very slowly at first, to drive off the water, and if you

are careful you will manage to do this without any spluttering. There should be enough fat to cover the bottom of the pan.

3. Heat the fat until a very faint blue haze rises. Then put in the prepared food and cook as directed. For details of different fried foods consult the index. If the food is thick and requires some time to cook through, lower the heat after it has browned on both sides. With thick veal and pork chops it is a good plan to cover the pan with a lid, as the steam helps to make the food tender (see No. 382).

4. Fat bacon and oily fish such as herrings and sprats may be fried without any fat in the pan, but heat it before adding the food. Overlap rashers of bacon so that only the fat parts touch the pan.

149. Deep-fat Frying

1. A good supply of a suitable fat is essential for this method. It is not much good trying to do deep-fat frying with less than $1\frac{1}{2}$ lb. (750 g.) of fat or 1 pint ($\frac{1}{2}$ l.) of oil.

2. Use a deep, heavy pan made of aluminium, iron, or steel. A deep pan is essential, as there must be room for fat to cover the food well, and at the same time the pan must not be more than half full. This is a safety measure, as fat bubbles when food is put in, and it may easily bubble over in a shallow pan. Many pans sold for frying are too shallow for safety.

3. Some utensil is needed for lifting cooked food out of the pan. There are special frying-baskets sold for the purpose, or you can use a perforated spoon or small strainer. If you are buying a frying-basket, choose one a little smaller than the pan, as it will swell on heating. When frying food coated in batter do not put it directly on the hot wires of the basket, or it will stick. Have the basket in the pan and drop the coated food in gently, using a fork or skewer.

4. Heat the fat slowly to begin with. It will bubble at first, showing that water is being evaporated. When it stops

bubbling the heat may be increased until frying temperature is reached. It is quite wrong to say food should be cooked in 'boiling hot fat', as fat does not bubble or boil when it is hot enough for frying. While it is bubbling the temperature is only 212° F (100° C). A candy or fat thermometer can be used for testing the temperature, and is a very useful piece of kitchen equipment to have. If you have no thermometer cut a one-inch cube of stale bread and drop it into the fat. The time this takes to brown tells you the temperature of the fat (see table below). Some people recommend looking for a faint blue haze, but as different fats produce a haze at different temperatures, this is a very rough-and-ready method, and will not always give good results.

TEMPERATURE AND TIME GUIDE FOR FRYING

Food	Time for bread to turn light brown	Temperature °F.	°C.	Cooking Time
Choux pastry . . .	2 mins.	320	160	15 mins.
Croquettes, fish cakes, and rissoles . . .	30 secs.	390	200	2–3 mins.
Cutlets, whole or thick pieces of fish, or doughnuts	1 min.	375	190	5–10 mins.
Fish fillets, small thin fish	1 min.	375	190	2–3 mins.
Fritters, uncooked filling .	1 min.	375	190	2–3 mins.
Fritters, cooked filling .	40 secs.	375	190	2–3 mins.
Potato chips . . .	30 secs.	390	200	8–10 mins.
Potato crisps . . .	30 secs.	390	200	1 min.
Whitebait . . .	30 secs.	390	200	2 mins.

N.B. Some fats burn at 400° F., so be careful when heating beyond 390° F.

5. Make sure the food is dry before putting it in the fat. This is to reduce spluttering and bubbling. Do not try to fry too much at once, or the temperature will fall and, instead of frying crisp and dry, the food will be flabby and greasy. 1 pint (½ l.) of oil will not take more than 3 fish cakes or a

good handful of potato chips. The amount largely depends on the degree of heat you are able to maintain under the pan to keep the fat hot. Foods which require 15 minutes cooking should be finished at a lower temperature. The fat should always be re-heated before a fresh lot of food is put in.

6. Have ready a flat tin covered with crumpled absorbent paper, and place the drained food on this, keeping the pieces apart so that they will stay crisp, and keeping them really hot in the oven or warming cupboard.

7. When frying is finished let the fat cool, and then strain into a clean jar. Provided it is not allowed to burn, the same fat can be used many times and added to as required. If there is any fine sediment on the bottom of the cake of fat scrape it off and put it with other fat to be clarified.

150. Potato Cakes, or Rissoles. Frying time 2–3 minutes

Fat temp. 390° F. (200° C.)

Quantities for 8 cakes:

1 lb. mashed potatoes (2 c.)
2 Tbs. milk
$\frac{1}{2}$ tsp. salt
Pinch of pepper
2 Tbs. chopped parsley
1 tsp. onion juice or grated onion

$\frac{1}{4}$ tsp. mace or nutmeg
1 egg
Crumbs for coating
Fat for frying

Measures level. These are easier to make if the potatoes are mashed while still hot, and nicer if the potatoes are freshly cooked. Mix with the milk and flavourings and leave until cold. Then mould into the required shapes, cylinders, balls, or flat cakes, and coat with egg and crumbs (see No. 146). Fry in shallow or deep fat, or grill or bake with a small knob of fat on each one. They will take about 10 minutes to grill and 15–20 minutes to bake in a hot oven, 450° F. (230° C.) Mark 8. It will be found that all mixtures of this kind keep their shape better if they are left to stand for half an hour after coating and before cooking.

Serve with fried or grilled meat or fish, poached egg, or with bacon for breakfast.

151. Meat Cakes or Rissoles

¾ lb. mashed potatoes (1½ c.)
3 oz. cooked minced meat (½ c.)
1 tsp. salt, or to taste
Pinch of pepper
Pinch of mace or nutmeg
1 tsp. Worcester sauce
1 tsp. onion juice
1 egg
Crumbs for coating
Fat for frying

Measures level. Mix and cook as for No. 150. Serve with a Brown Sauce, No. 73, or Tomato Sauce, No. 89.

152. Fish Cakes

8 oz. mashed potatoes (1 c.)
8 oz. cooked or canned flaked fish (1 c.)
½ tsp. salt, or to taste
Pinch of pepper
Pinch of mace or nutmeg
1 tsp. onion juice
1 Tbs. chopped parsley
Few drops vinegar or lemon juice
1 egg
Crumbs for coating
Fat for frying

Measures level. Mix and cook as for Recipe No. 150. Serve with Tomato Sauce, No. 89, or Anchovy Sauce, No. 72.

153. Cheese Cakes

¾ lb. mashed potatoes (1½ c.)
4 oz. grated cheese (125 g.)
½ tsp. salt
Pinch of pepper
Pinch of ground mace
1 Tbs. chopped parsley
1 egg
Crumbs for coating
Fat for frying

Measures level. Mix and cook as for No. 150. Serve with Tomato Sauce, No. 89, and Lettuce Salad, No. 563.

Other Recipes for Frying are:

Fritters, Nos. 865–70.
Fish, Nos. 263–9.
Meat, Nos. 378–89.
Omelets, Nos. 201–13.
Pancakes, Nos. 859–61.

CHAPTER 9

Milk, Cream, and Cheese

154. Food Value

MILK is a cheap source of many nutrients, the most important being protein of excellent quality, calcium, and vitamins A, D, riboflavine and thiamine (B_1). It is a specially important food for children, expectant and nursing mothers, adolescents, the sick and the aged. Aim to have 1 pint ($\frac{1}{2}$ l.) of milk a day for each adult in the family and $1\frac{1}{2}$–2 pints (1 l.) a day for children, adolescents, expectant and nursing mothers. This includes milk used for cooking as well as drinks and need not be fresh bottled milk.

Canned and dried milks are usually cheaper than fresh milk and are very suitable for most purposes as well as being an emergency store. The canned and dried whole milks contain the same nutrients as fresh milk but the skimmed milks lack fat, and vitamins A and D. This loss can be made good by the addition of a little margarine or butter during cooking.

CREAM is simply the fat removed when milk is skimmed or separated. It also contains vitamins A and D.

CHEESE contains all the important nutrients found in milk, but it is a very concentrated food; 1 pint ($\frac{1}{2}$ l.) of milk makes 2 ounces (50 g.) of hard cheese. It is a cheap alternative to meat and fish in main meals, 2 ounces (50 g.) of cheese being equal in protein value to 4 ounces (100 g.) of meat. Cottage and soft cheeses are less concentrated, while cream cheese has the same nutritive value as cream.

MILK

155. Pasteurizing and Scalding

Milk is an ideal medium for the growth of disease-producing bacteria and care is therefore essential to see that it is kept clean and free from infection.

Milk for drinking should be heat treated to make sure it is safe. Pasteurized, Homogenized, Sterilized, and Ultra Heat Treated (UHT) milks have all been heated; but the grades known as Untreated and Untreated Farm Bottled do not have any heat treatment.

Unpasteurized milk can be scalded in the home to make it safe for drinking. Heat it over boiling water until it reaches a temperature of 162° F. (72° C.). Keep it at that heat for 15 seconds and then stand the container in cold water to cool the milk quickly.

If you have no thermometer, heat the milk in an uncovered pan until bubbles begin to appear round the edges. If possible do this over boiling water. After heating, pour the milk into a jug which has been scalded by rinsing it out with boiling water. Cool the milk quickly by standing the jug in cold water.

Keep the scalded milk covered from dust and flies and in a cold place.

156. Keeping Milk Fresh

Milk should always be kept in as cool a place as possible. If you have no refrigerator or very cold larder, stand the jug or bottle in a basin of cold water with a piece of clean, damp muslin over the top, with the ends in the water. Stand it in a draught to encourage evaporation of the water, for this keeps the milk cool.

If milk comes in bottles, it is best to leave it there until you are ready to use it, but wipe the outside of the bottles.

All jugs and containers for milk should be kept very clean.

After ordinary washing with first cold and then hot water, rinse out with boiling water and turn upside down to dry. Do not dry with a cloth, as this may introduce germs and undo the good done by scalding.

Always keep milk covered from dust and flies and, as it absorbs odours readily, keep it away from any food with a strong flavour.

Do not mix new milk and old unless it is to be used at once, and even then you should be sure the old milk is still quite sweet.

157. Dried Milk

Full-cream dried milk is the best, but it does not keep as long as dried skim milk, because the fat or cream tends to become rancid, especially after the container has been opened.

Mix dried milk according to the directions on the container, but after mixing, do not try to keep it longer than fresh milk.

For cakes, puddings, and sauces the milk may be mixed dry with the other dry ingredients, and so save the trouble of reconstituting.

Store dried milk in an airtight jar or tin in a cool, dry place, away from foods which have a strong flavour. The time it will keep depends on its age when you bought it.

158. Evaporated Milk

This is full cream or skim milk from which some of the water has been evaporated. To bring it to the consistency of fresh milk, add water according to the directions on the can, generally an equal amount. It can then be used in any recipe requiring fresh milk, except junket. After the can has been opened evaporated milk will not keep any longer than fresh milk.

159. Condensed Milk

This is like evaporated milk, but with still more water removed and some sugar added. It should be diluted according to the directions on the can, and used for sweet sauces and puddings. Because of the sugar, it will keep longer than evaporated milk after the can has been opened.

160. Sour Milk

Milk which has been pasteurized or scalded will not sour, but does eventually go bad. Milk which has not been heated sours because it contains bacteria which feed on the small amounts of sugar in milk and produce lactic acid. This acid makes the milk clot.

Sour milk may be used in place of fresh milk for mixing cakes, scones, and puddings. The curd alone may be used for cottage cheese. The whey can be used in place of fresh milk for mixing.

TO SEPARATE THE CURD AND WHEY. Put the sour milk in a basin and heat it over hot water until the curd separates. Scald a piece of butter muslin in boiling water. Wring out well. Place it in a strainer and pour the sour milk carefully into the centre. Gather the ends together into a bag, tie with clean string, and hang the bag over a basin to drip for 24 hours.

TO MAKE COTTAGE CHEESE. Remove the curd from the bag and mash it with a fork, seasoning well with salt and pepper. A few chopped chives may be added for extra flavour. In some countries cottage cheese seasoned with salt is eaten with jam and hot rolls for breakfast, and is very good too. Cottage cheese may be used for sandwich fillings, see No. 890. It may also be made from fresh milk set with rennet or by warming 1 pt. of fresh milk with the juice of $\frac{1}{2}$ lemon.

YOGURT. This is milk that has been fermented by the use of heat and different bacteria from those causing ordinary souring. Many people claim medicinal properties for

Yogurt, but it is doubtful whether it has any advantages over ordinary milk as a source of nutrients. In cooking, plain or natural Yogurt can be used to take the place of sour cream, giving an excellent flavour to the dish without increasing the fat content to the same extent.

161. Cream

By law single cream must contain not less than 18 per cent butterfat; double cream not less than 48 per cent; canned and sterilized cream not less than 23 per cent; and clotted cream not less than 48 per cent.

For whipping there should be about 35 per cent fat; too much tends to produce a buttery cream, while if the cream is too thin it will not whip at all. Two parts double cream to one part single cream makes a very good mixture. Have the cream as cold as possible, use a rotary beater, and stop beating as soon as it is as thick as you want it, being particularly careful as it begins to thicken.

Reconstituted cream made from butter and milk, using a cream machine, can be whipped after it has been refrigerated for 24 hours.

Undiluted evaporated milk makes a good substitute for cream in cooking and, when chilled and whipped, it may be used in place of whipped cream. It whips to a greater volume than cream and less is usually needed.

Cultured or soured cream is prepared from pasteurized cream with a special culture added to give an acid flavour, traditional in many continental recipes. It is used for sauces, salad dressings, and in cooking, and can replace double cream in most recipes, though it has a lower fat content. Yogurt is a low-fat alternative to cultured cream in cooking, and evaporated milk made acid with lemon juice is another alternative.

UHF cream with a long shelf life is available as single or double cream and can be used to replace ordinary fresh cream.

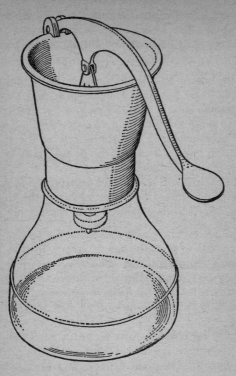

cream machine

162. Reconstituted Cream

Using a cream machine to reconstitute butter and milk to
cream can be a real economy as well as providing the means
of having cream at hand whenever you want it. You can
work out the saving for yourself. The thin cream recipe
makes about $\frac{3}{4}$ pint ($1\frac{1}{2}$ c.) of coffee cream, while the thick
cream recipe makes $\frac{1}{2}$ pint (1 c.) of whipping cream, both
indistinguishable from fresh cream. For soups and savoury
sauces margarine can replace the butter.

Thin cream: 4 oz. unsalted butter (125 g.) and ½ pint milk (1 c.)

Thick cream: 4 oz. unsalted butter (125 g.) and ¼ pint milk (½ c.)

Warm the butter and milk together until melted. Then cool it a little by pouring it backwards and forwards between the pan and a jug. Then pour it into the cream machine in small lots and pump quickly until all is through. It is not necessary to screw the nozzle of the machine so tight that it is hard work to do the pumping. A little experience soon shows the right position.

Stir the cream with a fork and put it aside to cool before storing in the refrigerator. After 24 hours the thick cream can be whipped and, provided it is thoroughly whipped, will keep its shape for some hours.

163. Cream Chantilly (for decorating sweets and serving with fresh fruit or fruit salad)

½ pt. whipping cream (1 c.)

1 oz. sifted icing sugar (¼ c.)

Vanilla or other essence or liqueur

Measures level. If the cream is for piping use double cream, otherwise use a mixture of half double and half single cream. Whip until the cream is thick but not buttery. Fold in the icing sugar and flavouring.

164. Milk Topping (a low-fat garnish to use in place of cream)

Quantities for 4 helpings:

8 Tbs. cold water

1 Tbs. lemon juice

1 oz. sugar (2 Tbs.)

3 oz. dried skim milk powder (75 g.)

Vanilla or other flavouring

Measures level. Put the water and lemon juice in a bowl and sprinkle in the sugar and milk powder. Beat until thick and light, preferably with a machine. Flavour to taste. Use within half an hour as it tends to become runny after this.

165. Junket. Time to set, 20 minutes–½ hour

Quantities for 4 helpings:

1 pt. milk (2 c.)	Rennet, junket powder, or
Pinch of salt	tablets, according to the
1 Tbs. sugar	maker's instructions
Flavouring to taste	

Measures level.

　　1. Heat the milk until it is just lukewarm (90–100° F. or 30–35° C.). Fresh milk is best for junket, but dried milk may be used if it is mixed a little thicker than usual, and if 1½ times the normal amount of rennet is used. Evaporated or condensed milk is not suitable, because heat used in the canning process destroys the power of the milk to clot.

　　2. Pour the milk into the serving dish and stir in the salt, sugar, and flavouring.

　　3. When the sugar is dissolved add the rennet. Leave in a warm place, and do not disturb until set.

166. Chocolate Junket

Mix 2 level Tbs. cocoa and 2 Tbs. boiling water. Add to the milk, and warm as in No. 165. Use vanilla essence for the flavouring.

167. Coffee Junket

Add 2 tsp. coffee essence or ½–1 Tbs. soluble coffee to the milk. Add vanilla essence for flavouring. Make as for No. 165.

168. Coloured Junkets

For children who are difficult about taking milk puddings it is a good plan to disguise the milk by adding a little vegetable colouring, such as a few drops of cochineal, and by flavouring with fruit essence. If the junket is set in a small individual dish it is made still more attractive to the child.

169. Jam Junket

Spread 2 Tbs. of red jam in the bottom of the dish before pouring in the junket. In this case the rennet should be mixed into the milk first, as the milk should not be disturbed after it has been poured on the jam.

CHEESE

170. General Information

In the past there has been much confusion over the naming of cheese, especially the use of the terms 'cottage', 'curd' and 'cream' cheese, but the labelling of cheeses is now controlled by law. The main types are: hard cheeses such as Cheddar and Cheshire and others less hard such as Caerphilly; blue-vein cheeses; soft cheeses which have a higher water content and a softer texture; cottage cheese which is softer still and is made from specially prepared pasteurized milk (it may be fat-free); curd cheese which is similar to cottage cheese but is made from naturally soured unpasteurized milk and may be skimmed, whole, or with added cream; cream cheese which is made from either single cream, and is like a rich curd cheese, or from double cream, when it resembles butter in texture; and processed cheese.

The most useful cheeses for cooking are Parmesan, a strong, dry Cheddar, or a hard Dutch or Swiss cheese. These can be grated finely and will blend with other ingredients and give a better flavour. The less hard and processed cheeses can be added to sauces and used for Welsh rarebit if they are first cut in small pieces.

When cheese is served as a course by itself, it is usually eaten with bread, biscuits, toast or rusks according to personal preference. Some use butter, others prefer not to. Some people like to eat pickles with mild cheese; others prefer a little green salad or some watercress, celery, radishes or fruit.

To keep cheese in a cupboard or larder for short periods, either store it in the box in which it was purchased or put it in a loose polythene bag and keep it cool. For longer storage, put cheese in a polythene bag and keep it in the refrigerator; but take it out some hours before using it, otherwise it will lack flavour.

A supply of ready-grated cheese can be stored in a covered jar, and will keep some weeks in a refrigerator. If grated cheese is to be stored in an ordinary larder it must be very dry, or the cheese will quickly become mouldy.

Cheese melts at a fairly low temperature, and if made very hot it soon becomes tough, stringy, and indigestible. When making cheese dishes for children, care should be taken to cook the cheese very lightly. In some cheese dishes the recipe calls for cooking at a very high temperature to brown the cheese. This should be done as quickly as possible.

171. Welsh Rarebit. Cooking time about 15 minutes

Quantities for 3 helpings:

½ oz. butter or margarine (1 Tbs.)	1 tsp. made mustard or Worcester Sauce
4 oz. grated Cheddar cheese (125 g.)	2 Tbs. milk or ale
	3 slices of toast

Measures level. Melt the butter or margarine in a small pan. Mix the other ingredients into the melted fat, and cook very gently until smooth and creamy. Spread on the hot toast, and serve at once or brown under the grill, according to taste.

172. Buck Rarebit

Serve a poached egg on top of each portion of Welsh Rarebit.

173. Cheese Tart. Cooking time ¾ hour

Temperature 400° F. (200° C.) Mark 6 for 15 minutes, then 325° F. (160° C.) Mark 2 for ½ hour.

Quantities for 4–6 helpings:

Short pastry, No. 807, using 4 oz. flour (1 c.)	4 oz. grated Swiss cheese (125 g.)
2 eggs	Pinch grated nutmeg
¼ pt. single cream (½ c.)	Few grains cayenne pepper

Measures level. Roll the pastry to line a 7–8 inch (18–20 cm.) flan ring. Put to chill. Beat the eggs and mix in the other ingredients. Pour into the pastry case and bake until the filling is golden brown and set. Serve hot or cold.

174. Chutneyed Cheese. Cooking time 5 minutes

Quantities for 4 helpings:

4 slices toast	2 Tbs. chutney
Margarine to spread	
3–4 oz. cheese (4 thin slices)	

Measures level. Spread the toast thinly with margarine. Cut the cheese in wafer-thin slices and place on the toast. Spread with chutney and heat under the grill or in a hot oven, 450° F. (230° C.) Mark 8, until the cheese melts. Serve hot.

175. Cheese Fondue. Cooking time 5 minutes

Quantities for 2 helpings:

2 fresh eggs
2 oz. grated Emmenthal
  or Gruyère (50 g.)

1 oz. butter or margarine
  (25 g.)
Salt and pepper to taste

Measures level. Beat the eggs thoroughly, and add the butter cut in small pieces, and the grated cheese. Season well. Put in a small saucepan and stir over a fairly quick heat until the mixture begins to thicken. It should be thick enough to eat with a fork. Serve in small hot dishes with bread or toast handed separately.

176. Cheese Pudding. Cooking time $\frac{1}{2}-\frac{3}{4}$ hour

Temperature 375° F. (190° C.) Mark 5.

Quantities for 4–6 helpings:

3 oz. fresh breadcrumbs
  (1$\frac{1}{2}$ c.)
1 pt. milk, scalded (2 c.)
4 oz. grated cheese (125 g.)

2 fresh eggs
$\frac{1}{2}$ tsp. salt
Pinch of pepper

Measures level. Soak the breadcrumbs in the milk for a few minutes. Then add the cheese, seasonings, and beaten egg yolks. Beat the whites stiffly and fold them into the mixture. Pour into a well-greased baking dish. Bake until risen and set.

177. Potted Cheese Spread. Cooking time 5 minutes

Quantities for about $\frac{1}{4}$ pt. ($\frac{1}{2}$ c.):

2 Tbs. flour
6 Tbs. water
2 oz. grated cheese (50 g.)
1 oz. margarine (25 g.)

$\frac{1}{2}$ tsp. salt
$\frac{1}{8}$ tsp. paprika pepper
1 Tbs. tomato purée or
  tomato juice

Measures level. Mix the flour and water to a smooth cream in a small saucepan and stir until it boils. Cook gently for 5 minutes. Add the cheese, margarine, seasonings, and tomato purée. Mix well and keep in small jars. The mixture may be used as a sandwich spread or as a savoury on toast.

178. Quiche Lorraine. Cooking time 1 hour

Temperature 450° F. (230° C.) Mark 8, then 375° F. (190° C.) Mark 5.

Quantities for 4–6 helpings:

Short Pastry, No. 807, using 4 oz. flour ($\frac{3}{4}$ c.)	$\frac{1}{2}$ pt. hot milk (1 c.)
2 eggs	2 oz. grated cheese (50 g.)
$\frac{1}{2}$ tsp. salt	3 rashers bacon, grilled
Pinch pepper	$\frac{1}{2}$ oz. butter (1 Tbs.)

Measures level. Roll the pastry to line a 7–8 inch (18–20 cm.) flan ring or sandwich tin. Bake blind, see No. 812. Beat the eggs and seasoning slightly, add the milk and cheese and the chopped cooked bacon and butter. Pour into the cooked pastry and bake in a moderate oven for 30–40 minutes or until the filling is set. Serve hot or cold.

For other Recipes using Cheese see the Index.

CHAPTER 10

Eggs

179. Food Value and General Information

Eggs are nutritionally one of the most valuable foods we have as they contain protein of very good quality, are a good source of vitamins A and B and also of iron. Two eggs are equivalent in protein value to 4 oz. (125 g.) meat.

In all recipes given in this book, standard size eggs have been used unless otherwise stated. Average weights for standard eggs are about 2 oz.; large about $2\frac{1}{4}$ oz.; medium $1\frac{3}{4}$ oz.; and small $1\frac{1}{2}$ oz. Thus a recipe requiring 3 standard eggs can have 4 small ones substituted.

Ducks' eggs may be used for making cakes and puddings, when one will be equivalent to $1\frac{1}{2}$–2 hens' eggs. Care must be taken to see that they are thoroughly cooked, as they are more likely to be infected with harmful bacteria than hens' eggs, and are not therefore suitable for light cooking – e.g. poached and coddled. Other eggs may be hard-boiled and used in salads or used in place of hens' eggs for cakes and puddings.

A fresh egg is heavy in proportion to its size, and becomes lighter with age. It sinks in cold water, while a stale egg floats. When broken, a fresh egg smells good, the yolk is firm and the white is viscid, while a stale egg will be known by the smell, a yolk that breaks easily, and a watery white.

It is advisable to break each egg separately into a cup or saucer, to make sure it is fresh. Hold the egg over the cup and give it a sharp tap with a knife to break the shell. Put the thumbs into the crack and break the egg apart. If the yolk and white are to be separated, tip the yolk from one half of the shell to the other until all the white has fallen into the cup below. Care must be taken not to let any yolk get in with the white, or it will not beat up well.

Eggs set, or 'coagulate', as it is called, at a temperature well below boiling point, and when heated above 160° F. (70° C.) become hard and tough. When adding eggs to a hot sauce or to milk for a custard you must be careful to see that the sauce or milk is below boiling point, or the eggs may set in small hard bits and 'curdle' the mixture.

180. Keeping Eggs

Because the shells are porous, eggs should be kept away from any food with a strong odour. They will keep a week in a cool larder but otherwise it is safer to keep them in the refrigerator. Egg yolks should be covered with a little cold water, plus a lid, and stored in a cold place. Before using them, the water can either be poured off or mixed in. Egg whites should be covered and stored in a cold place. Both whole eggs (out of the shell), and egg yolks and whites can be stored in the freezer.

181. Beating Eggs

They should be at room temperature for best results. If you have taken them straight out of the refrigerator, warm the bowl first. An electric beater is the easiest tool to use for beating a number of eggs, but for just one a small wire whisk is ideal. Beating will be quickest when the bowl is of such a size and shape that the blades of the beater are at least half covered by egg. Do not beat them in advance as they tend to lose air with standing.

182. Boiled Eggs

1. Do not use eggs with cracked shells. You can test this by tapping the eggs lightly together when the sound will

tell you if one is cracked. Put the eggs in a pan with cold water to cover, bring to the boil, lower the heat and boil gently to prevent cracking. Do not use a lid.

2. Count the time from boiling point:

Soft boiled (*soft whites, liquid yolks*)
Large 3 minutes, standard 2¾ minutes, medium 2½ minutes.
Medium boiled (*firm whites, soft yolks*)
Large 4½ minutes, standard 4 minutes, medium 3½ minutes.
Hard boiled (*firm whites and yolks*)
Large 8–10 minutes, standard 7 minutes, medium 6 minutes.

Less time is required for eggs which are not so fresh and for those below the average size.

3. If the eggs have been hard-boiled, crack the shells as soon as they are cooked, plunge them into cold water and leave until quite cold. This helps to prevent the dark ring which sometimes shows round the yolk, and which is generally due to over-cooking.

183. Coddled Eggs

This is the best way of cooking eggs for children and invalids, as there will be no danger of the white being tough and indigestible.

Proceed as before, but when the water boils turn down the heat and cook below boiling. The time required will be a little longer, e.g. for large eggs allow:

Soft boiled, 4 minutes.
Medium boiled, 6–7 minutes.
Hard boiled, 15–20 minutes.

184. Curried Eggs. Cooking time ½ hour

Quantities for 4 helpings:

4 hard-boiled eggs   4–8 oz. rice (½–1 c.)
½ pt. Curry Sauce, No.
  76 (1 c.)

Cut the eggs in half and pour the sauce over them. Serve
with the rice boiled, see No. 613.

185. Eggs Lyonnaise. Cooking time 20 minutes

Quantities for 4 helpings:

4 hard-boiled eggs   Salt and pepper
½ pt. Onion Sauce, No. 85   2 oz. cheese, grated (½ c.)

Measures level. Slice the eggs and heat them in the sauce.
Place in a fireproof dish and cover with the grated cheese.
Place in the oven or under the grill to melt the cheese.
Serve very hot.

186. Scotch Eggs. Cooking time 7–8 minutes

Frying Temperature 375° F. (190° C.).

Quantities for 4 helpings:

4 eggs, hard-boiled and   1 beaten egg
  shelled   Fine white breadcrumbs
Seasoned flour   Oil for frying
8 oz. sausage meat or
  skinned sausages (250 g.)

Make sure the outsides of the eggs are dry and dust them
with seasoned flour. Divide the sausage meat into four
pieces, flatten each piece and mould it round an egg to coat
it evenly and smoothly. Brush with beaten egg and roll it in
the crumbs to coat thoroughly. Fry, see No. 149. Do not

try to hurry the frying process as it is important to allow time to cook the sausage thoroughly. Drain on absorbent paper and serve hot with a sauce or cold with salad.

187. Fricassée of Eggs. Cooking time 20 minutes

Quantities for 4 helpings:

4 hard-boiled eggs
½ pt. Brown Sauce, No. 73
    (1 c.)

4 rashers streaky bacon
1 Tbs. chopped parsley
Toast

Measures level. Cut the eggs in half and heat them gently in the sauce. Roll the rashers of bacon and fasten them on a skewer. Grill or bake. Put the eggs and sauce on a hot dish, garnish with the bacon and parsley and serve hot with toast.

188. Stuffed Eggs

Fresh eggs only should be used, as stale eggs are apt to have the yolk lying to one side, and that spoils the shape for a stuffed egg. Hard boil the eggs and allow to become cold. Shell, cut in half, and remove the yolks. Mash the yolks and mix with one of the stuffings given below, season highly and then press back into the whites. Serve with a salad or as a savoury for a supper party, or press the halves together for carrying in the picnic-basket.

  1. For 4 eggs allow 2 level Tbs. grated cheese, 1 Tbs. vinegar, ¼ level tsp. mustard, salt and pepper, and 1 tsp. melted butter or margarine.

  2. For each egg allow 1 level Tbs. minced ham. Season well and add some chopped parsley.

  3. Beat in anchovy essence and a little lemon juice to taste.

  4. Mix with an equal amount of minced cooked chicken or veal and season to taste with salt and pepper. Add mayonnaise to moisten.

189. Poached Eggs

1. Place enough water in a frying-pan or saucepan to cover the eggs. Bring to the boil.

2. Break the egg into a saucer and slide it gently into the water. Only fresh eggs should be used for poaching, as if the whites are watery they will spread badly.

3. Turn down the heat so that the water is just below boiling. Leave 5 minutes or until the egg is lightly set – that is, when the white becomes opaque.

4. Lift out with a fish slice and rest the slice on a clean cloth for a second to drain off the water. Then slide on to buttered toast. Serve at once.

190. Eggs Mornay

Allow 5 pt. (2 Tbs.) Cheese Sauce, No. 75, for each egg, or use a packet sauce.

Place the very lightly poached eggs on a fireproof dish and cover with the cheese sauce. Brown under the grill.

191. Poached Eggs on Anchovy Toast

Spread the toast with Anchovy Sauce, No. 72, or paste.

192. Poached Egg with Potato Cake

Use any of the Potato Cake Recipes, Nos. 150–53, and shape into flat cakes about the size of a poached egg. Fry in shallow fat and serve a poached egg on each one. Cover with Tomato Sauce, No. 89, or Brown Sauce, No. 73.

193. Poached Eggs in Aspic

Poach the eggs lightly, drain and trim them to a round. Place in cold water to chill them. Trim thin slices of lean ham, allowing two per egg. Arrange half these on a flat dish and put an egg on each. Cover with the second slice of ham. Cover with just-melted Aspic Jelly, No. 716, or with ready-prepared aspic jelly, which can be bought from most stores. When firmly set cut out each with a large round cutter the size of the pieces of ham. They may be served plain or with a green salad. The yolks should still be soft inside.

194. Steamed Eggs or Eggs en Cocotte

Special egg steamers are sold for this purpose, also little earthenware dishes called 'cocottes'. Small round patty-tins may be used too. Grease the dishes before adding the eggs and then stand them in a frying-pan with water coming half-way up the sides. Keep the water just below boiling and cook for the same time as poached eggs. Serve in the same way, or, if cocottes are used, leave the eggs in the dishes and serve toast or bread separately.

195. Scrambled Eggs. Cooking time 5 minutes

Quantities for 4 helpings:

4 or 5 eggs	1 oz. margarine or butter
½ tsp. salt	(25 g.)
Pinch of pepper	4 slices of toast
6 Tbs. milk	

Measures level.

1. Beat the eggs enough to mix them well and add the milk and seasoning.
2. Melt the fat in a small saucepan, but do not allow it to become hot. Add the eggs and cook over a very low heat or over hot water. Do not stir the eggs more than is necessary to keep them from sticking to the pan, because stirring makes them granular instead of letting them set in large, creamy clots.

3. Serve as soon as they are set. If allowed to cook longer they will become tough and hard with a watery liquid separating out. Serve on the hot toast.

196. Cheesed Eggs

Add 1 oz. grated cheese (25 g.) and 1 Tbs. chopped parsley to Scrambled Eggs, No. 195, before cooking.

197. Curried Scramble

Use Recipe No. 195 for scrambled eggs and fry 1 small chopped onion in the fat. Then add 1 level Tbs. curry powder, mix well and allow to cool a little. Then add the eggs and finish in the usual way.

198. Portuguese Eggs

Cut 1 lb. tomatoes in pieces (500 g.) and cook them gently in ½ oz. fat (1 Tbs.). Season well. Scramble eggs as described in No. 195 and dish them in a ring on a hot dish. Pour the tomatoes in the centre and serve hot, sprinkled with chopped parsley.

199. Scrambled Eggs with Bacon

Chop one rasher of bacon and fry it gently in the fat before adding the eggs. Cook as described for Scrambled Eggs, No. 195.

200. Scrambled Eggs Lyonnaise

Chop one medium-sized onion finely and fry it in margarine. Add the eggs and proceed as for Scrambled Eggs, No. 195.

201. French Omelet. Cooking time about 2 minutes

Quantities for 4 helpings:

8 eggs	Pinch of pepper
1 tsp. salt	1 oz. butter (25 g.)

Measures level.

1. Beat the eggs just enough to mix them thoroughly, and add the seasoning.

2. Be sure that the pan is perfectly clean and dry. The ideal is to keep a pan just for omelets and to wipe it out instead of washing it. If yours is a general-purpose pan you will find it a help to heat the pan and fat slowly at first in order to draw off any moisture. A damp pan causes omelets to stick. Heat enough butter to cover the bottom of the pan. It is nicer to make individual omelets, but for a family it is more practical to make a large one. This recipe is about right for a pan 10 inches (25 cm.) across, and the omelet may then be divided into four for serving.

3. When the butter begins to brown pour in the eggs and keep a good heat under the pan to cook the omelet quickly. As soon as the underside begins to set start lifting the edge first in one place and then in another, tilting the pan slightly to let the liquid egg run underneath. The omelet is done when no more liquid will run under, but it should still be quite moist on top.

4. Using a knife, roll the omelet over, away from the handle, and tip it out on to a hot plate. It should be golden-brown on the outside and still moist inside, unless you prefer them dry, when you will naturally cook the omelet a little longer. If the omelet is a stuffed one, the filling should be put on before it is rolled up.

202. Bacon Omelet

Add 1 level Tbs. chopped parsley to Omelet, No. 201, before cooking, and fry one or two rashers of chopped bacon in the fat before adding the eggs. If the bacon is very salty this method may make the omelet stick to the pan, so it is better to cook the bacon separately and mix it with the eggs before pouring them into the omelet pan.

203. Cheese Omelet

Mix 2 oz. grated cheese (50 g.) with the eggs before making Omelet, No. 201.

204. Herb Omelet

Add 2 level Tbs. chopped parsley and 2 level Tbs. chopped chives to the eggs before cooking Omelet, No. 201. If no fresh herbs are available add 1 tsp. dried herbs instead.

205. Kidney Omelet

Chop 2 sheep's kidneys into small pieces and cook them for a minute or two in a separate pan with $\frac{1}{2}$ oz. fat (1 Tbs.). Add 1 level Tbs. flour, mix well and then pour on $\frac{1}{4}$ c. stock. Stir until it boils, and cook gently for 5 minutes. Make the omelet, according to No. 201, and spread the kidney mixture on before rolling up.

206. Mushroom Omelet

Peel and chop 4–6 oz. mushrooms (125–175 g.) and cook for a few minutes in the fat before adding the eggs and cooking as for No. 201.

207. Onion Omelet

Peel and chop two small onions finely. Cook in the fat until brown before adding the eggs and cooking as for No. 201.

208. Sweet Omelet

Half Recipe No. 201 is enough for 4 helpings. Leave out the salt and pepper and spread on 2 or 3 Tbs. hot jam before rolling it up.

209. Rum Omelet

Quantities for 4 helpings:

Use half Recipe No. 201, leaving out the salt and pepper. When the omelet is served sprinkle with 2 tsp. sugar and pour over 2 Tbs. rum. Set light to the rum and baste the omelet with it.

210. Omelette à la Crème. Cooking time 15 minutes

Quantities for 1 helping:

1–2 oz. mushrooms (25–50 g.)	1 Tbs. thick cream
1 oz. butter (25 g.)	2 eggs
¼ pt. Cheese Sauce, No. 75 (½ c.)	Salt and pepper

Measures level. Wash the mushrooms and chop coarsely. Stew in ½ oz. butter in a small pan until tender. Add the cream to the sauce and keep hot. Make the omelet as in No. 201, adding the mushrooms before cooking. Fold on to a hot, fireproof dish and pour the sauce over. Brown lightly under the grill.

N.B. This omelet may be made twice or four times the size in a large pan and cut in portions for serving.

211. Soufflé Omelet. Cooking time 15 minutes

Quantities for 1 large or 4 small omelets:

4 fresh eggs	Pinch of pepper
¼ c. water	½ oz. melted butter (1 Tbs.)
½ tsp. salt	Chopped parsley

1. Separate the yolks and whites of the eggs and beat the yolks with the water until thick and lemon-coloured. Add the seasonings.

2. Beat the egg whites stiffly.

3. Melt the fat in the pan.

4. Fold the egg yolks into the whites very gently and pour into the pan. Cook very slowly for about 5 minutes, when the omelet should be golden underneath and beginning to rise up in the pan. If the heat is too great it will rise up quickly and then collapse and be tough.

5. Continue cooking in a moderate oven or under a slow grill for 8–10 minutes, until the top looks dry. Do not cook too long, or it will shrivel and be tough.

6. Fold in half and turn on to a hot dish. Sprinkle with chopped parsley and serve at once.

N.B. For variety this omelet may be served with a sauce poured over – e.g. Onion Sauce, No. 85; Tomato Sauce, No. 89; Cheese Sauce, No. 75; Mussel Sauce, No. 83; or Mushroom Sauce, No. 82.

212. Spanish Omelet. Cooking time about 5 minutes

Quantities for 2 helpings:

3 eggs	$\frac{1}{2}$ oz. fat (1 Tbs.)
$\frac{1}{2}$ tsp. salt	$\frac{1}{2}$ c. mixed cooked or
Pinch of pepper	canned vegetables, diced
1 Tbs. chopped parsley	

Measures level. Beat the eggs. Add seasoning and parsley. Heat the fat and toss the vegetables in it. Any vegetables are suitable, and may include some sliced raw tomato or chopped pimentos. Pour the eggs over the vegetables and cook, without stirring, until the egg is brown underneath. Place in the oven or under the grill to set the top lightly. Fold over and serve at once.

213. Swedish Omelet. Cooking time 25–30 minutes

Temperature 350° F. (180° C.) Mark 3.

Quantities for 3–4 helpings:

2 oz. diced bacon (50 g.)	½ pt. milk (1 c.)
2 eggs	Salt and pepper

Measures level. Grease a shallow baking-dish. Add the bacon. Beat the eggs and season well. Add the milk and pour over the bacon. Bake in a moderate oven until set. This may be varied by using chopped, smoked fish in place of the bacon.

214. Fried Eggs. Cooking time 2–3 minutes

　1. Heat enough fat to cover the bottom of the frying-pan.
　2. When it is melted, but not very hot, add the eggs, which should each be broken separately into a saucer and then slid into the fat. This is to make sure you do not drop a bad egg into the fat.
　3. Cook gently – much more slowly than ordinary frying – basting the egg with the hot fat until the white is set. Lift out with a fish-slice. If the fat is too hot and the cooking too fast, the egg will be tough and unpleasant to eat.

215. Eggs with Brown Butter. Cooking time 3–4 minutes

Quantities for 2–4 helpings:

1 oz. butter (25 g.)	Salt and pepper
4 eggs	1 Tbs. vinegar

Heat the butter in a frying-pan until it turns nut-brown. Break in the eggs, and season each with a pinch of salt and pepper. Cook gently until the whites are firm. Place on a hot dish. Add the vinegar to the butter and pour over the eggs.

216. Custards

The true custard is made with egg, milk, and a little flavouring, and depends entirely on the eggs to thicken it.

When making custards, care must be taken to have the proportions of eggs and liquid correct, or the custard will not set. Adding too much sugar also prevents setting, and cooking too fast or for too long produces curdling.

It is recommended that hot milk be used, as this hastens the cooking process.

Soft Custard or Custard Sauce. See Sauces, No. 105.

217. Baked Custard. Cooking time about ¾–1 hour

Temperature 250–350° F. (120–180° C.) Mark ¼–3.

Quantities for 4 helpings:

2 large or 3 standard eggs	Pinch of salt
1 pt. milk (2 c.)	Flavouring to taste
1 Tbs. sugar	Nutmeg

Measures level.

1. Beat the eggs, salt, and sugar enough to mix well.
2. Heat the milk. Pour the hot (not boiling) milk on to the eggs and stir well. Add flavouring to taste.
3. Pour into a greased pie-dish. When using the higher temperature, place the pie-dish in a baking-tin with hot water to come half-way up the sides of the pie-dish. Sprinkle a little nutmeg on top of the custard.
4. Bake until set. To test for setting, slip the blade of a knife into the custard half-way between the centre and the side, and if it comes out clean with no custard sticking to it, the baking is finished. The custard may not be quite done in the middle, but there will be sufficient heat in it to finish the cooking, and taking it out at this stage prevents over-cooking and curdling.

The time required depends to some extent on the type of dish used. It will take longer in a narrow, deep dish than in a shallow, wide one. In a pressure cooker allow 4 minutes: reduce pressure slowly.

218. Caramel Custard

Use Recipe No. 217, omitting the sugar. Boil 2 oz. sugar (4 level Tbs.) and 2 Tbs. water together until toffee-coloured. Add the hot milk and stir until dissolved. Then add to the eggs and proceed as usual. Add 1 tsp. vanilla for flavouring.

219. Caramel Mould or Crème Caramel. Cooking time 35–45 minutes

Temperature 250–350° F. (120–180° C.) Mark ¼–3.

Quantities for 4–6 small moulds:

4–5 eggs	*Caramel*
1 Tbs. sugar	4 oz. sugar (8 Tbs.)
1 pt. milk (2 c.)	4 Tbs. water
Vanilla essence	

Measures level.

1. Individual moulds are the most satisfactory to use, as the mould is less likely to break on turning out. The moulds may be metal or earthenware. Grease them well.

2. Boil the sugar and water, without stirring, until it goes a good toffee colour. Pour quickly into the moulds. Hold the moulds in a cloth and twist round to coat well with caramel.

3. Mix the custard as for Baked Custard, No. 217, and pour into the moulds.

4. Bake according to No. 217, or place in a saucepan with hot water coming half-way up the sides of the moulds.

Cover the moulds with greased paper and put a lid on the pan. Cook gently below boiling until the custard is set.

5. It is advisable to leave the custards in the moulds to cool. They will then turn out more easily and the caramel will coat the mould. If turned out hot, there is a tendency for some of the caramel to stay in the mould.

N.B. An eggless mould may be made using Recipe No. 645 for a cornflour mould. Pour into the caramel-lined mould and leave to set overnight.

220. Coffee Mould

Flavour the milk with coffee essence or strong black coffee and make Recipe No. 219, leaving out the caramel. Turn out and decorate with whipped cream and chopped nuts.

221. Orange Baked Custard. Cooking time 1–1½ hours

Temperature 250–350° F. (120–180° C.) Mark ½–4.

Quantities for 4 helpings:

3 eggs
Pinch of salt
1 oz. sugar (2 Tbs.)
1 pt. hot milk (2 c.)
Grated rind 1 orange

Fine light brown sugar
Small tin mandarin
oranges, or 2 fresh
oranges

Measures level. Beat the eggs, salt, and sugar slightly. Add the hot milk and the orange rind. Pour into a pie-dish, 1½–2-pint size (1 l.), and bake (see No. 217) until set. Sprinkle the top thickly with brown sugar and place under the grill to melt the sugar. Arrange overlapping slices of mandarins or oranges on top and leave to become cold. Serve plain or with cream.

222. Soufflés. Cooking time: large ones $\frac{1}{2}$–$\frac{3}{4}$ hour; small ones 15–20 minutes

Temperature 375° F. (190° C.) Mark 5.

Quantities for 4 helpings:

1 oz. butter or margarine (25 g.)
1 oz. plain flour (3 Tbs.)
$\frac{1}{4}$ pt. milk ($\frac{1}{2}$ c.)

3 eggs or 3 yolks and 4 whites
Flavouring, see Nos. 223–8

Measures level. Grease a 2-pint (1 l.) soufflé dish or 4–5 small ones. Use the fat, flour and milk to make a sauce by the Roux Method, No. 69. Add the egg yolks beaten with 1 Tbs. of cold water, and the flavouring. Fold in the stiffly beaten egg whites and pour the mixture into the prepared dish. Bake until the soufflé is risen and brown. It should still be soft inside and must be served at once, or it will begin to shrink as it cools. Serve in the soufflé dish with the sauce handed separately.

223. Cheese Soufflé

Add 3 oz. finely grated cheese (75 g.), preferably Parmesan, and a pinch of salt, nutmeg, mustard, and cayenne pepper.

224. Fish Soufflé

Add 4–6 oz. (125–175 g.) finely flaked cooked fish to the sauce. Season with a pinch of salt and pepper and 1 Tbs. of lemon juice. To make a smoother soufflé, the fish and sauce may be rubbed through a sieve before adding the egg whites. Coat the soufflé with Parsley Sauce, No. 87, or Anchovy Sauce, No. 72.

225. Chocolate Soufflé

Dissolve 1 oz. (25 g.) grated chocolate in the milk before making the sauce. Add 1 oz. sugar (2 Tbs.), a pinch of salt, and 1 tsp. vanilla essence. Serve with Chocolate Sauce, No 99, flavoured with a little rum.

226. Vanilla Soufflé

Add 2 oz. sugar (4 Tbs.), a pinch of salt, and 1 tsp. vanilla. Serve with Jam Sauce, No. 101, or Custard Sauce, No. 105.

227. Lemon Soufflé

Add a pinch of salt, the finely grated rind of 1 lemon, and 2 oz. sugar (4 Tbs.). Serve with a purée of fresh raspberries, see No. 602, or Melba Sauce, No. 110.

228. Strawberry Soufflé

Add a pinch of salt, 5 Tbs. strawberry purée (see No. 602), and 2 oz. sugar (4 Tbs.). Serve with sliced fresh strawberries which have been sprinkled with caster sugar and chilled.

229. Zabaglione. Cooking time about 10 minutes

Quantities for 4–6 glasses:

3 egg yolks	¼ pt. Marsala, Madeira,
1½ oz. sugar (3 Tbs.)	or Sherry (½ c.)

Measures level. Put the egg yolks and sugar in a quart-size pudding-basin. Beat with a rotary egg-whisk until thick and light. Add the wine and mix well. Place the basin over a pan of boiling water and continue beating until the mixture has risen well and is thick. Pour into individual glasses and serve hot or cold with small macaroons.

230. Chocolate Mousse. Cooking time 10 minutes

Quantities for 4–6 glasses:

4 oz. chocolate (125 g.)	Vanilla essence to taste or
3 Tbs. water	1 Tbs. rum or brandy
4 eggs	

Melt the chocolate in a pan over hot water or a very gentle heat. Add the water and mix well. Add the egg yolks beaten with another tablespoon of water until light. Remove from the heat and add the flavouring. Then fold in the stiffly beaten egg whites (beaten with a pinch of salt). Pour into small glasses. This is very much improved by being kept in the refrigerator for 12 hours.

231. Pink Foam. Cooking time about 10 minutes

Quantities for 3–4 helpings:

½ lemon	1 Tbs. red currant jelly
¼ pt. Burgundy (½ c.)	2 egg yolks
2 oz. sugar (4 Tbs.)	

Measures level. Grate the lemon rind finely and put in the top of a double boiler or in a basin to fit in the top of a saucepan. Add the other ingredients and mix well. Cook over boiling water, beating hard all the time with an egg-whisk until the mixture is thick and light and has increased in volume. Pour into individual glass dishes and chill for several hours. Serve with biscuits or macaroons made with the egg-whites, see Nos. 785–6.

CHAPTER 11

Fish

232. Food Value

Fish is an excellent food for protein. Some fish, such as herrings, kippers, bloaters, mackerel, sardines, sprats, pilchards, eels, and salmon, are a good source of Vitamin D. These are generally known as the 'oily' fish because they contain fat. White fish, such as sole, plaice, cod, halibut, etc., do not contain fat and are not a good source of Vitamin D, though the livers of some are – for example, cod liver and halibut liver.

Because Vitamin D is needed to build strong bones and teeth, children and expectant mothers are always advised to take cod-liver oil or one of the other fish-liver oils rich in this vitamin. Everybody needs some Vitamin D, and it is wise therefore to serve oily fish as often as possible.

The same fish are also a good source of Vitamin A, one of the vitamins which protect the body against ill-health. The most important nutrients in fish are not affected by preserving.

233. Choosing Fish

The ideal is to have fish straight from sea, lake or river but very few of us are able to do that. However, modern methods of keeping and transporting fish have very much improved the quality of fish available inland.

When buying fish there are some points to watch for to ensure that you buy it as fresh as possible. It should have a pleasant smell of the sea or fresh water. Whole fish should have bright clear gills, difficult to open, and the eyes should be full and bright, not dull and sunken. The flesh should be firm and no impression left when it is pressed. Fillets and steaks should be firm with a pleasant colour and odour. Avoid any which is flabby and watery. Do not buy packets of deep frozen fish if the wrapper is damaged or if there is a lot of frost inside the package. Frozen fish of poor quality will have white or brown patches on the surface and be stringy, tasteless and dry when cooked.

For best flavour cook fresh fish on the day of purchase; smoked fish will keep up to 3 days in a refrigerator. Put the fish in a polythene bag or other container in the coldest part of the refrigerator. Both fresh and smoked fish purchased from the fishmonger are perfectly satisfactory if stored for a week or so in the home freezer. Cook it either frozen or thawed.

234. Suggestions for Cooking Various Kinds of Fish

BLOATERS. Grilled.

BREAM. Boiled, steamed, grilled, baked (stuffed or plain).

BRILL. Boiled, baked, grilled.

CARP. Boiled, stuffed, baked.

COCKLES. Boiled, pickled.

COD and COLEY. If fresh, any method. Also good for 'made-up' dishes. If salt, soak for 24–48 hours, then boil and use in 'made-up' dishes. If smoked, grill, boil, bake, or steam.

CONGER EEL. If large, use for soup. If small, fry or stew like fresh-water eels.

CRAB. Salads, sandwich fillings. Generally sold cooked.

DAB. Boiled, steamed, fried, baked.

EELS. If fresh, boiled, fried, stewed, jellied, pies. If smoked, raw.

FINNAN HADDOCK. Grilled, boiled.

FLOUNDER. Fried, grilled.

GRAY MULLET. As Mackerel.

GURNET. Stuffed, baked, boiled (stuffed or plain), stewed.

HADDOCK. Boiled, stuffed, baked, stewed, fried.

HAKE. As Haddock.

HALIBUT. Boiled, baked, fried, grilled.

HERRING. Steamed, grilled, stuffed, baked, soused.

JOHN DORY. Boiled, steamed, baked.

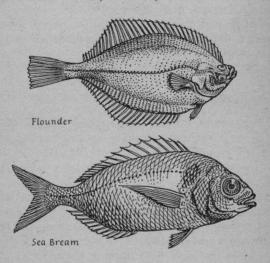

Flounder

Sea Bream

KIPPERS. Grilled.

LING. As Cod.

LOBSTER. Generally sold cooked and used in salads, sauces, and sandwich fillings.

MACKEREL. Boiled, steamed, soused, stuffed, baked.

MUSSELS. Boiled, fried, soups, stews.

PERCH. Fried, boiled, stewed.

PIKE. As Carp.

PILCHARDS. Fresh, as Herrings.

PLAICE. Fried, boiled, steamed, grilled, stuffed, baked.

PRAWNS. Generally sold cooked and used in salads and curry.

RED MULLET. Grilled or baked.

ROCK SALMON. As Cod.

SALMON. Boiled, steamed, grilled. If smoked, uncooked.

SCALLOPS. Fried, creamed.

SKATE. Steamed, boiled.

SMELTS. Fried, soused.

SOLE. As Plaice.

SPRATS. Grilled, fried, soused.

TROUT. Boiled, fried, grilled, stuffed, baked, soused.

TURBOT. Boiled, steamed, fried, grilled.

WHITEBAIT. Fried.

WHITING. Grilled, fried.

235. Using Frozen Fish

When fish is to be thawed before cooking this is best done slowly in the refrigerator, allowing about 6 hours per pound ($\frac{1}{2}$ kg.). It is essential to thaw at least partially fish required for coating with batter, otherwise the batter will be liable to fall off.

Fillets and steaks to be cooked by other methods are better if used while still frozen or partially thawed. If allowed to thaw completely these small pieces tend to lose a lot of moisture and flavour.

Whole fish are better if completely thawed.

Methods of cooking are the same as for fresh fish, although it is better to cook frozen fish more slowly, at a lower temperature, for about a quarter as long again if it has been thawed and about double the normal time if it is still frozen. Test a piece in the centre to make sure that it is cooked right through.

236. Preparing Fish for Cooking

SCALING

Do this on a piece of paper, to catch the scales. Hold the fish by the tail and, with a knife in the other hand, scrape

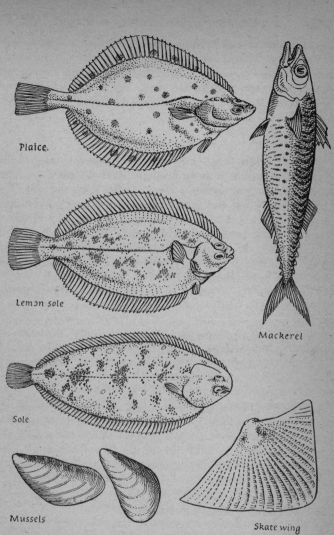

Plaice.

Lemon sole

Mackerel

Sole

Mussels

Skate wing

firmly from the tail towards the head. Wash to remove any loose scales. With certain fish, such as perch, the scales are very difficult to remove, and in this case the fish should either be cooked with the scales on and skinned before serving, or plunged into boiling water for a minute or two, and then the scales removed.

CLEANING

ROUND FISH (e.g. cod, whiting, mackerel, etc.). With kitchen scissors or a sharp knife slit the belly from the head towards the vent, remove the entrails: keep the roe. The black skin lining the inside of some fish can be removed by rubbing with a little cooking-salt. Wash well and drain.

Small fish, such as herrings, may be cleaned without cutting the belly. Cut behind the back of the head, not quite through to the belly, and pull away from the fish, when the inside should come away with the head.

Red mullet and smelts are cleaned by pulling out the gills, when the inside should come with them.

FLAT FISH (e.g. soles, plaice, etc.). Cut away the gills and make a small opening just behind the head. Pull out the inside, and wash the fish well. Remove any dark skin as described above.

SKINNING

FILLETS. Place, skin side down, on a board. Hold the tail end in one hand, but first rub salt on the fingers to prevent them from slipping. Take a knife in the other hand and use it to scrape and roll the fillet from the skin.

ROUND FISH. Remove the fins and cut off a thin strip of skin down the back. Slit the skin along the belly from the vent to the tail. Cut the skin by the gills and pull off gradually, first one side and then the other.

FLAT FISH. Slit the skin across the tail end. Rub salt on the fingers to prevent them slipping and grasp the skin firmly. Pull quickly towards the head. Do the other side in the same way.

EELS. Hold the head in a cloth and cut through the skin round the neck. Turn back about an inch, and then pull the head with one hand and the skin with the other. It should pull off easily.

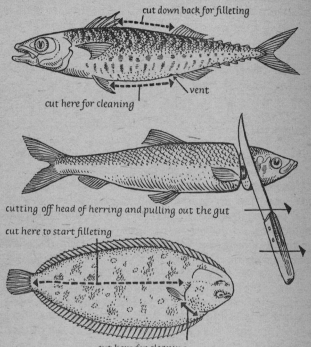

cut down back for filleting

cut here for cleaning   vent

cutting off head of herring and pulling out the gut

cut here to start filleting

cut here for cleaning

FILLETING

It is essential to have a sharp knife. Cut the fish down the backbone and slide the knife along close to the bones, cutting off the flesh. A flat fish will give four fillets, a round fish two. Use the bones and trimmings for Fish Stock, No. 34.

With a herring, after cutting down the backbone, open the fish with the finger and thumb and lift up the bone with the knife. If care is taken the small bones will come away with the backbone.

When carving or eating a whole cooked fish the same method of cutting down the backbone should be followed. The cooked flesh can then be easily removed from the bone.

BOILING AND STEAMING

237. Boiled Fish. Cooking time 7 minutes per lb. (500 g.) plus 7 minutes for thin fish; 10 minutes per lb. plus 10 minutes for thick fish. Fillets, steaks, small whole fish: 10–15 minutes.

Quantities: ½–¾ lb. (250 g.) per person

1. For suitable fish see list, No. 234. Whole fish or cuts of large round fish are suitable, but thick steaks may also be boiled, although steaming, No. 246, is the more satisfactory way for these.

2. Use a pan just large enough to hold the fish and only enough water to cover. To each pint (2 c.) of water add ½ Tbs. vinegar, 1 tsp. salt, 2 peppercorns, 1 sprig parsley, ½ bay leaf, 1 small sliced carrot, and 1 small sliced onion.

3. For small pieces of fish the water should be boiling, but whole fish should go into warm water, as the shrinkage caused by putting it into boiling water will cause the fish to lose its shape.

4. The water should not be allowed to boil after the fish has been added, for this needs to be 'poached' like an egg. You will find it easier to handle the fish if it is placed on a rack (sold for the purpose) or tied in a clean cloth.

5. To see if the fish is cooked test it at the thickest part with a fork, and if the flesh seems to come away easily from the bones it is done. Try not to overcook the fish, as this makes it dry and tasteless, and the flakes fall apart, spoiling

the appearance. Lift out carefully and drain very thoroughly.

6. Serve with a sauce made with some of the fish stock, e.g. Parsley Sauce, No. 87; Cheese Sauce, No. 75; Anchovy Sauce, No. 72; Egg Sauce, No. 77; Hollandaise Sauce, No.

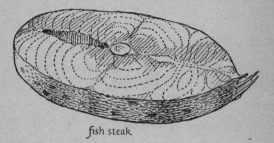

fish steak

94; Lobster or Shrimp Sauce, No. 81; Mussel Sauce, No. 83.

Plain boiled potatoes are generally considered the best, and any of the following vegetables are suitable: parsnips, green peas or beans, carrots, spinach, celery, tomatoes, green salad, beetroot, or cucumber salad. Left-over boiled fish may be used in Recipes Nos. 248–50 and 152.

238. Fish Boiled in Milk. Cooking time, see No. 237

Quantities: see No. 237.

1. Suitable for steaks, fillets, or small whole fish. This method is generally the one used for smoked fish.

2. Allow about $\frac{1}{2}$ pt. milk (1 c.) for $1\frac{1}{2}$ lb. fish (750 g.). Add salt, and cook the fish very gently below boiling point until the flakes begin to show signs of separating.

3. Drain well, and use the milk to make a sauce to serve with the fish, as for Boiled Fish, No. 237. Use any of the vegetables given for Boiled Fish. Mustard Sauce, No. 84, is good with smoked fish.

239. Boiled Cod

The head and shoulders make the best piece for boiling. Slices may be steamed. It keeps its shape better and is not so inclined to be watery if sprinkled with salt and left to stand for a couple of hours before cooking.

240. Boiled Eels

Skin the eels and cook them as directed in No. 237. Serve with Parsley Sauce, No. 87, or Anchovy Sauce, No. 72.

241. Boiled Finnan Haddock

Cook in milk or water according to No. 238. Keep hot, and use the milk to make Parsley Sauce, No. 87, or the water for Mustard Sauce, No. 84.

For smoked haddock with poached eggs, the eggs should be poached in the milk in which the fish has been cooked. Serve on top of the fish, allowing them to break over it.

242. Boiled Fresh Haddock

Cut four or five gashes about an inch deep on the sides of the fish and sprinkle well with salt. Leave for 2 hours, then boil according to No. 237. Serve with boiled parsnips sprinkled with chopped parsley and serve Egg Sauce, No. 77, separately.

243. Boiled Mackerel

These must be very fresh. Boil according to No. 237, and serve with Fennel Sauce, No. 78.

244. Boiled Salmon

This may be boiled in slices or in a whole piece. The latter is better for serving cold, as it keeps more moist. Serve with Cucumber Salad, No. 561, and boiled potatoes. The best sauces are Hollandaise, No. 94; Lobster or Shrimp Sauce, No. 81; Tartare Sauce, No. 117; or Brown Butter Sauce, No. 111.

Cold boiled salmon may be served with Mayonnaise, No. 113, or Tartare Sauce, No. 117. For Salmon Salad see No. 570.

245. Boiled Skate

Skate needs to be very fresh, and the thick pieces are the best to buy. It should be boiled according to No. 237, and served with a Caper Sauce, No. 74, or Brown Butter Sauce, No. 111.

246. Steamed Fish. Cooking time: see No. 237

Quantities: see No. 237.

1. For suitable fish, see list No. 234. Steaming is suitable for whole fish, cuts of fish, steaks, or fillets.
2. If no steamer is available, steaks or fillets may be cooked in a soup plate or deep dish over a pan of boiling water, using the lid of the pan to cover the fish.
3. Place the fish in the steamer or plate, sprinkle with salt, and cook until the flesh leaves the bones easily or until the flakes begin to separate.

Serve with a sauce and any of the vegetables given for Boiled Fish, No. 237. Any liquid with the fish should be added to the sauce.

247. Steamed Herrings

Cook the herrings according to No. 246 and serve with
Mustard Sauce, No. 84; or Caper Sauce, No. 74; or
Fennel Sauce, No. 78.

Steamed herrings are also very good cold with salad.

248. Fish Pie. Cooking time $\frac{3}{4}$–1 hour

Temperature 400° F. (200° C.) Mark 6.

Quantities for 4 helpings:

1 lb. smoked fish fillet (500 g.)	1 hard-boiled egg, chopped
$\frac{1}{2}$ pt. milk (1 c.)	Lemon juice
1 oz. butter or margarine (25 g.)	Pepper
1 oz. flour (3 Tbs.)	1 lb. hot mashed potato (500 g.)
1 Tbs. chopped parsley	Little milk
	Margarine

Measures level. Poach the fish in the milk. Drain and flake
fish, making the milk up to $\frac{1}{2}$ pt (1 c.). Melt the butter or
margarine in a pan. Add the flour and mix and cook for
a minute. Add the milk and whisk until it boils. Boil 5
minutes. Add the fish, parsley, egg, lemon juice and pepper
to taste. Put in a greased pie-dish. Mash the potato with
milk to make it soft enough to spread or pipe on top of the
fish. Dot with margarine and bake until hot and brown.

249. Fish au Gratin. Cooking time 30–40 minutes

Quantities for 4 helpings:

1 lb. boiled, steamed, or canned fish, flaked (2 c.)	1$\frac{1}{2}$ oz. grated cheese (6 Tbs.)
$\frac{3}{4}$ pt. Parsley Sauce, No. 87 (1$\frac{1}{2}$ c.), or use packet sauce	3 Tbs. dried breadcrumbs
	Margarine
1 lb. freshly cooked mashed potatoes (500 g.)	

Measures level. Mix the fish and sauce and make sure it is well seasoned. Make a border of the mashed potato on a fireproof dish; pour the fish mixture into the centre and sprinkle the cheese and crumbs over it. Dot with a little margarine and brown under a hot grill or in a hot oven.

250. Dry Fish Curry. Cooking time 5–10 minutes

Quantities for 4 helpings:

3 small onions
2 oz. butter (50 g.)
1 Tbs. desiccated coconut
1 apple, finely chopped
Pinch of salt
½ Tbs. curry powder

1 Tbs. chutney
1 lb. cooked fish or shell-
  fish (500 g.)
Juice of ½ lemon
Boiled rice

Measures level. Peel and slice the onions. Fry them brown in the butter. Add the coconut, apple, salt, curry powder, and chutney. Stir and heat until it is a deep brown. Add the fish and heat gently for a few minutes. Add lemon juice and serve with the boiled rice.

251. Fish Fillets with Lemon Sauce. Cooking time ½ hour

Quantities for 4 helpings:

1½ lb. fillets of sole or
  plaice (750 g.)
1 oz. margarine (25 g.)
1 oz. flour (3 Tbs.)
¼ pt. milk (½ c.)
½ pt. fish stock (1 c.)
Salt and pepper

Juice of ½ lemon
1 egg yolk
2 Tbs. cream
2 Tbs. chopped parsley
½ pt. shelled shrimps or
  prawns (1 c.)

Measures level. Use the fish trimmings to make Fish Stock, No. 34. Roll the fillets and fasten with a tooth-pick. Poach them in a little stock, see No. 237, drain and place on a hot dish. Remove tooth-picks. Make a sauce by the Roux Method, No. 69, adding the lemon, egg, and cream at the end and cooking until thick, without boiling. Pour over the fish and decorate with the parsley and shrimps or prawns.

252. Sole or Plaice Mornay. Cooking time ¾ hour

Quantities for 2 helpings:

1 medium-sized sole
About ½ pt. white wine and
    water (1 c.)
1 sprig parsley
1 slice onion
Salt and pepper

1 oz. butter (25 g.)
3 Tbs. flour
3 oz. finely grated cheese
    (75 g.)
Lemon juice

Measures level. Skin and fillet the fish. Put bones and skin in a pan with white wine and water to cover, about half and half. Add parsley, onion, and some salt and pepper. Boil gently for ½ hour. Strain and use for poaching the fillets for 5–6 minutes or until tender. Keep them hot. Make a sauce by Roux Method, No. 69, with the remaining ingredients, using about ½ pt. (1 c.) of the fish stock. If necessary make up with more water, or milk. The sauce should be thick enough to coat the fish. Grease a heat-resisting serving dish and coat the bottom with a thin layer of the sauce. Arrange the cooked fillets in a single layer and cover with remaining sauce. Brown under the grill or in a hot oven.

253. Sole or Plaice with Cream and Grapes. Cooking time ½ hour

Quantities for 2 helpings:

1 large sole or 8 oz. fillets
    (250 g.)

Salt and pepper
4 oz. white grapes (125 g.)

About ½ pt. dry white wine   ¼ pt. double cream (½ c.)
  (1 c.)   ½ oz. butter (1 Tbs.)
½ small chopped onion
Sprig of parsley

Skin and fillet the fish. Place in a shallow pan with white
wine to cover and add the onion and parsley. Cook very
gently until the fish is done, about 6 minutes. Remove fish
and keep hot in the serving dish. Add salt and pepper to the
wine and boil until reduced by half. Strain through a fine
sieve. Return to the pan and add the grapes and cream. Boil
until it thickens and then add the butter in small pieces. Mix
well and pour over the fish.

STEWING

254. Stewed Fish

This is a very good method of using thick fillets of cod or
other fish.

1. Cut the fish in 2-inch pieces and put in a deep dish.
Sprinkle well with salt and leave for half an hour or longer.
This draws out some of the moisture and makes the flesh
firmer. Drain well.

2. Stewed fish is generally a very savoury dish, the
foundation being some fried onions or leeks. Fry them
brown in a little dripping, then add any other flavouring
and a very little stock.

3. Add the fish and cook, below boiling, until the fish is
tender. It may then be served with the cooking liquor,
thickened if necessary.

255. Hungarian Fish Stew. Cooking time 15 minutes

Quantities for 4 helpings:

1½ lb. fillets of fish (750 g.)   2–3 Tbs. tomato purée or
1 oz. dripping (2 Tbs.)   juice
4 oz. onions, sliced (125 g.)   ½ tsp. paprika pepper

Measures level. Make according to No. 254, adding the tomato and paprika just before the fish. Shake the pan occasionally, and take care not to overcook, or the liquid will be watery. It should not need thickening. Serve with boiled potatoes and any green vegetable.

256. Soused Fish (suitable for herrings, mackerel, trout, pilchards, sprats, smelts). Cooking time 1½–2 hours

Temperature 275° F. (140° C.) Mark ½.

Quantities for 4 helpings:

8 herrings or similar amount of other fish	1 tsp. salt
1 onion, sliced	1 tsp. sugar
6 cloves	1 bay leaf
1 tsp. peppercorns	½ pt. vinegar (1 c.)

Measures level.

1. Clean the fish, removing the heads and tails, but leaving the roes inside. Pack into a casserole.
2. Sprinkle with the seasonings and pour over the vinegar.
3. Cover and bake for at least 1½ hours in a slow oven. Longer cooking improves the flavour and makes the bones soft, so that they can be eaten.
4. Leave in the dish to become cold, and serve with some of the strained liquor as a sauce. Serve with boiled potatoes and lettuce salad.

GRILLING

257. Grilled Fish. Cooking time 5–25 minutes according to thickness

Quantities: One steak or small fish per person.

1. If small whole fish are being cooked, cut two or three deep gashes on either side to allow the heat to reach the centre. For suitable fish, see No. 234.

2. The fish may be dipped in seasoned flour or left plain.

3. Heat the grill and grease the grid. Cutlets or white fish should be brushed with melted fat or basted with fat during cooking. Oily fish, such as herrings, mackerel, trout, and salmon, need no fat.

4. Grill gently until brown on one side, turn, and finish cooking. The fish is done when the flesh easily leaves the bones.

5. Serve at once with Tartare Sauce, No. 117, or Brown Butter, No. 111, or Parsley Butter, No. 123. Garnish with parsley or watercress and slices of lemon. Serve with fried or boiled potatoes; the best vegetables are parsnips, carrots, green peas or beans, grilled tomatoes, cucumber, beetroot, or green salad.

258. Grilled Bloaters

Slit down the backbone and grill for about 6 minutes; or remove the heads, slit down the backbone, open out, and remove the roes and bone. Grill out flat until brown on both sides. Fry the roes golden in a little fat, and serve with the bloaters.

259. Grilled Finnan Haddock

Serve hot with oatcakes and butter.

260. Grilled Kipper

Steep in hot water for 1–2 minutes. Drain well. Place the fish on the grill, skin side down, put a little margarine on top, and cook for 5–8 minutes. Sprinkle with pepper and serve with lemon and brown bread-and-butter.

261. Grilled Salmon

The steaks should be cut $1-1\frac{1}{2}$ inches (2–4 cm.) thick, and will need about 20–25 minutes to cook. Serve with Parsley Butter, No. 123, and Cucumber Salad, No. 561.

262. Grilled Sprats

Quantities: 1 lb. (500 g.) for 3 people.

Thread on to skewers, run through the eyes, and grill quickly for 3–4 minutes. Serve very hot with lemon and brown bread-and-butter.

FRYING

263. Fried Fish

General directions for frying fish will be found in Chapter 8, Nos. 142–9. Sauces and accompaniments should be the same as for Grilled Fish, No. 257.

In addition to the ordinary methods, there are the two famous French methods of frying fillets and small fish called 'doré' and 'à la Meunière'. In both these the fish is fried in butter, which naturally gives a delicious flavour. For 'doré' the fish is dipped in flour and then fried brown in a little butter. For 'à la Meunière', after frying in this way, the fish is sprinkled with lemon juice, salt and pepper, and chopped parsley. Then a little more butter is cooked until it goes brown, and quickly poured over the fish, which should be served at once. This is the best way of cooking trout and fillets of sole.

264. Fried Eel

Skin the eel and cut it in 3-inch (8 cm.) pieces. Egg and crumb and fry. Serve with Tartare Sauce, No. 117.

265. Fried Herrings with Oatmeal

The herrings may be boned and opened out flat or fried whole. Sprinkle with salt and pepper and toss in coarse oatmeal until thoroughly coated. Fry in hot dripping until brown on both sides – about 10 minutes. Garnish with parsley and lemon. Serve with boiled potatoes.

266. Fried Smelts

To clean, pull out the gills; the insides should then come too. Coat with egg and crumbs and fry brown.

267. Sole Meunière with Orange. Cooking time 8–10 minutes

Quantities for 4 helpings:

4 fillets sole, skinned	1 large orange
2 oz. butter (50 g.)	Flour
Salt and pepper	

Sprinkle the sole with salt and pepper and then with flour to coat it lightly. Heat half the butter in a pan and fry the fillets until lightly browned. Place on a hot dish. Arrange slices of orange on each, the orange being very carefully peeled and as much white pith removed as possible. Heat the rest of the butter until light brown, pour over the fish and serve at once.

268. Fried Whitebait

Toss the fish in a mixture of flour and fine breadcrumbs until the fish are well separated. Fry for 1 minute in deep fat. Serve with lemon and brown bread-and-butter.

269. Fried Whiting. Cooking time about 10 minutes

Cut three gashes in each side of the fish. Dip in milk and then in flour to coat it evenly. Fry until golden brown in hot lard or oil. Sprinkle with salt and pepper and chopped parsley and serve lemon separately.

BAKING

270. Baked Stuffed Fish

This method is most suitable for whole fish. Steaks or fillets may be stuffed and baked, but do not look as attractive as the whole fish. For names of suitable fish turn to No. 234.

Cooking time ¾–1 hour for large fish, 20–30 minutes for small fish.

Temperature 375° F. (190° C.) Mark 5.

Quantities: ¾ lb. (375 g.) per person for whole fish.

1. Clean the fish in the usual way, but leave the head on, merely removing the eyes.
2. Make a well-seasoned stuffing, such as No. 130 or 128. Fill the cleaned belly of the fish and sew up with a needle and coarse thread. Do not fill too full, as the stuffing swells during cooking, and may burst the fish. If you are stuffing a flat fish such as sole or plaice, cut the fish down the backbone as if you were going to fillet it, and push the stuffing in under the fillets. In this case the fish is not sewn up afterwards, and the stuffing is allowed to show through the centre.
3. The fish may either be brushed with melted fat or coated in egg and breadcrumbs; see No. 146.
4. Place in the baking-dish in a little hot fat, and cook in a moderate oven until tender. Before baking, the fish is sometimes skewered into the form of a letter 'S', or the tail is twisted round and fastened in the mouth.
5. Remove skewer and thread and garnish with parsley and lemon. Serve a sauce separately. Suitable ones are Nos. 73 or 89. Boiled or baked potatoes are best, and any of the following vegetables: parsnips, carrots, celery, spinach, tomatoes, green beans or peas, green salad, beetroot, or cucumber salad.

271. Baked Fish au Gratin

This method is most suited to fillets, steaks, and small whole fish. The dish does not necessarily contain cheese, as 'gratin' really means the crisp crust formed on top by the crumbs and fat.

Cooking time 20–30 minutes.

Temperature 375° F. (190° C.) Mark 5.

Quantities: One steak or small fish per person.

1. Prepare the pieces of fish and place them in a fireproof dish. A shallow dish is best, as the fish will be served in it.
2. Cover with the sauce, which can be Cheese Sauce, No. 75; Tomato Sauce, No. 89; Parsley Sauce, No. 87; Anchovy Sauce, No. 72; Brown Sauce, No. 73; Egg Sauce, No. 77; Mustard Sauce, No. 84; or Sour-Sweet Onion Sauce, No. 88. With herrings and mackerel, Horse-radish Sauce, No. 80. Packet sauces or condensed soups may be used instead.
3. The sauce should be of coating consistency, and there should be just enough to cover the fish. Sprinkle the top with browned breadcrumbs and dot with butter, margarine, or dripping.
4. Bake in a moderate oven until the fish is cooked. Test with a fork to see if the flakes separate easily.
5. Serve with fried or mashed potatoes and any of the vegetables given for No. 270.

272. Fish Baked in Stock or Wine (suitable for fillets or small whole fish). Cooking time 20–30 minutes

Temperature 375° F. (190° C.) Mark 5.

Quantities: One small fillet or whole fish per person.

1. Prepare the fish and season it well. Whole fish may be stuffed, as in No. 270. Fillets may be spread with a thin layer

of stuffing and then rolled up tightly. Fillets of sole and plaice are generally folded in two before baking.

2. Use a shallow baking-dish. Place the fish in a single layer. For extra flavour, it may be put on a bed of finely chopped or minced shallots and parsley, with some chopped mushrooms, if available.

3. Pour over very little liquid – only just enough to moisten, as it should be nearly all evaporated by the time cooking is finished. Suitable liquids are: Fish Stock, No. 34, red or white wine, cider, Mushroom Stock, No. 35, or lemon juice and melted butter.

4. Bake in a moderate oven until the flesh is tender and the flakes part when tested. Baste once or twice during cooking.

5. Drain the fish and add any liquid to the sauce. This fish is always served with a sauce poured over it, and may be decorated with a border of Duchess Potatoes, No. 518, or small Stuffed Tomatoes, No. 541, or other vegetables. Suitable sauces are the same as for No. 271 or use Oyster or Mussel Sauce, No. 83, or Shrimp or Lobster Sauce, No. 81.

273. Smoked Fish Hot Pot. Cooking time 20 minutes

Temperature 375° F. (190° C.) Mark 5.

Quantities for 4 helpings:

¾ lb. smoked fish fillets (375 g.)	¼ tsp. pepper
	1 Tbs. water
¾ lb. tomatoes, skinned (375 g.)	2–4 thin rashers bacon
1 oz. butter or margarine (25 g.)	

Measures level. Put the fish in a greased pie-dish and cover with the tomatoes, sliced. Sprinkle with pepper and dot with the butter. Add the water and cover with the rashers of bacon. Bake until the fish is tender. Serve with mashed potatoes.

274. Fish en Papillote. Cooking time 30 minutes

Temperature 375° F. (190° C.) Mark 5.

Quantities: 1 small fish or 1 steak per person.

This method is suitable for herrings and other small fish or for steaks of salmon, turbot, hake, cod and other fish. It is the best method of keeping small pieces of fish moist and retaining the flavour.

The fish may be baked just with salt and pepper for seasoning or can have additional flavourings such as chopped mushrooms, parsley, lemon juice, and a knob of butter.

Clean and remove heads and tails of small fish. Put seasonings inside small fish and on top of steaks. Wrap each portion in a loose parcel of foil, put on a tray and bake. Remove from the foil and serve with any cooking liquid; or add the liquid to an accompanying sauce.

275. Whiting à la Bercy. Cooking time 15–20 minutes

Temperature 375° F. (190° C.) Mark 5.

Quantities for 4 helpings:

4 small whiting
2 shallots, finely chopped
¼ c. white wine and Fish
    Stock, No. 34

2 oz. butter or margarine
    (50 g.)
½ lemon
1 Tbs. chopped parsley

Measures level. Remove heads and fins from the whiting and slit them down the backbones to allow the heat to penetrate easily. Grease a shallow baking-dish and sprinkle in the shallots. Add the liquid and the butter and bake in a moderate oven, basting frequently with the juice. By the time the fish is done all the liquid should have evaporated. Sprinkle with the lemon juice and parsley and serve at once.

276. Swedish Baked Herrings. Cooking time 20–25 minutes

Temperature 375° F. (190° C.) Mark 5.

Quantities for 4 helpings:

4 herrings	Pinch of pepper
2 tsp. salt	Pinch of ground cloves
2 Tbs. vinegar	2 Tbs. browned bread-
2 Tbs. water	crumbs
1½ Tbs. sugar	

Measures level. Fillet the herrings and rub them well with the salt. Put in a shallow baking-dish, letting the fillets overlap slightly. Mix the vinegar, water, sugar, pepper, and cloves together and pour over the fish. Sprinkle the crumbs on top. Bake until the flesh flakes easily. Serve with boiled potatoes.

277. Fish à la Bretonne (suitable for mackerel, whiting, herrings, and sole). Cooking time 20 minutes

Temperature 375° F. (190° C.) Mark 5.

Quantities for 4 helpings:

4 small fish	Pinch of pepper
Flour to coat	2 oz. butter (50 g.)
1 tsp. salt	½ lemon

Measures level. Slit the belly and flatten round fish, after removing heads and fins. Dry and coat in the flour and seasoning. Melt the butter in a casserole and when very hot add the fish, skin side up. Cook for a few minutes. Turn the fish over, and then put the lid on the casserole and cook until the fish is tender. Sprinkle with lemon juice before serving.

CANNED FISH

278. General Information

Canned fish should keep for several years in a cool, dry place, but the tins must not be allowed to become damp or rust will eat through and make them leak. Turn the cans over occasionally to keep the contents well mixed with the liquid. Discard any tins which are 'blown' – that is, bulge at the ends instead of being flat.

After opening, canned fish will not keep any longer than cooked fresh fish.

The bones of canned fish are soft, and can be eaten. They contain calcium, which the body needs for strong bones and teeth.

279. Suggestions for Using Canned Crawfish or Crab

Salad, No. 293   Patties, No. 294
Curry (heat fish in Sauce,
   No. 76)

280. Suggestions for Using Canned Herrings or Pilchards

Fish Cakes, No. 152   Salad, No. 562
Open Sandwich, No. 892

281. Herrings or Pilchards for Breakfast

Method 1. Place the fish on slices of toast and heat under the grill.
Method 2. Heat the fish in a frying-pan and serve on slices of fried bread.

282. Suggestions for Using Canned Oysters or Mussels

Sauce for fish, No. 83

Soup, No. 54

Hors-d'œuvre, No. 961

Fried in batter, Nos. 147–9

283. Suggestions for Using Canned Prawns

Hors-d'œuvre, No. 310

Heat in Curry Sauce, see
    No. 76

Salad, No. 309

284. Suggestions for Using Canned Salmon or Tuna

Fish Cakes, No. 152

Fritters, No. 867

Fish Pie, No. 248

Sandwich, Nos. 890 and
    892

Au Gratin, No. 249

Salad, No. 570

Flan, No. 834

Mousse, No. 286

285. Salmon or Tuna Loaf. Cooking time ¾ hour

Temperature 375° F. (190° C.) Mark 5.

Quantities for 4 helpings:

8 oz. mashed fish (1 c.)

¼ pt. milk (½ c.)

2 oz. breadcrumbs (1 c.)

2 eggs

1 tsp. salt

1 tsp. lemon juice

Pinch of pepper

Pinch of mace

Measures level. Mash the fish, including the bone, which is quite soft. Heat the milk and pour on to the breadcrumbs. Soak for a minute or two. Add the egg yolks, fish, and the seasonings. Add the beaten egg whites. Pour into a well-greased 1-lb (500 g.) loaf tin and bake in a moderate oven until set. Turn out.

Serve with boiled or mashed potatoes and green peas or

baked tomatoes. Mask with Parsley Sauce, No. 87, or Tomato Sauce, No. 89.

286. Fish Mousse (for salmon, tuna, cooked smoked fish, or fresh or smoked cod's roe)

Quantities for 4 helpings:

½ oz. gelatine (1½ Tbs.) Pinch of paprika pepper
⅛ pt. hot water (5 Tbs.) ⅛ pt. whipping cream
8 oz. fish (250 g.) (5 Tbs.)
1 Tbs. tarragon vinegar

Measures level. Dissolve the gelatine in the hot water and mash it with the fish, vinegar and pepper; or put in the blender. Whip the cream and fold it into the fish mixture. Taste for seasoning and pour into a mould. When set unmould and serve with salad and lemon wedges. Suitable for a main dish, hors d'œuvre or buffet meal.

287. Suggestions for Using Canned Sardines

Fish Cakes, No. 152 Sandwich, No. 892
Hors-d'œuvre, No. 965

288. Sardines on Toast with Cheese Sauce. Cooking time 10 minutes

Quantities for 4 helpings:

6–8 sardines Chopped parsley
4 slices toast
½ pt. Cheese Sauce, No.
  75 (1 c.) or use packet
  sauce

Arrange the sardines on the toast and warm under the grill. Pour the hot sauce over and decorate with chopped parsley.

289. Suggestions for Using Canned Anchovies

Fish Stuffing, No. 130
  (use 1 or 2 anchovies
  in place of the essence)

Hors-d'œuvre, No. 948
Cauliflower Mayonnaise,
No. 560

SHELL-FISH

290. General Information

With the exception of oysters and mussels, shell-fish are usually sold cooked. The live fish is thrown into boiling water, the boiling time varying with the size: 5 minutes for shrimps, 7–8 minutes for prawns, 15–20 minutes for lobsters or crabs. Frozen cooked shell-fish should be allowed to thaw completely and then used as soon as possible.

Crabs, lobsters, prawns, and shrimps are all regarded as rather indigestible. Vinegar, or a sauce containing vinegar, or lemon juice, is generally served with them, as the acid present in these helps to soften the fish fibres and to stimulate the flow of digestive juices, making for better digestion.

291. Crabs

Medium-sized crabs (6–10 inches (15–25 cm.) across in the widest part) are generally regarded as the best buy. They should have large claws, and all the claws should be on, because if a claw comes off during cooking, water seeps in and makes the inside damp. Another indication of good quality is for the crab to be heavy in proportion to its size and for the shell to be rough and bright in colour. The claws should be stiff.

To prepare crabs pull off the claws, crack them, using a hammer or nut-crackers, and pick out the flesh.

Turn the crab on its back, and, with a sharp-pointed knife, remove the 'apron', the small pointed piece at the lower part of the shell. Separate the upper and lower shells.

Pick out the flesh from the shell, taking out any hard pieces of tendons. The yellow liver is used as well as the white flesh, but the gills, stomach, and green intestine should be discarded.

292. Dressed Crab

Quantities for 3 helpings:

1 medium-sized crab
2 Tbs. vinegar
2 Tbs. oil

Salt, mustard, and cayenne
  pepper
Lemon and parsley

Mix the flesh with the oil and vinegar and season well. Wash the shell, dry it thoroughly, and put the flesh back inside. Decorate with slices of lemon and the parsley. If preferred, the crab may be prepared in individual portions and served in small scallop-shells, or in a nest of lettuce leaves.

293. Crab Salad

Use the same mixture as No. 292 and serve it on a bed of lettuce and decorate with cress and tomatoes.

294. Crab Patties

Mix 1 c. crab meat with 1 c. Parsley Sauce, No. 87. Season well, and add a little lemon juice or vinegar to taste. Serve in Patty-cases, No. 810.

295. Hot Buttered Crab. Cooking time 5 minutes

Quantities for 3 helpings:

1 medium-sized crab
1 Tbs. cream or top milk

2 tsp. lemon-juice
2 tsp. vinegar

2 tsp. chopped parsley
3 Tbs. breadcrumbs
½ oz. butter or margarine
   (1 Tbs.)

Pinch of cayenne pepper
½ tsp. anchovy essence
Paprika pepper
Toast

Measures level. Mix the crab meat with the other ingredients and heat in a pan. Serve in hot scallop-dishes and decorate the top with paprika pepper. Serve hot toast separately.

296. Lobsters

A good lobster should be heavy in proportion to its size, and the tail should feel springy if pulled back a little.

To prepare a lobster for serving break off the claws. If there is any spawn 'coral' under the tail, keep it for decorating the dish. Crack the claws with a hammer.

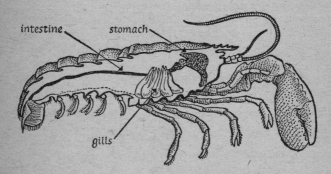

Remove the small intestinal vein which runs down the centre of the tail. Cut the body and tail lengthwise through the middle and remove the flesh, discarding the stomach and the green liver, also the gills at the sides of the body. The shell of the body and tail may be washed and dried and used to hold the meat for serving.

297. Cold Lobster

This is usually served split in half and decorated with the claws arranged neatly round and with parsley or lettuce heart. A French Dressing, No. 118, or Mayonnaise, No. 113, is served with it.

298. Lobster Mayonnaise

Arrange pieces of lobster on a nest of fresh, crisp lettuce and cover the lobster with Mayonnaise, No. 113. Decorate with the coral.

299. Lobster au Gratin. Cooking time $\frac{1}{4}$–$\frac{1}{2}$ hour

Quantities for 4 helpings:

1 medium lobster (about 2 lb. or 1 kg.)
1½ oz. butter or margarine (3 Tbs.)
2 tsp. chopped onion
2 Tbs. flour
½ pt. milk (1 c.)
Cayenne pepper

Salt to taste
2 Tbs. chopped parsley
2 tsp. lemon juice
½ tsp. anchovy essence
1 egg yolk
3–4 Tbs. fresh bread-crumbs

Measures level. Save the four pieces of lobster shell and clean them for serving. Cut the meat in slices. Melt the butter or margarine and cook the onion for a minute or two without browning. Add the flour, mix well, and then add the milk. Stir until it boils. Boil for 5 minutes. Then add the seasonings and the egg and cook for another minute or two. Mix in the lobster. Fill the lobster-shells and cover the top with bread-crumbs. Dot with a little butter or margarine and bake in a moderate oven for 20 minutes or brown under the grill.

300. Lobster Patties

Mix 1 c. lobster meat with 1 c. thick Tomato Sauce, No. 89. Use to fill Patty-cases, No. 810.

301. Mussels

The shells should be closed tightly. Discard any which are even slightly open, as this indicates staleness.

Wash the mussels in several waters, brushing off as much of the sand as possible. To make the shells open, put the mussels in a pan with a very little water and put the lid on. Cook gently until the shells open. Then strain the liquor and keep it for the sauce. Remove any weed there may be under the black tongue.

302. Mussels Served Cold

Cook as described in No. 301. Leave in one half of the shell. Serve vinegar and brown bread-and-butter with them.

303. Mussels Served Hot. Cooking time 10 minutes

Quantities for 2 helpings:

1 qt. of mussels (1 l.)	Salt and pepper
1 oz. butter or margarine (25 g.)	1 Tbs. lemon juice
	1 tsp. Worcester Sauce

Measures level. Prepare the mussels as described for No. 301. Mix the liquor with the other ingredients and pour over the mussels. Serve hot with brown bread-and-butter.

304. Moules Marinières. Cooking time 15 minutes

Quantities for 3 helpings:

3 pt. mussels (1½ l.)	2 Tbs. fine breadcrumbs
2 oz. butter or margarine (50 g.)	1 c. water and liquid from fish
1 tsp. chopped chives	Juice of ½ lemon
1 tsp. chopped parsley	

Measures level. Cook the mussels as described in No. 301, saving the liquor. Remove half the shells, leaving the

mussels attached to the other halves. Make the liquor up to
1 cup with water and mix in a pan with the butter, chives,
parsley, and breadcrumbs. Boil for 2 minutes with the
mussels. Squeeze over the lemon-juice and serve hot, with
bread-and-butter.

305. Oysters

If oysters are fresh they should be difficult to open and
should close hard on the knife when inserted for opening.

To open, hold the oyster in a cloth with the deep shell at
the bottom to catch the juice. Slide the knife in with a see-
saw movement.

306. Oysters au Naturel

Prepare as described in No. 305, and leave the oysters in
the deep shell with their juice. Stand on crushed ice for an
hour before serving. Serve with vinegar or lemon, pepper,
and brown bread-and-butter.

307. Prawns

If fresh they have a sweet smell.

When cooked prawns are stale, the tails are limp and the
fish pale and clammy with a pungent smell.

Shelling is very difficult if the prawns are at all stale. Hold
the head and part of the body in the thumb and forefinger
of the right hand. Hold three joints of the tail with the left
hand and bend back a little. Then pull the end of the tail,
and the tail-shell should come off. Hold the body and gently
pull out of the head and body-shell.

308. Curried Prawns. Cooking time ½ hour

Quantities for 4 helpings:

1 pt. prawns (2 c.)   4 oz. rice (½ c.), boiled
½ pt. Curry Sauce, No. 76
  (1 c.)

Make the curry sauce and heat the prawns in it. Let them stand for 5 or 10 minutes to absorb the flavour of the curry. Serve with the boiled rice.

309. Prawn Salad

Arrange prawns on a bed of crisp lettuce. Squeeze lemon or lime juice over them and cover with Mayonnaise, No. 113.

310. Prawns for Hors-d'œuvre

Sprinkle with lemon juice or lime juice, and serve very cold with brown bread-and-butter.

311. Scallops

These are generally sold already opened, but must be very fresh. Cut off the beards, but leave the black, white, and orange parts. The deep shells are useful for serving various savoury dishes.

312. Fried Scallops

Allow two scallops per person. Dry them well, dip in seasoned flour, and then in Fritter Batter, No. 865. Fry in deep fat until brown: see No. 149. Serve with lemon or with Tomato Sauce, No. 89.

313. Scalloped Scallops. Cooking time 20 minutes

Temperature 375° F. (190° C.) Mark 5.

Quantities for 4 helpings:

8 scallops	Chopped parsley
¼ pt. White Sauce, No. 69	Lemon juice
(½ c.)	Breadcrumbs
Cayenne pepper and salt	

Grease four deep scallop shells and strew on a few bread-crumbs. Put two scallops in each, and sprinkle on a few grains of cayenne pepper, a little lemon juice, and chopped parsley. Cover the scallops with the well-seasoned sauce and sprinkle with breadcrumbs. Put a small knob of butter or margarine on top of each. Bake for about 20 minutes in a moderate oven. Serve hot.

314. Scampi, also known as Norway Lobster, Dublin Bay Prawn, Scampo, Scampolo (Italy), Langoustine (France)

They are sold fresh-cooked or deep-frozen (raw or cooked). The fleshy tails are the part eaten. Frozen raw scampi should be thawed before separating from each other. To fry, dry well, coat with flour and batter and deep fry, see No. 149. Otherwise poach them for 3–4 minutes in boiling salted water, taking care to avoid over-cooking. Then serve in the same way as prawns.

315. Shrimps

Prepare and use in the same way as Prawns, Nos. 307–310.

316. Potted Shrimps

Shell the shrimps and mash them with just enough butter to bind them well, or, an alternative method, put the shrimps in small jars and pour over melted butter to cover. Serve with toast or brown bread-and-butter.

FISH ROES

317. Fried (suitable for herring or other small roes)

Hard or soft roes may be used. Dip in flour or in egg and breadcrumbs and fry in shallow fat until light brown. Serve on toast with lemon.

318. Creamed Soft Roes. Cooking time 20 minutes

Quantities for 4 helpings:

8 soft roes	Salt and pepper
¼ pt. milk (½ c.)	Lemon juice
4 slices toast	Chopped parsley
1½ Tbs. flour	

Measures level. Stew the roes in the milk until they are opaque and firm. This takes about 10–15 minutes. Place two roes on each piece of toast and keep hot. Mix the flour to a paste with a little cold water. Add the hot milk. Return to the pan and stir until it boils. Cook for 5 minutes. Season well, add lemon juice, and pour over the roes. Garnish with chopped parsley.

319. Fried Cod's Roe

Cod's roe is usually sold cooked or canned and ready for frying, but, if raw roe is purchased, proceed as follows.

Tie the roe in a thin cloth to keep it in shape. Put into boiling salted water and cook very gently for about half an hour. Lift out of the pan, but leave in the cloth until quite cold. Cut in ½-inch slices and dust with flour. Fry in hot fat until well browned and crisp. Serve with slices of lemon.

CHAPTER 12

Meat, Poultry, and Game

320. Food Value

As a group, meat, game and poultry are all important sources of protein, vitamins of the B group, and iron. Liver is one of the richest sources of vitamin A as well as of B vitamins and iron, while beef (particularly corned beef) is noted for its iron content, and pork and chicken as sources of B vitamins.

The only nutrients lost to any significant extent when meat is canned are B vitamins and these are also lost through the action of preservatives used in sausages. The loss of nutrients during the curing of ham and bacon, or the freezing of meat, is small.

Because meat can be a source of infection there is always a health hazard when it is eaten raw or under-done. It is particularly important that sausages, minced meat and pork be cooked thoroughly.

321. General Information

Lean meat is made up of bundles of fibres or long cells which contain protein, water, salts, and extractives. Extractives are the substances which give meat its particular flavour, and the meat from old animals contains more than that from the young. Therefore beef has more flavour than veal.

These bundles of fibres are held together by a substance called connective tissue. Muscles which have a great deal of use, such as leg-muscles, have more connective tissue than others, and it can be easily seen as gristle. The less connective tissue meat has, the more tender it is. Heat and moisture soften connective tissue, allowing the muscle-fibres to fall apart, and thus the meat becomes tender. Cuts of meat containing a lot of gristle must always be cooked by one of the moist methods, such as stewing or braising, so that they will be sure to be tender. Only the cuts of meat which do not contain much connective tissue are suitable for 'dry' methods of cooking, such as roasting, grilling, and frying.

The alternative method of making tough meat tender is by mincing, which breaks up the connective tissue, and the same idea lies behind the custom of beating steaks before cooking.

During the process of hanging meat after slaughter, softening of the connective tissue takes place naturally due to the presence of lactic acid, and makes the meat more tender. This process can be helped by treating the meat with a 'tenderizer' which contains the juice of pawpaw with its tenderizing enzyme. Preparations containing this enzyme are sold under various trade names.

Another effect of cooking is to make the meat shrink and, in shrinking, it squeezes out juice. With the juice go some of the extractives or flavour and some of the salts, and water. These are not lost, as they help to form the gravy. With dry methods of cooking, such as roasting and grilling, some of the extractives and salts stay on the outside of the meat to form a crust, which gives the particularly attractive flavour to meat cooked by this method.

322. Quantities of Meat to Buy

Meat without bone, 4–6 oz. per person (125 g.)
Meat with bone, 6–8 oz. per person (175–250 g.)
Brains, 1 small per person
Ears, pig's, 2 per person
Kidney, sheep's and pig's, 1 per person

Kidney, calf's, serves 2
Liver, 4 oz. per person (125 g.)
Ox-tail serves 3–4
Sausages, 4 oz. per person (125 g.)
Sweetbreads, 1 per person
Tongue, sheep's, 1 per person

Tongue, ox, serves 6 or more

Tripe, 4 oz. per person (125 g.)

Blackcock and Widgeon serve 3–4

Chicken, oven-ready, allow ½ lb. per portion (250 g.)

Feet, calf's and pig's, 1 per person

Head, sheep's, serves 2–3

Head, calf's, serves 10 or more

Head, pig's, serves 7–8

Heart, calf's, serves 4–5

Heart, sheep's, serves 1

Duck, oven-ready, allow ½ lb. per portion (250 g.)

Duckling serves 4–5

Goose, oven-ready, allow ¾ lb. per portion (375 g.)

Grouse serves 3

Guinea-fowl serves 4–5

Hare serves 5–6

Partridge serves 2–3

Pheasant serves 2–4

Pigeon serves 2–3

Plover serves 2

Quail and Ortolan, allow 1 each

Rabbit serves 4–5

Teal, Ptarmigan, Snipe, and Woodcock serve 1–2

Turkey, oven-ready, allow ¾ lb. per portion (375 g.)

323. Carving

Good carving is not difficult if you have a really sharp carving-knife. The important thing to remember is that meat must always be carved ACROSS the grain, and not with it. One cut with the knife should be sufficient to show if it is going in the right direction. If you are cutting the wrong way – that is, with the grain – you will clearly see the long fibres of meat, instead of the fine surface produced by cutting across the fibres. A little experience will soon tell you which way to start tackling any joint.

Beef is nicer if cut in very thin slices, but lamb and pork are generally cut a little thicker.

When carving game and poultry, begin by cutting off the legs at the joint closest to the body. The breast is then cut in slices upwards.

With a calf's or pig's head the cheek is the meaty part, and should be carved from mouth to ear.

CHOOSING MEAT

324. General Information

The ideal is to be able to make up your mind in advance exactly what cut you want to buy and how you are going to cook and serve it, but in practice it seldom works out like that. If you are new to shopping, the best thing to do is to ask the butcher's advice. Either ask him the name of the cut you are buying and then look in your cookery book for the best way of treating it, or else ask him whether it is suitable for roasting or stewing. If he says it will roast, 'but cook it slowly', you will be well advised to treat it like a tough cut, and braise or pot roast it.

The ideal place to keep meat, poultry, and game is in a refrigerator; otherwise in a cold larder or a safe hung in a cool, airy place. It must always be protected from flies. Do not wrap raw meat for storage in the refrigerator unless the wrap is close-fitting film or foil. Enclosed air tends to make raw meat become slimy and bad-smelling. A better way is to put it on a plate with a piece of foil on top. Wrap bacon or cooked meat in foil or polythene.

325. Choosing Beef

Good-quality beef is light red, fine in grain, firm, and elastic to touch, and marbled with fine, cream-coloured fat. Poor quality beef is flabby, dark, and coarse, with yellow fat.

If the meat contains any gristle it is not suitable for grilling, frying, or ordinary roasting.

CUTS SUITABLE FOR GRILLING AND FRYING: Rump, fillet, sirloin.

SUITABLE FOR ROASTING: Round, rump, top side, sirloin, fore ribs, wing ribs, standing ribs.

SUITABLE FOR POT ROASTING AND BRAISING: Aitch-
bone, middle rump, ribs, shoulder, chuck, brisket.

SUITABLE FOR STEWING, BOILING, PIES, AND
PUDDINGS: Leg, shin, flank, skirt, neck, shoulder.

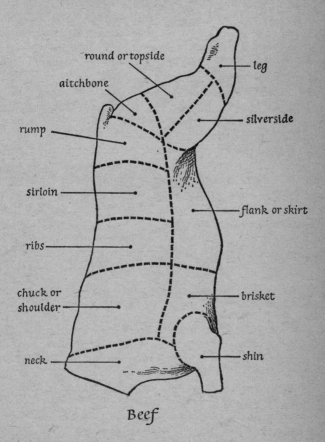

Beef

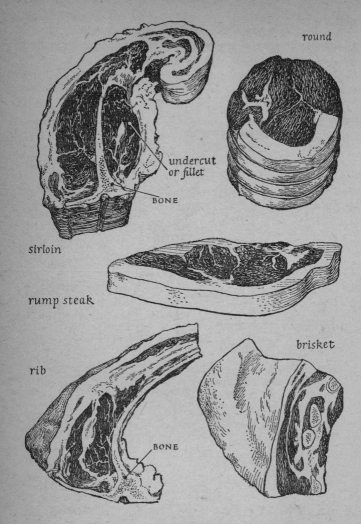

round

undercut
or fillet

BONE

sirloin

rump steak

rib

BONE

brisket

326. Choosing Lamb and Mutton

Lamb should be red with white fat and the bones should be moist and red at the joints.

Mutton should be bright red with yellowish fat and the bones white.

SUITABLE FOR GRILLING AND FRYING: Best end of neck, loin.

SUITABLE FOR ROASTING: Leg, loin, best end of neck, shoulder.

SUITABLE FOR POT ROASTING AND BRAISING: Middle neck, scrag, breast.

SUITABLE FOR BOILING AND STEWING: Leg, neck, scrag, breast (stuffed and rolled).

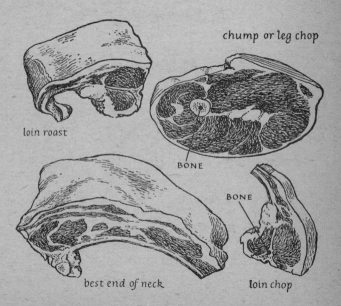

chump or leg chop

loin roast

BONE

best end of neck

BONE

loin chop

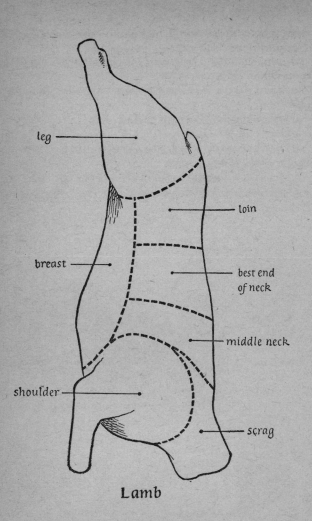

leg

loin

breast

best end
of neck

middle neck

shoulder

scrag

Lamb

327. Choosing Pork

Good-quality pork should be pale brownish-red with firm flesh and white, firm fat.

SUITABLE FOR GRILLING AND FRYING: Loin chops (thorough cooking needed).

SUITABLE FOR ROASTING: Leg, loin.

SUITABLE FOR POT ROASTING AND BRAISING: Spare ribs, best end of neck, blade bone.

SUITABLE FOR BOILING AND STEWING: Leg, spare ribs, best end of neck, blade bone, belly, hand and spring, head.

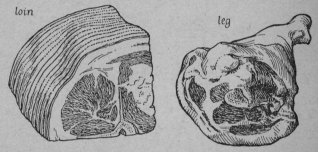

loin

leg

328. Choosing Veal

Good-quality veal should be pale pink with clear, firm, white fat.

SUITABLE FOR GRILLING AND FRYING: Fillet, loin, best end of neck. (Thorough cooking needed.)

fillet

chop

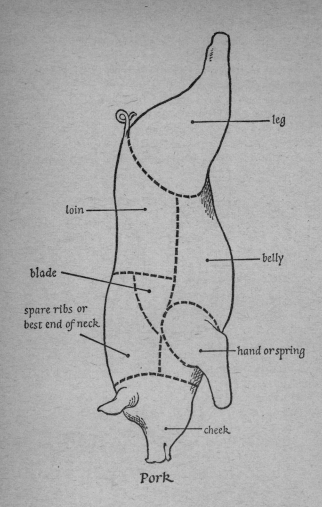

leg

loin

belly

blade

spare ribs or
best end of neck

hand or spring

cheek

Pork

SUITABLE FOR ROASTING: Leg, loin, shoulder or oyster.

SUITABLE FOR POT ROASTING AND BRAISING: Best end of neck, breast (rolled and stuffed).

SUITABLE FOR BOILING AND STEWING: Breast, scrag, shoulder, knuckle.

veal

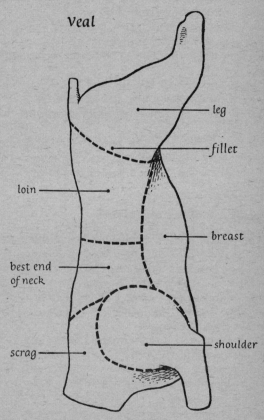

329. Choosing Offal and Sundries

BRAINS: Suitable for boiling, and may then be fried.

FEET: Suitable for stewing, braising, soups, brawn.

HEAD: Suitable for boiling, brawn, soups.

HEARTS: Suitable for stewing (cut up and mixed with other meat) and braising (stuffed or plain).

KIDNEYS: Suitable for stews, puddings, pies, soups. Lamb's kidneys suitable for frying and grilling.

LIVER (LAMB'S AND CALF'S): Suitable for frying, stewing, braising.

OX LIVER: Suitable for stewing and braising.

OX-TAIL: Suitable for soups, stews, braising.

SAUSAGES: Suitable for frying, grilling, stewing, loaves, and pies.

SWEETBREADS: Suitable for braising, frying, grilling.

TONGUES: Suitable for boiling, braising, brawn.

TRIPE: Suitable for stewing, boiling, braising.

330. Choosing Poultry and Game

Most 'oven-ready' poultry is labelled as suitable for either frying, roasting or boiling. Otherwise, it is best to buy it from a reliable butcher, first telling him how you want to cook the bird.

CHICKENS are roasted or fried if very young.

FOWLS are stewed, braised, or boiled but may be steamed and then roasted.

DUCKS OR DUCKLINGS are roasted or braised.

GEESE are roasted.

GUINEA-FOWL are roasted.

PIGEONS are stewed or grilled (if young).

TURKEYS are roasted.

Young hares and rabbits have smooth, sharp claws, ears that are tender and easily torn, and a short, stumpy neck. Cultivated rabbit is usually tender.

Roasting is the favourite method of cooking all game, but if it is old, stewing or braising is advisable. Venison is usually hung for 14 days, and then roasted. Neck chops may be grilled as veal or pork chops. Venison may also be stewed.

PREPARING MEAT, POULTRY, AND GAME FOR COOKING

331. Preparing Meat

FRESH MEAT. Trim off surplus fat and keep it for rendering down (see No. 138). In warm weather, if the meat has a slight smell wipe the surface with a cloth dipped in vinegar.

FROZEN MEAT. Thaw all meat completely unless you know it has been specially prepared for cooking without thawing. Well hung home-frozen meat can be cooked without thawing.

SALT MEAT. If very salt, soak in cold water for 3–4 hours or longer.

BRAINS. Soak in cold water until all the blood is removed. Remove skin and fibres.

EARS (pig's). Soak in cold water for 5–6 hours.

FEET (cow's and calf's). Usually sold ready for cooking.

FEET (pig's and sheep's). Wash well.

HEAD (calf's). Ask the butcher to cut it in half lengthwise. Remove the brains, and soak head and brains in cold water until all the blood is removed. Change the water several times. Then blanch the head by boiling 15 minutes. See No. 12.

HEAD (pig's). If salted, soak in cold water.

HEAD (sheep's). Wash in several waters and then soak in salt water for 1 hour. Then blanch by just bringing to the boil. See No. 12.

HEART. Wash in several waters and leave to soak in cold water for 1 hour. Squeeze out all blood.

KIDNEYS. Remove fat, skin, and hard core.

LIVER. Wash and dry.

OX-TAIL. Wash, dry, and cut in joints.

SWEETBREADS. Soak in cold water for 1 hour to remove the blood. Blanch, as in No. 12, just bringing lamb's sweetbreads to the boil but boiling calf's sweetbreads for 10–12 minutes. Leave to become cold. Remove all gristle and tissue before completing the cooking.

TONGUE (OX). Soak in cold water for 2–3 hours; (sheep's and pig's): soak in cold water for 2 hours, and then blanch, see No. 12; (calf's): cooked with the head.

TRIPE. Usually sold ready for cooking.

332. Preparing Poultry

1. Either pluck the bird directly after killing and while it is still warm, or else put it in a bucket and pour boiling water over it, when the feathers will be found to come out quite easily. Be careful not to tear the skin. Remove the short pin-feathers with the aid of a knife. Singe off the hairs by holding the bird over a gas-flame, lighted taper, or spill of paper.

2. Cut off the head. Cut the neck-bone off close to the body, but first pull back the skin, as you want this left long to fold over neatly. The neck should be kept to cook with the other giblets for stock. Remove the crop and wind-pipe from the neck end and loosen the top of the entrails by working round the body with your forefinger.

3. Turn the bird on its back. Lift up the skin just above the vent and make a long cut in it. Then cut round the vent. Loosen the fat and then loosen the entrails by passing the right hand gently between the inside walls of the body and the entrails. Hold the bird firmly with the other hand while you do this. Then take hold of the gizzard, which can easily be felt, as it is big and hard, and gently draw out the entrails. Try not to damage the little gall-bladder attached to the liver, as, if the gall gets on the liver, it makes it bitter

and unusable. You will be able to tell if this has happened, as there will be a green patch on the liver. The lungs and kidneys do not always come out with the entrails, so put in your hand again and feel for them in the hollows by the backbone. Wash the inside in cold running water and drain thoroughly.

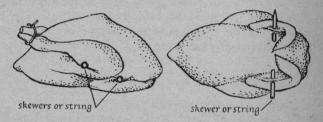

skewers or string   skewer or string

4. Break the legs at the lower joint and bend them back. This exposes the tendons. Lever up the exposed part with a skewer and pull out the tendon, taking care not to tear the flesh.

5. Stuff from the neck end until the breast is plump. Draw the skin back over the neck-opening and sew or skewer it firmly to seal the opening. For sewing use a coarse needle and thick white cotton. Stuff the body from the tail end. Push the tail through the slit and skewer it there firmly.

6. To truss, draw the thighs close to the body and cross the legs over the tail. Tie them together with string. Fold the wings backwards and inwards over the neck-skin and tie or skewer them.

7. The giblets consist of the neck, feet, heart, liver, and gizzard. Clean them in the following way. Cut through the thick muscle of the gizzard, lengthwise. Peel it off the rough, wrinkled lining and discard the lining and contents. Cut the heart open lengthwise. Remove the gall-bladder very carefully from the liver and, if it should be broken, cut away any discoloured liver. Scald the feet in boiling water for a minute or two and then peel off the skin. Wash all the giblets and boil them in water with an onion, a carrot, and

seasonings for 1–2 hours, and use the liquid for gravy or stock.

333. Frozen Poultry

Joints may be cooked without thawing but whole birds should be completely thawed, preferably in the refrigerator or cold larder. Chickens, ducks and geese will need 24–36 hours, and turkeys 2–4 days, depending on the size. They take less time in a warm room.

334. Preparing Hares and Rabbits

1. Cut off the legs at the first joints.
2. Slit the skin all along the belly and loosen it from the body.
   Pull it off the hind legs. Then pull towards the head and off the front legs.
3. Slit the belly and draw out the entrails. Keep the liver and heart to use for making stock. Wash the animal well in cold water. Truss for roasting by skewering or tying the legs close to the body; or joint as follows.
   Cut off the head. Cut out the eyes and split the head in half lengthwise. Use it for stock.
   Cut off the hind legs close to the body. The joints are quite easy to find.
   Cut the body in three or four pieces through the backbone. The piece with the forelegs should be cut in half lengthwise.

BOILING

335. General Information

Boiling is best suited to whole joints, breast of lamb or veal, rabbits or fowls, tongues, salt meat, and similar foods. Smaller pieces of meat lose so much flavour to the liquid that they are better cooked by one of the other methods unless they are boiled with the deliberate idea of flavouring the liquid for soup. This method is popular in many countries, the Scotch Broth being one example, and the French Pot au Feu another. The boiled meat is served as one course, together with the vegetables cooked in the same liquid, and the stock is used to make a soup.

You will find a list of suitable cuts of meat for boiling in Nos. 325–330.

N.B. Boiled meat may be cooked in a pressure cooker, when $\frac{1}{4}$–$\frac{1}{3}$ the normal times will be required.

336. Boiled Fresh Meat, Game, or Poultry

1. It is advisable to choose a pan just big enough to hold the meat, as the less liquid you have with it the better will be the flavour of both meat and stock.

2. Boil the liquid and add a bouquet garni, and an onion stuck with 3 or 4 cloves.

3. Add the meat and boil rapidly for 5 minutes. Skim well and cover the pan.

4. Lower the heat and cook just below boiling (simmering) until the meat is tender. A fine skewer will go in easily if the meat is tender. For times see No. 338.

5. If vegetables are being cooked with the meat they should be cut in large pieces and added $\frac{1}{2}$–1 hour before the end of cooking, depending on the kind of vegetable. Add about 1 level Tbs. salt with the vegetables. Dumplings should be added $\frac{1}{2}$ hour before serving.

6. Use the liquid for a sauce to serve with the meat and the remainder as stock for soup.

337. Boiled Salt Meat (bacon, ham, pork, beef, tongue, etc.)

This differs from fresh meat in that it is started in cold water in order to draw out the salt. If the meat is very salty it should be soaked in cold water for 3–4 hours or longer before cooking. If the meat is to be served cold, cool it as quickly as possible, and store it in the refrigerator or cold larder.

338. Boiling Time Table

Bacon and Ham: Pieces under 1 lb. ($\frac{1}{2}$ kg.) 45 minutes; pieces of 1–2 lb. ($\frac{1}{2}$–1 kg.) 1–1$\frac{1}{2}$ hours; pieces of 3 lb. and over (1$\frac{1}{2}$ kg.) allow 30 minutes per lb. Pressure cooking allow 12 minutes per lb.

Beef, salt: 1 lb. ($\frac{1}{2}$ kg.) or less 1 hour; 2–3 lb. (1–1$\frac{1}{2}$ kg.) 2–3 hours; 4–5 lb. (2–2$\frac{1}{2}$ kg.) 3–4 hours; more than this 20 minutes per lb. ($\frac{1}{2}$ kg.) plus 20 minutes.

Beef, fresh, as for salt. Pressure cooking allow $\frac{1}{4}$–$\frac{1}{3}$ these times.

Brains, calf's: 20 minutes, or 10 minutes if to be fried afterwards.

Brains, ox: 30 minutes.

Brains, sheep's and pig's: 15 minutes.

Ears, pig's: 1$\frac{1}{2}$ hours.

Feet, calf's and cow's: 2–3 hours.

Feet, pig's: 2 hours.

Fowl: 1–2$\frac{1}{2}$ hours depending on age and size.

Head, calf's: 3–4 hours.

Head, pig's (half): 1$\frac{1}{2}$–2 hours.

Head, sheep's: 1$\frac{1}{2}$–2 hours.

Mutton or Lamb: 15–20 minutes per lb. (500 g.) (breast, rolled, 1–1$\frac{1}{2}$ hours).

Pork, salt: 25–30 minutes per lb. (500 g.).

Rabbit: 40–60 minutes.

Tongue, calf's: Cooked with the head or 2–3 hours.

Tongue, ox: 3–3$\frac{1}{2}$ hours.

Tongue, sheep's and pig's: 1$\frac{1}{2}$–2 hours.

Veal: 20–25 minutes per lb. (500 g.) (breast, rolled, 1–1$\frac{1}{2}$ hours).

339. What to Serve with Boiled Meat, Poultry, or Game

BEEF. Boiled potatoes. Onions, carrots, swedes, turnips, cabbage (cut in quarters), beetroot (cooked separately). Dumplings. Tomato Sauce, No. 89; Parsley Sauce, No. 87; Horse-radish Sauce, No. 80.

BOILED BACON OR SALT PORK. Boiled potatoes. Cabbage, carrots, turnips, beetroot (cooked separately), beans. Pease Pudding, No. 553; Parsley Sauce, No. 87; Tomato Sauce, No. 89.

BRAINS. After boiling, these are often sliced and fried. They should be allowed to become cold, and then sliced and dipped in egg and crumbs. If served boiled make a Parsley Sauce, No. 87, with some of the stock. Any vegetables may be served.

CALF'S FEET. The bones are removed after cooking, the feet cut in pieces and served in a Parsley Sauce, No. 87, made from the cooking liquor, with some chopped cooked ham or bacon in it. Serve with any vegetable.

CALF'S HEAD. Boiled potatoes. Vinaigrette Sauce, No. 119, with the cooked, mashed brains added. Slices of the tongue are served with slices of the meat. A lettuce salad, No. 563, is generally served afterwards.

FOWL. Boiled potatoes. Any green or root vegetables. Onion Sauce, No. 85; Bread Sauce, No. 121; Egg Sauce, No. 77; Parsley Sauce, No. 87.

LAMB AND MUTTON. Boiled jacket potatoes. Swedes, carrots, turnips, onions, and any green vegetables. Caper Sauce, No. 74; Parsley Sauce, No. 87; Onion Sauce, No. 85; Fennel Sauce, No. 78; Red-currant jelly.

PIG'S EARS. These are generally cooked with the feet, then cut in strips, and served with a Parsley Sauce, No. 87, made from the cooking liquor. Any vegetables are suitable.

RABBIT. Boiled jacket potatoes. Onions, carrots, turnips, and any green vegetable. Dumplings. Boiled salt pork or bacon. Parsley Sauce, No. 87; Mint Sauce, No. 120.

SHEEP'S HEAD. The brains are added 15 minutes before the end of cooking, and then mashed and added to a sauce made from some of the cooking liquor. Root vegetables are cooked and served with the head. Boiled potatoes are the best.

TONGUE. These are generally served cold with salad. After cooking they are pressed in a basin or mould with a weight on top and left until quite cold. If served hot, a Parsley Sauce, No. 87, or Tomato Sauce, No. 89, is suitable, and any vegetables.

340. Boiled Breast of Lamb or Veal

Ask the butcher not to chop the breast in pieces. Remove the small bones and any surplus fat. Place the meat skin side down and spread the inside with Veal Forcemeat, No. 135, or Mint Stuffing, No. 131. Roll up tightly and tie with fine string. Boil as in No. 336.

Serve hot with a sauce made from the liquid, for example, Parsley Sauce, No. 87; Caper Sauce, No. 74; Brown Sauce, No. 73; Tomato Sauce, No. 89; Paprika Sauce, No. 86; or (with lamb) Fennel Sauce, No. 78.

Serve cold after pressing between two plates with a heavy weight on top. Leave until cold, remove the string, and glaze, see No. 717. Cut in slices to serve.

341. Boiled Beef and Horse-radish Sauce. Cooking time 2 hours

Quantities for 8–10 helpings:

1½–2 pt. water (3–4 c.)	1 parsnip
2–2½ lb. lean brisket beef (1 kg.)	1 stalk of celery
½ Tbs. salt	1 onion
1 carrot	5 whole allspice

Measures level. Heat just enough water to cover the meat, and when it is boiling add the meat and other ingredients. Cook until tender. Serve the meat sliced and surrounded by the vegetables. Use the stock to make Horse-radish Sauce, No. 80, or use half stock and half milk. Serve with boiled potatoes and some extra vegetables.

342. Chicken Blanquette. Cooking time ¾ hour

Quantities for 4–6 helpings:

1 boiling fowl, cooked
2 oz. butter or margarine (50 g.)
2 oz. flour (6 Tbs.)
1 pt. stock (2 c.)
Salt and pepper

Bouquet garni, see No. 12
8 small onions
¼–½ lb. button mushrooms (125–250 g.)
2 Tbs. chopped parsley

Measures level. Make a sauce by the Roux Method, see No. 69, using the fat, flour, stock, and seasonings. Add the onions and the mushrooms, including the chopped stalks. Cook gently for ¾ hour. Add the chicken, which has been jointed and, if preferred, removed from the bone. Heat gently without boiling until the chicken is heated through. Serve sprinkled with chopped parsley.

343. Creamed Rabbit (for vol-au-vent, patties, or to serve in a border of potato). Cooking time 20 minutes

Quantities for 6 helpings:

1 boiled rabbit, see No. 336
1 medium onion, chopped
2 rashers bacon, chopped
3 stalks celery, chopped
1 oz. margarine or dripping (25 g.)

4 Tbs. flour
¾ pt. rabbit stock (1½ c.)
Salt and pepper
1 Tbs. lemon juice
2 Tbs. chopped parsley

Measures level. Fry the vegetables and bacon in the fat for a few minutes, without browning. Add the flour and mix well. Add the stock and stir until it boils. Boil for at least 10 minutes. Cut the meat off the bone and dice it. Season the sauce well, add the meat, and heat for 10 minutes, without boiling. Add the parsley and serve.

344. Veal Galantine. Cooking time 2–3 hours

Quantities for 12 helpings:

3 lb. breast of veal (1½ kg.)   1 lb. pork sausage-meat
½ tsp. salt   (500 g.)
Sprig of parsley   3 hard-boiled eggs
Sprig of thyme   2 Tbs. gelatine
½ bay leaf   Gravy browning
½ lb. gammon bacon
  (250 g.)

Measures level. Bone the veal. Put the bones in a pan with cold water to cover. Add the salt, parsley, thyme, and bay leaf. Bring to the boil and simmer for a few minutes. Cut the bacon in cubes and mix with the sausage-meat. Put the veal on a board, skin side down, and spread with half the sausage-meat. Add the sliced eggs and the rest of the sausage-meat. Roll up and tie in a clean cloth. Place in the stock and simmer for 2–3 hours or until tender. Take out the meat, tighten the cloth, and press between two dishes with a weight on top. Leave until cold. Dissolve the gelatine in 1½ pt. (3 c.) of the stock and boil quickly until reduced to ½ pt. (1 c.). Add a few drops of browning and cool. Brush thickly over the galantine.

STEWS AND CASSEROLES

345. General Information

Stews and casseroles are among the simplest and most useful of meat dishes. They are economical because the cheapest cuts of meat can be used, and, although the cooking time is long, very little fuel is required; and yet they can be rich and savoury, and you need not be ashamed to serve them at any meal. Stews and casseroles include Ragoûts, Curries, Hot Pots, Goulash, Jugged Hare, and many other well-known dishes. They all depend for success on the following three important points.

1. The use of very little liquid, so that the gravy is rich and full of flavour.

2. Good flavouring. The use of vegetables, herbs, and spices to combine with the meat for a savoury flavour.

3. Long, slow cooking. A stew should never be allowed to boil. It should simmer, which is below boiling and just keeps the surface of the liquid agitated, with an occasional bubble showing. Most stews need at least 2 hours' cooking, preferably 3 hours or longer, as the long cooking gives a rich flavour. This is most easily done in a casserole in the oven, 300° F. (150° C.) or Mark 1. You can arrange to cook other dishes with it, and not waste oven space. Most casseroles are sufficiently attractive to go to the table, so you save on the washing-up too.

4. If you cook the stew in a saucepan on top of the stove you may find a thickened liquid tends to catch, unless you have a thick pan and a gentle heat. In that case it is better to thicken the liquid by the Blending Method, No. 95, after cooking is finished.

Any of the recipes for stews are suitable for a pressure cooker, allowing about 20 minutes or according to the instructions for stewing given with the cooker. It is always better to thicken these stews after cooking is finished, otherwise they will stick and burn.

346. Quickly Prepared Casserole or Stew

To save time in preparation use condensed soups and/or canned vegetables in place of fresh vegetables, stock and thickening. Wine, beer, cider, herbs and other seasonings can be added to taste. The fresh meat is cut up and browned in hot oil or fat in the usual way, then the condensed soup, diluted with half a can of stock, water or milk, is added and the whole stewed gently as in No. 345. Canned vegetables are either added with the soup or put in near the end of cooking. Frozen peas and other frozen vegetables make a useful addition, as do canned tomatoes, juice or paste, and canned red peppers, beans or mushrooms.

Suggestions:

BEEF: with condensed oxtail, vegetable, beans with bacon, minestrone or tomato soup.

LAMB: with tomato, cream of celery, Scotch broth, or green pea soup.

CHICKEN: with cream of mushroom, asparagus, cream of tomato soup.

347. Basic Brown or White Stew. Cooking time 3 hours or longer

Quantities for 4 helpings:

1 lb. meat without bone (500 g.) or 1½ lb. meat with bone (750 g.)	¾ pt. stock or water (1½ c.) or use some beer, wine or cider
3 Tbs. flour	Pinch of thyme
1 lb. mixed vegetables (500 g.)	1 bay leaf
2 oz. fat or oil (50 g. or 4 Tbs.)	Sprig of parsley
	1 tsp. salt
	Pinch pepper

Measures level

1. Cut the meat in pieces, removing as much fat as possible.

2. Prepare and slice or dice the vegetables.

3. Put the flour in a paper or polythene bag and shake the meat in it until well coated.

4. Heat the fat or oil and fry the meat brown; add the vegetables and fry for a few minutes longer.

5. Add any remaining flour and then stir in the liquid and seasonings. Cook slowly until the meat is tender. Add gravy browning if necessary for a good rich colour.

6. If dumplings are added they should go in half an hour before serving, see No. 806.

7. Serve with boiled or mashed potatoes and a green vegetable.

WHITE STEW

1. Melt the fat in a saucepan and stir in the flour, cooking until it turns yellow.

2. Add liquid and mix well.

3. Add remaining ingredients and cook very slowly until tender.

348. Casserole of Tripe. Cooking time 2–3 hours

Quantities for 4 helpings:

1 lb. dressed tripe (500 g.)	$\frac{1}{2}$ tsp. mixed dried herbs
1 oz. lard or dripping (25 g.)	$\frac{1}{4}$ tsp. each of ground ginger, nutmeg, and cloves
2 Tbs. flour	
$\frac{3}{4}$ pt. stock (1$\frac{1}{2}$ c.)	Pinch of cayenne pepper
2 carrots	1 tsp. salt
2 turnips	1 tsp. chopped marjoram
2 sticks celery	2 Tbs. grated cheese
1 onion	

Measures level. Cut the tripe in pieces about 2 inches (5 cm.) square, and cook as for White Stew, No. 347. Serve with the marjoram and cheese sprinkled on top. Boiled potatoes go with it.

349. Goulash (beef, veal, or lamb). Cooking time 2–3 hours

Quantities for 4 helpings:

2 onions, sliced
1 oz. fat (25 g.)
1 lb. lean meat (500 g.)
2 tsp. paprika pepper
1 tsp. salt
¼ c. tomato juice or 2
  tomatoes

Pinch of carraway seeds
½ c. stock
1–1½ lb. potatoes (4–6
  medium)

Measures level. Fry the onions and fat in a saucepan. Cut the meat in 1–2-inch (2–5 cm.) cubes and add to the onions. Cook until brown, and then add all the other ingredients except the potatoes. Cover and cook very slowly for 2–3 hours. It may need a little more stock during cooking. Boil the potatoes for 15–20 minutes and cut them in quarters. Add them to the goulash for the last 10 minutes' cooking. Mix carefully. Serve with boiled cabbage.

350. Curry. Cooking time 2–3 hours

Quantities for 6–8 helpings:

2 lb. beef or mutton (no
  bone) (1 kg.) or 1
  rabbit
6 Tbs. flour
2 tsp. salt
2 medium-sized onions
½ clove garlic
2 apples
1 tomato

2 oz. fat (50 g.)
2 Tbs. curry powder
¾ pt. stock (1½ c.)
Rind and juice of ½ lemon
1 tsp. brown sugar
1 Tbs. desiccated coconut
2 Tbs. raisins or sultanas

Measures level. Cut the meat in pieces and roll them in the flour and salt mixed together.

Chop the onions, garlic, apple, and tomato. Heat the dripping in a saucepan and fry the vegetables and meat.

Pour off any excess fat. Add the curry powder and any flour left. Mix well and stir in the stock. Add gravy browning if a dark curry is preferred. Add the lemon juice, coconut, fruit, and sugar, and cook slowly for 2–3 hours. Serve with boiled rice and chutney. Follow with a salad.

351. Jugged Hare, Rabbit, Venison, or Pigeons. Cooking time 3–4 hours

Temperature 300° F. (150° C.) Mark 1.

Quantities for 6–8 helpings:

1 hare or 2 small rabbits or 2–3 pigeons or 2 lb. venison (1 kg.)	1 tsp. grated lemon rind
	1 oz. butter or margarine (25 g.)
1 oz. fat (25 g.)	4 Tbs. flour
2 onions, sliced	½ pt. stock (1 c.)
Bouquet garni	¼ pt. vinegar (½ c.)
6 cloves	½ pt. red wine, cider, or beer (1 c.)
3 whole allspice	
Pinch of pepper	Forcemeat Balls, No. 135, or use packet stuffing
2 tsp. salt	

Measures level. Joint the meat and fry the pieces brown in the dripping. Put in a casserole with the onion and seasonings. Melt the butter or margarine and add the flour. Mix well and stir in the liquid. Stir until it boils and pour over the hare. Cover and cook in a slow oven for 3–4 hours.

Serve with fried forcemeat balls, boiled potatoes, red-currant jelly, and any vegetable.

352. Les Carbonnades Flamandes (steak stewed with beer). Cooking time 2–3 hours

Quantities for 6–8 helpings:

2 lb. steak (1 kg.)	¾ pt. beer (1½ c.)
4 Tbs. flour	¼ clove garlic, chopped

3 tsp. salt
Pinch of pepper
2 oz. fat (50 g.)
1 lb. onions, sliced (500 g.)

Bouquet garni
1 tsp. sugar
2 Tbs. vinegar

Measures level. Cut the steak in slices about ½ inch (1 cm.) thick and 3 inches (8 cm.) square. Coat them well in the flour, salt, and pepper. Fry the meat in the fat until brown. Transfer to the casserole and fry the onions. Add the rest of the flour and mix well. Pour the beer into the frying-pan and stir until it boils. Pour over the meat and add the garlic, bouquet garni, and sugar. Cover and cook slowly for 2–3 hours. Add the vinegar just before serving.

Serve with boiled potatoes. Follow with a salad.

353. Stewed Ox-tail. Cooking time 2–3 hours

Quantities for 5–6 helpings:

1 ox-tail
4 Tbs. flour
2 tsp. salt
Pinch of pepper
2 oz. fat (50 g.)
1 onion, sliced

1 carrot, sliced
1 stick celery, chopped
1 small turnip, sliced
Bouquet garni
1 pt. stock or water (2 c.)

Measures level. Joint the ox-tail and cook as for Brown Stew, No. 347. Cook slowly for 2–3 hours or until the meat will easily leave the bones. Serve with boiled potatoes and a green vegetable.

354. Liver Provençale. Cooking time 35 minutes

Quantities for 4–6 helpings:

2 oz. bacon (50 g.)
1 lb. onions (500 g.)
2 tsp. salt
Pepper

2 Tbs. flour
½ pt. stock (1 c.)
1 lb. sheep's liver (500 g.)
Chopped parsley

Measures level. Cut the bacon in small pieces and fry it gently, adding a little fat if the bacon is lean. Remove the bacon. Slice the onions and fry them in the fat until they are just beginning to colour. Add the seasoning, using less salt if the bacon is salty. Add the flour and mix well. Add the stock and stir until it boils. Return the bacon and add the liver cut in small pieces. Cover and simmer for ½ hour. Serve sprinkled with chopped parsley.

355. Ragoût of Kidneys. Cooking time 20 minutes

Quantities for 4 helpings:

6 lamb's or 4 veal kidneys	½ Tbs. finely chopped onion
Salt and pepper	¾ pt. stock (1½ c.)
1 oz. fat (25 g.)	2 oz. mushrooms (50 g.)
3 Tbs. flour	

Measures level. Skin and trim the kidneys and cut in slices. Sprinkle with salt and pepper. Melt the fat and fry the kidneys for 5 minutes. Remove and keep hot. Brown the onion in the fat, add the flour, and mix well. Cook for a few minutes and add the stock. Stir until it boils and then add the sliced mushrooms. Return the kidneys and cook for a few minutes longer. Serve in a border of mashed potatoes.

356. Beef-steak Stewed with Olives. Cooking time 1½–2 hours

Quantities for 4 helpings:

1½ lb. stewing steak (750 g.)	½ a red or green sweet
1 oz. fat or oil (25 g. or 2 Tbs.)	pepper, chopped
1 onion, chopped	¼–½ pt. tomato juice (½–1 c.)
3 oz. stuffed olives, sliced (75 g.)	

Cut the steak in small pieces, removing fat. Fry the meat and onions in the fat or oil until they begin to brown. Add the olives and sweet pepper and enough tomato juice to moisten. Cover and cook gently on top of or in the oven until the meat is tender, adding more tomato juice as necessary. No salt or pepper is needed, but garlic may be added to taste. Serve with either boiled potatoes, rice or noodles.

357. Beef Rolls. Cooking time about 1 hour

Temperature 350° F. (180° C.) Mark 4.

Quantities for 4–6 helpings:

1 lb. topside beef, cut in thin slices (500 g.)
4 bacon rashers
Fresh sage leaves or dried sage
2 oz. fat or oil (50 g. or 4 Tbs.)

¼ pt. red wine (½ c.)
¼ pt. stock (½ c.)
2 Tbs. tomato paste
Salt and pepper

Measures level. Cut the beef slices in 8–12 pieces and cut bacon pieces slightly smaller. Put a piece of bacon on each slice of beef and a sage leaf or pinch of dried sage on top. Roll it up and secure with string or a cocktail stick. Heat fat or oil and fry the rolls brown. Put the rolls in a casserole with the wine, stock, tomato paste blended with 2 Tbs. water, and salt and pepper to taste. Cover and simmer until the meat is tender, about ¾ hr. Remove strings before serving.

358. Casserole of Pork with Apple Sauce. Cooking time 1½ hours

Quantities for 4–6 helpings:

1½ lb. boneless pork (750 g.)
2 onions, peeled and sliced
2 Tbs. flour

Pinch of chopped fresh or dried rosemary
2 chopped fresh or dried sage leaves

1 tsp. salt

Pinch of pepper

½ tsp. dry mustard

Pinch of ground ginger

¼–½ pt. white wine (½–1 c.)

Apple sauce, No. 108, or
use canned

Measures level. Trim any fat from the meat, cut meat in small pieces and coat it in the flour, salt, pepper and mustard mixed. Heat the pieces of fat in a pan until the fat flows, or heat some lard. Fry first the onion and then the meat until brown. Transfer to a casserole and add the herbs. Swill out the pan with the wine and pour it over the meat. Cover and cook until tender. Serve with the apple sauce.

359. Veal Olives. Cooking time 1¼ hours

Quantities for 4 helpings:

1 lb. fillet veal (500 g.)

Veal Forcemeat, No. 135

1 Tbs. chopped onion

1 oz. butter or margarine
  (25 g.)

3 Tbs. flour

¾ pt. stock (1½ c.)

1 Tbs. chopped parsley

1 tsp. salt

Pinch of pepper

Measures level. Have the veal cut in 4 thin slices about 4 × 3 inches (10 × 8 cm.). Spread each with some of the forcemeat and roll up tightly. Fasten with a wooden tooth-pick or tie with fine white string. Melt the fat in a pan and fry the onion and meat until brown all over. Remove and place in a casserole. Add the flour and mix well. Add  the stock and stir until it boils. Add parsley and seasoning and pour over the olives. Cover and cook very gently until tender, about 1 hour. Remove string or tooth-picks and arrange on a dish. Pour the sauce over and serve with mashed potatoes and spinach or peas.

360. Chicken Casserole. Cooking time 2½–3 hours

Temperature 300° F. (150° C.) Mark 1.

Quantities for 4–6 helpings:

1 chicken or boiler, jointed	2 sticks celery, chopped
3 Tbs. flour	2–3 carrots, sliced
2 tsp. salt	2 Tbs. tomato paste
Pinch of pepper	½ pt. water or stock (1 c.)
1–2 oz. fat (25–50 g.)	8 oz. rice (250 g.)
12 small onions	

Measures level. Dredge the pieces of chicken with the flour and seasoning. Fry in the fat until brown. Place in a casserole with the onions, celery, and carrots. Add the tomato and liquid. Cover and cook slowly until tender. Serve with the rice, boiled, see No. 613.

361. Paprika Chicken. Cooking time 1–2 hours

Quantities for 4–6 portions:

1 oz. oil or lard (2 Tbs. or 25 g.)	2 tomatoes or 2 tsp. purée
1 large onion, sliced	2 Tbs. sour cream or Yogurt
1 tsp. paprika pepper	1 Tbs. chopped parsley
1 tsp. salt	1 small chicken

Measures level. Melt the lard and fry the onion in it for a few minutes. Cut the chicken in pieces and add to the onions, together with the paprika pepper. Fry for a few minutes. Add salt and tomatoes. Cover and cook until tender, adding a very little water if necessary. It will take 1–2 hours, depending on the age of the chicken. Add the cream or Yogurt and sprinkle with chopped parsley.

362. Veal Blanquette. Cooking time 1½–2 hours

Quantities for 6 helpings:

2 lb. breast of veal or pie veal (1 kg.)
6 small onions or shallots
Bouquet garni
1 oz. butter or margarine (25 g.)

1 oz. cornflour (3 Tbs.)
1 pt. water (2 c.)
1 egg yolk
2 Tbs. cream
2 Tbs. lemon juice
Chopped parsley

Measures level. Cut the meat in small pieces and skin the onions. Melt the butter or margarine in a stew-pan or casserole and add the cornflour. Mix and cook for a few minutes. Add the water and stir until it boils. Add the meat, onions and bouquet garni, cover, and cook gently on top or in the oven until the meat is tender. Remove the bouquet garni. Mix egg, cream and lemon. Add to it a spoonful of the sauce from the meat, mix, and stir into the meat, stirring until it thickens but do not allow to boil. Serve with chopped parsley to garnish.

363. Mutton or Lamb Casserole. Cooking time 1½–2 hours

Quantities for 3–4 helpings:

1 lb. lean lamb or mutton without bone (500 g.)
Seasoned flour
1 oz. butter or margarine (25 g.)
1 small chopped onion
½ clove chopped garlic

1 Tbs. chopped parsley
⅛ pt. stock (¼ c.)
⅛ pt. cider (¼ c.)
2 tsp. Worcester sauce
Salt and pepper to taste

Cut the meat in small pieces and coat it with seasoned flour. Heat the butter or margarine and fry the meat until brown. Remove meat to a casserole and add the onion, garlic and parsley. Add stock, cider and sauce to the frying pan and simmer for 5 minutes. Pour over the meat, cover and cook gently until the meat is tender. Taste the sauce for seasoning.

364. Spanish Cutlets. Cooking time $\frac{1}{2}$–$\frac{3}{4}$ hour

Temperature 350° F. (180° C.) Mark 4.

Quantities for 4 helpings:

1 oz. fat (25 g.)	1 onion, sliced
4 lamb cutlets	1 lb. tomatoes, sliced
Salt and pepper	(500 g.)
1 rasher bacon, chopped	8 small sausages

Trim the cutlets, removing as much fat as possible. Fry brown in the dripping. Place in a casserole and season with salt and pepper. Fry the onion and bacon in the same fat and, when the onion begins to brown, add the tomatoes. Cook for 10 minutes. Add to the cutlets and cook in a moderate oven for $\frac{3}{4}$ hour, with the lid on the casserole. Bake the sausages separately and serve with the meat and tomatoes. Serve with baked or mashed potatoes.

365. Spiced Steak. Cooking time $1\frac{1}{2}$ hours

Temperature 325° F. (160° C.) Mark 2.

Quantities for 3–4 helpings:

1 lb. beef steak (500 g.)	1 onion, sliced
Salt and pepper	$\frac{1}{4}$ bay leaf
1 oz. fat (25 g.)	$\frac{1}{2}$ tsp. grated nutmeg

Measures level. Beat the steak well to flatten it, and then season with salt and pepper. Fry in the dripping until well browned on both sides. Add the onion, bay leaf, and nutmeg. Cover with a fitting lid and cook slowly for $1\frac{1}{2}$ hours. If necessary, add a very little water during cooking. Cooking may be in the oven or on top. Serve with mashed potatoes and any green vegetable.

GRILLING

366. General Information

As already mentioned in No. 321, only the most tender cuts of meat are suitable for grilling. For suitable meat, see Nos. 325–30.

367. Grilled Beef Steak

1. The meat should be cut across the grain and not less than an inch thick. It is generally grilled in pieces weighing about 6 oz. (175 g.), but is also often cut in pieces about 2 inches (5 cm.) square. These are called Tournedos, Mignons, or Noisettes, and may be tied with string to keep them in shape. Fat should be left on, as this helps to keep the meat moist during cooking. The fat should be cut through at intervals, and so should any skin round the meat. This is because the fat and skin shrink more than the meat and, if not cut, will make it curl up, instead of staying flat. Beating well with the handle of a rolling-pin, or the edge of a saucer, a couple of hours before grilling helps to make the steak tender. If the meat is very lean it should be brushed with melted butter or olive oil. For Marinaded Steak see No. 369.

2. Heat the grill very thoroughly and if using an open fire, it should be clear and red. Grease the bars of the grilling rack.

3. Place the prepared steak on the rack and cook 1 minute each side. The heat should be fierce enough to give the meat a good coating of brown in this time. Then reduce the heat slightly and continue to cook, turning it every 2 minutes. Do not pierce with a fork during turning, or juice will escape.

4. The steak will take from 10 to 15 minutes, depending on its thickness and whether you like it well or lightly done. The usual test is to press the steak lightly, and if it resists the pressure but still feels spongy, it is ready. Another indication is given by small beads of blood which appear on the surface when the steak is done.

5. Serve at once on a very hot dish with the vegetables and garnish, which you will have prepared in advance so as not to keep the steak waiting. If a sauce is to be served with it, put it in a sauce-boat, not over the steak, as this makes the meat flabby. The only garnish which goes straight on the meat is Parsley Butter, No. 123, or a grating of horse-radish.

6. The following are suitable accompaniments for grilled steak: fried or mashed potatoes, fried onions, fried or grilled mushrooms or tomatoes, watercress, lettuce, peas, beans, diced carrots, spinach, cauliflower, spaghetti, noodles, Parsley Butter, No. 123; Watercress Butter, No. 124; grated horse-radish; Mushroom Sauce, No. 82; Onion Sauce, No. 85.

368. Tournedos Vert Pré

Grill tournedos as described in No. 367 for steak, and serve with Parsley Butter, No. 123, on top. Surround with alternate heaps of Straw Potatoes, No. 517, and watercress.

369. Marinaded Beef Steak

For each pound (500 g.) of steak allow 1 Tbs. olive oil, 1 Tbs. vinegar, salt, and pepper.

Mix the oil, vinegar, and seasoning and let the steak lie in this for 24 hours, turning it occasionally. Then grill in the usual way. See No. 367.

370. Grilled White Meat (veal, lamb, pork, chicken)

The only difference between these and Grilled Beef Steak is that white meat needs cooking more slowly and thoroughly, and the browning and cooking should be finished together.

Lamb cutlets, 7–10 minutes.
Lamb chops, 10–20 minutes.
Pork or veal chops, 10–20 minutes.
Spring chicken (skewered out flat), 20 minutes.

White meat needs constant basting with melted fat or oil or with a Basting Sauce, see No. 122. It is served with the same garnishes and vegetables as steak.

371. Lamb Chops with Cucumber. Cooking time 15–20 minutes

Quantities for 4 helpings:

1 medium-sized cucumber	½ tsp. salt
1 oz. margarine or butter (25 g.)	Pinch of pepper
	4 lamb chops

Measures level. Peel the cucumber and cut in dice. Melt the fat in a saucepan, add the cucumber, cover and cook gently until tender. Add the seasoning. While the cucumber is cooking, grill the chops, see No. 370. Put the cucumber in the centre of a serving-dish and arrange the chops round it.

372. Lamb Shashlik. Cooking time 15 minutes

Quantities for 3 helpings:

1 lb. lamb from leg or shoulder (500 g.)	Juice of 1 lemon
1 small onion	1 Tbs. wine or cider
½ tsp. salt	6 or 8 small tomatoes
Pinch pepper	6 or 8 small mushrooms

Cut the meat in 1½-inch (4 cm.) cubes, trimming off most of
the fat. Place in a bowl with the sliced onion, seasoning,
lemon juice, and wine. Stand overnight. Put the meat on
skewers, alternating pieces of meat with a small whole
tomato or a mushroom. Grill for 15 minutes and serve on
the skewers. Serve with vegetables and potatoes or savoury
rice (Risotto, No. 615).

373. Grilled Liver and Kidneys. Cooking time 5–10 minutes

Cut the liver in slices and leave the kidneys whole, or, if
large, cut in half and skewered out flat. Grill fairly slowly
and keep basted with fat. They are cooked when small
beads of blood appear on the surface. Serve with grilled
bacon or as part of a mixed grill.

374. Kidneys en Brochette

Slice and thread on skewers, alternately with bacon and
mushrooms. Grill and serve with fried potatoes and watercress.

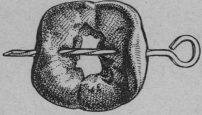

Kidney cut and skewered

375. Grilled Bacon. Cooking time 3–5 minutes. Gammon rasher 10–20 minutes, depending on thickness.

Remove the rind. With a gammon rasher cut the fat at
intervals to prevent the rasher from curling up during
cooking. Grill fairly slowly until the fat is clear.

376. Grilled Sausages. Cooking time 15–20 minutes

Grill fairly slowly, turning frequently, until well browned. Serve with grilled bacon, mashed or fried potatoes, any vegetable, and apple, onion, or bread sauce.

377. Kebabs. Cooking time 20 minutes more or less according to ingredients. Meat is grilled on skewers of a special kind, and is similar to Shashlik No. 372. The kebabs can be cooked under a grill, over an open fire, or on a rôtisserie. The meat, which should be tender, is cut in pieces about an inch (3 cm.) or more cubed. Suitable meats are lamb, beef, pork, liver, kidney, bacon, ham, sausages or chicken. Pieces of fruit or vegetable are alternated with the meat, for example, tomatoes, sweet pepper, pineapple, onions, bay leaves, mushrooms, pieces of apple. The kebabs are brushed with oil or with one of the basting sauces, see No. 122. They can be served with vegetables, but the traditional accompaniment is rice.

FRYING

378. General Information

As already mentioned in No. 321, only the most tender cuts of meat are suitable for frying. For suitable meat, see Nos. 325–30. You will also find general instructions for frying in the chapter on fats, Nos. 148–9.

379. Fried Beef Steak

1. Prepare the steak as described for grilling, No. 367, except that there is no need to brush with oil or fat, and the meat can be cut in thinner slices.

2. Use a thick frying-pan and heat in it a very little lard, dripping, or oil. When it is very hot put in the steak and brown for 1 minute on each side. Keep cooking over a

fierce heat, turning every minute or two. Cooking times are the same as for grilling. Minute steaks 1 minute each side.

3. Serve on a hot dish with any of the vegetables and garnishes given for grilled steak. The frying-pan is generally swilled out with a little liquid, such as wine, lemon juice, or mushroom stock, and the liquid poured over the meat.

380. Fried Steak and Onions. Cooking time 10–15 minutes for the onions and 5–15 minutes for the steak, depending on its thickness and whether it is preferred well-done or rare.

Quantities for 4 helpings:

1–2 lb. rump steak	Salt and pepper
($\frac{1}{2}$–1 kg.)	Butter
1$\frac{1}{2}$ lb. onions (750 g.)	

Cut the meat in four portions. Trim off excess fat and cut the fat in small pieces. Skin and slice onions thinly. Season the meat. Put the chopped fat in a heavy frying pan and heat gently until the fat runs, or use other frying fat. Remove fat and add onions. Reduce the heat and cook slowly, stirring frequently until the onions are tender and lightly browned. Remove and keep hot. Put a small knob of butter in the pan and turn up the heat. When the butter begins to brown add the steaks. Brown each side quickly and continue to cook over a good heat, turning every minute, until the meat is cooked to taste. Put on a hot dish with the onions. Add a little water or stock to the pan and simmer until all the sediment is dissolved. Pour over the meat and serve.

381. Fried Lamb Cutlets

These are cut from the best end of neck, and all surplus fat should be trimmed off, leaving about an inch of clean bone. Beat the cutlets to flatten them a little, and then dip in egg

and breadcrumbs and fry in deep fat as described in No.
149.

Serve with any vegetables and a sauce, such as Onion,
No. 85; Tomato, No. 89; Brown, No. 73; or Mushroom,
No. 82.

382. Fried Chops (veal, lamb, or pork)

These are fried in the same way as steak, but the cooking
should be very much slower, taking at least 20 minutes.
After the meat has been browned on both sides reduce the
heat and finish the cooking more slowly. It is often an
improvement to cover the pan with a lid and let the steam
help to cook the meat. When the meat is cooked, gravy
may be made in the pan by the Roux Method, as described
for roast meat in No. 79.

With Pork Chops serve: Mashed or fried potatoes.
Onions, carrots, celery, tomatoes, or turnips. Fried apple-
rings, or tart jelly.

With Lamb Chops serve: Mashed or fried potatoes.
Spinach, peas, beans, tomatoes, or mushrooms.

With Veal Chops serve: Mashed or fried potatoes,
macaroni, or spaghetti. Tomatoes, carrots, celery, or
beans. Tomato Sauce, No. 89; Apple Sauce, No. 108; or
lemon.

383. Fried Liver, Kidneys, Bacon, and Sausages

The same rules apply as for grilling, see No. 373. Gravy may
be made in the pan in the same way as for roast meat, see
No. 79.

384. Escalopes of Veal

These are very thin slices of meat cut from the fillet and are
delicious fried, either plain or coated in egg and breadcrumbs. The veal should be pounded well to flatten it before

cooking, and is then fried in butter, fat, or oil until brown on both sides.

Serve with any of the vegetables and accompaniments given for Veal Chops, No. 382.

385. Escalopes of Veal with Lemon

Fry the uncoated veal in butter. Remove from the pan and keep hot. Add a very little hot water to the pan and boil hard for a minute or two. Then for every four escalopes, add the juice of $\frac{1}{2}$ lemon and pour over the meat.

386. Wiener Schnitzel

Coat veal escalopes in egg and breadcrumbs and fry in butter or hot fat. Serve with slices of lemon and anchovy on each escalope. Other garnishes sometimes used are olives, capers, hard-boiled eggs, mushrooms, tomatoes.

387. Chicken Sauté. Cooking time 40–45 minutes

Quantities for 4 helpings:

4 pieces of frying chicken
Seasoned flour
Butter or oil for frying
$\frac{1}{8}$ pt. red wine ($\frac{1}{4}$ c.)
1 small onion, chopped
2 oz. sliced mushrooms
   (50 g.)

1 Tbs. chopped green
   pepper
2 sliced tomatoes
1 rasher bacon, chopped

Wash and dry the chicken pieces. Coat them in seasoned flour. Fry in a little butter or oil until the pieces are brown on both sides. Pour off surplus fat, add the other ingredients, and simmer for 30 minutes or until the chicken is tender. It helps to cover the pan with a lid of foil and if the pan becomes too dry, moisten with a little stock or wine.

388. Liver and Onions with Red Wine. Cooking time 10 minutes

Quantities for 4 helpings:

1 onion, thinly sliced	Salt and pepper
4 Tbs. oil	1 oz. flour (3 Tbs.)
1 lb. lamb's or calf's liver, thinly sliced (500 g.)	¼ pt. red wine (½ c.)

Measures level. Heat the oil and fry the onion until tender, about 3 minutes. Sprinkle the liver with salt and pepper and toss in the flour to coat it well. Remove the onion and keep hot. Fry the liver quickly, 2–3 minutes each side. Return the onion, add the wine and cook at high heat for a minute. Serve at once with boiled potatoes and Lettuce Salad, No. 563.

389. Pork Cutlets à la Charcutière. Cooking time 30–40 minutes

Quantities for 4 helpings:

1 oz. lard or butter (25 g.)	½ tsp. salt
1 large onion, chopped	4 peppercorns
1 Tbs. flour	4 Tbs. chopped gherkins
½ pt. stock (1 c.)	1 tsp. French mustard
¼ pt. white wine or cider (½ c.)	4 pork cutlets

Measures level. Melt the fat in a saucepan and add the onion. Cook until tender, without browning. Add the flour and mix well. Cook until yellow. Add the stock and wine or cider and the salt and peppercorns. Boil gently for 30–40 minutes. Just before serving add the gherkins and mustard. Grill or fry the cutlets for 20–25 minutes. Put on a dish and pour the sauce over. Serve with Mashed Potato, No. 511.

ROASTING

390. General Information

There are many different methods used for roasting meat but the two most useful are low-temperature roasting and high-temperature roasting.

LOW-TEMPERATURE ROASTING
350° F. (180° C.) Mark 3.

This is the best method because it gives a tender, juicy result, even with the less expensive cuts such as those listed as suitable for Pot Roasting and Braising, see Nos. 325–30. In addition the oven is not splashed by the fat.

Put the meat in a roasting-pan; if it is lean add some extra fat or dripping. Very lean meat like veal, game and poultry needs to have either a piece of pork or bacon fat put on top, or a loose lid of foil, or wrap the meat in cooking film. Remove this for the last half hour to allow browning.

When the meat is cooked (for times see No. 391), lift it out and put to keep hot while making gravy by the Roux Method as in No. 79.

To cook Yorkshire pudding and brown roast potatoes, raise the oven temperature to 450° F. (230° C.) Mark 8 for the last half hour of cooking. It is better to have the potatoes in a separate tin and not round the meat. If desired, the meat can be left in during this high-temperature cooking.

HIGH-TEMPERATURE ROASTING
425–450° F. (220–230° C.) Mark 7–8.

This is the best method to use when pastry and pies are being cooked with the meat. For this kind of roasting it is advisable to use a covered roasting pan or to wrap the meat in foil. This prevents fat from the meat from splashing on the oven walls, which is inevitable at high temperatures. The cover may need to be removed for the last half hour to allow browning.

When the meat is cooked make gravy by the Roux method, see No. 79.

High-temperature roasting is also used when meat is preferred under-done but with a well-browned exterior. In this case the meat is not covered. The method is only suitable for the more expensive cuts of beef such as rump roasts and sirloin on the bone.

ROASTING PORK. 375° F. (190° C.) Mark 5.

Pork needs special treatment to ensure good crisp crackling. It should not be covered during roasting and should be placed on a rack in such a way that the skin is kept above the drippings. Rubbing the skin with salt or brushing it with oil before cooking helps to give crisp crackling.

Roast potatoes should brown readily at this temperature.

USING A RÔTISSERIE or SPIT-ROASTING

This method is suitable for boned and rolled ribs of beef, thick pieces of steak, legs of lamb, chicken and other birds, and any cuts of an even shape. It is also excellent for Kebabs, No. 377, and Shashlik, No. 372. The meat does not need to be basted unless it is very lean and then the better method is to tie a piece of fat over the lean surface to act as a self-baster. Alternatively, brush the meat with melted butter or oil, or with a Basting sauce, No. 122, at the beginning of cooking, and during cooking too if it seems necessary.

Cooking times recommended by the makers of rôtisseries should be followed, but are generally the same as for low-temperature roasting or grilling.

391. Roasting Time Table

The times given below are for joints between 3 and 8 lb. in weight (1½–4 kg.). With boned joints weighing less than 3 lb. you should allow 1½–2 hours. With the exception of small chickens and game birds and small loin roasts of lamb, veal or pork, very small pieces of meat are not really satisfactory roasted and I would advise instead Braising, No. 404, or Pot Roasting, No. 403. All boned and rolled, or stuffed meat should be cooked very thoroughly to avoid any danger of food poisoning caused by infection introduced during boning. Pork should always be thoroughly cooked and lamb and veal are usually considered indigestible and unpalatable if under-done. Chicken and other birds should also be thoroughly cooked, particularly when spit-roasted.

COOKING TIMES
(for wrapped or unwrapped meat)

BEEF: Unboned ribs and thin pieces, 40 minutes per lb. ($\frac{1}{2}$ kg.). Boned and rolled and thick pieces, 45 minutes per lb. For under-done meat, use about two thirds of these times.

LAMB or MUTTON: 45 minutes per lb. ($\frac{1}{2}$ kg.).

PORK: Spare ribs and loin, 35 minutes per lb. ($\frac{1}{2}$ kg.). Leg, 40 minutes per lb. ($\frac{1}{2}$ kg.).

VEAL: Pieces with bone, 30 minutes per lb. ($\frac{1}{2}$ kg.). Boned and rolled pieces, 40 minutes per lb. ($\frac{1}{2}$ kg.).

CHICKEN, RABBIT, DUCK, BLACKCOCK, GUINEA FOWL: 2 hours.

GROUSE or PHEASANT: $1\frac{1}{2}$ hours.

GOOSE: drawn weight 6 lb. (3 kg.), 1 hour 40 minutes, 12 lb. (6 kg.), 2 hours 20 minutes, 18 lb. (9 kg.), 3 hours 10 minutes, 24 lb. (12 kg.), 4 hours.

TURKEY: drawn weight 7–10 lb. ($3\frac{1}{2}$–5 kg.), 3 hours, 10–12 lb. (5–6 kg.), 4 hours, 15–20 lb. ($7\frac{1}{2}$–10 kg.), $4\frac{1}{2}$ hours.

Smaller game birds such as teal, quail, and woodcock are best cooked at 400° F. (200° C.) Mark 6 for about 30 minutes. Do not cover.

Large geese and turkeys and very large joints of meat are more satisfactory cooked by the Low-temperature method.

392. What to Serve with Roast Meat, Poultry, Game

BEEF. Roast or boiled potatoes. Any green vegetables. Baked parsnips, marrow, pumpkin. Brown Gravy, No. 79; Horse-radish Sauce, No. 80; Yorkshire Pudding, No. 862.

LAMB or MUTTON. Roast or boiled potatoes. Any green vegetable. Mashed turnips or swedes. Savoury stuffing. Currant jelly. Brown Gravy, No. 79; Onion Sauce, No. 85.

PORK. Boiled, roast, or mashed potatoes. Any green vegetable. Celery, onions, tomatoes. Brown gravy. Sage and Onion Stuffing, No. 133. Baked or fried apples or Apple Sauce, No. 108; Cranberry Sauce, No. 109. Tart jelly.

VEAL. Boiled, roast, or mashed potatoes. Spinach, tomatoes, onions, or beetroot. Veal Forcemeat, No. 135; Brown Gravy, No. 79; Boiled or grilled bacon or salt pork.

CHICKEN. Mashed, fried, or roast potatoes. Cauliflower, celery, peas, beans, onions, watercress, green salad. Stuffing, No. 135. Currant jelly. Bread Sauce, No. 121; Brown Gravy, No. 79. Bacon rolls.

DUCKLING OR DUCK. Boiled or roast potatoes. Peas, carrots, turnips, Orange Salad, No. 564. Apple Sauce, No. 108; Sage and Onion Stuffing, No. 133; or Veal Stuffing, No. 135. Tart jelly.

GOOSE. Roast or boiled potatoes. Any green vegetable. Onions or carrots. Sage and Onion Stuffing, No. 133; or Prune and Apple Stuffing, No. 132. Apple Sauce, No. 108; Brown Gravy, No. 79; currant jelly. Cranberry Sauce, No. 109.

RABBIT OR HARE. Roast or boiled potatoes. Any green vegetable. Onions, carrots. Red-currant jelly. Brown Gravy, No. 79. Savoury stuffing.

TURKEY. Boiled, fried, or roast potatoes. Onions, peas, pumpkin, sprouts. Sausages. Grilled bacon rolls. Cranberry Sauce, No. 109; Brown Gravy, No. 79. Stuffing, No. 134; Bread Sauce, No. 121.

GAME. Any of the accompaniments already given for poultry. Game is not usually stuffed for roasting.

VENISON. Any potatoes and vegetables. Brown Gravy, No. 79. Red-currant jelly.

393. Re-heating Roast Meat

Slice the cold meat very thinly, and place the pieces overlapping on a hot dish. Pour over well-seasoned boiling gravy or sauce. There will be sufficient heat in the sauce to warm the meat. The flavour is spoiled if meat is re-cooked. Serve at once.

394. Roast Stuffed Veal

The most suitable cuts to use are the loin or shoulder, which should be boned. Veal Forcemeat, No. 135, gives the best flavour. The stuffed loin should be skewered or tied into a roll.

Another method of stuffing loin is to separate the meat from the bone just enough to make a pocket for the stuffing. Fasten up the opening.

395. Roast Stuffed Pork

The most suitable cuts to use are loin or leg. Sage and Onion Stuffing, No. 133, is the usual one, but Prune and Apple, No. 132, is also very good. The leg should be boned for stuffing, but the loin can be boned or not as described for Veal, No. 394. To make crisp crackling, rub salt into the skin before roasting.

396. Roast Stuffed Lamb

The most suitable cuts are loin, leg, or shoulder. The following stuffings are the best: Veal Forcemeat, No. 135, or Mint or Watercress, No. 131. The joint is usually boned for stuffing, but the loin may be treated as for Veal, No. 394.

397. Savoury Roast Pork

Score the skin of a 4-lb. (2 kg.) roast in lines $\frac{1}{4}$ inch ($\frac{1}{2}$ cm.) apart. Mix the following seasonings together, and rub them well into the pork before roasting in the usual way.

Measures level.

$\frac{1}{2}$ tsp. powdered sage	$\frac{1}{4}$ tsp. pepper
$\frac{1}{2}$ tsp. mustard	1 finely chopped onion
$\frac{1}{2}$ tsp. salt	

398. Roasting a Boiling Fowl

Stuff in the usual way, and then roast in a very hot oven, 475° F. (250° C.) Mark 9, until brown. Then steam for 1–2 hours or pressure cook for 15–20 minutes, or until tender. Keep the roasting-pan and fat to make the gravy by the Roux Method as in No. 79.

399. Baked Bacon or Gammon

Specially prepared cuts of gammon or bacon are sold ready for baking and usually with cooking instructions attached; but any cut can be used if it is first boiled for half the cooking time, see No. 338. Drain, remove the rind, and score the fat in a diamond pattern, using the point of a sharp knife. Stick a clove in each diamond, pressing it into the fat. Put the meat in a baking dish with a thin layer of treacle, syrup, honey or brown sugar on top, and pour round the meat $\frac{1}{2}$ pint (1 c.) of either cider, stout or orange juice. Bake at 325° F. (160° C.) Mark 3 for the remainder of the time, basting frequently with the liquid. Serve the liquid as a sauce.

400. Roast Pork or Veal with Orange Sauce

Roast a $3\frac{1}{2}$–4 lb. ($1\frac{1}{2}$–$1\frac{3}{4}$ kg.) piece of pork or veal. Remove it from the pan and put to keep hot. Pour the fat from the

pan, leaving the juice behind. Add the juice of 2 oranges to
the pan before making gravy in the usual way, see No. 79.

401. Baked Lamb with Rosemary

For a 4–5 lb. (1¾–2¼ kg.) joint of lamb put 2 sprigs of rosemary and 2 bay leaves under the meat. Season the meat
with salt and pepper and put ¼ pint stock (½ c.), or white
wine, in the pan. Baste the meat frequently with the juices
to make sure the flavour of the herbs penetrates. Make
gravy in the pan in the usual way, see No. 79.

POT ROASTING AND BRAISING

402. General Information

These are both useful methods for treating a joint which is
not sufficiently tender for ordinary roasting. For suitable
cuts, see Nos. 325–30. They are also very useful ways of
cooking the not-so-young game and poultry, or for steaks
and chops, especially those which require thorough cooking,
such as veal or pork chops.

Although both pot roasting and braising were originally
carried out in saucepans on top of the stove, they may
equally well be done in a slow oven. In both cases the meat
is browned in a little fat, and then cooked slowly with the
lid on. If you want to cook it in the oven and have no
casserole which will stand frying heat, brown the meat in a
frying-pan, and then transfer it to the casserole. If cooking is
done on the top of the stove, a heavy pan must be used,
otherwise the meat will stick and burn.

Using a covered roasting pan, see No. 390, gives very
similar results to pot roasting.

403. Pot Roasting. Temperature 325–350° F. (160–180° C.) Mark 3.

1. Melt enough fat to cover the bottom of the pan. Then
fry the meat over a good heat until it is well browned.

2. Put on the lid, which should be a good fit, and reduce the heat. Cook slowly until tender, turning the joint over occasionally. Allow the same times as for Slow Roasting, No. 390, with a minimum time of 2 hours for joints weighing less than 3 lb. (1½ kg.). Potatoes and vegetables may be cooked round the meat but will not brown.

3. Lift out the meat and pour off surplus fat, making the gravy by the Roux Method, as described in No. 79. Serve with any of the accompaniments given for Roast Meat, No. 392.

404. Braising. Temperature 325–350° F. (160–180° C.) Mark 3.

1. Begin by trimming off all surplus fat. You can render this down as described in No. 138. The reason for cutting off the fat is to avoid having the finished dish too greasy, which would make it unappetizing and indigestible.

2. Peel, and dice or slice enough vegetables to make a layer about 2 inches (5 cm.) thick, on the bottom of the pan. If you want the dish to have a special flavour, use just one vegetable alone, for example, onions or tomatoes; or use a mixture of vegetables such as onions, carrots, celery, turnips, tomatoes, parsnips, peas, and swedes.

3. Heat enough fat to cover the bottom of the saucepan. Put in the meat and cook over a good heat until it is brown all over.

4. Lift out the meat and fry the vegetables until they are slightly browned. Then pour off any fat.

5. Put the meat on the bed of vegetables and add just enough stock to moisten, or to come almost level with the top of the layer of vegetables. Add salt and pepper and herbs such as bay leaf, sprig of parsley, and thyme, or their equivalent in dried herbs.

6. Put on a lid which fits tightly, and cook very gently until the meat is tender. The times are the same as for Roasting, Low-temperature No. 390, with a minimum

time of 2 hours for a joint weighing less than 3 lb. ($1\frac{1}{2}$ kg.),
$\frac{3}{4}$–1 hour for chops, $1\frac{1}{2}$–2 hours for pieces of steak.

7. Braised meat looks best if cut in slices and arranged on
a dish with the vegetables round it. Put in a warm place
while the gravy is prepared. First skim off as much fat as
possible. The liquid may then be used as it is or thickened
with flour by the Blending Method, see No. 95. Colour
with gravy browning according to taste. The same vegetables and accompaniments as for Roast Meat, No. 392,
are suitable for braised meat, game, or poultry.

405. Continental Pot Roast of Beef

Pot roast the beef as in No. 403, using olive oil instead of
fat. When the meat is cooked, lift it out and pour off the fat.
To the remaining juices add $\frac{1}{4}$ pint ($\frac{1}{2}$ c.) of white or red
wine, 1 tablespoon tomato paste, $\frac{1}{4}$ pint stock ($\frac{1}{2}$ c.) and 12
olives. Boil for a few minutes. Slice the meat and serve it
with the sauce poured over it.

406. Pot-roasted Chicken. Cooking time $1\frac{1}{2}$ hours

Temperature 350° F. (180° C.) Mark 4.

Quantities for 4–6 helpings:

1 chicken	1 tsp. salt
2 oz. butter (50 g.)	Pinch of pepper

Measures level. For extra flavour put a sprig of rosemary or
tarragon inside the chicken. Melt the butter in a casserole.
When hot add the chicken, and fry until brown all over.
Sprinkle with the salt and pepper. Cover and cook gently
until tender. Cook the chicken lying on its side and turn
two or three times during cooking. Pour the juice and butter
over the chicken before serving. The best way of serving is to
carve the chicken and arrange it on a large platter before
pouring over the juice. Serve with green peas and new
potatoes.

MINCED MEAT

407. General Information

Mincing is a very useful way of making tough meat tender without long, slow cooking. The mincer breaks up tough connective tissue, making the meat easy to chew. An interesting fact about mincing is that the smaller the meat is minced the less natural flavour it has. On the other hand, fine mincing makes a smoother and more tender mixture, and herbs and seasoning can be added for flavour. Either buy lean, ready-minced meat, or ask the butcher to mince a piece for you. Unless you have a very efficient or a power-driven mincer, it is very hard work to do it yourself.

One kind of meat can be used alone, or a mixture of two or more kinds. Fat bacon goes very well with beef and veal, and a mixture of beef, pork, and veal is very good. Liver, heart, sausage, etc., may also be mixed with the meat to make up the weight.

408. Minced Meat. Cooking time 15 minutes or longer depending on how used

Quantities for 4–6 helpings:

1 lb. lean raw meat (500 g.) (see No. 407)
½ c. fresh breadcrumbs or 4 Tbs. dried crumbs
1 tsp. salt
Pinch of pepper
2 Tbs. onion, chopped and fried

¼ tsp. ground mace
4–8 Tbs. milk or wine
Chopped or dried herbs (marjoram, basil, savory, thyme, etc.) to taste

Measures level.

1. Put the meat once or twice through the mincer, or until it is fine enough to hold together smoothly, or buy ready-minced meat.

2. Add the bread and flavourings. There is no need to fry the onion first if the meat is to be cooked in a loaf or mould for some time, although frying does improve the flavour. It is essential to fry the onion for meat cakes and meat balls, as otherwise it will not cook in time and there will be raw onion in the middle of the meat cake. Flavourings can be added according to taste, and any fresh or dried herbs are suitable, also spices, which can be blended to give individual flavours, or a minute speck of garlic.

3. Mix well, using a wooden spoon, and working until the mixture is smooth, adding liquid as needed. The mixture should be moist without being difficult to handle.

4. Shape on a board with floured hands, and use in any of the ways suggested in Nos. 409–412.

409. Grilled or Fried Meat Rissoles. Cooking time 10–15 minutes

Divide mixture No. 408 into eight equal portions, and pat and shape each into a flat rissole $\frac{1}{2}$–1 inch thick (1–2 cm.). Do not make them too thick, or the outsides will be hard before the insides are cooked.

GRILLED. Cook under a fierce heat until brown and then more slowly to finish.

FRIED. Brown in a little hot fat and finish the cooking more slowly. Keep hot while making gravy in the pan according to No. 79.

Serve either fried or grilled rissoles with fried or mashed potatoes, and any vegetable. Brown Gravy, No. 79, or Tomato Sauce, No. 89. Fried onions.

410. Baked Meat Rissoles. Cooking time 20–30 minutes

Temperature 450° F. (230° C.) Mark 8.

Use Recipe No. 408. The nicest way of baking is to wrap a thin rasher of streaky bacon round each rissole, fastening it

with a tooth-pick or small skewer. Place on slices cut from
a large onion and pre-cooked in a little fat for 5 minutes.
Serve with fried potatoes and spinach, peas, beans, or
tomatoes. Gravy may be made in the pan in the same way
as for Roast Meat, see No. 79.

411. Casserole of Pork Rissoles. Cooking time $\frac{3}{4}$ hour

Temperature 375° F. (190° C.) Mark 5.

Use pork for the meat in No. 408, and flavour with a pinch
each of ground nutmeg, ginger, cloves, and mace. Fry
brown and put in a casserole. Fry in the same fat:

1 sliced onion
2 stalks celery, chopped
2 tomatoes, chopped

Add 2 Tbs. flour and mix well and then stir in $\frac{1}{2}$ pt. (1 c.)
stock, 1 tsp. salt, $\frac{1}{4}$ tsp. pepper, and 2 Tbs. wine vinegar.
Pour over the meat, cover, and cook in a slow oven for
$\frac{3}{4}$ hour. Serve with boiled or baked potatoes and cabbage or
other green vegetables.

412. Meat Rissoles Jardinière. Cooking time 10–15 minutes

Fry the meat rissoles as in No. 409 and serve surrounded
with heaps of two or three different vegetables, such as diced
carrots, peas, diced turnip, beans, etc.

413. Swedish Meat Balls. Cooking time 10–15 minutes

Quantities for 20–30 balls:

1 lb. lean raw beef or beef and pork mixed (500 g.)	Pinch of pepper
1 large boiled potato, mashed	2 Tbs. onion, chopped and fried
1 tsp. salt	$\frac{1}{4}$ tsp. ground mace
	4–8 Tbs. milk or water

Measures level. Mince the meat three times to make it very smooth, or buy ready minced. Add the other ingredients and shape into small balls. Fry in a little hot fat, taking care not to crowd them in the pan, and turning until brown all over. Put in a dish to keep hot. Pour 2–3 Tbs. water in the pan and swill it round. Pour over the meat balls. Serve with boiled or browned potatoes and any vegetable.

414. Meat Balls in Tomato Sauce. Cooking time 10–15 minutes

Make according to No. 413 and, when cooked, put in ¾ pt. (1½ c.) Tomato Sauce, No. 89, and heat for a few minutes. Serve with mashed or boiled potatoes and spinach, peas, beans, or any green vegetable.

415. Grilled Meat Balls with Cheese. Cooking time 10–15 minutes

Make meat balls from Recipe No. 413, leaving out the onion, but adding 2 oz. (50 g.) grated cheese. Thread these on skewers alternately with mushrooms and small tomatoes and grill for 10–15 minutes. Serve with fried potatoes, or Risotto, No. 615.

416. Meat Loaf. Cooking time ¾ hour

Temperature 375° F. (190° C.) Mark 5.

Make according to No. 408, adding a tiny speck of garlic for extra flavour. Shape into a loaf and bake in a moderate oven with a little fat round and a piece of greased paper on top. Remove the paper for the last 10 minutes to allow the top to brown. Make gravy in the pan in the same way as for roast meat, No. 79, or serve the loaf with Tomato

Sauce, No. 89. For serving, cut in slices about $\frac{3}{4}$ inch (2 cm.) thick. Any vegetables are suitable.

417. Meat Shape to Serve Cold. Cooking time 2 hours

Make according to Recipe No. 408, and put the mixture in a greased basin, or stone jar, or tin with straight sides. Cover with greased paper and steam for 2 hours. Turn out and roll in dried breadcrumbs, and cut in thin slices when cold. This cold shape is nicest if a little bacon can be used with the meat. Pork mixture No. 411 also makes a very good loaf, and so does a mixture of liver, sausage, and bacon.

418. Moussaka. Cooking time 1 hour

Temperature 375° F. (190° C.) Mark 5.

Quantities for 4 helpings:

2–4 oz. butter or margarine (50–125 g.)
$\frac{3}{4}$ lb. minced raw meat (375 g.)
8 oz. chopped onions (250 g.)
4 Tbs. chopped parsley
8 oz. chopped tomatoes (250 g.)
$1\frac{1}{2}$ lb. potatoes (750 g.)
4 Tbs. wine
2 Tbs. flour
$\frac{1}{2}$ pt. milk (1 c.)
1 egg
4 Tbs. grated cheese

Measures level. Melt about 2 oz. (50 g.) of the butter or margarine and fry in it the meat, onions, parsley, and tomatoes. Season well. Grease an 8-inch (20 cm.) cake-tin. Peel and slice the potatoes very thinly. Put a layer of potatoes on the bottom of the tin, add a layer of meat, and repeat the layers, finishing with potato. Sprinkle with the wine. Melt $\frac{1}{2}$ oz. (1 Tbs.) butter or margarine in a small pan. Add the flour, mix, and cook for a minute. Add the milk and stir until it boils and thickens. Remove from the heat and add the slightly beaten egg and the grated cheese. Pour over the potatoes and meat. Bake in a moderate oven for 1 hour. Cut in wedges or squares for serving.

USING COOKED AND CANNED MEAT

419. General Information

Always bring re-heated meat to boiling point, otherwise there is danger of food poisoning. Re-heated meat is apt to be tasteless and needs additional flavourings, best provided by a well-seasoned sauce. I have already suggested, in No. 393, how to re-heat roast meat. Cold roast, braised or boiled meat, and canned meat, such as corned beef or other whole meat, may be served with salad or hot vegetables, such as Browned Potatoes, No. 510, or fried or roast potatoes, and a vegetable mixed with a well-flavoured sauce. This is an opportunity to use some of the more elaborate vegetable dishes. Chutney, pickles, sweet pickled pears, pickled walnuts, or gherkins all add zest to this sort of meal.

420. Cold Meat Hash. Cooking time 10–15 minutes

Quantities for 4 helpings:

1½ c. Brown Sauce, No. 73; or Curry Sauce, No. 76; or Tomato Sauce, No. 89, or use a packet sauce or condensed canned soup

2 c. minced cooked meat

Measures level. Make the sauce and heat the meat in it without boiling. Make sure it is well seasoned. A little Worcester Sauce or Mushroom Ketchup improves the flavour. Serve with boiled potatoes and any vegetable.

421. Shepherd's Pie. Cooking time 20 minutes

Temperature 450° F. (230° C.) Mark 8.

Quantities for 4 helpings:

Meat and sauce as for
  No. 420.

1½ lb. mashed potatoes
  (750 g.)

Put the meat and sauce in a pie-dish and cover with the
mashed potatoes. Decorate the top by roughing with a
fork or piping potato through a forcing-tube. Bake in a hot
oven until brown on top. This is always nicer if the potatoes
are freshly cooked.

If the sauce and meat are heated before putting the
mixture in the dish it can be finished off under the grill
instead of going into the oven.

422. Corned Beef Hash. Cooking time 10 minutes

Quantities for 2–3 helpings:

1 c. diced corned beef
2 c. diced cooked potatoes
Fat for frying

1 small onion, sliced
1 Tbs. milk

Measures level. Mix the meat and potatoes. Fry the onion
brown in the fat. Add the meat mixture and sprinkle over
the milk. Stir well, and then leave on a very low heat until
brown underneath. Fold over. Turn out and serve hot.
Follow with a salad.

Red Flannel Hash

Add ½ c. diced cooked beetroot to mixture No. 422.

423. Fricassée of Cooked Veal or Poultry. Cooking time 10–15 minutes

Quantities for 3–4 helpings:

¾ lb. cooked diced meat (3 c.)

½ pt. Sauce, No. 69, made with meat stock or milk (1 c.)

Salt and pepper to taste

Pinch of nutmeg

2 egg-yolks

Juice of ½ lemon

1 Tbs. chopped parsley

3 or 4 rolls fried or grilled bacon

Measures level. Heat the meat in the sauce and season well. Just before serving stir in the eggs and cook for a minute or two longer. Add the lemon and parsley and garnish with the bacon rolls. Serve with mashed potatoes and spinach, peas, or carrots.

424. Fried Chicken with Almonds. Cooking time 15–20 minutes

Quantities for 4 helpings:

¾ lb. cooked chicken without bone (375 g.)

Oil for frying

2 oz. blanched almonds (50 g.)

1 small sliced onion or shallot

4 oz. sliced mushrooms (125 g.)

1 Tbs. cornflour

¼ pt. stock (½ c.)

1 tsp. Worcester or soya sauce

Salt and pepper

Measures level. Cut the chicken in small pieces. Fry the almonds in a little oil until they are lightly browned. Remove from the pan and fry the chicken, mushrooms and onion until the onion is cooked. Remove from the pan. Mix the cornflour into the remaining fat in the pan, add the stock, sauce and seasoning, and stir until it boils. Return the almonds and chicken and make sure it is hot before serving. Rice is a good accompaniment.

Other Recipes using Cooked Meat are:

Meat Cakes or Rissoles, No. 151.
Stuffed Pancakes, No. 861.
Meat Fritters, No. 867.

CHAPTER 13

Vegetables, Herbs, and Salads

425. Food Value

Vegetables are important foods for a number of reasons; they give variety and colour to meals; they are bulky and filling but of a lower carbohydrate and calorific value than many other foods; they contain cellulose which helps maintain normal peristalsis, and prevent constipation; and many have a high vitamin and mineral content.

Green leafy vegetables provide vitamins B, C, and carotene while watercress is a good source of calcium and iron. Iron is also found in parsley, mustard and cress, and the majority of green vegetables. Carrots are valuable for carotene, peas, beans and lentils for vitamin B and protein, and potatoes, especially new ones, are a useful source of vitamin C.

Unfortunately, when vegetables are badly cooked a lot of their value is lost. They are drowned in water, over-cooked, and the water-soluble nutrients poured down the sink. Quite apart from the loss in food value, this is a foolish method of cooking, for it destroys the natural flavour and makes the vegetables unpalatable.

Canned vegetables lose some of their vitamins and minerals to the liquid, and some of the vitamins B and C are destroyed by the high temperatures used in canning. However, canned carrots are still a good source of carotene, canned beans of protein, canned tomatoes of vitamin C and carotene and the others will provide at least some of the nutrients of the original vegetable and probably more than stale and badly cooked fresh vegetables.

If deep-frozen vegetables are cooked carefully according

to the manufacturer's directions their nutritive value compares very favourably with that of fresh ones.

426. Choosing and Keeping Fresh Vegetables

For maximum flavour and food value take the vegetables straight from the garden to the kitchen. The next best thing is to take care to buy only fresh vegetables and to use them as soon as possible. Good-quality vegetables are crisp and firm, but not hard. Those of a medium size are the best, as if too small the flavour will not be fully developed; if too large they will be inclined to be coarse and tough. Cabbage, cauliflower, and lettuce should be heavy in proportion to their size, and should feel solid to the touch.

If you have to keep green vegetables for any length of time they can be prevented from wilting by putting them in a covered saucepan or other container and standing it on a cool floor. If you have a refrigerator, wash the vegetables, drain well, and put them in the drawer provided for this purpose or in a polythene bag. Care must be taken not to freeze them, or they will be spoiled. Wilted green vegetables can be revived, if not too far gone, by soaking in cold water for $\frac{1}{2}$ hour and then hanging up in a draught in a wire salad-basket or clean cloth. Some of the goodness and flavour will be lost, so avoid soaking too long. Sometimes washing and putting in the refrigerator will revive them.

Root vegetables should be kept in a dark, cool, airy place and, if to be stored for any length of time, should be put on ventilated shelves or racks.

427. Recipe for Boiling All Fresh Vegetables (except potatoes, artichokes, whole beetroot, and asparagus)

1. Wash green vegetables thoroughly, separating the leaves of cabbages so as to get them clean without soaking. Cut cauliflower and broccoli into sprigs. Scrub root vegetables and then peel thinly or scrape with a sharp knife.

Keep outer leaves of cabbage, and trimmings from other vegetables for the stock-pot, see No. 33.

2. Slice root vegetables or dice them. Shred green vegetables, except spinach.

3. Heat about an inch ($2\frac{1}{2}$ cm.) of water in a saucepan with 1 level tsp. salt to each pound (500 g.) of vegetables. When the water is boiling add the vegetables and cover with a lid, which should fit well to keep in the steam needed to help cook the vegetables.

4. Boil for 10–20 minutes, giving the pan an occasional shake to prevent sticking. Do not boil too rapidly, or the water will boil away and the pan will burn. Just keep a good steady boil.

5. When the vegetables are tender, but not mushy, drain off any liquid, keeping it for stock.

6. Serve the vegetables at once, as keeping spoils the flavour and destroys vitamin C.

7. Melt a little margarine, butter, or dripping in the pan and return the vegetables, tossing them for a few minutes to dry out any moisture and mix them well with the fat. They may also be served with Sauce, No. 71, made with vegetable stock alone, or with some milk added.

428. Pressure Cooking Vegetables

All vegetables may be cooked under pressure according to instructions provided with the cooker. The greatest saving is with vegetables which normally require fairly long cooking. Care must be taken not to exceed the time recommended, or the vegetables will be over-cooked, with loss of vitamin C and flavour.

429. Cooking Frozen Vegetables

Instructions are usually given on the packet but, if not, proceed as follows. Vegetables should be cooked while frozen, the only exceptions being corn-on-the-cob, whole green peppers, and vegetables in large solid packs where partial thawing is necessary to separate the pieces. Use the minimum amount of water for cooking, $\frac{1}{4}$–$\frac{1}{2}$ pint ($\frac{1}{2}$–1 c.) for each pound of vegetables ($\frac{1}{2}$ kg.). Put the vegetables in the slightly salted boiling water and keep the pan on a high heat until the water comes back to the boil. Cooking times are less than with fresh vegetables, because frozen vegetables have already been blanched before freezing. Cook until just tender.

Approximate boiling times are:

3–4 minutes: Brussels sprouts, loose corn, spinach.
5–8 minutes: Asparagus, broccoli, carrots, cauliflower sprigs, corn-on-the-cob, peas, sliced runner beans or chopped green beans.
12–15 minutes: Broad beans, whole French beans.

Frozen vegetables are also suitable for cooking in fat, No. 433, in a casserole, No. 434, au gratin, No. 432, and in place of fresh vegetables in most recipes.

430. Using Canned Vegetables

To serve them as a separate vegetable, tip into a pan and heat gently in their own liquid, drain and dress with butter or margarine. Better still, thicken the cold drained liquid as for a sauce for vegetables, No. 71, or Macedoine, No. 437, and heat the vegetables in the sauce. Also use them for soups, in recipes needing cooked vegetables, and in stews and casseroles.

With some canned peas and beans, the flavour may be better if the vegetables are drained and rinsed before being used. Heat either with a little butter or margarine or in a sauce.

431. Using Dehydrated and Accelerated Freeze Dried Vegetables

These are sold in packets with the cooking instructions. The vegetables may be added to soups, stews and casseroles without previous cooking and cooked with the other ingredients. Dried onions and dried mushrooms are particularly useful for this purpose.

432. Vegetables au Gratin. Cooking time ½ hour

Temperature 450° F. (230° C.) Mark 8.

Quantities for 4 helpings:

1–1½ lb. any vegetable (500–750 g.), fresh, canned, or frozen

½ pt. Cheese Sauce, No. 75 (1 c.), or use packet sauce

Buttered breadcrumbs, No. 876

Boil the vegetables as in No. 427, saving any liquid for the sauce. Put vegetables and sauce in layers in a pie-dish, finishing with a layer of sauce. Cover with buttered breadcrumbs. Brown in a hot oven or under the grill.

433. Recipe for Stewing Vegetables in Fat (suitable for all except potatoes, beetroot, and asparagus)

1. Prepare the vegetables as for No. 427.
2. Heat sufficient fat (butter, lard, dripping, or oil) to cover the bottom of the pan and, when hot but not smoking, add the vegetables. Add ½ level tsp. salt for each pound (500 g.) of vegetables. Cover with a tightly fitting lid.
3. Cook over a moderate heat, shaking the pan occasionally. When the vegetables are tender – in about 10–20 minutes – serve with any liquid in the pan. Sprinkle with chopped parsley.

434. Baking in a Covered Dish or Casserole (suitable for all except green vegetables and potatoes)

1. Prepare the vegetables as for No. 427.
2. Put in a casserole with ½ oz. fat (1 Tbs.) to each pound (500 g.) of vegetables, ½ level tsp. salt, and a pinch of pepper. Add 1–2 Tbs. water and cover with a fitting lid.
3. Cook in a slow–moderate oven, 275–375° F. (140–190° C.) Mark 2–5, for ½–1 hour or until tender. Serve sprinkled with chopped parsley.

435. Roast Vegetables (suitable for potatoes, carrots, parsnips, marrow, pumpkin, turnip, onions, artichokes, and swedes)

1. Peel the vegetables and cut them in pieces or leave whole. Place in the hot fat round a roast joint or in a little hot fat in a separate pan.
2. Bake in a hot oven, 450° F. (230° C.) Mark 8, turning occasionally. They will take 40 minutes to 1 hour, depending on the size. Drain from the fat.

436. Vegetable Ragoût or Stew. Cooking time ¾–1 hour

Quantities for 4–5 helpings:

1 oz. fat (25 g.)	2 lb. mixed vegetables,
2–4 oz. bacon, chopped	sliced or diced (1 kg.)
(50–125 g.)	Bouquet garni
1 onion, sliced	3 Tbs. wine vinegar
1 Tbs. flour	Salt and pepper
½–¾ pt. stock (1–1½ c.)	Chopped parsley

Measures level. The vegetables may be any in season. If mostly root vegetables are used, the larger amount of stock will be needed, otherwise use ½ pt. (1 c.) only. Melt the fat in a saucepan, and fry the onion and bacon until they are just beginning to brown. Add the flour and cook until it turns yellow. Then add the stock, stir until it boils, and add the vegetables and flavourings. Boil gently, stirring occasionally until the vegetables are tender. Add the vinegar and taste for seasoning. Serve with chopped parsley sprinkled over.

437. Macedoine of Vegetables. Cooking time ½ hour

Quantities for 4 helpings:

½ pt. diced carrots (1 c.)	1 eggyolk
¼ pt. diced turnips (½ c.)	Chopped parsley
½ pt. peas (1 c.)	
½ pt. Vegetable Sauce, No. 71 (1 c.)	

Measures level. Boil the vegetables and make the sauce. Add the egg to the sauce and cook for a minute or two. Combine sauce and vegetables and serve with chopped parsley sprinkled over.

438. Vegetables Jardinière. Cooking time 1½ hours

Quantities for 4–5 helpings:

½ lb. lean salt pork or bacon, diced (250 g.)	2 lb. green peas, shelled (1 kg.)
½ oz. butter or margarine (1 Tbs.)	1 lb. new potatoes, scraped (500 g.)
1 lb. young carrots, sliced (500 g.)	1 tsp. salt
5 small onions	Pinch of pepper
½ Tbs. flour	Bouquet garni, see No. 12

Measures level. Fry the bacon or pork. Add the carrots, onions, and flour and fry 5 minutes. Add water to cover and cook slowly for ½ hour. Add peas, potatoes, and seasonings and cook slowly for 1 hour or until all the vegetables are tender. The cooking may be done in a casserole in a moderate oven and the vegetables served in the casserole.

SUGGESTIONS FOR COOKING AND USING DIFFERENT KINDS OF VEGETABLES AND HERBS

439. Artichokes, Globe

Allow 1 small, or half a large one, for each person.

Artichokes must be very fresh. They are no good if they have hard, sharp, brown tips.

Prepare by cutting off the stalk and removing the outer row of tough leaves. Trim the tops of the other leaves with scissors to make a neat shape. Wash in several changes of water, or soak in salted water for an hour to remove any insects. Drain well, upside down.

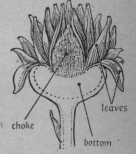

Cook in boiling, salted water for $\frac{1}{2}$–$\frac{3}{4}$ hour for small ones and up to an hour for large ones. They are done when the leaves pull out easily. If over-cooked they become tasteless. Drain upside down.

To serve, remove the 'choke' – that is, the bunch of small fluffy leaves in the centre. The centre may then be filled with Hollandaise Sauce, No. 94, or serve the sauce separately. Cold artichokes are generally served with Vinaigrette Sauce, No. 119.

Artichoke bottoms are obtained by pulling off all the leaves. When the whole artichoke is served, the juicy bits at the end of each leaf are dipped in the sauce and eaten.

440. Artichokes, Jerusalem

Allow ¼ lb. per person (250 g.).

Prepare by scrubbing and then scraping or peeling thinly. Put at once in cold water to cover, with 1 Tbs. vinegar to every quart (4 c.). This helps to keep them a good colour. Leave in the water for ½ hour. They may also be boiled in their jackets and peeled afterwards.

Cook by putting in boiling salted water to cover, and boil until tender when pierced. Over-cooking makes them soggy. Time 20–30 minutes. They may also be roasted as in No. 435 or fried like Potato Crisps, No. 516.

To serve, make Sauce, No. 71, with some of the vegetable water, or serve au gratin, No. 432, or use for soup, Nos. 38 and 52.

441. Asparagus

Allow 6 or 8 medium-sized pieces per person.

Prepare and use as soon as possible after cutting. Stale asparagus has very little flavour and is inclined to be bitter. Never buy it with drooping or dry heads. Wash well, scrubbing the white ends and scraping them downwards with a sharp knife. Place in bundles of twelve large or twenty-four small heads with the tops level, and trim the ends. Use the ends for Vegetable Stock, No. 33.

Cook in boiling salted water to cover the thick ends, but leave the heads in steam. If possible, use a tall, deep pan, so that they can stand upright. If you cook asparagus often, it is worth while buying a special asparagus boiler. The asparagus takes anything from 15 to 30 minutes to cook, depending on its condition. It should still be crisp at the thick ends. If over-cooked the tips will fall off. Drain carefully.

To serve, place on a hot dish and serve either Hollandaise Sauce, No. 94, or Brown Butter Sauce, No. 111, separately.

It may be served cold, in salads or with Vinaigrette Sauce, No. 119, or in Rolled Sandwiches, No. 886, with grated cheese or Cheese Sauce, No. 75, or the tips mixed with sauce may be used to fill patties, No. 810.

442. Balm

The finely chopped raw leaves are used for flavouring salads, soups, and stews. Allow 2 Tbs. chopped balm to 1 pt. liquid (2 c.).

443. Basil

Small amounts of the fresh leaves are used for flavouring soups, salads, stews, and savoury meat dishes. It can be bought and used dried. A little is very good in minced-meat patties or loaves.

444. Bay Leaves

A bay leaf forms part of the bouquet garni used for flavouring savoury dishes, see No. 12. Bay leaves are fairly strong in flavour, and a piece of a leaf is generally sufficient for flavouring a dish for 4 people. Alternatively a whole leaf may be used and removed when the desired flavour is obtained.

445. Beans, Broad

Allow ½–1 lb. per person (250–500 g.), depending on the fullness of the pods.

Prepare by shelling. If the pods are young and tender, they can be sliced and cooked with the beans; if old, use them for Vegetable Stock, No. 33.

Cook in a little boiling salted water as in No. 427.

To serve, toss in a little melted butter or margarine and

sprinkle with chopped parsley or savory; or serve with
Sauce, No. 71, made with some of the cooking liquid and
some chopped parsley or savory. For a supper dish garnish
with rolls of fried or grilled bacon.

Serve cold for salads or hors-d'œuvres.

446. Broad Beans and Bacon. Cooking time 20–30 minutes

Quantities for 4 helpings:

3–4 lb. beans (1½–2 kg.)
2 oz. butter or margarine
  (50 g.)
3 Tbs. flour
¾ pt. vegetable water
  (1½ c.)

2–4 oz. chopped bacon
  (50–100 g.)
Salt and pepper to taste
1 tsp. sugar
2 Tbs. chopped parsley
2 Tbs. vinegar

Measures level. Shell the beans. Melt the fat in a saucepan
and mix in the flour. Add the water and stir until it boils.
Add the chopped bacon and the beans, and cook gently
until the beans are tender. Season to taste. The amount of
salt required will depend on the saltiness of the bacon. Add
the sugar, parsley, and vinegar, and serve hot.

447. Beans, French or Runner

Allow 6–8 oz. per person (175–250 g.).

Prepare by removing tops and tails. If they are old
remove the stringy vein which develops along the rib. Small,
young beans should be cooked whole, otherwise break
them into 2-inch (5 cm.) lengths or slice them.

Cook by boiling in a little salted water, as in No. 427.

To serve, drain well and toss in a little melted fat. Use
cold boiled beans for salads or hors-d'œuvres.

448. Beans Béarnaise. Cooking time 15–20 minutes

Quantities for 4 helpings:

1 lb. runner beans (500 g.) 2 tomatoes, chopped
½ oz. fat (1 Tbs.) Salt and pepper to taste
1–2 oz. chopped bacon
  (25–50 g.)

Measures level. Prepare and cook the beans as in No. 447. Drain and keep hot. Fry the bacon and tomatoes in the fat for a few minutes. Add the beans and mix well. Season to taste and serve hot.

449. Beetroot

Allow 6–8 oz. per person (175–250 g.).

Prepare by scrubbing well to remove all soil, but taking care not to break the skin, or they will lose their colour during cooking. Leave the root on, but cut the stalks to about 2 inches.

Cook by putting in boiling water to cover with 1 Tbs. salt to 2 lb. (1 kg.) vegetables. Boil until tender. Test by pinching the skin, and if it comes off easily, the beetroot is done. They are excellent cooked in a pressure cooker for 10–40 minutes, depending on the size.

To serve, remove the skins and slice or dice. They may be served cold for salad or hot with a sauce.

450. Harvard Beets. Cooking time 10 minutes

Quantities for 4 helpings:

1 lb. cooked beetroot 1 Tbs. sugar
  (500 g.) ½ tsp. salt
1 oz. margarine (2 Tbs.) Pinch of pepper
2 Tbs. flour
3 Tbs. vinegar made up
  to ½ pt. (1 c.) with water

Measures level. Skin the beetroot and cut in cubes. Use the other ingredients to make a sauce by the Roux Method, No. 69, adding the sugar and seasoning at the end. Add the beetroot and cook gently for 5 minutes. Serve hot.

451. Broccoli

Prepare and cook in the same way as cauliflower, see Nos. 464–7.

452. Brussels Sprouts

Allow 6–8 oz. per person (175–250 g.).

Prepare by trimming off any damaged outer leaves and washing well in salted water. Do not buy badly blighted sprouts, as it is very difficult to get them clean. Cut large sprouts in half before cooking.

Cook by boiling in a little salted water, as in No. 427.

To serve, toss in a little melted margarine or butter or serve with Sauce, No. 71, made with the cooking liquid, or au gratin, No. 432.

Raw, finely shredded sprouts are very tender and sweet in salads.

453. Sprouts Lyonnaise. Cooking time 20 minutes

Quantities for 4 helpings:

1½ lb. sprouts (750 g.)   1 oz. butter or dripping
2 Tbs. chopped onion   (25 g.)

Measures level. Boil the sprouts in a little salted water, as in No. 427. Drain well. Fry the onion in the fat, and then add the sprouts and fry for a minute or two longer.

454. Cabbage and Savoys

Allow 6–8 oz. per person (175–250 g.).

Prepare and boil in a little salted water, as in No. 427, or cook in fat, as in No. 433.

To serve boiled cabbage or savoy, add a little melted margarine or butter and toss well. The addition of a little vinegar is an improvement. Cabbage may also be served au gratin, No. 432, or shredded raw in salads.

455. Fried Cabbage

Cook in a little fat, as in No. 433, adding 1 medium-sized chopped onion for each pound (500 g.) of cabbage, and a pinch of ground mace or nutmeg. A little chopped bacon may also be added with the onion.

456. Sour-Sweet Cabbage. Cooking time 20 minutes

Quantities for 4 helpings:

1½ lb. cabbage, shredded (750 g.)	6 Tbs. vinegar
	1 Tbs. sugar
1 oz. bacon fat or dripping (2 Tbs.)	Pinch of ground cloves

Measures level. Boil the cabbage in a little salted water, as in No. 427. Drain well.

Boil the other ingredients in a small pan for a few minutes. Pour over the cabbage and serve at once. This is very good with pork or sausages.

457. Cabbage and Bacon. Cooking time ½ hour

Quantities for 4 helpings:

1½ lb. cabbage, shredded (750 g.)	1 tsp. meat extract
	1 oz. fat (25 g.)

4 leeks, chopped, or small onions

4 rashers bacon, chopped

3 Tbs. flour

½ pt. stock (1 c.)

Salt and pepper to taste

Boil the cabbage, leeks, and bacon in about ½ pt. water (1 c.) for 15–20 minutes, or until tender. Drain and keep hot. Use ½ pt. (1 c.) of the liquid, fat, and flour, to make the sauce by the Roux Method, No. 69. Season well and add the extract. Pour over the cabbage.

458. Stuffed Cabbage Leaves. Cooking time ½ hour

Quantities for 4 helpings:

4 large cabbage leaves

For the stuffing use half the Risotto recipe, No. 615, or half the Minced Meat recipe, No. 408.

Serve with ½ pt. (1 c.) Cheese Sauce, No. 75, or Tomato Sauce, No. 89.

Pour boiling water on the cabbage leaves to soften them. Place some stuffing on each and roll up tightly. Pack closely in a pan and add a very little stock or water. Cook gently for 20 minutes to ½ hour. Add any liquid to the sauce and serve with the sauce poured over.

459. Red Cabbage. Cooking time ½–¾ hour

Quantities for 4 helpings:

1 oz. fat (25 g.)

1 lb. red cabbage, shredded (500 g.)

1 large onion, sliced

1 large apple, sliced

2 Tbs. stock or water

2 Tbs. vinegar

1 tsp. salt

Pinch of pepper

1 Tbs. brown sugar

Measures level. Melt the fat in a saucepan and add all the other ingredients. Cover with a tight-fitting lid and boil gently for $\frac{1}{2}$–$\frac{3}{4}$ hour or until the cabbage is tender. Stir occasionally, and do not cook too quickly, or the pan will boil dry. There should be hardly any liquid left at the end of cooking. This is very good served with pork or sausages.

460. Carrots

Allow 6–8 oz. per person (175–250 g.).

Prepare by scrubbing well and then scraping. If the carrots are freshly dug and young, they will only need washing. Young ones may be cooked whole, otherwise slice or dice them.

Cook by boiling in a little water, as in No. 427, or stew in fat, as in No. 433, or cook in a casserole, as in No. 434, or use one of the recipes given below.

Serve according to the method of cooking, sprinkling with chopped parsley. Cold cooked, diced carrots may be used in salads, or use raw grated carrot. A favourite method of serving boiled carrots is with Parsley Sauce, No. 87.

461. Carrots Vichy. Cooking time 15–20 minutes

Quantities for 4 helpings:

1 oz. butter or margarine (25 g.)	$\frac{1}{2}$ tsp. salt
	1 tsp. sugar
1 lb. young carrots, sliced (500 g.)	1 Tbs. chopped parsley

Measures level. Melt the butter or margarine in a saucepan, and add the other ingredients, except the parsley. Cover and cook gently until tender. Serve with the chopped parsley sprinkled over.

462. Carrot Purée (for veal or lamb cutlets). Cooking time ½ hour

Quantities for 4 helpings:

1½ lb. carrots, sliced (750 g.)   ½ oz. dripping (1 Tbs.)
1 small onion, chopped   Salt and pepper
   very finely

Measures level. Boil the carrots in a little water, as in No. 427. Fry the onion in the dripping until brown. Rub the carrots through a sieve or put in the blender. Add to the onions and heat well, stirring all the time. Season to taste.

463. Carrots and Sprouts

Boil equal quantities of sliced carrots and whole sprouts together in a little water, as in No. 427.

464. Cauliflower

Allow 1 large head for 4 portions.

Prepare by removing the outer leaves and stalk, which should be used for Vegetable Stock, No. 33. Divide the cauliflower into sprigs or leave whole and wash well. When left whole cauliflower takes longer to cook and has a stronger flavour.

To cook, boil in a little water, as in No. 427.

To serve, make a sauce with the vegetable water, as in No. 71. Cauliflower may also be served au gratin, No. 432, cooked or raw in salads, or with Hollandaise Sauce, No. 94.

465. Cauliflower with Bacon Sauce. Cooking time 30 minutes

Quantities for 4 helpings:

1 large cauliflower	2 oz. flour (6 Tbs.)
2 oz. fat (50 g.)	1 pt. stock (2 c.)
2 oz. chopped bacon (50 g.)	Salt and pepper
1 Tbs. chopped onion	4 Tbs. chopped parsley

Measures level. Boil the cauliflower in a little salted water, as in No. 427. Fry the bacon and onion in the fat in a small saucepan. Add the flour and finish the sauce according to the Roux Method, No. 69. The outside leaves and stalks of the cauliflower should be used to make the stock and add milk to make up to the pint. Season to taste, add the parsley and pour over the cauliflower.

466. Cauliflower Lyonnaise

Boil the cauliflower in a little water, as in No. 427. Drain well. For 1 large cauliflower melt 1 oz. dripping (2 Tbs.) in a pan and fry in it 1 large chopped onion, together with the drained cauliflower. Serve when brown.

467. Cauliflower Milanaise. Cooking time 20–30 minutes

Quantities for 4 helpings:

1 large cauliflower	2 oz. grated cheese (50 g.)
2 oz. butter or margarine (50 g.)	

Measures level. Boil the cauliflower in small pieces, as in No. 427. Drain well and place in a shallow, greased, fireproof dish, which has been sprinkled with a little of the cheese. Sprinkle the cauliflower with the rest of the cheese and half the butter cut in small pieces. Place in a hot oven or under the grill to melt and brown the cheese. Heat the rest of the butter in a small pan until light brown and pour over the cauliflower. Serve at once.

468. Celery

Allow 1 large head for 2–3 people.

Prepare by removing any damaged outside stalks and the green leaves. Use these in Vegetable Stock, No. 33. Pull off the stalks and trim the root. Wash very thoroughly in cold water, using a small brush if necessary.

To cook, cut in pieces and boil in a little water, as in No. 427, or stew in a little fat, as in No. 433, or cook in a casserole, as in No. 434.

To serve, make a Sauce, No. 71, from the cooking liquid, or serve au gratin, No. 432. The tender centre stalks are used raw in salads or eaten with cheese.

469. Celeriac

Allow 6–8 oz. per person (175–250 g.).

Prepare by scrubbing and peeling. Cut in slices or dice.

To cook, boil in a little water, as in No. 427, or cook in fat, No. 433, or in a casserole, No. 434.

To serve, make a sauce from the cooking liquid, as in No. 71. They may also be used raw, grated in salads.

470. Chicory

Allow 4 oz. per person (125 g.).

Prepare by cutting off any damaged leaves and washing well.

To cook, put in hot water to cover, bring to the boil and boil for 5 minutes. Drain well. Then boil in a little water, as in No. 427, or cook in fat, No. 433, squeezing a little lemon juice over to help keep a good colour. Cooking takes about 30–35 minutes. To serve, drain well.

Chicory is also used sliced in salads, but may sometimes be found too bitter to eat raw. It is advisable to try a little first.

471. Chicory with Cheese and Ham. Cooking time 1 hour

Temperature 400° F. (200° C.) Mark 6.

Quantities for 4 helpings:

1 lb. chicory (500 g.)
1 Tbs. lemon juice
½ pt. Cheese Sauce, No. 75 (1 c.)

4 oz. cooked ham (125 g.)
4 Tbs. buttered crumbs, No. 876

Measures level. Boil the chicory until tender in a little salted water with the lemon juice. Drain and put in a baking-dish in layers with the sauce and ham, finishing with a layer of sauce. Cover the top with the crumbs and bake in a moderate oven for 20 minutes.

472. Chives

Chives are used to replace onion where a milder flavour is desired. They are chopped finely and used in salads, omelets, scrambled eggs, mashed potatoes, cottage cheese, and sandwich fillings.

473. Chervil

Chervil is a very delicate herb which wilts quickly and is seldom on sale in a greengrocer's. It is used chopped with cucumber salad and in soups and sauces.

474. Corn Salad

Use in green salads in the same way as lettuce.

475. Cucumbers

These are usually served raw in salads, see No. 561, but when cheap and plentiful may be cooked and served in the same way as Vegetable Marrow, Nos. 544–7.

476. Eggplant or Aubergine

FRIED. Peel and cut in ¼-inch (6 mm.) slices. Coat the slices in egg and breadcrumbs and fry in hot fat. Serve with Tomato Sauce, No. 89.

BAKED STUFFED. Boil 5 minutes in salted water. Cut in half and scoop out the centre. Discard the seeds if they are

big. Mix the pulp with an equal amount of chopped tomato cooked in fat with a little onion. Season well and put back in the shells. Cover the tops with browned breadcrumbs and bake in a hot oven until browned on top.

GRILLED. Peel and cut in slices. Mix 1 Tbs. oil with ¼ level tsp. salt and pinch pepper. Dip the slices in this and grill 3 minutes each side. Serve with fried eggs or Tomato Sauce, No. 89.

STEWED. Peel, slice, and stew in Tomato Sauce, No. 89.

477. Endive

This is generally used raw in salads in the same way as lettuce. Wash thoroughly, removing any damaged leaves, and then drain well.

478. Fennel

Use the chopped leaves in sauce to serve with fish or boiled mutton. It may also be used to flavour stews and soups.

Florence fennel has a swollen leaf-base which is used raw or cooked in salad, sliced finely. It is also used as a vegetable, boiled in water or stock and served with a White Sauce (Nos. 69, 90) or Tomato Sauce (No. 89).

479. Garlic

As it is very strong, only minute amounts should be used. Each bulb of garlic consists of a number of cloves, and half a small one of these is plenty to flavour a soup or stew for 4 people. It is specially good in dishes made with lamb or mutton, and a cut clove of garlic rubbed round the salad bowl gives a slight flavour which is very pleasant. Also available dried, or as garlic salt.

480. Gherkins

Immature cucumbers of a special variety used for pickling. Small ridge cucumbers are also pickled. Gherkins are used for garnishing purposes and in sauces such as Tartare, No. 117, and Vinaigrette, No. 119.

481. Horse-radish

Grated horse-radish is used to make Sauce, No. 80, to serve with roast beef, or with fatty fish such as herrings. A little is nice on grilled steak or in sandwich fillings. For the best flavour it should be grated, just before use, and grate the sides, not across the cut end, which is very difficult.

482. Kale

Allow ¼ lb. per person (250 g.).

Prepare by washing well and stripping the green from the coarse stalks, unless the kale is very young, when the stalks will be tender enough to eat.

To cook, shred large leaves, and cook in the same way as cabbage, see No. 454.

483. Kohl Rabi

Allow 6–8 oz. per person (175–250 g.).

Prepare by removing the green leaves and stalks and peeling fairly thickly, to remove the outer skin.

Cook and serve in the same way as turnips, see No. 542.

484. Leeks

Allow ½–¾ lb. per person (250–375 g.).

Prepare by removing the roots and coarse outer leaves. Cut the tops off about 2 inches above the white part and use them for Vegetable Stock, No. 33. Cut the leeks in half lengthwise, and wash thoroughly, opening up the outer leaves to remove all dirt. Drain well.

To cook, boil in a little salted water, as in No. 427.

To serve, drain well and serve with Sauce, No. 71, made with some of the cooking liquid, or with Cheese Sauce, No. 75, or Tomato Sauce, No. 89, or Caper Sauce, No. 74. Cold, boiled leeks with French Dressing, No. 118, or Vinaigrette Sauce, No. 119, make an excellent salad or hors-d'œuvre.

485. Lettuce

Allow 1 medium-sized lettuce for 3 people.

Prepare by removing any damaged leaves and then washing the rest in cold water. Drain well and hang up in a towel in a cold place to get crisp, or put in a covered dish in the refrigerator.

To serve, see Salad recipes, Nos. 554–579.

486. Maize or Sweet Corn

Allow 1 ear per person.

Prepare by boiling in a little salted water until tender. This will take anything from 10 to 20 minutes, depending on the age of the corn. It may also be stripped from the cob before cooking, but only if the corn is fairly well developed. It is nicest when fairly young and freshly picked. If it takes more than 20 minutes to cook it is too old to be nice. It may also be baked in the oven with a little fat.

To serve, add a little butter or margarine, toss well, and season with salt and pepper. Or it may be served with a well-seasoned Sauce, No. 69, made with milk, or used to make fritters, see No. 865, using 6–8 oz. corn (250 g.).

487. Corn and Tomatoes. Cooking time, about ½ hour

Quantities for 4 helpings:

1 oz. butter or margarine (25 g.)	1 small sprig thyme
2 c. cooked or canned corn	¼ bay leaf
2 c. chopped tomatoes	1 tsp. sugar
1 sprig parsley	Salt and pepper to taste

Measures level. Melt the butter or margarine in a saucepan and add the tomatoes and chopped herbs. Cook for 10 minutes. Add the corn and cook for 20 minutes. Season well and serve hot.

488. Marjoram

The fresh or dried herb is used for flavouring sauces, stews, soups, meat rissoles, and other savoury dishes.

489. Mint

Use to make Mint Sauce, No. 120, and to cook with new potatoes and green peas. It should be used with discretion, or the flavour will drown the natural flavour of the vegetables. It is excellent with salads, and for stuffing lamb or mutton, see No. 131, and to serve sprinkled over cooked carrots or peas. Mixed with jam or dried fruit and sugar it makes an unusual filling for sweet patties.

490. Mushrooms

Allow 2–4 oz. per person (50–125 g.).

Prepare by removing the stalks, and peeling off the outer skin, using a small sharp knife. Discard any which have worm-holes or are old and blackened. The stalks and peelings should be used to make Mushroom Stock, No. 35.

Cook by grilling with a small knob of fat in the centre, or frying; or use to make Mushroom Sauce, No. 82, or for flavouring soups and stews.

491. Mousseline of Mushrooms. Cooking time 10–15 minutes

Quantities for 4 helpings:

½ medium-sized onion, chopped
2 oz. butter (50 g.)
1 lb. mushrooms (500 g.)

½ pt. thick cream (1 c.)
½ tsp. salt
Pinch of cayenne

Measures level. Heat the butter and cook the onion in it without browning. Peel the mushrooms and chop them coarsely. Add to the onions, and cook until almost tender. Add the cream, and cook very gently until thickened. Add the seasoning and serve.

492. Mustard and Cress

This is generally used in salads, or served plain with bread-and-butter. It should be thoroughly washed and any split seeds removed. Drain well.

493. Nasturtiums

Young nasturtium leaves are very good in salads or for a sandwich filling. Wash the leaves well before using. The seeds may be pickled and used in place of capers.

494. Okra or Gumbo or Ladies' Fingers

The immature green pods of the plant are the parts eaten, available fresh or canned. Fresh okra are boiled whole in a little salted water, drained and dressed with melted butter or cream. They can also be stewed in a little butter with water to moisten.

495. Onions

Allow 4–6 oz. per person (125–175 g.).

Prepare by peeling off the brown skin. If this is done under water it helps to prevent the eyes from watering.

Cook by boiling in salted water to cover, until tender. This will take anything from $\frac{3}{4}$ to $1\frac{1}{2}$ hours, depending on the size. Drain well and use the water for stock. They may also be roasted in fat, see No. 435, or baked in their jackets by standing them on a baking-shelf in a moderate oven 400° F. (200° C.) Mark 6, and cooking until they are soft when squeezed. This will take 40–60 minutes. They may also be cooked in a pressure cooker for 5–10 minutes, or longer if very big.

To serve boiled onions make Sauce, No. 71, using some of the cooking liquid, or serve au gratin, No. 432.

496. Sugared Onions (to serve with roast beef, lamb, or pork)

Cooking time ¾ hour.

Quantities for 3–4 helpings:

1 lb. small onions or shallots (500 g.)	2 Tbs. sugar
2 oz. butter or margarine (50 g.)	

Measures level. Peel the onions and boil until nearly done. Drain well. Melt the fat in a saucepan and cook the onions in it until they are brown. Then sprinkle on the sugar and cover the pan. Cook gently for a few minutes longer until the onions are quite tender. Serve hot.

497. Onion Toast. Cooking time 20 minutes

Quantities for 4 helpings:

1 oz. fat (25 g.)	Salt and pepper
4 medium-sized onions, sliced	4 slices cheese
4 slices hot buttered toast	French mustard

Fry the onions in the hot fat until tender. Spread on the toast, and sprinkle with salt and pepper. Spread the slices of cheese with mustard, and place on top of the onions. Grill, or bake in a hot oven until the cheese melts. Serve at once.

498. Parsley

Ordinary parsley may be used for decorating and flavouring all savoury dishes.

Hamburg parsley leaves are used in the same way, but the roots are cooked like parsnips.

499. Parsnips

Allow 6–8 oz. per person (175–250 g.).

Prepare by scrubbing and peeling.

Cook by boiling in a little water, as in No. 427, or in a pressure cooker, stewing in fat, as in No. 433, roasting in fat, No. 435, or cooking in a casserole, No. 434.

To serve boiled parsnips, mash well with a little butter or margarine and season with salt and pepper. Carrots and parsnips cooked and mashed together are a very good mixture. Parsnips, cooked by any method, go well with fish.

500. Parsnip Balls (to serve with fish)

Boil the parsnips in a little water, as in No. 427. Mash well and season with salt and pepper to taste. Dry over a gentle heat. Shape in balls and roll in breadcrumbs. Bake in a hot oven for 20 minutes, either with the fish or in a dish by themselves.

501. Peas

Allow ½ lb. per person (250 g.), but the amount varies according to the fullness of the pods.

Prepare by shelling. If the pods are fresh and young, use them to make Vegetable Stock, No. 33.

Cook in a little water, as in No. 427. It is traditional to cook a little mint with peas, but this is a pity when they are young, as the mint disguises the natural sweet flavour. In France they are cooked with lettuce leaves and a few small onions, which is an excellent method.

To serve, add a little butter or margarine and toss well.

502. French Method of Cooking Peas. Cooking time about ½ hour. Suitable for fresh or frozen

Quantities for 4 helpings:

2 lb. peas (1 kg. or 2½ c. shelled)
1 oz. butter or dripping (2 Tbs.)
4 or 5 outside leaves of lettuce

4 or 5 small onions
½ tsp. salt
Pinch of pepper
2 rashers bacon, chopped
2 or 3 Tbs. water

Put all the ingredients in a saucepan and cook gently until the peas are tender. Add more water if necessary to prevent burning.

503. Carrots and Peas. Cooking time ¾ hour

Quantities for 4 helpings:

½ lb. young carrots, diced (250 g.)
¼ pt. water (½ c.)
1 tsp. salt

1 Tbs. sugar
1 oz. butter or margarine (25 g.)
1½ lb. peas (750 g.)

Measures level. Place the carrots in a saucepan with all the other ingredients except the peas. Cook gently for 5 minutes, and then add the peas and continue cooking until the peas and carrots are tender. There should be hardly any water left in the pan.

504. Spanish Peas. Cooking time ½ hour

Quantities for 4 helpings:

2 lb. peas (1 kg. or 2½ c. shelled)
1 oz. lard or dripping (25 g.)
A speck of garlic

2 Tbs. tomato purée
2 Tbs. water
1 tsp. salt
Pinch of pepper
2 oz. bacon (50 g.)

2 Tbs. chopped parsley   8 oz. chipolata sausages
1 Tbs. flour   (250 g.)

Measures level. Put all the ingredients, except the bacon and sausages, in a pan. Put on the lid and cook gently until the peas are tender. Ten minutes before serving add the bacon, which has been grilled or fried and cut in small pieces, and the sausages, which have been grilled or fried and cut in slices. Mix well and serve hot.

505. Sugar Peas or Edible-podded Peas or Mangetout

These are eaten whole while the pods are still very young and flat. Wash, cut off the stem end and cook and serve in the same way as French beans.

506. Peppers or Capsicums

These may be the very small hot ones known as Chillies, from which cayenne pepper is made, and which are used dried in

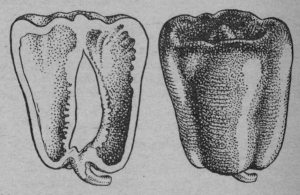

pickles; or the large sweet ones, which may be green or red in colour, and are used as a vegetable.

These are prepared by cutting in half and scraping out the seeds and membranes. They are generally served stuffed, or sliced and used in stews and vegetable soups, or raw in salads.

507. Stuffed Sweet Peppers. Cooking time $\frac{3}{4}$–1 hour

Quantities for 4 helpings:

4 peppers
1 small onion, chopped
1 oz. fat (25 g.)
1½ oz. rice (1½ Tbs.),
  boiled, or ⅓ c. bread-
  crumbs
4 oz. minced meat or
  ham (125 g.)

1 egg
Salt and pepper
1 Tbs. chopped parsley
½ pt. Tomato Sauce, No.
  89 (1 c.)

Measures level. Prepare the peppers, as in No. 506. Fry the onion in the fat and add the meat, rice or breadcrumbs, egg, and seasonings. Fill the peppers and place them in a baking-dish or saucepan. Pour round the sauce and cook gently until they are tender, about $\frac{3}{4}$ hour. Serve hot with mashed potatoes and lettuce salad.

508. Potatoes

Allow ¼ lb. per person (250 g.).

Prepare by scrubbing well. New potatoes should be scraped, if the skins do not come off with scrubbing. Old potatoes are peeled thinly. Both new and old potatoes are very good cooked in their skins, and have much more flavour than when peeled.

Cook according to any of the methods given below.

509. Boiled Potatoes

Peel, or leave the skins on, and put in enough boiling salted water to cover. Cook with the lid on and keep boiling gently, as rapid boiling makes the potatoes break and become mushy. When tender, drain carefully and shake over a low heat for a minute or two to make them floury and dry. New potatoes may be cooked with a sprig of mint for extra flavour.

510. Browned Potatoes

Boil small or medium-sized potatoes in their jackets, until almost cooked, as in No. 509. Peel while hot. Melt enough fat to cover the bottom of the pan and cook the potatoes in it until brown all over. Turn frequently.

511. Mashed Potatoes

Boil according to No. 509. If unpeeled, remove the skins by holding the potatoes on a fork and peeling with a sharp knife. Mash well or rub through a sieve. Return to the pan and beat with 1 Tbs. milk and 1 oz. (25 g.) margarine for each pound ($\frac{1}{2}$ kg.). Season with salt and pepper and add a little chopped parsley or chives for extra flavour. Beat well to make them white and smooth, keeping the pan over a gentle heat to make sure the potatoes are still hot.

512. Baked Potatoes

Choose medium or large potatoes without blemishes. Scrub them well dry, and rub the skins with greased paper. Place on a baking-shelf in a moderate–hot oven 400–450° F. (200–230° C.) Mark 6–8, and cook for 45 minutes or until tender. They are done if they feel soft when squeezed in a cloth. Prick well to allow steam to escape and make them floury. The most attractive way of serving them is to prick the top in the shape of a cross. Then squeeze the sides of the potatoes gently, and the cross will open into four points. Put in a knob of butter or margarine, a little salt and pepper or paprika pepper, and a sprig of parsley.

513. Baked Stuffed Potatoes

For each potato allow:

1–2 Tbs. milk
½ tsp. butter or margarine
Pinch of pepper
¼ tsp. salt

1 Tbs. chopped parsley or minced ham or corned beef or grated cheese, or ½ Tbs. chopped fried onion

Measures level. Bake the potatoes as in No. 512. Cut in half lengthwise and scoop out the inside carefully. Mash with the milk, fat, seasonings, and chosen flavouring. Put back into the shells. Brown in a hot oven 450° F. (230° C.) Mark 8, for a few minutes.

514. Roast Potatoes

Cook in a little hot fat in the oven according to No. 435, rolling the potatoes in seasoned flour before putting them in the fat.

515. Chip Potatoes

1. Choose large potatoes. Scrub and peel them and cut into ⅜-inch (1 cm.) slices lengthwise and then again lengthwise; or use a potato chipper.
2. Put into cold water to cover until ready for frying.
3. Drain well and dry thoroughly on a clean towel.
4. Fry in hot, deep fat, see No. 149, or in a shallow fat, No. 148. Drain well on absorbent paper and sprinkle with salt. Serve as soon as possible, as they become flabby with keeping.

516. Potato Crisps or Game Chips

Cut the potatoes in thin shavings on a vegetable slicer or with a sharp knife. Fry in deep fat, as in No. 149.

517. Straw Potatoes

Cut the potatoes in very thin strips about $\frac{1}{4}$ inch (6 mm.) wide and about 3 inches (8 cm.) long. Fry in the same way as Chip Potatoes, No. 515.

518. Duchess Potatoes

Boil the potatoes, sieve while hot, return to the pan and dry over a gentle heat or in the oven. For each pound (500 g.) of potato add 1 oz. (25 g.) butter or margarine, 1 egg or 2 yolks, grated nutmeg, salt, pepper, and hot cream or milk to make the mixture soft enough for piping. Beat thoroughly. Pipe in rosettes on a greased baking tray and bake in a hot oven until brown. The mixture may also be used for ornamenting savoury dishes.

519. Parisian Potatoes. Cooking time 10–15 minutes

Shape raw potatoes in balls with a vegetable scoop or cut in cubes and fry in shallow fat until well browned and cooked. Drain and sprinkle with chopped parsley, salt and pepper.

520. New Potatoes Fried with Mint

Boil the potatoes according to No. 509, and let them cool a little. Then fry brown in shallow fat. Drain and sprinkle with mixed chopped parsley and mint.

521. Potatoes with Cheese

Slice cold boiled potatoes and fry them brown in shallow fat. Sprinkle liberally with grated cheese, and allow the cheese to begin to melt before serving.

522. Potato Ragoût. Cooking time ¾ hour

Quantities for 4 helpings:

2 lb. small potatoes (1 kg.)	Salt and pepper
3 large onions	1 sprig thyme
1 oz. fat (25 g.)	1 bay leaf
2 Tbs. flour	2 sprigs parsley
1 pt. water or stock (2 c.)	

Measures level. Peel the potatoes and onions and cut them in quarters. Heat the fat in a saucepan and stir in the flour. Stir and cook until it begins to turn yellow. Add the stock and stir until it boils. Add the rest of the ingredients, cover and boil gently for ¾ hour or until the potatoes are tender. Serve hot. This may be served as a separate dish for lunch or high tea.

523. Paprika Potatoes with Smoked Sausages. Cooking time 40–50 minutes

Quantities for 4 helpings:

1 oz. fat (25 g.)	2 tsp. salt
4 oz. chopped onion (1 medium)	½ pt. stock or water (1 c.)
2 Tbs. flour	1½ lb. new potatoes (750 g.)
1 tsp. paprika pepper	1½ lb. smoked sausages (750 g.)
1 Tbs. wine vinegar	

Measures level. Melt the fat and fry the onion in it. Add the flour and paprika and mix well. Add the vinegar, salt, and stock, and stir until it boils. Scrape the potatoes and cut in pieces, about half the size of an egg. Add to the sauce. Cover the pan and boil gently, stirring occasionally, until tender. Cook the sausages separately or heat them with the potatoes during the last 10 minutes of cooking.

524. Pumpkin or Squash

Treat the same way as marrow, see No. 544, except that to have the best flavour, pumpkin should be really ripe.

525. Radishes

Wash well and serve very cold. They are generally eaten as hors-d'œuvre at the beginning of a meal or with cheese at the end; but may be used in salads and for decorations. To cut radish roses, use a sharp-pointed knife and cut slashes from the root end to within $\frac{1}{4}$ inch (6 mm.) of the stalk and $\frac{1}{8}$ inch (3 mm.) deep, cutting to make petal shapes. Ease the red skin away from the rest and put in iced water until required.

BLACK RADISH is grated or sliced very thinly and used in salads or eaten with cheese. Large ones may be cooked and served in the same way as turnips.

526. Sage

This is a strongly flavoured herb, and should be used in small amounts. It is used for a stuffing for pork or duck, in lentil soup, and with dried beans.

527. Salsify

Allow 1 lb. for 3 people (500 g.).

Wash and scrape the roots and treat in the same way as Jerusalem Artichokes, see No. 440.

528. Savory

This herb is used in stuffings for veal or poultry, in sausages and meat rissoles, and with lentil soup or broad beans.

529. Seakale

Allow 1 lb. for 3 people (500 g.).

Prepare by cutting off any discoloured leaves and peeling the stump.

To cook, tie in bundles, put in boiling salted water, and cook for 20–30 minutes.

To serve, use the liquid to make Sauce, No. 71, or serve with Hollandaise Sauce, No. 94.

530. Seakale Beet, Silver Beet, or Swiss Chard

Cook and serve in the same way as Cabbage, No. 454. The leaves and chopped stalks may be cooked together, or separately to make two different dishes, but the former method gives the best flavour.

531. Shallots

Treat in the same way as Onions, see No. 495.

532. Spinach

Allow ½ lb. per person (250 g.).

Prepare by removing any decayed leaves and weeds and washing in several changes of water until the last water is clean. Lift the spinach out each time to allow the sand to collect in the water. Let the water away, run in fresh, and then add the spinach again.

Cook without adding water, as there is sufficient left on the leaves after washing.

When tender, drain well, pressing out all moisture. Return to the pan and heat gently to dry it further. Add a little butter or margarine, pepper, and a pinch of ground mace or nutmeg.

533. Creamed Spinach. Cooking time 20 minutes

Quantities for 4 helpings:

2 lb. spinach (1 kg.)
2 oz. butter or margarine
    (50 g.)
Salt and pepper to taste

Pinch of grated nutmeg or
    mace
Squeeze of lemon juice

Boil the spinach as directed for No. 532. Drain well. Rub
through a sieve. Melt the fat and add the spinach and other
ingredients. Heat gently until thick.

534. Spinach with Poached Eggs

Boil the spinach, as in No. 532. Drain well. Make a bed of
it on each plate and put a poached egg on top. If liked, pour
over a little Cheese Sauce, No. 75, and brown under the
grill.

535. Spinach au Gratin. Cooking time 15–20 minutes

Quantities for 2–3 helpings:

1 lb. spinach (500 g.)
2 oz. butter or margarine
    (50 g.)

4 oz. grated cheese (125 g.)
Pinch of pepper

Measures level. Cook the spinach as described in No. 532.
Drain and chop. Return to the pan with half the butter and
cook quickly until well dried. Add three-quarters of the
cheese and mix well. Place in a greased, fireproof dish and
sprinkle with the rest of the cheese and the butter, melted.
Put in a hot oven or under the grill for the cheese to melt
and brown.

536. Spring Onions

Cut off the roots and trim off any damaged leaves. Wash
well and use in salads, with cheese, to flavour mashed

potatoes, or in place of onions in stews and savoury dishes. Welsh onions are used in the same way.

537. Swedes

Allow 6–8 oz. per person (175–250 g.).

Prepare by scrubbing and peeling thickly to remove the outer skin. Cut in chunks, slices, or dice.

Cook by boiling in a little water, as in No. 427, or in a casserole, No. 434, or stew in fat, No. 436.

To serve, mash well with a little pepper and butter or margarine.

538. Tarragon

Use the finely chopped leaves in salads (especially tomato), sauces, stews, and pickles.

539. Thyme

Use in small amounts in stuffings and savoury dishes. It forms a part of the traditional bouquet garni used extensively in cooking, see No. 12.

540. Tomatoes

Allow 4–6 oz. per person (125–175 g.).

Prepare by removing the green flowers and washing well. If they are to be skinned, plunge them in boiling water for a minute or two and then into cold water, when the skins should peel off quite easily.

Cook by stewing without any liquid. Season with salt, pepper, and sugar; or prick well to prevent bursting and bake in a moderate oven for 20 minutes; or cut in half and grill for 10–15 minutes; or dip the cut sides in seasoned flour and fry in shallow fat until tender.

541. Stuffed Tomatoes. Cooking time 20 minutes

Temperature 400° F. (200° C.) Mark 6.

Quantities for 6 helpings:

6 large tomatoes (about
   1 lb. or 500 g.)
½ oz. fat (1 Tbs.)
½ onion, chopped
1 oz. chopped bacon
   (25 g.)
1 Tbs. grated cheese

1 tsp. chopped parsley
¼ tsp. salt
Pinch of pepper
Pinch of sugar
Pinch of grated nutmeg
½ c. fresh breadcrumbs

Measures level. Cut a slice off the stem end of the tomatoes. Remove the pulp carefully, using a small teaspoon, and rub it through a sieve. Fry the bacon and onion in the fat and mix with the pulp and other ingredients. Stuff the tomatoes with this and sprinkle the tops with crumbs. Bake in a moderate oven for 20 minutes. Serve hot.

542. Turnips

Allow 6–8 oz. per person (175–250 g.).

Prepare by scrubbing well and peeling thickly to remove the outer skin. Small turnips should be left whole, others cut in chunks or slices, or diced.

Cook according to Nos. 427–435.

Serve as cooked, or mashed with a little pepper and fat.

543. Ragoût of Turnips. Cooking time 45 minutes

Quantities for 2–3 helpings:

10 small young turnips
½ oz. dripping (1 Tbs.)
1 Tbs. flour
½ pt. stock (1 c.)

½ tsp. salt
Pinch of pepper
2 tsp. sugar

Measures level. Peel the turnips. Melt the fat and add the flour, cooking until it turns yellow, stirring well all the time. Add the stock and stir until it boils. Add the turnips and seasonings and cook gently until tender, about 45 minutes.

544. Vegetable Marrow

Allow 1 medium-sized marrow 2–3 lb. (1–1½ kg.) for 4 people, or use 1 lb. Courgettes (½ kg.).

Marrows about 9 inches (24 cm.) long are delicious cooked whole with the skin on, and the whole marrow may be eaten. Smaller marrows, called 'Courgettes', are grown in France specially for this purpose. The bigger a marrow is allowed to grow the less flavour it has.

Prepare large or medium marrows by cutting in pieces and removing the seeds. The skin may be left on.

Cook by boiling in a little water, as in No. 427, cooking in a casserole, No. 434, roasting in fat, No. 435, stewing in fat, No. 436.

To serve, season with pepper and put a small knob of fat on top, or mash well. They may also be served with a vegetable sauce, No. 71, or au gratin, No. 432.

545. Stewed Marrow and Tomatoes. Cooking time 35 minutes

Quantities for 4 helpings:

2 lb. marrow (1 kg.) or 1 lb. courgettes (½ kg.)	Salt and pepper
	Pinch of mixed herbs
8 oz. tomatoes, sliced (250 g.)	½ tsp. sugar
	¼ pt. stock (½ c.)
1 medium onion, sliced	2 Tbs. chopped parsley
1 oz. fat (25 g.)	

Measures level. Prepare the marrow or courgettes and cut in small pieces. Fry the tomatoes and onion in the dripping for

5 minutes, using a saucepan. Add the other ingredients, except the parsley. Cover and cook gently for 30 minutes or until the marrow is tender. Turn into a hot dish and sprinkle with parsley.

546. Stuffed Marrow

For 1 medium marrow allow 1 lb. (500 g.) sausage meat or Minced Meat, No. 408. Peel the marrow and cut a slice off the top. Scoop out the seeds and fill with the stuffing. Tie on the end again. Put in a baking-dish with a little fat and cook in a moderate oven 375° F. (190° C.) Mark 5, until tender – about ¾ hour. Baste often with the fat or cover the dish with a lid. Serve with Brown Sauce, No. 73, or Tomato Sauce, No. 89.

547. Marrow Lyonnaise

Mix cooked marrow or courgettes, cut in small pieces, with half its bulk of onions, fried in a little fat.

548. Watercress

This is generally used for salads, either by itself or mixed with other vegetables, or as a garnish for grilled or fried meats. It may also be chopped and mixed with mashed potato, or used for Soup, No. 44, Stuffing, No. 131, or Butter, No. 124.

549. Yams

Allow 6–8 oz. per person (175–250 g.).

Prepare by washing and peeling.
Cook by rolling in flour and baking in fat. Season well.

DRIED VEGETABLES

550. Boiling Dried Vegetables (peas, beans, lentils, and split peas)

Allow 4 oz. (dry) (125 g.) per person. 1 lb. (500 g.) dried peas or beans gives 2 lb. cooked (1 kg.).

1. The treatment to be given dried vegetables depends on their quality (age and condition before drying), and the hardness of the water to be used for cooking. Good-quality dried vegetables do not need soaking, nor do lentils and split peas, but poor-quality peas and beans should be soaked in warm water for about 1½ hours before cooking. If the water is hard it prevents the vegetables from softening quickly, and it is advisable to add a little bicarbonate of soda to soften it. 1 level tsp. of soda to each pound (500 g.) of dried vegetables is plenty. If too much is used, the flavour and colour are spoiled, and the beans will fall to pieces on the outside before the inside is cooked. Dried vegetables need 2–4 times their bulk of water for cooking, depending on the length of time taken.

2. Bring the vegetables and water to the boil and cover the pan. Cook very slowly until tender. Peas and beans take from 2 to 3 hours and lentils and split peas ½–¾ hour.

3. For extra flavour cook a sprig of mint or a pinch of dried mint with peas. With beans, lentils, or split peas, cook an onion stuck with a few cloves, a carrot, and some bacon rinds.

4. Use the cooking liquid for soups, sauces, and gravy.

N.B. Much time is saved by cooking dried vegetables in a pressure cooker. Add four times their bulk of water, and be careful not to fill the pan more than half full, to allow for swelling. Cook for 25–30 minutes.

551. Beans à la Bretonne

Cook the beans as directed in No. 550, or use canned beans. Drain well. For each pound of dried beans fry 2 medium sliced onions in dripping, and when brown add the beans and mix well. Sprinkle with chopped parsley and serve hot.

552. Italian Beans. Cooking time 2 hours or longer

Quantities for 4 helpings:

8 oz. beans (250 g.)
4 Tbs. oil or dripping
2 fresh sage leaves

2 Tbs. tomato purée
Salt and pepper

Measures level. Boil the beans according to No. 550, or use canned beans. Drain well. Heat the oil or dripping and the chopped sage leaves. When hot add the beans and cook until the fat is absorbed. Add the tomato and season well.

553. Pease Pudding

To each pound (500 g.) of dried peas or split peas allow 1 oz. (25 g.) margarine and 1 egg. Cook the vegetables as in No. 550, and rub through a sieve. Beat with the margarine and egg and season well. Put in a greased basin and steam for 1 hour. Turn out and serve with meat or with a Tomato Sauce, No. 89, or Brown Sauce, No. 73.

SALADS

554. General Information

Salads can be used to give variety all the year round and not just in the summer months. They are excellent in hors-d'œuvre, or as a first course and as an accompaniment to hot meat or fish and other savoury dishes, as well as with cold dishes. A salad containing meat, fish, cheese or eggs can make a substantial main course for lunch or high tea and is acceptable even in the winter, especially if it is preceded by a good bowl of hot soup.

Winter vegetables such as cabbage, Brussels sprouts,

carrots, celery, leeks, beetroot and celeriac, all make good salads. The ideal is to make salads of raw vegetables to give crispness, but if you do not like raw winter vegetables the next best is to use them cooked or canned. A raw salad is not necessarily of higher nutritive value than a portion of cooked vegetable, and it should be regarded as something to eat for pleasure and variety.

555. Salad Ingredients

COOKED VEGETABLES. Potatoes, cabbage, sprouts, beetroot, turnip, parsnip, kohl rabi, swede, onions, leeks, peas, beans, cauliflower, broccoli, artichokes.

RAW VEGETABLES. Lettuce, watercress, cabbage heart, sprouts, spinach, endive, chicory, radishes, cucumber, onions, celery, cauliflower, sweet peppers.

FRUIT. Any fruit, fresh or dried, is suitable.

MEAT AND FISH. Use any kind, cooked or canned.

EGGS. Hard-boiled or scrambled are suitable.

CHEESE. Use any kind grated or cut in slices or cubes.

FLAVOURINGS. Use green herbs, chives, parsley, mint, spring onions, nasturtium leaves, young celery leaves, mustard and cress, garlic, gherkins, pickles.

DRESSINGS. See Nos. 113–119.

556. Making Salads

1. All raw green salad vegetables should be as fresh and crisp as possible. Wash well under running water, and hang them up in a clean, damp cloth in a draughty place to drain. If you have a refrigerator, put them in a covered dish in the least cold part. They should be dried first, and the best way of doing this is to use a wire salad-basket and shake or twirl the greens in it gently until all moisture is thrown off.

2. Cooked vegetables should be quite cold and well drained from all moisture. Cut cooked vegetables in slices or dice.

3. Raw vegetables, with the exception of lettuce and watercress, should be finely shredded with a sharp knife, or grated.

4. Fish and meat are improved in flavour if mixed with the salad dressing and allowed to stand some time before using. Potatoes are better if mixed with the dressing while they are still warm. Lettuce or similar raw green salads are better not dressed until just before serving, or they will become limp and slimy.

5. Serve salads in a large bowl, or arranged on a big flat dish, or serve individual portions in nests of curly lettuce leaves.

557. Bean and Apple Salad

Quantities for 4 helpings:

3 c. cooked or canned $\frac{1}{2}$ tsp. salt
   French or runner beans   Salad dressing
$\frac{1}{2}$ c. diced raw apple
$\frac{1}{2}$ c. sliced raw or cooked
   cabbage

Measures level. Mix the vegetables with the salt and moisten with salad dressing.

558. Beetroot and Mint Salad

Make individual nests of lettuce leaves or line a salad bowl with them. In the centre arrange thin slices of beetroot. Sprinkle with finely chopped mint and serve with French Dressing, No. 118.

559. Brussels Sprouts Salad

Quantities for 4–5 helpings:

1½ lb. cooked sprouts   1 small cooked beetroot
  (750 g.)
French Dressing, No. 118

Toss the cold sprouts in the dressing in a salad bowl. Decorate with the beetroot, cut in slices or diced.

560. Cauliflower Mayonnaise

Quantities for 4 helpings:

1 medium-sized cauliflower   6–8 strips of anchovy fillets
Mayonnaise, No. 113

Boil the cauliflower sprigs in a little water, as in No. 427, cooking some of the small green leaves with it. Arrange these round the bowl with the flowers in the centre. Dress with mayonnaise and decorate with the strips of anchovy.

561. Cucumber Salad

Quantities for 4–6 helpings:

1½ lb. cucumbers (1 large   1 Tbs. water
  or 2 medium size)   Pinch of pepper
1 Tbs. salt   2 Tbs. sugar
4 Tbs. vinegar   2 Tbs. chopped parsley

Measures level. The fat field, or ridge, cucumbers make the best salads. Peel the cucumbers and slice them very thinly, the thinner the better. Arrange them in layers in a deep dish and sprinkle over the salt. Leave for 2 hours for the moisture to come out. Pour away the liquid. Rinse and drain the cucumber. Mix the vinegar, water, pepper, and sugar together and pour over the cucumbers. Sprinkle with chopped parsley.

562. Herring Salad

Quantities for 2–4 helpings:

1 salt or 1 fresh herring
1½ c. diced cooked potatoes
⅓ c. chopped gherkins
½ c. chopped apples
1½ c. chopped cooked
  beetroot
1 Tbs. chopped onion

4 Tbs. vinegar
2 Tbs. water
1 Tbs. sugar
Pepper to taste
Hard-boiled egg
Chopped parsley

Measures level. If salt herring is used, clean, remove the head, and soak in cold water overnight. Drain, skin, fillet, and dice. Skin, fillet, and flake cooked herring. Mix all the ingredients together and pack into a basin or mould. Unmould on the serving dish and decorate with the egg and parsley.

563. Lettuce Salad

The lettuce should be very dry, fresh, and crisp, see No. 554. For best flavour it should not be cut or broken, but the leaves left whole. French dressing is the best to use, but should not be added until just before serving, and use just enough to moisten. Turn the leaves over and over in the dressing, using a spoon and fork, until the lettuce is well coated. For extra flavour the salad bowl may be rubbed with a cut clove of garlic or chopped mint, or other herbs may be sprinkled on the leaves.

564. Orange Salad

Quantities for 4 helpings:

3 or 4 oranges
1 lettuce
1 c. chopped apple

1 c. chopped celery
1 Tbs. chopped nuts
Salad dressing

Measures level. Peel the oranges and remove the pith. Slice them or divide them into sections. Arrange in individual portions on the lettuce leaves. Cover with the apples and celery and sprinkle with chopped nuts. Serve with Mayonnaise, No. 113, or French Dressing, No. 118.

565. Potato Salad

Quantities for 4 helpings:

1½ lb. potatoes (750 g.)
1 Tbs. finely chopped onion
¼ pt. Mayonnaise, No. 113,
   or Vinaigrette Sauce,
   No. 119 (½ c.)

1 Tbs. chopped mint,
   parsley, or other green
   herbs

Measures level. Boil the potatoes in their jackets, see No. 509. Peel and slice or dice while still warm. The waxy type of potato is best for salads, as the floury ones do not cut in clean slices. Canned new potatoes may be substituted. Warm them before adding dressing. Add the chopped onion and mix well with the salad dressing. Sprinkle with the chopped herbs. Leave until cold. Instead of using onion, the bowl may be rubbed with a cut clove of garlic before putting in the potatoes.

N.B. If the potatoes are floury it is better to dress the salad when cold.

566. Russian Salad

Quantities for 3 helpings:

1 c. cooked or canned
   diced potatoes
1 c. cooked diced beetroot
1 c. cooked haricot beans
   or canned peas

2–3 Tbs. French Dressing,
   No. 118
Chopped parsley

Measures level. Mix all the ingredients together and sprinkle with chopped parsley.

567. Spring Salad

Quantities for 2 helpings:

4 oz. watercress (125 g.)   2 Tbs. French Dressing,
½ cucumber   No. 118
6 spring onions

Wash and dry the watercress and cut the cucumber in thin slices. Chop the onions. Mix all with the dressing just before serving.

568. Stuffed Egg Salad

Use Recipe No. 188, allowing one egg per person. Place in a nest of lettuce leaves and decorate with slices of tomato and cucumber and some thick salad dressing.

569. Waldorf Salad

Quantities for 1 helping:

3–4 lettuce leaves   1 Tbs. chopped walnuts
1 red apple, diced   1–2 Tbs. salad dressing
1 stick celery, chopped

Arrange the lettuce in a nest. Mix the other ingredients together and pile in the leaves. Decorate with a little red apple.

570. Salmon Mayonnaise

Quantities for 3–4 helpings:

8 oz. fresh or canned   1 lettuce
    salmon (250 g.)   Chopped parsley
1 small beetroot or 3 or 4   3–4 Tbs. mayonnaise
    tomatoes   1 hard-boiled egg

Make a nest of the lettuce leaves. Place the salmon in the centre and mask with the mayonnaise. Decorate with the other vegetables.

571. Swiss Salad

Quantities for 4 helpings:

1 c. diced cooked chicken or rabbit	1 c. chopped walnuts
1 c. peeled and diced cucumber	1 c. cooked green peas
	1 lettuce
	Salad dressing

Arrange nests of lettuce leaves on 4 plates. Mix the other ingredients with enough salad dressing to moisten. Pile in the centre of the lettuce and serve at once.

572. Carrot and Apple Salad

Quantities for 4 helpings:

2 c. raw grated carrot	1 lettuce
2 c. raw grated apple	Salad dressing
$\frac{1}{2}$ c. raisins or other dried fruit	

Arrange nests of lettuce leaves on 4 plates. Mix the carrot, cheese, and fruit together and pile in the centre of the lettuce. Mask with salad dressing and serve at once.

573. Celery and Cheese Salad

Quantities for 4 helpings:

1 lettuce	4 small tomatoes
3 c. sliced celery	Salad dressing
$1\frac{1}{2}$ c. diced cheese	

Line the salad bowl with lettuce leaves. Mix the celery and cheese with enough dressing to moisten and put in the centre. Decorate with sliced tomatoes. Serve at once.

574. Asparagus Salad

Serve cold boiled asparagus with Mayonnaise, No. 113, or Vinaigrette Sauce, No. 119. If liked, arrange each portion in a nest of lettuce leaves.

575. Ham Roll Salad

Spread thin slices of cold, cooked ham with cottage cheese. Roll up loosely. Arrange in a nest of lettuce leaves and serve with salad dressing.

576. Creole Potato Salad

Quantities for 4 helpings:

1 lb. potatoes (500 g.)	1 tsp. salt
2 c. shelled prawns	Pinch of pepper
4 Tbs. oil	2 hard-boiled eggs
2 Tbs. vinegar	

Boil the potatoes in their jackets. Peel and slice. Mix with the prawns. Mix the salt, pepper, oil, and vinegar together and combine with the potato and prawns while still warm. Leave to cool and decorate with the sliced eggs.

577. Curried Salad

Quantities for 4–6 helpings:

8 oz. cooked chicken or other meat, diced (250 g.)	3 hard-boiled eggs, coarsely chopped
8 oz. canned or cooked diced carrots (250 g.)	8 Tbs. mayonnaise
½ tsp. chopped or grated onion	1 Tbs. curry powder
2 apples, peeled and chopped	Salt to taste
	Lettuce

Measures level. Combine the chicken or meat, carrots, onion, apples and eggs. Mix the curry into the mayonnaise and add salt to taste. Combine this with the other ingredients and serve in a bowl lined with lettuce leaves. Also suitable for hors-d'œuvre.

578. Shrimp and Egg Salad

Quantities for 4 helpings:

1 lettuce, large
4 hard-boiled eggs
½ pt. Mayonnaise, No. 113 (1 c.)

Chopped chives or parsley
1½ pt. cooked shrimps (1½ c. shelled)

Measures level. Make a nest of crisp lettuce leaves on each plate. Cut the eggs in half and place in the centre, cut side up. Cover the eggs with mayonnaise and sprinkle with the chives or parsley. Surround the eggs with the shrimps and serve at once.

579. Tongue Salad

Quantities for 4 helpings:

4 hard-boiled eggs
6 oz. cooked or canned tongue, diced (175 g.)
1 medium beetroot, diced
1 apple peeled and diced
Pinch of pepper

½ tsp. salt
½ tsp. mustard
2 Tbs. vinegar
2 Tbs. cream or evaporated milk
Lettuce or chicory leaves

Reserve two of the egg yolks for the dressing and chop the remainder. Mash the yolks with the seasoning and mix to a smooth cream first with the vinegar and then the cream or milk. Combine with the other ingredients and serve in a bowl lined with lettuce or chicory. Also suitable for hors-d'œuvre.

CHAPTER 14

Fruit and Nuts

580. Food Value

For many generations it has been known that certain fruits are valuable foods. Sailors knew how important it was to have lemon juice or other citrus fruits, and our grandfathers were great believers in the use of fruits for medicinal purposes. We know now that many fruits contain vitamin C, which the body needs for good health and vitality. Fruits which are a good source of this vitamin are oranges, lemons, grapefruit, rosehips, strawberries, black and red currants, gooseberries, loganberries, raspberries, and some apples (especially the skins). In addition, the red and yellow fruits contain carotene, from which the body makes vitamin A, and all provide roughage and bulk.

While fresh fruits have the highest vitamin C content, some preserved fruits are also a useful source, for example, frozen black currants, blackcurrant syrup, rosehip syrup, and frozen strawberries. Canned fruits lose some vitamin C, but canned citrus fruits and juices are a good source and tomato juice is useful for carotene as well.

Nuts provide protein, oil, B vitamins, minerals and cellulose. Chestnuts are an important exception as they contain a higher proportion of carbohydrate and less protein and oil than most other nuts. Peanuts have a very high nutritive value and peanut butter is also good value. Nuts are important in vegetarian diets as a substitute for animal protein.

581. Suggestions for Preparing Different Kinds of Fruit. For detailed recipes using each kind of fruit see Index.

APPLES. If they are to be used for dessert or to be cooked with the skins on, wash and dry well just before using. To prevent discolouring when peeling, use a silver or stainless-steel knife and, if the apples are not to be cooked at once, put them into salted water to cover. Allow 1 level Tbs. salt to each quart (4 c.) of water. Put a plate on top to keep the pieces under the water. Drain well and rinse before using.

For stewing, peel, core, and leave whole or cut in quarters.

For puddings and pies, peel, core, and slice.

For purée, wash and cut in sections. The cores and skins are removed when the pulp is sieved.

Dried apples, see No. 592.

APRICOTS. Wipe and dry carefully. They are generally stewed with the stones in, but may be cut in half and the stones removed. Crack some stones and cook the kernels with the fruit.

Dried apricots, see Nos. 592–4.

BANANAS. Do not peel until they are to be used, as they turn brown very quickly. This may be prevented to some extent by covering the sliced fruit with lemon-, orange-, or pineapple-juice. They are generally served raw in salads, or with custard, but may be used to make a purée or fried and served with bacon.

BILBERRIES AND BLUEBERRIES. Wash, and use to make pies and puddings, and the purée or juice for fruit fools and other cold puddings.

BLACKBERRIES. Pick over carefully, removing stalks, hulls, and any grubs and mouldy berries. Just before using wash by putting the berries in a colander and gently running cold water through. Drain well.

If the berries are not to be used at once, spread them on a shallow dish, as they keep better if not left in a heap. They may be put in a refrigerator. To serve raw, sprinkle with caster sugar and stand in a cold place or in the refrigerator for $\frac{1}{2}$ hour.

BOYSENBERRIES. Prepare and use in the same way as blackberries.

CHERRIES. Wash well and leave the stalks on if the fruit is for dessert. For fruit salad remove stalks and stones. For stewing and pies remove the stalks.

CHINESE GOOSEBERRIES. Peel off the brown, furry skin and use the soft inside as raw fruit, or in salads, or to make a flan.

CRANBERRIES. Prepare in the same way as blackberries, removing the stalks and leaves.

CURRANTS (black, white, and red). Wash well while still on the stalks, using the same method as for blackberries, and store in the same way. Do not remove the fruit from the stalks until you are ready to use it, as it keeps better this way. To stalk use a fork, holding the bunch in your left hand and using the fork in your right to pull off the berries.

DAMSONS. Wash well and remove stalks, leaves, and any damaged fruit.

ELDERBERRIES. Prepare in the same way as currants.

FIGS. Fresh figs should be washed well and served whole or sliced.

For stewing remove the stalks.

Dried figs are treated in the same way as other dried fruit, see No. 592.

GOOSEBERRIES. Wash well and remove the tops and tails, using a pair of kitchen scissors or a small knife.

GRAPES. Wash carefully and drain well, removing the seeds if the fruit is to be used for a salad.

GRAPEFRUIT. To prepare grapefruit sections peel the fruit, removing pith and skin at the same time. Hold the fruit over a dish to collect the juice. Remove the skins round the sections by cutting close to the membrane on each side. A very sharp knife is needed to do this. To prepare *halves* of grapefruit for serving, cut in half across. Remove the seeds.

Using a sharp vegetable knife, cut along each side of the membrane between the sections. Use the same knife or a special curved grapefruit knife, and cut round and under the fruit, separating it from the skin. Then cut out the core with a pair of scissors or a knife and lift it out with the membrane. Rearrange the sections and sprinkle with caster sugar or add a little honey.

GREENGAGES. Wash well and remove the stalks. If they are to be used in fruit salad remove the stones.

LEMONS. Wash the skin. Grate the rind before squeezing out the juice. Grate only the yellow part, as the white pith is bitter.

Use a lemon squeezer or juice extractor to get all the juice out.

LOGANBERRIES. Treat in the same way as blackberries.

MELONS. Wash the outside. Cut in sections lengthwise and remove all seeds. Serve very cold with a little caster sugar. Cantaloupe melons are sometimes served with a portion of vanilla ice-cream on top of each slice. To prepare melon for a fruit salad remove the skin and seeds and cut it in cubes.

NECTARINES. Wash and dry carefully. For fruit salad or pies remove the stones and cut the fruit in slices.

ORANGES. Use the rind and juice in the same way as for lemons. For serving in the skin prepare in the same way as grapefruit.

PASSIONFRUIT OR PURPLE GRANADILLA. Cut in half and remove seeds and pulp. Use together to flavour fruit salads or as a sauce for ice-cream. To remove seeds, boil and strain.

PEACHES. Wash and dry carefully. To remove the skins plunge the fruit into boiling water for a minute and then into cold water, when the skins should peel off quite easily.

PEARS. Prepare in the same way as apples.

PINEAPPLES. Peel thickly to remove all the skin. Take out the hard core and cut the pineapple across in $\frac{1}{2}$-inch

(1 cm.) slices or in dice. Serve very cold with a little caster sugar sprinkled over or add to fruit salad.

PLUMS. Prepare in the same way as greengages.

POMEGRANATES. Cut in halves and serve with a spoon. The seeds and juice are eaten.

QUINCES. Peel, core, and slice thinly.

RASPBERRIES. Prepare in the same way as black-berries.

RHUBARB. Wash well and trim the ends. It keeps a better colour if the skin is left on.

STRAWBERRIES. Prepare in the same way as black-berries. Serve very cold.

582. Suggestions for Preparing Different Kinds of Nuts

Unless you can purchase fresh, good-quality nuts at the beginning of the season it is usually better to buy shelled ones instead. About half the weight of most nuts is shell and the wastage can be much higher if there are many poor-quality nuts. Unfortunately, the quality can rarely be judged by the shells and it is important to buy from a reliable source and to pay a fair price.

To shell nuts, use a good strong pair of nut-crackers or a small hammer.

To chop nuts, use a sharp knife on a board, or one of the patent choppers or grinding machines. If finely chopped or ground nuts are required an electric blender is an ideal tool to use.

For recipes using nuts see the Index.

ALMONDS are sold in the shells, shelled, blanched, salted, split, as nibs (small pieces), or ground to a powder. To skin or blanch almonds, put them in a basin and cover with boiling water, leave for a few minutes, strain and cover with cold water. The skins can then easily be removed. Dry the nuts before use.

BRAZIL NUTS usually have the skin left on and may be chopped or ground and used in the same ways as almonds or walnuts.

CASHEW NUTS require no preparation. They may be used chopped or ground.

CHESTNUTS (sweet) are sold fresh in the shell, dried shelled, or canned purée or glacé (marrons glacé). To shell chestnuts, cut off the pointed end and either bake them in a moderate oven for 20 minutes or grill gently until the shells split. Remove shells and skins. Do only a few at a time as they are easier to shell while hot. To cook dried chestnuts, cover them with water and simmer gently until they are tender.

COCONUT OR COCOANUT Fully ripe coconuts are hollow inside but unripe ones contain 'milk' which can be drunk or added to curries and other cooked dishes. Fresh coconut is chopped in pieces and removed from the shell. It may be eaten in pieces or shredded or chopped. Dried coconut is sold coarsely shredded or as fine desiccated coconut, used for flavouring cakes, puddings, and for making sweets.

FILBERTS OR KENTISH COBS are usually picked and sold green and served for dessert. The nuts are cracked, shelled and peeled which is quite easy to do when they are fresh. They can be prepared in the same way as salted almonds and, when ripe, are used in the same way as hazel nuts.

HAZEL NUTS OR COB NUTS are sold ripe in the shell, or shelled and sometimes roasted as well. To skin the shelled nuts, spread them on a tray and bake in a moderate oven until the skins can easily be rubbed off. This process also toasts them and improves the flavour. They can be chopped or ground and used in the same way as almonds and walnuts, including for making marzipan.

PEANUTS OR GROUND NUTS are sold fresh or roasted, shelled or unshelled, salted, or as peanut butter. Roasted peanuts can be skinned by rubbing. They are excellent in cooking when used chopped or ground in the same way as almonds or walnuts.

PECAN NUTS. Prepare and use as walnuts.

PINE KERNELS are sold ready for use as dessert nuts or in cooking.

PISTACHIO NUTS are usually reserved for garnishing because of their attractive green colour. Where they are cheap and plentiful they are often salted.

WALNUTS are used green and whole to make pickled walnuts. With ripe nuts the flavour is better if the skins are left on but they may be removed by blanching in the same way as with almonds. For cooking, they are used sliced, chopped or ground.

583. Using Frozen Fruit

If the fruit is to be served raw, thaw it slowly in the refrigerator allowing 8–10 hours per pound ($\frac{1}{2}$ kg.). For quicker thawing, empty the fruit into a bowl and thaw it at room temperature for 3–4 hours.

Fruit for cooking can be used either frozen or partially thawed, the latter being preferable for pies and tarts.

When a little frozen fruit is being added to a fruit salad, put it into the syrup with the other fruit and leave it to thaw.

584. Fruit Salad

This may be made with one kind of raw fruit or with a mixture of different kinds, either all raw, or with some frozen, bottled or canned fruit. Syrup from canned fruit will be used to moisten the salad.

1. For a raw fruit salad make a syrup by boiling together $\frac{1}{2}$ pt. (1 c.) water, or $\frac{1}{2}$ cider and $\frac{1}{2}$ water, and 2–4 oz. (4–8 Tbs.) sugar or honey. This is sufficient for a salad for 4 people. When the sugar is dissolved, allow to cool. In countries where brandy and other spirits are cheap, these

are used instead of the syrup. The fruit is sprinkled with caster sugar and the spirit poured over.

2. Fruit for a salad may be sliced or diced, but when mixed fruit is used it is better cut in fairly small, even-sized pieces.

3. Serve all salads very cold. They may be put in the refrigerator for half an hour or so beforehand. Serve with a sweet biscuit and cream or custard.

585. Pear and Ginger Salad

Peel ripe pears and cover them with the syrup described in No. 584. Sprinkle with chopped, preserved ginger or, if none is available, cook some root ginger with the syrup until it is well flavoured.

586. Orange and Apple Salad

Use equal amounts of sliced, peeled oranges and sweet apples. Pour over syrup and if possible add 1 Tbs. brandy or rum to it.

587. Plum and Melon Salad

Quantities for 4 helpings:

1 lb. ripe plums (500 g.)   1 oz. honey (1 Tbs.) or to
½ small ripe melon   taste
6 oz. orange juice (¾ c.)

Wash and stone the plums and cut in small pieces. Remove seeds and pulp, peel and dice the melon. Mix the fruits and add the orange juice mixed with the honey to dissolve it. Chill before serving.

588. Frozen Strawberries in Orange Juice

Quantities for 4–5 helpings:

1 lb. frozen strawberries   1 Tbs. caster sugar
  (500 g.)
½ pt. canned orange juice
  (1 c.)

Put the frozen berries in a bowl with the orange juice, sprinkling any exposed fruit with sugar. Cover the bowl and put it in the refrigerator to allow the berries to thaw slowly. Serve when they are only just thawed. This will take about 4 hours.

589. Stewed Fresh Fruit or Fruit Compote

1. For each pound of fruit heat together 4 oz. (½ c.) sugar and ½ pt. (1 c.) water. Stir until the sugar dissolves and bring to the boil. More or less sugar may be used according to personal taste.

2. Prepare the fruit as described in No. 581, and add it to the boiling syrup. Reduce the heat to keep it just below boiling, and cook until tender. If the syrup is allowed to boil hard, the fruit will break and be unsightly. Cherries should be allowed to cook until the skin breaks, otherwise the sugar will not be absorbed.

3. The time varies with the kind and ripeness of the fruit, but the following table will be a guide:

Berries and other soft fruit, 15–20 minutes.
Quartered apples, plums, etc., 20–30 minutes.
Cooking pears, ½–1 hour (2–3 hours for hard kinds).
Quinces, 1½–2 hours.

When the fruit is just tender, drain from the syrup and place in the serving-dish.

4. Boil the syrup hard to make it thick. Then pour over the fruit and serve hot or cold.

5. For variety, flavourings may be added to the syrup and the fruit. For example, lemon or orange peel, cloves, spices, ginger, or use some cider in place of the water.

6. Serve stewed fruit with cream or custard, with milk puddings or with a biscuit or piece of cake.

590. Stuffed Stewed Apples

Peel and core small apples, and cook them in syrup in a saucepan, as in No. 589, turning them occasionally and taking care not to over-cook or break them. Place in a serving-dish and fill the centres with red jam mixed with chopped nuts or dried fruit. Boil the syrup to thicken it, and pour round the apples. Serve cold with custard or cream.

591. Pears Armandine. Cooking time 30 minutes or more

Quantities for 4 helpings:

$\frac{1}{2}$ pt. water (1 c.)	Toasted almonds
4 oz. sugar ($\frac{1}{2}$ c.)	8 oz. frozen or fresh
Vanilla essence	strawberries (250 g.)
4 pears, peeled, halved and cored	Whipped cream

Measures level. Boil the sugar and water for 3–4 minutes. Add the vanilla and poach the pears in this until they are just tender. Turn frequently. Put them in a serving dish, round sides up, and stick with slivers of almonds. Boil the syrup to reduce it by half. Add the strawberries and boil until tender and mashed. Sieve. Spoon over the pears and chill. Serve with cream.

592. Stewed Dried Fruit

1. Wash the fruit well and soak for 24 hours in warm water. It will need 2–4 times its bulk of water.

2. Cook very gently in the soaking water until tender, $\frac{1}{2}$–1 hour. Lemon or orange peel or some cinnamon or cider may

be used for extra flavour, and a little sugar should be added towards the end of cooking. If added too soon it prevents the fruit from softening properly.

3. Serve in the same way as fresh fruit or use in recipes requiring cooked fruit.

593. Dried Fruit Salad

Quantities for 8 helpings:

4 oz. dried apricots (125 g.)   8 oz. prunes (250 g.)
8 oz. dried figs (250 g.)   Sugar to taste
8 oz. dried peaches or
    pears (250 g.)

Prepare and cook as in No. 592.

594. Mixed Fruit Compote

Quantities for 8 helpings:

1 lb. dried apricots (500 g.)   1-inch piece of lemon peel
1 qt. water (4 c.)   1 large or 2 small apples
8 oz. seedless raisins
    (250 g.)

Wash the apricots and put in a pan with the water, raisins, and peel. Cook gently until tender. Core the apple and cut into eighths. Lay the sections on top of the other fruit, cover the pan, and cook until the apples are tender.

595. Stewing in a Casserole

1. Prepare the fruit as for ordinary stewing and put it in a casserole or any oven-dish with a lid.

2. Add 2–4 oz. (4–8 Tbs.) sugar or honey to each pound (500 g.) of fruit and just enough water to moisten the bottom of the dish. With juicy fruits like berries, rhubarb, and ripe

plums no water is needed; quinces and hard pears will need
½ pt. (1 c.) water per pound (500 g.) of fruit.

3. Cover the dish and cook in a moderate or slow oven
375–300° F. (190–150° C.) Mark 5–2, until the fruit is
tender. The times are about the same as for stewing, see No.
589, but may take twice as long in a slow oven.

596. Rhubarb and Orange Compote. Cooking time 20–30 minutes

Temperature 300–350° F. (150–180° C.) Mark 2–4.

Quantities for 4 helpings:

1 lb. rhubarb (500 g.)   2–3 oz. sugar (4–6 Tbs.)
2 oranges

Cut the rhubarb in 1-inch (2½ cm.) pieces and put it in
layers in a casserole with the sliced, peeled oranges and the
sugar. Cover and cook in a slow-moderate oven until the
rhubarb is tender. Serve hot or cold with custard or cream.

597. Baked Apples

1. The apples may be peeled, or baked with the skins on.
It is better to remove the core with an apple-corer. If the
skins are left on, slit them in a ring about half-way down the
apple, using the point of a sharp knife. This prevents the
skin from bursting during cooking.

2. The centres may be stuffed with any one of the following: dates, honey and ground cloves, cinnamon, brown
sugar, treacle, or raisins. Place in a shallow baking-dish and
add 1 level Tbs. sugar for each apple and about ¼ inch
(6 mm.) water.

3. Bake in moderate oven 400° F. (200° C.) Mark 6, until
the fruit is tender, basting occasionally with the liquid. They
will take about 40–50 minutes. Serve hot or cold.

598. Special Baked Apples, with Meringue. Cooking time about 1 hour

Quantities for 4 helpings:

2 oz. syrup (2 Tbs.)
¼ pt. water (½ c.)
¼ tsp. cinnamon
1 tsp. grated lemon rind
½ oz. margarine (1 Tbs.)
4 cooking apples

1 egg white
2 Tbs. sugar
12 blanched and shredded almonds
4 glacé cherries, chopped

Measures level. Heat the first five ingredients together and bring to the boil. Core the apples and peel the upper half. Place in a baking-dish with the syrup, and cook as in No. 597. Beat the egg white until stiff, and beat in the sugar. Put ¼ on top of each apple, and decorate with the almonds and cherries. Bake until lightly browned in a moderate oven 350° F. (180° C.) Mark 4. Serve hot.

599. Baked Bananas and Prunes. Cooking time 20 minutes

Temperature 375° F. (190° C.) Mark 5.

Quantities for 2–3 helpings:

2 bananas
1 tsp. grated lemon rind
2 Tbs. lemon juice

8 oz. cooked or canned prunes or red plums (250 g.)

Peel the bananas and cut in four lengthwise. Arrange in a shallow baking-dish. Sprinkle with the lemon rind and juice. Drain and stone the prunes or plums and put on top of the bananas. Pour over enough juice barely to cover. Bake in a moderate oven for 20 minutes. Serve warm or chilled.

600. Baked Pears. Cooking time 2–3 hours

Temperature 300° F. (150° C.) Mark 3.

Quantities for 4 helpings:

1 lb. stewing pears (500 g.)   3 oz. syrup (3 Tbs.)
1 c. buttered crumbs, No.   ¼ pt. water (½ c.)
  876

Measures level. Peel and halve or quarter the pears. Remove the cores. Coat in the buttered crumbs and pack in a casserole. Add the syrup and water. Cover and cook slowly until the pears are tender. Serve with custard or cream.

601. Baked Spiced Rhubarb. Cooking time 25 minutes

Temperature 400° F. (200° C.) Mark 6.

Quantities for 4–6 helpings:

2 lb. rhubarb (1 kg.)   4 cloves
6–8 oz. sugar (¾–1 c.)
1 inch stick of cinnamon or
  a little ground cinnamon

Measures level. Cut off the tops of the sticks and trim the root ends. Wash rhubarb and cut in 1 inch pieces. Put in a casserole. Sprinkle on the sugar, add spice. Cover and bake until tender but not mushy. Leave it covered while cooling and serve cold.

602. Preparing Fruit Pulp or Purée (1 lb. fruit gives about ½ pt. purée or 1 c.)

Fruit Pulp may be made from fresh ripe fruit rubbed through a sieve. When cooked fruit is used the oven method No. 595 is the best for flavour. When the fruit is quite tender rub it through a fine sieve. If possible use a nylon sieve, as metal sieves sometimes affect the flavour and colour of the fruit. Pulp may also be made from stewed dried fruit or canned fruit, straining off some of the juice before sieving. Raw or cooked frozen fruit is also suitable.

603. Fruit Fool. Cooking time ½ hour

Quantities for 4 helpings:

½ pt. raw or cooked Fruit
  Purée, No. 602 (1 c.)
½ pt. evaporated milk
  or cream, whipped (1 c.)

Sugar to taste
Flavour with lemon or
  orange juice or with
  essence

Sweeten the fruit pulp to taste and allow to become quite cold. If evaporated milk is used, scald the tin in a pan of boiling water for ½ hour, cool and then chill. Beat the milk and then fold in the fruit pulp. With whipped cream, fold the pulp into the cream. Flavour to taste and serve very cold in individual glasses. If necessary, a little colouring may be added.

604. Fruit Soufflé. Cooking time 20 minutes

Temperature 375° F. (190° C.) Mark 5.

Quantities for 4 helpings:

½ pt. Fruit Purée, No. 602
  (1 c.)
2 egg whites

Pinch of salt
1 oz. sugar (2 Tbs.)
½ tsp. grated lemon rind

Measures level. Beat the egg whites with the salt until they are stiff. Then beat in the sugar. Fold in the fruit pulp and the lemon rind. Pour into a baking-dish and cook in a moderate oven until risen and lightly set. Serve at once with cream, or a custard made with the egg-yolks. Serve a piece of cake or a biscuit separately.

605. Cinnamon Apples

Make apple pulp according to No. 602. Sweeten to taste with sugar and add cinnamon (1 tsp. to 2 lb. (1 kg.) apples) when cooking the apples. Serve cold in individual dishes with biscuit or cake and cream.

606. Apple Crisp or Crumble. Cooking time 1–1½ hours

Temperature 350° F. (180° C.) Mark 4.

Quantities for 3–4 helpings:

1 lb. cooking apples (500 g.)	3 oz. flour (⅔ c.)
¼ tsp. ground cinnamon	2 oz. sugar (4 Tbs.)
⅛ pt. water (¼ c.)	1 oz. margarine or butter (25 g.)

Measures level. Peel and slice the apples finely and put in a baking-dish. Sprinkle with the cinnamon and add the water. Mix the flour and sugar and rub in the fat until the mixture looks like fine crumbs.

Sprinkle on top of the fruit and bake in a slow–moderate oven until golden-brown. Do not have the oven too hot or the juice will bubble up and spoil the top.

N.B. This recipe may also be made with rhubarb and other fruits. If the fruit is very sour it should have extra sugar sprinkled on before the crumble.

607. Grilled Grapefruit. Cooking time 5–7 minutes

Allow half a grapefruit per person. Prepare the halves as described in No. 581. Sprinkle with brown sugar. Place about ¼ oz. (½ Tbs.) butter over the hole in the centre. Grill gently for 5–7 minutes or until lightly browned. Serve hot.

608. Banana and Chocolate Creams

Quantities for 4 helpings:

4 bananas
2 Tbs. caster sugar
¼ pt. double cream (½ c.)
Vanilla essence

Juice of 1 lemon
2 oz. grated chocolate
  (50 g.)
Glacé cherries

Measures level. Mash the bananas with a fork and add the sugar, cream, and vanilla essence to taste. Add the lemon juice and mix well. Put in individual dishes and cover the top with a layer of grated chocolate. Decorate with glacé cherries and serve cold, but do not put it in the refrigerator.

609. Caramel Oranges. Cooking time about 5 minutes

Quantities for 6 helpings:

6 oranges
Caster sugar
Brandy or liqueur
  (optional)

¼ pt. water (½ c.)
4 oz. gran. sugar (½ c.)
Whipped cream
Chopped nuts

Measures level. Peel the oranges, taking care to remove all the pith. Cut in slices or divide into segments. Arrange in layers in a heat-resisting serving-dish, sprinkling each layer with a little caster sugar and liqueur, if used. Heat the sugar and water, stirring until dissolved, and then boil rapidly, without stirring, until it turns a pale-brown caramel. Pour over the oranges and leave in a cold place for several hours. The caramel will gradually dissolve and form a syrup round the oranges. Decorate with whipped cream and chopped nuts.

610. Lemon Delicious Pudding. Cooking time 45 minutes

Temperature 350° F. (180° C.) Mark 4.

Quantities for 4 helpings:

2 eggs
1 tsp. grated lemon rind

2 Tbs. flour
¼ pt. milk (½ c.)

2 Tbs. lemon juice   2 tsp. melted butter
5 oz. caster sugar ($\frac{2}{3}$ c.)

Measures level. Separate the whites and yolks of the eggs. Mix ingredients in this order; lemon rind, lemon juice, sugar, flour, beaten egg yolks, milk and butter. Mix thoroughly and fold in the stiffly beaten egg whites. Pour into a greased baking dish and cook until set. The mixture separates into a frothy top and custardy base.

CHAPTER 15

Cereals and Starch Foods

611. Food Value

Arrowroot, sago, and tapioca consist almost entirely of starch. Cereals contain starch, protein, calcium, iron, and B vitamins. Whole-grain cereals have the highest vitamin content, but they contain phytic acid which hinders the absorption of calcium and iron. Refined cereals like white flour and white rice have a lower nutritive value than the whole grain. In the United Kingdom, white and brown flours are enriched with calcium, iron, and B vitamins (thiamine and niacin). They contain more calcium than whole-grain flour but slightly less iron and B vitamins.

612. General Information

CEREALS include:

Wheat which is used for making flour, semolina, spaghetti, macaroni, vermicelli, and for certain prepared breakfast foods.

Oats which are used for making rolled oats and oatmeal.

Rice which is used as the whole grain with the outer husk removed, or as ground rice.

Maize which is used to make maize flour (corn meal), hominy, polenta, and cornflour.

Barley which is used as pearl barley to make barley flour and barley flakes.

Rye which is used to make flour for rye bread and for crisp breads.

STARCH FOODS include:

Arrowroot which is made from the root of a plant which grows in the West Indies and India.

Potato starch, fecule or flour.

Sago which is made from the pith of the sago palm.

Tapioca which is made from the root of a tropical plant.

As they readily absorb moisture and become mouldy, cereals must be stored in dry containers with airtight lids. Whole-grain cereals do not keep as long as the refined ones. Do not put fresh cereals on top of old ones in the container, as the old may spoil the new.

When they are cooked, heat and moisture soften the starch grains in cereals and make them swell. As they swell moisture is absorbed, and we say they thicken the liquid. Cooking also makes the grains more digestible and improves the flavour. Many packet puddings made from cereals and starch are very much improved by giving them longer cooking than the instructions generally advise.

613. Boiling Rice

Long-grain rice is usually the best for boiling but others are sometimes used. Some rice is specially treated for quick and easy cooking and sold in packets with cooking instructions. The method below is the best to use for cooking other types of rice.

Quantities: allow 2 oz. ($\frac{1}{4}$ c.) per person.

1. Put the rice in a strainer and hold it under the cold tap allowing water to run through and wash away loose starch which tends to make the grains stick together during cooking.

2. For each 2 oz. ($\frac{1}{4}$ c.) rice allow $\frac{1}{4}$ pt. ($\frac{1}{2}$ c.) water and $\frac{1}{4}$ level teaspoon salt.

3. Put rice, water and salt in a pan, bring to the boil, stir, put on the lid and reduce the heat to simmering. Cook 15 mins. without stirring or lifting the lid. If more convenient,

this part of the cooking can be done in a double boiler or in a moderate oven.

4. Test a few grains by squeezing them between the thumb and fore-finger. If the rice is done there will be no hard core of starch. By this time all the water should have been absorbed.

5. Remove the lid, fluff the rice up with a fork and keep it in a warm place for 5–10 mins. to dry, but do not let it cook any more.

614. Re-heated and Fried Rice

Cold boiled rice keeps well in a tightly covered dish in the refrigerator for up to a week, or in the larder for 2–3 days.

To re-heat it, put the rice in a covered saucepan with a few tablespoons of water and stand the pan over a low heat. Shake the pan occasionally until the rice is hot and fluffy.

To fry the rice, first fry a little chopped onion in butter or oil until it begins to brown. Add the rice and heat until the fat is absorbed and the rice is beginning to brown. Add chopped green herbs and season to taste. Optional additions: chopped canned pineapple and chopped salted almonds; raisins and chopped almonds; chopped green or red sweet peppers; chopped tomato; chopped celery and mushroom fried with the onion.

615. Risotto. Cooking time 25–30 minutes

Quantities for 2–3 helpings:

2 oz. fat (50 g.)	2 oz. chopped cooked
3 oz. chopped onion ($\frac{1}{2}$ c.)	mushrooms, liver, or
6 oz. rice ($\frac{3}{4}$ c.)	tomatoes (50 g.)
1 pt. stock (2 c.)	2 oz. grated cheese (50 g.)

Measures level. Use a thick frying-pan, and fry the onion in the fat until it begins to brown. Add the rice and cook for 3 minutes longer.

Add a quarter of the stock and cook for 15–20 minutes or until the rice is tender, adding the rest of the stock gradually. All the stock should be absorbed by this time. Add the cooked mushrooms, liver, or tomatoes a few minutes before serving. They should be fried in a little fat. Serve the grated cheese separately, to be sprinkled on at table.

616. Kedgeree

Quantities for 2–3 helpings:

1–2 oz. butter or margarine (25–50 g.)
2 c. cold, boiled rice No. 613
8 oz. cooked, flaked fish (fresh, smoked, or canned) (1 c.)

1 hard-boiled egg
Salt and pepper to taste
Pinch of nutmeg
1 lemon

Measures level. Melt the butter or margarine and stir in the fish and rice. Add the seasonings and chopped egg white. Heat gently until thoroughly hot through. Pile on a dish. Rub the egg yolk through a sieve and sprinkle over the top. Serve with sliced lemon.

617. Raisin Rice (to serve with poultry or meat). Cooking time 15–20 minutes

Quantities for 4 helpings:

8 oz. long-grain rice (1 c.)
1 oz. butter (25 g.)
1 small, sliced onion
2 oz. seedless raisins ($\frac{1}{4}$ c.)

2 oz. blanched, sliced almonds ($\frac{1}{4}$ c.)
Salt

Measures level. Boil the rice, see No. 613. Meanwhile, heat the butter and fry the onion and almonds until brown. Add the raisins, rice, and salt. Make sure it is hot before serving.

618. Liver Pilaf. Cooking time 45 minutes

Quantities for 4–6 helpings:

2 oz. butter (50 g.)	8–12 oz. liver, diced
1 pt. chicken stock (2 c.)	(250–375 g.)
8 oz. long-grain rice (1 c.)	1–2 oz. butter (25–50 g.)
Salt and pepper	

Measures level. Put 2 oz. (50 g.) butter and the stock in a large pan. Bring to the boil and add the rice. Stir, and then cook slowly until the rice is tender and all the stock absorbed, about 20–30 minutes. This can be done in a slow oven, 350° F. (180° C.) Mark 4. Season the rice to taste. Dish on a hot plate or pack into a ring mould. Keep hot. Heat 1–2 oz. (25–50 g.) butter in a frying pan and fry the liver very quickly, turning it frequently until it is lightly browned, about 5 minutes. Season with salt and pepper and either pile on the rice or put it in the centre of the un-moulded border. If preferred more moist, the liver may be mixed with a little hot brown or mushroom sauce.

619. Boiling Macaroni, Spaghetti, Vermicelli, and Noodles (*pasta*).

1. Allow 4 oz. (125 g.) per person. Boil 1 qt. (4 c.) of water in a large saucepan with 1 level Tbs. salt.
2. The macaroni or spaghetti may be cooked whole or broken in pieces. Other pasta are cooked as purchased. Add to the boiling water and cook rapidly without a lid on the pan, or it will boil over. With long pieces put one end in the pan, and the rest will coil up as it softens.
3. Boil until the pasta is tender. Try to avoid overcooking, as this makes the pieces stick together in a mass, instead of being separate. The time varies from 5 to 15 minutes.
4. Drain in a colander and pour boiling water through to separate the pieces.

5. Reheat in a little melted butter or margarine or serve with tomato or cheese sauce.

620. Macaroni Cheese. Cooking time ¾ hour

Temperature 375° F. (190° C.) Mark 5.

Quantities for 4 helpings:

4 oz. macaroni (125 g.)
1 pt. Cheese Sauce, No. 75 (2 c.)

Buttered breadcrumbs, No. 876

Measures level. Boil the macaroni according to No. 619. Put in a pie-dish in layers with the sauce, finishing with sauce. Sprinkle the top with the breadcrumbs and bake in a moderate oven until brown on top or brown under the grill.

621. Macaroni Cheese with Ham

Make according to No. 620, adding 2 oz. (50 g.) cooked chopped bacon or ham to the sauce.

622. Noodles with Cultured Cream or Yogurt. Cooking time 10 minutes

Quantities for 4 helpings:

1 lb. egg noodles (500 g.)
8 oz. cooked, sliced ham (250 g.)
2 oz. butter (50 g.)

½ pt. cultured (soured) cream or yogurt (1 c.)
Salt and pepper
Grated Parmesan cheese

Measures level. Boil the noodles and drain. Put the slices of ham in a pile and cut in strips lengthwise and then across to give small pieces. Melt the butter. Add the noodles and ham and mix. Add cream or yogurt and seasoning. Make sure it is hot. Serve on a hot dish and hand the cheese separately.

623. Spaghetti and Meat Sauce. Cooking time 1 hour

Quantities for ½–1 lb. of spaghetti (250–500 g.):

2 Tbs. olive oil
8 oz. minced lean beef
  (250 g.)
1 chopped onion
2 oz. chopped mushrooms
  (50 g.)

14 oz. can tomatoes
  (400 g.)
Garlic salt or fresh or
  dried garlic to taste
Salt and pepper to taste
Grated Parmesan cheese

Heat the oil and fry the beef until it changes colour. Add the onion and mushrooms and fry gently for 10 minutes, stirring occasionally. Add the tomatoes and seasoning and simmer gently for 40 minutes or until the sauce is thick and the ingredients well blended. Either mix with the boiled spaghetti, see No. 619, or serve on top of it. Sprinkle with the cheese.

624. Boiling Sago and Tapioca

These are generally cooked in just enough liquid to be all absorbed by the end of cooking. To wash the cereal, put it in a basin with cold water, stir, and then leave to settle. Pour off the water carefully. Add the cereal to the boiling liquid in a saucepan and cook gently until clear. Sago and small tapioca takes about 15 minutes. If milk is used for the liquid, it is easier if the cooking is done over boiling water allowing about 20 minutes. There is then no danger of boiling over or burning.

625. Sago or Tapioca Cream. Cooking time 25 minutes

Quantities for 4–6 helpings:

2 oz. sago or small tapioca
  (4 Tbs.)
¼ tsp. salt
1 pt. milk (2 c.)

1–2 oz. sugar (2–4 Tbs.)
2 eggs
Vanilla essence to taste

Measures level. Heat the milk in the top of a double boiler. Add the sago to the milk with the salt and sugar. Bring to the boil and then cook over boiling water until the sago is clear, about 20 minutes. Add the beaten egg yolks and cook for 5 minutes. Add the flavouring and fold in the stiffly-beaten egg whites. Serve hot or cold with jam, or a fruit sauce.

626. Lemon Sago or Tapioca. Cooking time 15 minutes

Quantities for 4 helpings:

2 oz. sago or small tapioca (4 Tbs.)
1 pt. water (2 c.)
Pinch of salt

Grated rind and juice 1–2 lemons
3 oz. syrup (3 Tbs.)

Measures level. Boil the sago as in No. 624, and add the lemon and syrup at the end. Serve cold in individual dishes with cream or fruit salad. The mixture thickens on cooling.

627. Date Butterscotch Pudding. Cooking time 15 minutes

Quantities for 4 helpings:

2 oz. sago or small tapioca (4 Tbs.)
1 pt. milk or water (2 c.)
2 oz. brown sugar (4 Tbs.)
Pinch of salt

$\frac{1}{2}$ c. chopped dates
1 oz. butter or margarine (25 g.)
$\frac{1}{2}$ tsp. mixed spice
Vanilla essence to taste

Measures level. Boil the sago according to No. 624, adding the sugar, salt, dates, butter, and spice during cooking. Flavour to taste and serve hot or cold with cream or custard.

628. Porridge

Traditional porridge is made with medium or coarse oatmeal. It must not be stale, or the flavour will be poor. Oatmeal enthusiasts often buy by mail order from the miller.

Rolled oats or porridge oats, on the other hand, keep better because they have been heated during the rolling process. They also need a shorter cooking time. Instructions for making rolled oat porridge are usually given on the packet, otherwise use the recipe below.

629. Oatmeal Porridge. Cooking time 15–20 minutes

Quantities for 4 helpings:

4–6 oz. medium or coarse oatmeal ($\frac{1}{2}$–$\frac{3}{4}$ c.)

2 pt. water (4 c.)
2 level tsp. salt

If thick porridge is required use the larger amount of oatmeal. Soak the oatmeal overnight in the water. Add the salt, bring to the boil, and cook for 15–20 minutes. Stir occasionally to prevent sticking.

630. Porridge with Rolled Oats. Cooking time 5–10 minutes

Quantities for 4 helpings:

6–8 oz. rolled oats (2–2$\frac{1}{2}$ c.)
2 pt. water (4 c.) or milk

2 level tsp. salt

If thick porridge is required, use the larger amount of cereal. Mix the cereal with a little of the cold water. Boil the rest and pour on to the cereal, stirring well. Add the salt. Return to the pan, stir until it boils, and occasionally during cooking.

631. Swiss Breakfast Dish (*Muesli*)

Quantities for 4 helpings:

4 oz. rolled oats (1$\frac{1}{3}$ c.)
$\frac{1}{2}$ c. cream or evaporated milk
$\frac{1}{2}$–$\frac{3}{4}$ lb. raw grated apple (2 medium)

2–4 Tbs. sugar
Lemon juice
Chopped nuts

Measures level. Soak the cereal overnight in barely enough water to cover. Beat up well with the other ingredients and serve without cooking. Add lemon juice and nuts to taste. This is specially suitable for summer breakfasts.

632. Prepared Breakfast Cereals

These include such things as wheat and cornflakes, puffed wheat and rice, and other similar preparations. Unless the packet is freshly opened and the cereal in good condition, it is improved by heating in a warm oven before serving. This makes it fresh and crisp again.

Breakfast cereals are served with milk or cream and fruit, or may be served with fruit juices instead of milk. Wheat or cornflakes may be crushed and the crumbs used in place of breadcrumbs in puddings and meat loaves. Fold the flakes in a clean towel and crush with a rolling-pin or use a blender. 4 c. flakes gives 1 c. crumbs.

633. Cereal Topping

½ c. cereal crumbs, see No. 632

¼ c. chopped nuts

2 Tbs. brown sugar

1 Tbs. melted margarine

Measures level. Mix the ingredients together and use them to sprinkle on top of a bread pudding or instead of the flour mixture for Apple Crisp, No. 606.

634. Cooking Semolina and Ground Rice

Fine semolina and ground rice may be used in the same way as cornflour. Either the fine or coarse semolina is suitable for puddings. Although coarse semolina can successfully be sprinkled into boiling liquid as directed in many recipes, I find the easier way with both fine and coarse is to mix it to a paste with a little of the cold liquid and then add the rest boiling, in the same way as using cornflour. Lumps are much less likely this way. Fine semolina will cook in about 5–8 minutes, coarse needs 15 minutes.

635. Semolina Pudding. Cooking time 5–15 minutes

Quantities for 4 helpings:

4½ Tbs. semolina	1½ pt. milk (3 c.)
2 Tbs. sugar	Flavouring
Pinch of salt	

Measures level. Mix the semolina, sugar, and salt with a little of the cold milk. Boil the rest and pour it on to the blended mixture. Return to the pan and stir until it boils. Boil for 5–15 minutes, or cook over hot water for 15–30 minutes. The latter method is easier, as there is no danger of the pudding catching. Stir occasionally during cooking. Add flavouring to taste. This plain pudding may be served hot or cold with fruit or jam, or may have a little grated nutmeg sprinkled on top and be baked in a moderate oven 375° F. (190° C.) Mark 5, for 20 minutes or until brown on top.

636. Creamed Semolina

Make according to No. 635, but do not add the sugar until near the end of cooking. Mix it with 1 egg and stir in for the last 5 minutes of cooking. Serve as before.

637. Baked Milk Pudding (using rice, tapioca, sago)

Cooking time 1–2 hours for sago and tapioca; 2–3 hours for rice.

Temperature 300° F. (150° C.) Mark 1.

Quantities for 3–4 helpings:

1½ oz. cereal (3 Tbs.)	Pinch of salt
1 Tbs. sugar	Grated nutmeg
1 pt. milk (2 c.)	

Measures level.

1. Wash the cereal by putting it in a dish and covering with cold water. Stir well and leave to settle. Then pour off the water. Coarse cereals may be put in a strainer, and cold water run through.

2. Put in a pie-dish with the milk, salt, and sugar, and grate a little nutmeg on top.

3. Bake in a slow oven. Long, slow baking gives a creamy pudding. The pudding should be stirred two or three times at the beginning of cooking, and any skin mixed in, as this helps to make it creamy. The last part of cooking should be undisturbed to allow a final skin to settle and brown.

638. Baked Chocolate Milk Pudding

Make according to No. 637, mixing 3 level Tbs. cocoa with a little of the cold milk and adding it to the rest of the milk, with a little vanilla essence and an extra 1 or 2 Tbs. of sugar. Leave out the nutmeg.

639. Baked Caramel Milk Pudding

Make according to No. 637, using 2 level Tbs. sugar. Heat the sugar with 1 Tbs. water in a small heavy pan until it turns a light caramel colour. Heat the milk and dissolve the caramel in the hot milk. Add a little vanilla essence and leave out the nutmeg.

640. Recipe for Making a Mould (using rice, small tapioca, or sago)

Cooking time 15–20 minutes.

Quantities for 4 helpings:

2 oz. cereal (4 Tbs.)
1 pt. liquid (2 c.)
3 Tbs. sugar
Pinch of salt

Flavouring to taste
½ oz. butter or margarine
   (1 Tbs.)

Measures level.

1. Milk, fruit juice, coffee, etc., are suitable for the liquid. Wash the cereal as in No. 637 and add to the boiling liquid, stirring well all the time.

2. Cook until sago and tapioca are clear or the rice tender. If milk is used it will be easier to prevent sticking and burning if you cook the mixture in a double boiler after it has come to the boil. In that case the cooking time will be half as long again.

3. Add the sugar, salt, and flavouring, and stir in the fat, which greatly improves the texture. Pour into a mould and leave to set.

641. Cereal Mould with Egg

Make Recipe No. 640, adding 1–2 beaten eggs with the sugar. Cook for a few minutes longer without boiling. As the eggs help to thicken the mould, less cereal need be used, $\frac{1}{2}$–1 oz. (25 g.) less depending on the number of eggs used.

642. Pear or Peach Condé

Make the mould according to No. 641, using rice. The mixture may either be set in a basin and then turned out, or formed into a mound on the serving-dish. Cook the pears gently in syrup according to No. 589, adding vanilla essence to flavour; or use canned fruit. Arrange the fruit round the mound of rice and serve very cold. Chopped preserved ginger is very good sprinkled on pears.

643. Banana Meringue. Cooking time 1 hour

Quantities for 6 portions:

1½ oz. rice (3 Tbs.)	½ pt. water (1 c.)
1 pt. milk (2 c.)	Vanilla essence
6 oz. sugar (¾ c.)	4 large bananas

2 eggs

Salt

½ oz. butter (1 Tbs.)

Red and yellow jam or
jelly

Measures level. Boil the rice in the milk with 2 Tbs. sugar, see No. 640. When tender add the egg yolks and the butter. Season with a pinch of salt and spread in a shallow heat-resisting serving dish. Make a syrup with 2 oz. (4 Tbs.) sugar and the water. Flavour well with vanilla. Peel the bananas and slice in half lengthwise and then across. Poach until tender in the syrup. Drain and arrange on the rice. Beat the egg whites with a pinch of salt and, when stiff, fold in the remaining 3 oz. (6 Tbs.) sugar. Put in small heaps over the bananas and bake in a slow oven 350° F. (180° C.) Mark 3 until the meringue is set and very lightly browned. Decorate between heaps of meringue with alternating colours of jam. Serve hot or cold.

644. Lemon Meringue Pudding. Cooking time 30–40 minutes

Quantities for 4 helpings:

1½ oz. rice, sago or small
   tapioca (3 Tbs.)

1 pt. milk (2 c.)

3 Tbs. sugar

2 egg yolks

Pinch of salt

½ oz. butter or margarine
   (1 Tbs.)

Grated rind 1 lemon

1½ Tbs. lemon juice

Meringue

2 egg whites

2 Tbs. sugar

Measures level. Cook the cereal in the milk as in Recipe No. 640, adding the egg yolks with the sugar. Add the lemon at the end and pour into a greased baking-dish. Cover the top with meringue, see No. 765. Bake in a slow oven 350° F. (180° C.) Mark 3, until the meringue is set. Serve hot.

645. Recipe for Making a Mould (using cornflour, arrowroot, fine semolina, or ground rice). Cooking time 5–8 minutes

Quantities for 4 helpings:

4 Tbs. cereal
2 Tbs. sugar
Pinch salt
1 pt. liquid (2 c.)

Flavouring to taste
½ oz. butter or margarine
    (1 Tbs.)

Measures level.

1. Mix the first three ingredients to a smooth paste with a little cold liquid. This may be milk, fruit juice, coffee, etc. Boil the rest of the liquid, and pour into the blended mixture, stirring well.

2. Return to the pan and stir until it boils. Cook gently for 1 minute for arrowroot and 5–8 minutes for the other cereals. Care should be taken not to use too much cereal, as this makes the mixture difficult to cook and unpleasant to eat.

If milk is used for the liquid you will find it easier to cook it over boiling water, in a double boiler. In that case allow about 20 minutes' cooking. Add flavouring to taste, and the fat.

3. Grease the mould lightly with oil, as this gives the finished mould a sheen. Pour in the mixture and leave until quite cold before turning out.

Serve with stewed or bottled fruit, Fresh Fruit Salad, No. 584, or Jam Sauce, No. 101.

646. Mould with Egg

Use 1 Tbs. less cereal for each egg added. Make according to No. 645, adding one or two beaten eggs at the end of cooking. Cook for 2 or 3 minutes longer without boiling. If preferred, the yolks only may be used and the whites beaten stiffly and folded in when cooking is finished.

647. Chocolate Mould

Make according to No. 645, adding an extra Tbs. of sugar and 2 Tbs. cocoa with the cereal. Flavour with vanilla essence. Serve with stewed fruit or a Fruit Sauce, No. 100. Rhubarb, pears, and plums are specially good with chocolate mould. For variety add 1 tsp. grated orange rind to the cooked mould.

648. Chocolate Mould with Raisins

Make as No. 647, and stir in 2 Tbs. raisins before pouring it into the mould. Turn out and serve with gooseberry or raspberry jam, or Jam Sauce, No. 101.

649. Coffee Mould

Make according to No. 645, using half milk and half strong black coffee. Flavour with vanilla. Serve with cream or decorate with cream.

650. Fruit Mould

Make according to No. 645, using milk for the liquid. Decorate the bottom of individual moulds with canned or stewed fruit drained from the liquid. Pour in the mould and leave to set. Serve with a sauce made with the fruit juice, see No. 100.

651. Ring Mould with Fruit

Make according to No. 645, using milk or fruit juice for the liquid. Pour into a greased ring or border mould and leave to set. Turn out and fill the centre with Fresh Fruit Salad, No. 584, or with Fruit Compote, No. 589.

652. Desserts

These are made in exactly the same way as the mould, No. 645, except that less cereal is used and the dessert is served in individual dishes instead of being moulded. They may be decorated by piping the top with whipped cream, and adding cherries, nuts, and chopped fruit.

2–3 Tbs. cornflour, arrowroot, fine semolina, ground rice, or custard powder	2 Tbs. sugar
	1 pt. liquid (2 c.)
	Flavouring
Pinch of salt	½ oz. butter or margarine (1 Tbs.)

Method as for No. 645.

653. Butterscotch Dessert

Make according to No. 652, but leave out the sugar and fat. Heat ½ oz. (1 Tbs.) of butter with 4 oz. brown sugar (½ c.) until liquid. Add this to the cooked pudding and stir until it dissolves. Flavour with vanilla essence and pour into individual dishes. Serve very cold. This is very much improved if you can spare 2 egg whites to beat stiff and add at the end. Fold them in gently. The yolks may be used, too, as in No. 646, or kept for some other dish.

654. Caramel Dessert

Heat 4 Tbs. sugar and 2 Tbs. water in a small heavy pan until it has turned a light caramel colour. Make the dessert according to No. 652, using milk for the liquid and dissolving the caramel in the hot milk before proceeding in the usual way. Flavour with vanilla essence.

655. Chocolate Peppermint Dessert

Make according to No. 652. Divide in two portions. Mix 3 Tbs. cocoa and an extra 2 Tbs. sugar with a little boiling water and stir into one half. Flavour with vanilla. Colour the other half pale green and flavour with peppermint essence. Put the two mixtures in alternate layers in individual glasses.

656. Mocha Dessert

Make according to No. 652, adding 2 Tbs. cocoa and an extra 2 Tbs. sugar with the cereal and using half milk and half coffee for the liquid. Flavour with vanilla. Less sugar may be used if a bitter-sweet mocha is preferred.

657. Dessert with Fruit Purée

Use 1 lb. (500 g.) fruit to make a purée as in No. 602. Make it up to 1 pt. (2 c.) with water and use this liquid to make the dessert. Any fruit may be used, but some of the best are blackberries, elderberries, quinces, raspberries, loganberries, black or red currants, cranberries, damsons, apples flavoured with spice or lemon rind, and rhubarb. Some extra sugar may be needed with sour fruits.

CHAPTER 16

Sugar, Sweets, Icings, and Cake Fillings

658. Food Value

Sugar is chiefly a source of calories. It is more easily digested than foods like fats, cereals, and starches, and is specially useful when the body needs an immediate supply of energy. It also relieves fatigue after strenuous exertion. Unfortunately, sugar eaten in excess dulls the appetite for other important foods, which is a serious matter where children are concerned. If more sugar is eaten than is needed for the energy we expend, the surplus is stored in the body as fat.

659. Kinds of Sugar and Ways of Using

BARBADOS SUGAR. A fine, dark-brown sugar used in making fruit cakes and gingerbreads of certain kinds. Also used for sprinkling on porridge. The flavour is too strong for it to be used for sweetening fruit.

CASTER SUGAR. A fine, white sugar useful for most sweetening purposes, especially for sprinkling on puddings and fresh fruit and for cake-making, when it produces a finer texture than granulated sugar.

DEMERARA SUGAR. A coarse, light-brown sugar mainly used on porridge and for sweetening coffee. It is too coarse to be used successfully in cake-making, but may be used to sweeten fruit.

GLUCOSE. Sold in powder or liquid form. Generally used for medicinal purposes, and mixed with other sugar to produce a fine texture in sweets and icings.

GRANULATED SUGAR. A coarse, white sugar used for general cooking purposes.

HONEY. Used mainly as a spread, but may also be used in cakes in the same way as syrup and for sweetening fruit.

ICING SUGAR. A powdered sugar used mainly for icings and for sprinkling on cakes and puddings for decoration. It is used in some kinds of cakes and biscuits where a specially fine texture is required.

LOAF SUGAR. This is granulated sugar in lumps convenient for serving with beverages. It is also useful for rubbing on oranges and lemons to obtain a slight flavour for a sauce or pudding.

MAPLE SUGAR OR SYRUP. This is made from the sugar maple tree, and is very much used in Canada and the U.S.A. The syrup can be used in the same way as golden syrup.

PIECES. A fine, light-brown sugar used for general cooking purposes where brown sugar is specified in the recipe. Also called soft brown sugar.

GOLDEN SYRUP. Used for a spread and for making cakes, puddings, sauces, and for sweetening fruit.

TREACLE. Darker than syrup, but can be used in the same way in any dish where the stronger flavour is not a disadvantage. It is a good source of iron.

JAM. Contains 60 per cent sugar, and can be used for sweetening sauces and puddings.

660. Sugar Temperatures Used in Making Sweets and Icings

When sugar is heated, either alone or with a little water, it first of all melts or dissolves in the water, and then comes to the boil. The longer it boils the hotter it becomes, until it turns brown or caramelizes, and finally chars or burns. Different kinds of sweets are made by stopping the cooking at different temperatures. Although these temperatures may be guessed at, it is much safer and more satisfactory to use a sugar thermometer. The same one is suitable for deep fat frying, see No. 149.

It is important to use the temperature recommended in the recipe if good results are expected.

THREAD STAGE. 225° F. (110° C.). When a little syrup is dropped from the spoon a very fine thread is seen.

SOFT BALL STAGE. 240° F. (115° C.). When a little syrup is dropped into a cup of cold water it can be gathered together in a small ball.

HARD BALL STAGE. 250° F. (120° C.). As for the soft ball, but instead the syrup forms a hard ball.

CRACK OR BRITTLE STAGE. 290° F. (145° C.). When the syrup is dropped into a cup of cold water it immediately hardens and crackles. With a plain sugar and water toffee this stage is reached when the mixture turns pale brown.

CARAMEL STAGE. 350° F. (180° C.). The syrup turns brown.

If the sugar and water syrup is stirred during boiling it forms crystals, therefore all sweets are made without stirring after the syrup has come to the boil. Some syrup crystallizes on the sides of the pan, and this can be washed down with a pastry-brush dipped in water. Lemon juice, glucose, or cream of tartar is sometimes added to recipes to keep the texture of the sweet from becoming coarse and granular.

Fudges and similar sweets are stirred and beaten after cooking, when they have cooled to 110° F. (45° C.). If a fine texture is desired, the sweets should never be beaten during or immediately after cooking has finished.

661. Glazing with Sugar

Certain sweet dishes, such as custards, sweet omelets, and fruit dishes, are improved by being glazed with sugar after cooking. This may be done by sprinkling with icing sugar and heating under a fierce grill until the sugar caramelizes.

Buns and other yeast mixtures are glazed by brushing

with a mixture of sugar and water as soon as they come out of the oven. To make the glaze mix 2 level Tbs. sugar with 2 Tbs. water and bring to the boil.

662. Coloured Sugar

This is used for decorating cold sweets and cakes. It is made by putting granulated sugar on a plate and adding a few drops of the required colour. Work it into the sugar with the fingers and spread in a warm place to dry thoroughly before storing in a covered jar ready for use.

663. Lemon or Orange Sugar

Rub lumps of sugar over the rind of an orange or a lemon until the sugar is well coloured. Crush, and dry in a warm place before storing. Use for flavouring puddings and sauces.

TOFFEE AND SWEETS

664. Plain Toffee

8 oz. granulated sugar (1 c.)	$\frac{1}{8}$ pt. of water ($\frac{1}{4}$ c.) Pinch of cream of tartar

Measures level. Heat together in a pan, stirring until the sugar is dissolved and the mixture boils. Boil, without stirring, until the toffee reaches the crack stage (290° F., 145° C.), see No. 660. Pour into a greased flat tin and mark in squares. Break when cold. To make nut toffee, put the prepared nuts in a greased tin and pour the toffee over. Almonds and peanuts should be blanched and roasted.

665. Toffee Apples

6 medium-sized apples	Toffee recipe, No. 664

Wash the apples and wipe them quite dry. Fasten each one on a stick or wooden skewer. Make the toffee, remove from the heat, and dip the apples in quickly before it has time to set, twisting each one round to coat it well. Stand on a greased tray to set, with the sticks upright.

666. Marzipan Toffees

Roll marzipan, No. 685, into small balls. If walnuts are available, press one half on each side of the marzipan, but the balls may be dipped alone. Make Toffee, No. 664. Remove the pan from the heat and dip each sweet in the toffee, using a cocktail stick or a small piece of wire with a loop on the end. Place on a greased baking-tray and leave to harden. You must work quickly, or the toffee will set before the sweets are all coated.

667. Cinnamon Drops

Quantities for 24 drops:

4 oz. granulated sugar ($\frac{1}{2}$ c.)	$2\frac{1}{2}$ tsp. ground cinnamon
	$\frac{1}{4}$ c. water

Measures level. Mix the cinnamon and sugar, add the water and cook as Plain Toffee, No. 664. Drop from the point of a teaspoon in small blobs on to a greased tray. Leave to harden.

668. Chocolate Fudge

$\frac{1}{4}$ pt. milk ($\frac{1}{2}$ c.)	3 Tbs. cocoa
1 oz. butter or margarine (25 g.)	Pinch of salt
$\frac{3}{4}$ lb. sugar ($1\frac{1}{2}$ c.)	$\frac{1}{2}$ tsp. vanilla essence

Measures level. Mix all the ingredients together, except the vanilla. Stir and heat until the sugar has dissolved and the mixture boils. Boil gently until it reaches the soft ball stage, see No. 660. Remove from the heat and allow to cool to 110° F. (45° C.). Then add the vanilla and beat hard until the mixture is thick. Pour into a greased tin and mark in squares. Leave overnight before cutting.

669. Crumb Fudge

2 Tbs. syrup
2 oz. margarine (50 g.)
2 oz. sugar (4 Tbs.)
1 tsp. salt
Vanilla essence

6 oz. cereal crumbs, No. 632, or sweet biscuit crumbs (1 c.)
2 oz. cocoa (6 Tbs.)

Measures level. Mix all the ingredients together very thoroughly and turn into a greased 7-inch (18 cm.) tin, spreading the mixture out smoothly with a palette knife. Mark into fingers or squares and leave overnight before cutting. For variety a dozen chopped dates or nuts may be added to the other ingredients.

670. Coconut Ice

1 lb. sugar (2 c.)
$\frac{1}{4}$ pt. milk ($\frac{1}{2}$ c.)

5 oz. coconut (1$\frac{1}{2}$ c.)
Colouring to taste

Measures level. Mix the sugar and milk in a pan and bring to the boil, stirring until dissolved. Boil gently until it reaches the soft ball stage, see No. 660. Add the coconut and colour to taste or leave white. Pour into a shallow greased tin, mark in squares, and leave to set. If desired the mixture may be divided in two after the coconut has been added. Pour one half into a tin, colour the other pink, and pour on top of the first lot to make two layers.

671. Marshmallows

8 oz. granulated sugar
    (1 c.)
$\frac{1}{2}$ pt. hot water (1 c.)

1$\frac{1}{2}$ Tbs. gelatine
$\frac{1}{2}$ tsp. cream of tartar
Vanilla or other flavouring

Measures level. Mix all ingredients except the flavouring, and heat, stirring until the sugar has dissolved. Boil for 2 or 3 minutes. Pour into a basin and leave to cool until a skin begins to form on top. Then beat hard until the mixture is thick and white. Add flavouring to taste and pour into a greased tin which has been dusted with icing sugar. When quite set cut in cubes and roll in icing sugar. This may be varied by adding chopped dates, cherries, or nuts to the mixture before pouring it into the tin.

672. Turkish Delight

1 oz. gelatine (3 Tbs.)
1 lb. sugar (500 g.)
½ pt. hot water (1 c.)

½ Tbs. lemon juice
Flavouring and colouring
 to taste

Measures level. Mix all ingredients except the flavouring and colouring and heat until the sugar has dissolved. Bring to the boil and boil gently for 2 or 3 minutes. Add flavouring and colouring and pour into a dish which has been rinsed with cold water. Leave to set. Cut in squares and roll in crushed and sieved icing sugar.

To make *Crème de Menthe*, flavour the mixture with a few drops of peppermint essence and colour a pale green.

ICINGS

673. General Information

The elaborate decorations confectioners make for wedding cakes are learnt by much practice, but it is possible to produce very artistic effects with simple home decorations. Sets of icing tubes may be purchased either with a forcing tube to match or you can use a cone-shaped nylon bag with a hole in the end just large enough to take the icing tube. If you have not used these before it is a good plan to practise the design you want to make, on a flat plate. The icing can be scraped off and used again on the cake. Suitable icings to use are Nos. 677–84 or 686–7, and the mixture should be stiff enough to hold its shape, but not so stiff that forcing is difficult. For writing, Water Icing, No. 674, is the best to use, and a tube with a small round hole in the end. If you are not skilled in writing in icing you will find it a help to prick the letters lightly on the cake with the point of a fine skewer or darning-needle and then follow the markings with the icing. In the same way you can mark the places for your decorations.

Ready-made decorations can be bought at most stores, and only require to be fixed in position on the moist icing.

The following are other useful decorations:

Coloured sugars, see No. 662.

Candied fruits and marzipan fruits.

Chopped or whole nuts.

Crystallized cherries and other fruit.

Angelica, green for stems of flowers.

Coconut, desiccated or shredded.

Chocolate shavings made by warming a bar of chocolate slightly and cutting thin shavings with a knife.

Coloured sweets.

Flavourings and colourings must be added very carefully. The easiest way with flavourings is to tip a little in a tea-spoon and add it drop by drop to the icing. Colours are generally stronger, and they should be added by dipping a metal skewer into the colour and letting a drop fall into the icing. Pale colours always look better than vivid ones.

When making orange or lemon icings use the juice for mixing, and also some of the finely grated yellow rind.

TO ICE WITH ROYAL ICING. Place the cake on an up-turned plate, with a piece of clean paper under to catch any icing that drops. Pour the icing into the centre of the cake and let it flow over the top and round the sides. Take a palette knife and dip it in hot water. Run it round the sides of the cake to give a smooth finish. It is better to leave the top alone, and it should be smooth with the icing which has flowed over.

If a glacé icing is used this should be poured over, and not smoothed with a knife. If a butter or fudge icing is used it is spread on with a knife dipped in hot water. The surface may be made smooth for decorating or roughed with the knife or a fork.

Small cakes should be put on a flat knife or a clean cake-rack and the icing poured over. Have a clean piece of paper under the knife or rack to catch icing as it falls. For putting a small blob of icing on biscuits or small cakes use a teaspoon and let the icing spread itself, or, alternatively, dip the top of the biscuit in the icing.

674. Glacé or Water Icing

8 oz. icing sugar (250 g.) Flavouring and colouring
Warm water or fruit   to taste
   juice – about 2 Tbs.

Measures level. Crush and sieve the icing sugar. Mix with warm liquid or mix over hot water. Add enough liquid to make the icing coat the back of a spoon without running off too freely. Beat well and add colouring and flavouring to taste. Pour over the cake as described in No. 673. The icing should dry with a shine, but will lose the shine if over-heated. $\frac{1}{2}$ oz. (1 Tbs.) butter or margarine may be added for each $\frac{1}{2}$ lb. (250 g.) of icing sugar used.

675. Chocolate Glacé Icing

Add to No. 674 4–6 level Tbs. cocoa mixed with a little boiling water. Flavour with vanilla. It may also be made by adding 2 oz. (50 g.) chocolate melted over hot water.

676. Coffee Glacé Icing

Make as No. 674, using coffee essence or strong black coffee for the liquid.

677. Butter Icing

Quantities for the inside and top of an 8-inch sandwich:

8 oz. icing sugar (250 g.)   Milk, water, or fruit juice
1–3 oz. butter or margarine   Colouring and flavouring to
  (25–75 g.)   taste

Measures level. Soften the fat and beat in the crushed and sieved icing sugar, adding enough liquid to give the desired consistency. It should be thick enough to hold its shape for piping or spreading, but thinner to spread over a cake. Flavour and colour to taste. This icing does not harden on standing.

678. Chocolate Butter Icing

Make as No. 677, adding 2 oz. (50 g.) melted chocolate or 6 level Tbs. cocoa mixed with a little boiling water. Flavour with vanilla.

679. Mocha Butter Icing

Make as No. 678, adding 1 tsp. soluble coffee.

680. Chocolate Orange Icing

Make as No. 678, adding the grated rind of half an orange and using the juice for mixing.

681. Coffee Butter Icing

Make as No. 677, adding soluble coffee to taste and flavouring with vanilla essence.

682. Orange or Lemon Butter Icing

Make as No. 677, adding the grated rind of 1 orange or lemon and using the juice for mixing.

683. Liqueur Icing

Make according to No. 674 or No. 677, adding wine, brandy, rum, or liqueur for the liquid.

684. Spicy Icing

Make according to No. 674, adding ¼ level tsp. each of ground nutmeg, cloves, and cinnamon.

685. Almond Paste, or Marzipan

Quantities for an 8-inch (20 cm.) cake:

8 oz. ground almonds (250 g.)
8 oz. icing sugar (250 g.) or 4 oz. icing sugar and 4 oz. caster sugar

2 egg yolks
2 tsp. lemon juice
Few drops almond essence
¼ tsp. rosewater

Measures level. Mix the almonds and sugar together. Add the beaten eggs and the flavouring and mix and knead very thoroughly. To cover a cake, turn upside down and brush over with melted jelly or a thick sugar-and-water syrup to make the paste stick. Roll a piece of paste into a circle the size of the top of the cake and roll strips for the sides. Leave overnight to set before covering with white icing.

686. Royal Icing

Quantities for an 8-inch (20 cm.) cake:

1 lb. icing sugar (500 g.)
2 egg whites

Juice of ½ lemon
Water if necessary

Measures level. Roll and sieve the icing sugar. Beat the egg whites and mix in the sugar and lemon, beating well until the mixture is thick and light. Use as described in No. 673.

687. Marshmallow Icing (may be used in place of Royal Icing)

Quantities for a 9–10-inch (22–25 cm.) cake:

3 tsp. gelatine
¼ pt. hot water (½ c.)
8 oz. icing sugar (250 g.)

Flavouring and colouring
    to taste

Measures level. Dissolve the gelatine in the hot water. Allow to cool, but not set. Roll and sieve the icing sugar. Beat in the liquid gradually and beat until the mixture is thick and shiny. Add flavouring and colouring to taste. This does not set hard like Royal Icing. It may be used for piping. This icing may also be made by using granulated sugar. Boil it with the water and gelatine for 2–3 minutes, cool until it begins to thicken, and then beat until thick enough to spread.

688. Fudge Icing

Quantities for a 6–8-inch (15–20 cm.) cake:

1 oz. margarine (25 g.)
8 oz. granulated sugar
    (250 g.)

½ pt. milk (1 c.)
Flavouring to taste

Measures level. Mix the ingredients together, and stir until the sugar is dissolved and the mixture boils. Cook to the soft ball stage, see No. 660. Then beat until the right consistency for spreading. Flavour to taste.

689. White Mountain Icing

Quantities for an 8-inch (20 cm.) cake:

8 oz. granulated sugar
    (250 g.)
Pinch of cream of tartar
Pinch of baking powder

¼ c. hot water
1 egg white
Pinch of salt
1 Tbs. lemon juice

Measures level. Mix the sugar, cream of tartar, and baking powder in a small pan. Add the water and stir until it boils. Beat the egg white and salt until stiff and beat in the sugar syrup a spoonful at a time. When half has been added, add the lemon juice and the rest of the syrup. Put the basin over boiling water and beat hard until it reaches the desired consistency. If it becomes too thick add a little boiling water and continue to beat over the hot water. Unlike Royal Icing, this does not set hard.

690. Milk Chocolate Icing

Quantities for a 6–8-inch (15–20 cm.) cake:

1 oz. margarine (25 g.)	1 c. sifted icing sugar
3 Tbs. cocoa or 1 oz. chocolate (25 g.)	Pinch of salt
2½ Tbs. milk	½ tsp. vanilla essence

Measures level. Melt the margarine and cocoa or chocolate over hot water. Scald the milk and pour it hot into the icing sugar and salt. Stir until the sugar dissolves and add the vanilla. Add the chocolate mixture and cool a little. Beat until thick enough for spreading.

691. Butter Cream

4 oz. butter or margarine (125 g.)	Milk
2–4 oz. caster sugar or icing sugar (4–8 Tbs.)	Flavouring

Measures level. Cream the butter and sugar until very smooth and fluffy. Gradually beat in cold milk until it is the required thickness. Flavour to taste. This is suitable for use as a cake-filling or for piping and decorations.

CAKE FILLINGS

692. Confectioner's Custard or Crème Pâtissière
(cake fillings, éclairs, etc.).

1 oz. cornflour (3 Tbs.)	1 egg
1 oz. sugar (2 Tbs.)	½ pt. milk (1 c.)
Pinch of salt	Vanilla essence to taste

Measures level. Make a sauce by the Blending Method, No. 95, adding the egg yolk to the sauce during making, and folding the stiffly-beaten egg white in at the end. If necessary, thin with a little cream or top milk. Add the vanilla and cool before using, stirring occasionally as it cools.

693. Coffee Filling

Add soluble coffee to taste to No. 692.

694. Lemon Curd

Rind and juice of 2 lemons	2 oz. butter or margarine
3 eggs	(50 g.)
8 oz. sugar (1 c.)	

Measures level. Grate the lemon rind and strain the juice. Beat the eggs slightly. Put all the ingredients in a pan and cook slowly over boiling water until the mixture thickens slightly. It will thicken more when it cools. If required for keeping pour at once into hot, sterilized jars and seal while hot.

695. Orange Filling

4 oz. sugar (½ c.)	½ Tbs. lemon juice
1 Tbs. cornflour	1 egg
Rind of ½ orange	1 tsp. butter
¼ c. orange juice	

Measures level. Mix the ingredients in the order given and cook for 15 minutes over boiling water, stirring occasionally. Leave until cold before using. This makes enough for two or three cakes and will keep quite well in a cold place.

696. Butter Cream Filling

Quantities for $\frac{3}{4}$ pt. (4 dl.):

2 Tbs. cornflour, custard
  powder, or arrowroot
$\frac{1}{2}$ pt. milk (1 c.)
2 oz. butter or margarine
  (50 g.)

2 oz. caster sugar (4 Tbs.)
Flavouring to taste

Measures level. Make the cornflour and milk into a sauce by the Blending Method, No. 95. Cook gently for 5 minutes, or 10 minutes over boiling water. Press a margarine paper over the top and leave to cool. The paper prevents a skin from forming. Cream the margarine and sugar until white and like whipped cream. Then beat in the cool, but not cold, cornflour mixture a spoonful at a time. Beat thoroughly before adding each spoonful and flavour to taste with essence, liqueur, grated orange or lemon rind.

CHOCOLATE CREAM. Add 2 level Tbs. of cocoa to the cornflour. Flavour with vanilla essence.

COFFEE CREAM. Add coffee essence or soluble coffee to the milk. Flavour with vanilla essence.

697. Honey and Almond Filling

4 oz. softened butter
  (125 g.)

4 oz. honey (4 Tbs.)
4 oz. ground almonds (1 c.)

Measures level. Beat together until creamy and soft and use to fill and ice a sandwich or layer cake. Decorate with almonds.

Other Recipes Suitable for Cake Fillings are Nos. 677–684 and 687–691.

CHAPTER 17

Jellies and Aspic

698. Food Value

Gelatine is a protein. As very small amounts are used, any value the dish may have as a food comes from additions made to the jelly, such as milk, cream, eggs, fruit, meat, fish, etc.

699. Kinds of Gelatine

The most popular are the prepared jellies, either jelly crystals or the solid form. In either case all that is required to make them is the use of boiling water to dissolve the gelatine. They consist of gelatine, sugar, flavouring and colouring.

Plain granulated gelatine sold in packets is useful for making all kinds of jellies, as you then add flavouring and colouring to suit your own taste.

700. Using Gelatine

It is advisable to follow the instructions issued by the manufacturer.

The general proportions of gelatine are $\frac{1}{2}$ oz. ($1\frac{1}{2}$ level Tbs.) to each pint (2 c.) of liquid. In very hot weather, if you have no refrigerator or cold larder in which to put the jelly, a little more gelatine may be needed, but it is important not to add more than is absolutely necessary, for too much not only spoils the flavour, but also makes the jelly stiff and unappetizing to eat. It should be stiff enough to hold its shape when turned out, but should quiver easily when the dish is shaken.

When gelatine is added to a milk mixture the powder should first be dissolved in hot water and should not be added to the milk until it is lukewarm, or it will curdle.

Acid liquids such as lemon juice and the juice from some bottled fruits need a little more gelatine. Fresh pineapple added to a jelly will prevent it from setting owing to an enzyme present in the fruit.

Plain jellies may be beaten and made light and fluffy. To do this let the jelly become quite cold and begin to thicken. Then beat hard with an egg-whisk until it is thick and light. It may be set in a mould in the usual way or piled up in individual glasses. Sometimes half the mould is set with one kind of plain jelly, and then another kind of whipped jelly is poured on top and left to set. This gives an attractive appearance when the jelly is turned out.

701. Moulding the Jelly

Metal moulds are the best, as jellies made in them are easier to turn out than from the thick porcelain or plastic moulds. They are sold in many different shapes and designs. A ring or border mould, one with a hole in the centre, is a very useful kind for special occasions.

To set a jelly with fruit and vegetables in it allow the jelly to cool until it just begins to thicken, then stir in the fruit or vegetables which have been well drained of all moisture. Stir well and pour into the mould. The slightly thickened jelly holds the fruit in place and prevents it from all sinking to the bottom or all floating on the top.

To make layers of different kinds of fruit or vegetables in the jelly, begin by pouring in a layer of about $\frac{1}{2}$ inch (1 cm.) of clear jelly. It is a great help to have some ice to put round the mould to hasten setting. Let the rest of the jelly cool until it just begins to thicken. When the layer of jelly is set, arrange the fruit or vegetables on it, making an attractive design. Then spoon the thickened jelly over in a thin layer.

Arrange alternate layers of thickened jelly and the rest of the fruit and vegetables, finishing with jelly. Leave to set.

If you want to decorate the sides of the mould also, press the decorations into the layer of thickened jelly, pushing them against the sides of the mould. The thickened jelly should hold them in position.

702. To Turn Out of the Mould

Have a basin of hot water deeper than the mould. Hold the mould in it for a few seconds with the water level with the top line of the jelly. Remove and wipe dry. Loosen the jelly round the edge with the point of a sharp knife. Twirl the mould and shake to loosen the jelly. If it still sticks, heat again, but be careful not to melt the jelly and thereby spoil the shape. Turn out on the dish.

703. Lemon or Orange Jelly

Quantities for 6–8 helpings:

1 oz. gelatine (3 Tbs.)
$1\frac{1}{2}$ pt. boiling water (3 c.)
2–4 oz. sugar (4–8 Tbs.)

$\frac{1}{4}$ pt. lemon or orange juice ($\frac{1}{2}$ c.)

Measures level. Dissolve the gelatine in the boiling water. Add the sugar and dissolve it. Add the strained juice. Pour into the mould, or use as a basis for setting fruit as described in No. 701.

704. Lemon or Orange Snow

Quantities for 3–4 helpings:

Rind and juice of $1\frac{1}{2}$ lemons or 1 orange
$1\frac{1}{2}$ oz. sugar (3 Tbs.)
$\frac{1}{2}$ pt. water (1 c.)

$\frac{1}{2}$ oz. gelatine ($1\frac{1}{2}$ Tbs.)
1 egg white
Whipped cream

Measures level. Peel off the yellow rind of the lemons very thinly, using a potato peeler. Put in a small pan with the sugar and water and bring to the boil. Strain on to the gelatine and stir until it dissolves, heating again if necessary. Allow to cool and then add the lemon juice and the egg white and whisk until stiff. Pile into glass dishes and garnish with whipped cream, slightly tinted if desired.

705. Crème de Menthe Jelly

Make Lemon Jelly, No. 703, or use a packet jelly. Colour it pale green and flavour with a few drops of peppermint essence, but do not add enough to take away the flavour of the lemon. Pour into a shallow glass dish and serve in the dish with cream or custard handed separately.

706. Milk Jelly (with evaporated milk)

Quantities for 3–4 helpings:

1-pt. packet jelly
$\frac{1}{4}$ pt. hot water ($\frac{1}{2}$ c.)
$\frac{1}{4}$ pt. cold water ($\frac{1}{2}$ c.)

$\frac{1}{2}$ pt. evaporated milk (undiluted) (1 c.)

Dissolve the jelly in the hot water and add the cold water. When the jelly is cold and just beginning to set, add the milk gradually. Pour into the moulds. Turn out and serve with stewed fruit.

707. Milk Jelly Squares

Make the milk jelly in two different flavours and colours. Set in two shallow dishes and then cut in squares. Serve with fruit salad.

708. Cream Whip

Quantities for 4 helpings:

1 Tbs. gelatine
$\frac{3}{4}$ pt. fruit-juice (1$\frac{1}{2}$ c.)
Sugar to taste
Colouring to taste

$\frac{1}{4}$ pt. undiluted evaporated milk, custard, or cream ($\frac{1}{2}$ c.)

Dissolve the gelatine in a little hot water. Add the fruit juice. Sweeten to taste and add colouring if necessary. Cool until the mixture is just beginning to set. Add the milk or cream and beat until light and frothy. Set in a mould or pile in individual dishes. Chopped fruit may be added.

709. Orange Mousse

Quantities for 4–6 helpings:

1 pt. packet orange jelly (2 c.)
¼ pt. evaporated milk or single cream (½ c.)

2 egg whites
1 oz. caster sugar (2 Tbs.)
Orange slices to garnish
Whipped cream (optional)

Measures level. Make the jelly with only half the usual amount of water. Cool, and when it begins to thicken, add the milk or cream and beat until light. Beat the egg whites stiff and beat in the sugar. Fold this into the jelly and put the mixture in a large bowl or individual dishes. Serve garnished with whipped cream and slices of fresh orange or canned mandarin segments.

710. Bavarois. Cooking time 10 minutes

Quantities for 6–8 helpings:

4 egg yolks
½ pt. milk (1 c.)
2 oz. gran. sugar (4 Tbs.)

¼ oz. gelatine (¾ Tbs.)
½ pt. whipping cream (1 c.)
1 oz. caster sugar (2 Tbs.)
Flavouring

Measures level. Mix egg yolks, milk, granulated sugar and gelatine and cook over boiling water or a very gentle heat. Stir with a wooden spoon until the mixture begins to thicken and coat the back of the spoon. Stand the pan in cold water and stir occasionally as it cools. Whip the cream until thick and light but not stiff. Add the caster sugar and whisk lightly into the cold egg mixture.

Flavourings: Add to the egg mixture either vanilla or almond essence; soluble coffee to taste; 3 oz. (75 g.) grated bitter chocolate; finely grated rind of 1 orange or lemon; kirsch, rum or any liqueur.

711. Prune Jelly

Quantities for 6–8 helpings:

1 lb. prunes (500 g.)
1½ pt. water (3 c.)
Strip of lemon rind
¾ oz. gelatine (2 Tbs.)

2 Tbs. sugar
1 Tbs. lemon juice or the
   grated rind of 1 orange

Measures level. Soak the prunes overnight in the water, add the lemon rind, and then cook until the fruit is tender. Rub through a sieve, re-heat, and add the gelatine. Stir until it dissolves. Add the sugar and lemon juice or orange rind, and pour into the mould. Serve with custard or cream.

712. Golden Jelly

Quantities for 4 helpings:

½ oz. gelatine (1½ Tbs.)
1 pt. hot water (2 c.)
6 oz. golden syrup (6 Tbs.)
Finely grated rind of 2
  lemons

4 Tbs. lemon juice
Custard sauce or cream

Measures level. Dissolve the gelatine in the hot water. Add the syrup and lemon rind and stir until the syrup is dissolved. Add the lemon juice and pour into a mould to set. Serve with custard sauce or cream.

713. Charlotte Russe

Quantities for a 2-pint (1 l.) soufflé dish:

1 pt. lemon jelly (2 c.)
Glacé cherries and
　angelica
1 packet sponge fingers
½ oz. gelatine (1½ Tbs.)

4 Tbs. hot water
½ pt. double cream (1 c.)
¼ pt. milk (½ c.)
2 oz. caster sugar (4 Tbs.)
Vanilla or liqueur

Measures level. Prepare the jelly and allow it to cool. Put a ¼ inch (6 mm.) layer in the bottom of a soufflé dish or similar dish. Chill to set the jelly. Arrange decorations of cherry and angelica on the jelly and spoon over more jelly to the depth of ½ inch (1 cm.) total. Chill to set. Trim the ends of the sponge fingers to make them fit upright round the sides of the dish. Dip each in jelly to make it stick in place. Chill again. Dissolve the gelatine in the water. Whip the cream lightly and gradually whip in the milk and sugar. Fold in the gelatine and add flavouring to taste. Pour carefully into the mould. Chill to set. Unmould and decorate with any remaining jelly, chopped. The recipe can be varied by adding chopped fruit to the cream mixture before putting it in the mould.

714. Cider Jelly

Quantities for 4–5 helpings:

¾ pt. water (1½ c.)
5 oz. sugar (10 Tbs.)
2 Tbs. gelatine

½ pt. dry cider (1 c.)
2 Tbs. lemon juice

Measures level. Heat the water and sugar. Dissolve the gelatine in the hot syrup and add the cider and lemon juice. Pour into moulds to set. The jelly may be used as a basis for setting fruit, see No. 701.

715. Norwegian Trifle

Quantities for 3–4 helpings:

¼ oz. gelatine (2 tsp.)	½ tsp. grated lemon rind
¼ pt. water (½ c.)	2 Tbs. lemon juice
2 eggs	Raspberry jam
2 oz. sugar (4 Tbs.)	Whipped cream

Measures level. Heat half the water and dissolve the gelatine in it. Beat the egg yolks with 1 oz. sugar (2 Tbs.), the lemon rind, and the remaining water. Put in a small pan over a very gentle heat, or in a double boiler, and cook gently, stirring frequently until the mixture begins to thicken a little. Add the gelatine and mix well. Remove from the heat and add the lemon juice. Whisk the egg whites in a bowl with a pinch of salt. Add the remaining ounce of sugar and beat until thick. Fold the lemon mixture into the egg whites and pour into one large or several individual dishes. When set, cover with a layer of raspberry jam and then decorate with whipped cream.

716. Aspic Jelly (with stock)

Use ready-prepared packet aspic, or canned consommé.

Aspic Jelly (without stock)

¼–½ oz. gelatine (¾–1½ Tbs.)	Juice of ½ lemon
⅛ pt. boiling water (¼ c.)	½ tsp. salt
½ pt. cold water (1 c.)	1 tsp. sugar
⅛ pt. vinegar (¼ c.)	Pinch of pepper

Measures level. Dissolve the gelatine in the boiling water. Add the other ingredients and use to set chopped vegetables, eggs, meat, etc.

717. Glaze (for cold dishes)

Use Aspic Jelly, No. 716. As the jelly begins to thicken it is poured over the food to be coated. If decorations are used dip them in melted glaze and then fix them in place on a layer of the glaze which has already set. Cover carefully with another layer of glaze.

718. Veal Mould or Jellied Veal

Quantities for 6–8 helpings:

1½ lb. stewing veal	Bouquet garni
Bacon rinds, bones, or trimmings	1 onion
	1 tsp. salt
1 carrot	1½ pt. water or stock (3 c.)
1 turnip	½ oz. gelatine (1½ Tbs.)

Measures level. Boil the veal, bacon rinds, seasoning, stock, and vegetables together as in No. 336; or for ½ hour in a pressure cooker. When the meat is quite tender, strain, and keep the liquid. Cut the meat in small pieces. Dissolve the gelatine in ½ pt. (1 c.) of the cooking liquid and cool until it is just beginning to set. Mix in the meat and pour into the mould, which may first be decorated with a clear layer of jelly at the bottom as in No. 701. Serve with salad. Use the rest of the stock for soup or sauces.

N.B. All meats suitable for brawn, see Nos. 325–30, may be prepared in the same way.

CHAPTER 18

Cakes, Puddings, Pastry, and Batters

719. Food Value

These all have a high calorie value which comes from the flour, sugar and fat used to make them. Other ingredients such as eggs, milk and dried fruit add to their nutritive value to a limited extent.

Cakes, puddings and pastry should be regarded as luxuries rather than necessities and not be eaten instead of more important foods like milk, cheese, meat, fish, fruits and vegetables. This is particularly important in the proper feeding of children who will sometimes eat large quantities of cakes, biscuits and puddings instead of having a well-balanced diet.

People who lead sedentary lives, or who are over-weight, are well advised to curtail their consumption of cakes, puddings and pastry.

720. Pre-Prepared Mixes and Machine Mixing

Cakes, puddings, pastry and batters are all available either completely prepared (fresh, canned or frozen), or as packet mixes which only have to be mixed up and cooked. All these can be given a personal touch by different methods of finishing and service, with sauces, icings, fillings and so on. Many people prefer to use their time and skill in this way rather than in preparing the basic mixture. Others find satisfaction in baking the old-fashioned way and today much of the hard work is removed by the use of electric mixing machines. Many people who could not make successful cakes by hand mixing now find new pleasure in home baking with the use of a machine.

Although the recipes in this book are designed for hand mixing, they can all be done with a machine, using the appropriate bowls and beaters as recommended by the manufacturer. A large mixer is necessary for heavy things like mixing flour and fruit into a rich cake, mixing yeast doughs and making choux pastry but a small portable mixer is suitable for the most important jobs of creaming fat and sugar and beating eggs, leaving only the final addition of dry ingredients to be carried out by hand. Wet mixtures like sponges and batters can be completely mixed by these smaller machines.

721. Choosing Flour

Wheat flour is the one most commonly used, and is sold as either plain or self-raising flour, which is plain flour with the raising agent already mixed in. Self-raising flour is suitable for scones, plain cakes, and any recipes which use 3-4 level tsp. baking powder to 8 oz. (250 g.) plain flour. Although it is widely used for pastry-making, it does not give a true short pastry, but a crust like a rich scone or biscuit. This is preferred by some people. Self-raising flour is not advisable for rich fruit cakes, as the large amount of raising agent tends to make the cakes rise up too much and then sink in the centre. Where the kind of flour is not specified in the recipes, either plain or self-raising may be used.

Plain flour is suitable for all cooking. It may be sold as a general-purpose flour for bread, cakes, and pastry or as flour specially prepared for either bread or cakes. A special cake-flour generally contains less gluten – the substance which makes flour tacky when it is mixed and kneaded. Too much gluten tends to make heavy cakes and pastry, especially if they are mixed or kneaded a lot.

A good flour for special cakes such as sponges can be made by mixing ordinary plain flour with some cornflour, arrowroot, or soya flour. These contain no gluten. Instead of 8 oz. flour ($1\frac{1}{2}$ c.) use 7 oz. flour ($1\frac{1}{3}$ c.) and 1 oz. corn-flour or soya flour (3 level Tbs.) sifted together. Scones and pastry which have been kneaded and rolled excessively become like rubber to handle, and are hard and tough when baked. This can be remedied in pastry by allowing the dough to 'rest' in a cool place for $\frac{1}{4}-\frac{1}{2}$ hour, when the gluten, which is responsible for the rubbery consistency, loses some of its elasticity.

Wheat-meal and whole-meal flours can be used in pastry, plain cakes, and scones, but are not suitable for rich and delicate cakes. They generally need more raising agent and more moisture than whiter flours.

Cornflour, arrowroot, and soya flour are not suitable to use alone, as they contain no gluten, and the cakes will not rise well, and will be dry and crumbly, but, as described above, they are useful for adding to ordinary wheat flour to make it suitable for special cakes. Soya flour also adds nourishment – particularly protein.

Semolina, ground rice, oatmeal, and barley products are used with a mixture of wheat flour to produce special results. They are not generally suitable for using alone.

Choosing Fats. See No. 141.

722. Choosing Sugar

For general notes on different kinds of sugar, see No. 659. Caster sugar is considered the best for cake making and for sweet pastry, as it dissolves more readily than the coarser sugars and gives a finer cake. Syrup, honey, and treacle can be used, and generally produce a closer, more moist texture, desirable in chocolate cakes and gingerbreads. Some syrup is added to fruit cakes for moistness and extra flavour.

723. Preparing the Dried Fruit

Dried fruit is sold ready-prepared for cooking and does not usually need to be washed. If this is necessary, see that the fruit is dried before it is used in cakes, although to leave currants slightly moist improves them. Damp fruit will sink. Dates may have stones to be removed before chopping them; prunes can be easily stoned if they are first put in a warm oven for a few minutes. Peel is most often sold ready cut and mixed, but if it is bought in large pieces, remove the surplus sugar and cut or mince the peel finely so that the flavour will mix well with the other ingredients. Crystallized and glacé fruits such as cherries and ginger are better if cut fairly small, because they are heavy fruits and inclined to sink.

Choosing and Using Eggs. See Nos. 179–81.

724. Choosing Flavourings

Cakes and puddings never need be dull in flavour, because of the wide variety of flavouring materials available. There are all the flavouring essences and spices, as well as chocolate and coffee. A pinch of salt, too, makes all the difference to the taste of sweet foods.

725. Raising Agents. How Mixtures are Made Light

BY AIR AND STEAM. Air is added to mixtures in three ways: by beating, as with a batter; by beating in eggs, as in sponges and creamed mixtures; and by folding a dough in layers, as when making flaky and puff pastry. When the mixture is cooked, it is made light by the expansion of cold air aided by the production of steam from water in the mixture. Mixtures which depend entirely on air and steam to make them light need careful handling in preparation and baking. They are: flaky and puff pastry, short pastry (using plain flour), true sponges, choux pastry, Yorkshire pudding, pancakes, and meringues.

BY CARBON DIOXIDE, which is a gas, and expands on heating in the same way as cold air, and so lightens the mixture. Carbon dioxide is produced in mixtures in the three following ways:

1. By using bicarbonate of soda and some acid such as cream of tartar, or the acid in sour milk, syrup, or treacle. The last three are not very accurate, as the amount of acid varies. 1 level tsp. bicarbonate of soda plus $2\frac{1}{2}$ level tsp. cream of tartar are equal to 4 level tsp. baking powder. These two should be used in the correct proportions, as if too much soda is used the flavour and colour of the mixture are spoiled. The use of extra soda is, however, liked by some, for example in soda bread and soda scones.

2. By adding baking powder or golden raising powder. These consist of bicarbonate of soda and an acid which may be cream of tartar or some other chemical. Their quality is controlled by law, and this is the most accurate way of raising mixtures.

Baking powders deteriorate if allowed to become moist, so always buy them in sealed tins and store in a dry place.

The amount of baking powder needed to raise a mixture depends on the method of mixing and the other ingredients used. A mixture containing a number of beaten eggs needs less baking powder than the same mixture with no eggs. One-stage cakes need more baking powder than well-beaten ones such as those made by conventional methods, especially when a machine is used. It is advisable to use the amounts recommended in the recipes. When plain flour is specified in a recipe this is because self-raising flour has rather too much baking powder for best results and can give a coarse texture and a sunken cake.

3. By using yeast, which is a plant, and feeds on the sugar in a mixture to give carbon dioxide. It also produces a flavour and texture peculiar to yeast goods.

726. Getting the Right Consistency

When mixing batters, cakes, and doughs, it is very important to have the right consistency. There are many ways of describing this, but the following terms are used in all the recipes in this book.

'*Mix to a thin batter*' means to add enough liquid to make the mixture the consistency of thin cream so that it flows easily when poured. It is used chiefly for Yorkshire pudding and pancakes.

'*Mix to a thick batter*' means to add enough liquid to make a mixture that will still pour but spreads slowly when dropped from a spoon. It is used for drop scones, Scotch pancakes, pikelets, fritters, some gingerbreads, and true sponges.

'*Mix to a soft cake mixture*' means to add enough liquid to make a mixture which will drop easily from the spoon with a sharp tap but is too thick to pour. This is the consistency used for most cakes.

'*Mix to a stiff cake consistency*' means to add enough liquid to make a mixture which is too sticky to handle and roll out, but stiff enough to keep its shape when put on a tray in small spoonfuls. Used for baking-powder breads, rock cakes, and similar mixtures.

'*Mix to a soft dough*' means to add enough liquid to make the mixture just stiff enough to handle and roll out. It should still be sticky to touch. It is used for scones, some biscuits, and yeast mixtures. The term 'elastic dough' is sometimes used for this consistency, but, with the exception of bread, the choice is unfortunate, for by the time a dough has become like elastic it is generally overmixed; see No. 721.

'*Mix to a stiff dough*' means to add only enough liquid to make the ingredients hold together. It is the most difficult consistency to get right, and is the cause of many failures in pastry-making. It is used for all kinds of pastry and for some biscuits.

727. Preparing Tins and Trays for Baked Goods

For notes on the choice of trays and tins see No. 24. Modern baking trays do not need to be greased unless the cake mixture contains a lot of sugar and very little fat. To grease, use a pastry brush dipped in oil or use well-oiled fingers.

Non-stick cake tins do not need greasing; others should be oiled and dusted with flour for plain cakes and sponges. A circle of non-stick paper in the bottom ensures easy removal of the cake.

Rich cakes are usually baked in tins lined with grease-proof or non-stick paper. Some people wrap the outsides of the tin with layers of brown paper but this is a relic of the past and is not necessary with modern ovens.

To line a tin with paper, put the tin on the paper, and mark round the bottom with the point of the scissors. Cut this piece out. Then cut a long strip to go round the sides of the tin and about ½ inch (1 cm.) wider. Bend up ½ inch (1 cm.) all along one side and snip at regular intervals. Put this side-piece in the tin, when the nicked edges should lie flat on the bottom. Put in the bottom piece to cover the nicked edges. This then makes a perfectly flat, smooth lining for the cake.

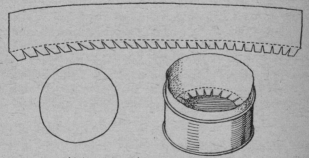

Lining a tin with greaseproof paper

728. Where to Place Tins and Trays in the Oven

Ovens vary a great deal in the way they are heated, and it is advisable to follow the maker's instructions. The following is intended only for a general guide.

Ovens heated from the bottom only (most gas ovens). Tarts, pies, small cakes, and sandwiches, between the middle and the top. Large cakes in the middle.

Ovens heated from the sides and bottom (electric). Tarts, pies, small cakes, and sandwiches, one tray top and one tray bottom. Large cakes in the middle.

Ovens heated from the sides only (electric). Pies, tarts, small cakes, and sandwiches, one tray middle and one tray top. Large cakes middle.

Ovens heated top and bottom (electric). The middle or a little below is best for all baking.

Solid fuel stoves. Small cakes and pastry near the top. Large cakes in the middle.

CAKES AND PUDDINGS
METHODS OF MIXING

729. The One-Stage Method

The ingredients are put in the mixing bowl all together, the fat used being one of the modern soft margarines or cooking fats, although butter, warmed to a soft consistency, can also be used.

The ingredients are then beaten together by hand or machine until smooth. Some people use both self-raising flour and extra baking powder in these cakes. I think this spoils the flavour and prefer to use a recipe such as No. 748.

730. The Melting Method

This is a very simple method of mixing, generally used for cakes containing syrup or treacle and for some steamed puddings.

　1. Sift the dry ingredients into the mixing-bowl and add any dried fruit in the recipe.

　2. Melt the fat and, if the recipe contains syrup or treacle,

melt it with the fat. Sometimes the sugar is heated too, but may be added to the other dry ingredients.

3. As soon as the fat and syrup are melted, but not boiling, stir into the dry ingredients and mix to a thick batter, see No. 726. Eggs are beaten and added at the same time as the melted syrup and fat. Mix until the ingredients are well blended, but do not over-beat.

4. The pan should be well greased, or lined with paper. Bake the cake as soon as it is mixed, and do not have the oven too hot, as cakes with syrup in them burn easily.

731. The Rubbing in Method

This method can be used for most mixtures where the amount of fat is not more than half the amount of flour by weight – for example, not more than 4 oz. fat to 8 oz. flour (125 g. to 250 g.).

1. The dry ingredients, such as flour, salt, baking powder, and any spices, are first sifted together to make sure they are well mixed.

2. Then the fat is rubbed in by hand or machine until the mixture looks like fine breadcrumbs. For good results, this must be done thoroughly.

3. Add the sugar and any dried fruit in the recipe.

4. Beat the eggs thoroughly and add them together with any other liquid in the recipe, and the flavouring. Any syrup or honey is added at this stage too. Mix thoroughly, but avoid over-mixing as this tends to make a heavy cake.

732. The Creaming Method

Best results are obtained if all ingredients are at room temperature.

1. Soften the fat, warming it if it is at all hard, but do not allow it to melt, or it will not cream well. Beat well with the sugar, using a wooden spoon, or mix by machine. Beat until

the mixture is white and light and the sugar no longer feels gritty. This is why caster sugar is recommended as it mixes more quickly than the coarser sugars. Any sugar or honey in the recipe should be creamed with the fat.

2. Sift all the dry ingredients together to mix them well and remove lumps.

3. Beat in the eggs one at a time, adding some of the flour if the mixture shows signs of curdling.

Add any flavouring essence.

4. Stir in the rest of the dry ingredients, together with any additional liquid in the recipe, to make a soft cake consistency, see No. 726.

5. Add any fruit and stir it in very gently. The cake should be mixed until the ingredients are smoothly blended.

733. The Sponge Method

A true sponge is made with beaten eggs, sugar, flour, and flavouring, and depends for its lightness on the air beaten in with the eggs. There are many variations of this method, some having a little melted fat added and some quite a lot.

1. Better results are obtained if all the ingredients are at room temperature or slightly warm. Stand the mixing bowl containing the eggs in another bowl of hot water for a few minutes before beginning to beat them. Beat the eggs until fluffy and then beat in the sugar until the mixture is thick and light, so that when the beater is withdrawn the surface takes some time to level out again. This is hard work unless you have an efficient beater such as an electric mixer.

2. The flour and any raising agent used should be sifted together and then cut and folded, see No. 12, into the egg mixture very gently, using a metal spoon. The object is to mix in the flour without losing any air, or more air than can be helped. The mixture should be a thick batter, see No. 726.

3. If there is any liquid or melted fat to be added it goes

in at the end, and should again be folded in carefully.

4. Turn the mixture into well-greased tins which have been dusted with flour.

5. Because of the large amount of egg they contain, sponges should be baked in a moderate oven, otherwise they become tough. A sponge is cooked if the impression made by the finger being lightly pressed on top springs back at once.

6. Run a knife round the edge of the cake to loosen it, and then turn out gently on a cake-rack, letting it fall out with its own weight.

734. How to Tell when a Cake is Cooked

A LARGE RICH CAKE. Insert a skewer or cocktail stick in the centre, and if it comes out clean, with no uncooked mixture sticking to it, the cake is done. Leave rich fruit cakes in the tin until cold; others are left to cool for a few minutes, and then turned out carefully on to a wire cake-rack.

SMALL CAKES AND SANDWICHES. Press the top lightly with the finger and, if the impression springs back quickly, the cake is cooked. It should also show signs of shrinking from the sides of the tin. Leave the cake to cool for a minute or two before turning it out. Turn carefully on to a wire cake-rack and leave to cool. Whether or not a cake turns out easily depends on how carefully you have prepared the tin, see No. 727.

The following results may be due to incorrect baking:
Oven too hot, cracked top, uneven rising, crust too brown.
Oven too slow, thick crust, coarse texture, or close heavy cake.
Not cooking long enough, heavy cake, sinking in the middle.
Cooking too long, thick crust, dry cake.
Moving while rising causes sinking in the middle.

735. Basic Mix for Large Cakes. Cooking time $1\frac{1}{4}$ hours
Temperature 350° F. (180° C.) Mark 4.

Quantities for a 7-inch (18 cm.) tin:

4 oz. margarine or other fat (125 g.)	8 oz. S.R. flour ($1\frac{1}{2}$ c.) Pinch of salt
4 oz. caster sugar ($\frac{1}{2}$ c.)	Flavouring Milk to mix, $\frac{1}{4}$ pt. ($\frac{1}{2}$ c.)
2–3 eggs	or less

Measures level. Mix to a soft cake consistency by the Creaming Method, No. 732. Bake in a greased and floured tin.

736. Cherry Cake. Cooking time $1\frac{1}{4}$ hours
Temperature 350° F. (180° C.) Mark 4.

Quantities for a 7-inch (18 cm.) tin:

Add 2 oz. (18) glacé cherries cut in halves to No. 735. Flavour with vanilla. Alternatively bake for $\frac{3}{4}$ hour in an oblong tin about 9 × 6 inches (22 × 15 cm.). When cold, ice and decorate and cut in squares.

737. Plain Fruit Cake. Cooking time $1\frac{1}{4}$ hours
Temperature 350° F. (180° C.) Mark 4.

Quantities for a 7-inch (18 cm.) tin:

Add 4 oz. of any dried fruit ($\frac{2}{3}$ c.), including some peel, to No. 735. Flavour with vanilla or lemon or 1 level tsp. mixed spice.

738. Lemon or Orange Cake. Cooking time $1\frac{1}{4}$ hours
Temperature 350° F. (180° C.) Mark 4.

Quantities for a 7-inch (18 cm.) tin:

Add the grated rind of 2 lemons or oranges to No. 735. The juice may be used for an icing. Alternatively bake for $\frac{3}{4}$ hour in an oblong tin about 9 × 6 inches (22 × 15 cm.) and when cold, ice and decorate the top.

739. Rock Cakes. Cooking time 10–15 minutes

Temperature 450° F. (230° C.) Mark 6–7.

Quantities for 18 cakes:

Make No. 735 using only 1 egg. Add 4–6 oz. dried fruit ($\frac{2}{3}$–1 c.) and $\frac{1}{2}$ level tsp. mixed spice. Add only enough liquid to make a stiff cake consistency and bake in small heaps on a greased tray.

740. Fruit Sponge

Put 2 lb. (1 kg.) sliced apples, or 1–2 lb. ($\frac{1}{2}$–1 kg.) of any other fruit, in a pie-dish. Cover with half Basic Mix No. 735, flavoured with vanilla or lemon; or use a packet sponge mix. Bake at 375° F. (190° C.) Mark 5 for $\frac{3}{4}$–1 hr. or until the fruit and pudding are cooked. Serve with Custard Sauce, No. 105, or Lemon Sauce, No. 102.

741. Basic Sandwich or Layer Cake Mix. Cooking time 20 minutes

Temperature 375° F. (190° C.) Mark 5.

Quantities for two 7-inch (18 cm.) sandwich tins:

4 oz. butter or margarine (125 g.)	2 eggs, beaten
4 oz. caster sugar ($\frac{1}{2}$ c.)	4 oz. S.R. flour ($\frac{3}{4}$ c.)
	Flavouring

Measures level. Grease the tins and line the bottoms with a circle of paper. Mix by the Creaming Method, No. 732. Bake until springy in the centre and beginning to shrink from the sides of the tins. Cool on a rack and join together with jam or a filling, and ice as desired.

742. Victoria Sandwich.

Make the Basic Mix, No. 741, and leave it plain, or flavour with vanilla. Fill with jam and dust the top with caster or sifted icing sugar.

743. Orange or Lemon Layer Cake

Flavour the Basic Mix, No. 741, with the finely grated rind of 1 small orange or lemon. When the cake is cold join with Lemon Curd or a Butter Cream, see Nos. 694, 696, and ice as desired. Each cake can be cut in two to give four layers. Chocolate icing goes well with this cake, see Nos. 675, 678 and 690.

744. Coffee Layer Cake

Mix 2–3 tsp. soluble coffee with a little warm water, and add to No. 741 with the creamed fat and sugar. Split the cold cake into four layers. Fill with Coffee Butter Cream, see No. 696, and ice. Decorate with chopped nuts.

745. Queen Cakes

Add 2–4 oz. sultanas ($\frac{1}{3}$–$\frac{1}{2}$ c.) to the Basic Mix, No. 741, and bake in 12–16 patty tins or small paper cases, for 15–20 minutes.

746. Fairy Cakes

Flavour the Basic Mix, No. 741, to taste and bake as for Queen Cakes, No 745. Ice and decorate.

The orange and lemon or coffee mixtures may also be baked as small cakes.

747. Upside-down Cake or Pudding. Cooking time $\frac{1}{2}-\frac{3}{4}$ hour

Temperature 350–375° F. (180–190° C.) Mark 4–5.

Quantities for a shallow tin approximately 6 in. (15 cm.) by 9 in. (22 cm.) or 8 in. (20 cm.) square:

1 oz. butter (25 g.)
Canned, fresh, or glacé
   fruits
Fine light brown sugar

One-stage recipe No. 748
  or Basic Sandwich Mix
  No. 741, or use a packet
  sponge mix

Melt the butter in the tin and sprinkle thickly with sugar. Arrange the fruit on the sugar to cover it closely with an attractive design. Spread the cake mixture smoothly over this and bake. Turn out on a large dish. Serve as a pudding, warm with cream, or as a cake.

748. Basic One-Stage Mix. Cooking time 20–30 minutes

Temperature 375° F. (190° C.) Mark 5.

Quantities for two 7 in. (18 cm.) sandwich tins:

6 oz. S.R. flour (1¼ c.)
Pinch salt
3 eggs
6 oz. caster sugar (¾ c.)

2 Tbs. milk
3 oz. soft butter or
  margarine (75 g.)
Flavourings, see Nos. 742–4

Measures level. Put all ingredients in a bowl and mix with a wooden spoon or with a hand mixer on slow speed for 2 minutes or until smooth. Spread evenly in the tins and bake. The mixture may also be used for Fairy Cakes, No. 746; Queen Cakes, No. 745, and Upside-down Cake, No. 747.

749. Madeleines. Cooking time 15–20 minutes

Temperature 400° F. (200° C.) Mark 6.

Quantities for 14 cakes:

4 oz. butter or margarine (125 g.)
4 oz. caster sugar ($\frac{1}{2}$ c.)
Vanilla essence or rind 1 lemon
2 eggs

4 oz. plain flour ($\frac{3}{4}$ c.)
$\frac{1}{2}$ tsp. baking powder
Apricot jam
Desiccated coconut
Glacé cherries

Measures level. Mix by the Creaming Method, No. 732. Fill greased dariole moulds two-thirds full with the mixture and bake in a moderate oven. When cold, paint with warm jam and roll in coconut to coat thoroughly. Stick a piece of cherry on top with a little jam or melted jelly.

750. Six Spice Cake. Cooking time 25–30 minutes

Temperature 350° F. (180° C.) Mark 4.

Quantities for two 8-inch (20 cm.) sandwich tins:

4 oz. margarine (125 g.)
4 oz. caster sugar ($\frac{1}{2}$ c.)
2 oz. syrup (2 Tbs.)
3 eggs
8 oz. S.R. flour ($1\frac{1}{2}$ c.)
Pinch of salt

$\frac{1}{4}$ tsp. each of ground ginger, mace and spice
$\frac{1}{2}$ tsp. grated nutmeg
$\frac{1}{2}$ tsp. each of ground cloves and cinnamon
About $\frac{1}{4}$ pt. milk ($\frac{1}{2}$ c.)

Measures level. Mix to a soft cake consistency by the Creaming Method, No. 732. Bake in greased and floured tins. When cold join together with Spicy Icing, No. 684, and ice the top.

751. Chocolate Layer Cake. Cooking time 25–30 minutes
Temperature 375° F. (190° C.) Mark 5.

Quantities for two 7-inch (18 cm.) tins:

2 oz. margarine or fat
   (50 g.)
4 oz. caster sugar ($\frac{1}{2}$ c.)
2 Tbs. syrup
1 egg
Vanilla essence

6 oz. plain flour ($1\frac{1}{4}$ c.)
1 tsp. baking powder
2 Tbs. cocoa
$\frac{1}{4}$ tsp. salt
1 tsp. bicarbonate of soda
$\frac{1}{4}$ pt. milk ($\frac{1}{2}$ c.)

Measures level. Mix by the Creaming Method, No. 732, to make a thick batter. The syrup is creamed with the fat and sugar and the soda added last, dissolved in the milk. Bake in two greased and floured 7-inch tins in a moderate oven. When cold sandwich together with Lemon Curd, No. 694, Butter Cream, No. 696. Ice the top with Chocolate Icing, No. 675 or 678.

752. Christmas or Birthday Cake. Cooking time 3 hours
Temperature 300° F. (150° C.) Mark 1.

Quantities for an 8–9 inch (20–22 cm.) tin:

8 oz. margarine or butter
   (250 g.)
8 oz. brown sugar ($1\frac{1}{3}$ c.)
5 eggs
$\frac{1}{2}$ tsp. almond essence
$\frac{1}{2}$ tsp. vanilla essence
$\frac{3}{4}$ lb. plain flour ($2\frac{1}{2}$ c.)

1 tsp. bicarbonate of soda
$\frac{1}{2}$ tsp. salt
2 tsp. mixed spice
2 lb. mixed dried fruit
   (1 kg.)
$\frac{1}{8}$ pt. brandy, rum, ale, or
   stout (4 Tbs.)

Measures level. Mix according to the Creaming Method, No. 732, but do not beat a lot. The mixture should not be too light, as there is a great deal of fruit to be held up. Mix to a stiff cake consistency. Put in a tin lined with paper and

spread with a slight depression in the middle so that it will
rise flat. Bake in a slow oven. Leave in the tin to cool.

753. Almond Fruit Cake. Cooking time 3 hours

Temperature 325° F. (160° C.) Mark 2.

Quantities for an 8-inch (20 cm.) tin:

8 oz. butter (250 g.)
8 oz. caster sugar (1 c.)
4 eggs
8 oz. ground almonds
  (2 c.)
4 oz. plain flour ($\frac{3}{4}$ c.)
Pinch of salt

$\frac{3}{4}$ lb. sultanas (2 c.)
3 oz. mixed peel, chopped
  ($\frac{1}{2}$ c.)
1 oz. preserved ginger,
  chopped ($\frac{1}{4}$ c.)
Grated rind 1 orange

Measures level. Mix by the Creaming Method, see No. 732,
using the ingredients in the order given in the recipe. Bake
in a tin lined with grease-proof paper in a moderate oven
for 3 hours. Leave in the tin to cool.

754. Dundee Cake. Cooking time 2 hours

Temperature 325° F. (160° C.) Mark 2.

Quantities for a 7-inch (18 cm.) tin:

6 oz. butter or margarine
  (175 g.)
5 oz. caster sugar ($\frac{3}{4}$ c.)
4 eggs
8 oz. plain flour ($1\frac{1}{2}$ c.)
$\frac{1}{2}$ tsp. baking powder
$\frac{1}{2}$ tsp. spice

3 oz. sultanas ($\frac{1}{2}$ c.)
1 oz. raisins (2 Tbs.)
2 oz. chopped peel ($\frac{1}{3}$ c.)
4 oz. currants ($\frac{2}{3}$ c.)
4 oz. almonds, blanched
  and chopped ($\frac{3}{4}$ c.)

Measures level. Mix by the Creaming Method, No. 732,
keeping half the almonds to sprinkle on top just before
baking.

755. Gingerbread. Cooking time ¾ hour

Temperature 350° F. (180° C.) Mark 4.

Quantities for a 9-inch (22 cm.) square tin:

8 oz. plain flour (1½ c.) or use half white and half wholemeal
1 tsp. mixed spice
1 Tbs. ground ginger
Pinch salt
2 oz. sultanas (⅓ c.)
1 oz. chopped peel or crystallized ginger (2 Tbs.)

1½ oz. brown sugar (3 Tbs.)
1 egg
1 tsp. bicarbonate of soda
¼ pt. milk (½ c.)
4 oz. butter or margarine (125 g.)
8 oz. golden syrup, treacle or honey (8 Tbs.)

Measures level. Mix by the Melting Method, No. 730. Grease the tin and line the bottom with non-stick paper. Pour in the mixture. Bake until it feels springy in the centre. Cool for 10–15 minutes and then turn out on to a rack.

756. Butter Sponge. Cooking time 20 minutes

Temperature 375° F. (190° C.) Mark 5.

Quantities for two 7-inch (18 cm.) sandwich tins:

3 eggs
4 oz. granulated sugar (½ c.)
4 oz. plain flour (¾ c.)

Pinch of salt
1 oz. butter or margarine (25 g.)
3 Tbs. hot water

Measures level. Mix by the Sponge Method, No. 733, adding the fat last, melted in the hot water. When cold, join together with jam or Butter Cream, Nos. 691, 696, or any sweet filling.

757. Genoese Sponge. Cooking time 25–30 minutes

Temperature 375° F. (190° C.) Mark 5.

Quantities for a 10 × 8-inch (25 × 20 cm.) tin:

3 eggs	3 oz. plain flour (⅔ c.)
3 oz. caster sugar (6 Tbs.)	2 oz. melted butter (50 g.)

Measures level. Mix by the Sponge Method, No. 733, beating the eggs and sugar over hot water and adding the butter last. Pour into the greased and floured tin and bake as for any sponge. Turn out carefully and use as a base for any of recipes Nos. 758–60 or for Refrigerator Cakes, Nos. 944–5.

758. Fruit Band

Trim off the edges of Genoese Sponge, No. 757. Arrange a layer of fresh or bottled fruit on top of the cake leaving ½-inch (1 cm.) margin round the edges. Cover the fruit carefully with a thin layer of thickened fruit juice or syrup, using 1 level Tbs. of arrowroot to each ½ pt. (1 c.) of liquid, as in Fruit Flan, No. 822. Pipe whipped cream round the edges. For serving, cut in slices.

759. Assorted Iced Cakes

Cut Genoese Sponge, No. 757, into small fancy shapes, using pastry-cutters. Cover with Glacé Icing as described in No. 674. Decorate by piping with Butter Icing, No. 677, or rolling in coconut or chopped nuts.

760. Truffles

Use the trimmings from the Genoese Sponge, No. 757. Rub through a sieve or put in a blender to make fine cake-crumbs. Bind to a firm consistency with sieved apricot or raspberry jam, flavoured with rum. Roll in the sieved jam and then in cocoa or chocolate vermicelli.

761. Sponge or Swiss Roll. Cooking time 7–10 minutes

Temperature 400° F. (200° C.) Mark 6.

Quantities for a 12 × 8-inch (30 × 20 cm.) tin:

2 eggs	1 tsp. baking powder
3 oz. granulated sugar	Pinch of salt
(6 Tbs.)	Warm jam
3 oz. plain flour ($\frac{2}{3}$ c.)	

Measures level. Grease the tin and line the bottom. Mix by the Sponge Method, No. 733, and spread evenly in the prepared tin. Bake in a moderately hot oven, taking care not to over-cook it, or the sponge will crack when you try to roll it. Have ready a piece of greaseproof paper sprinkled with sugar and placed on top of a damp cloth. Turn the sponge on to it and cut off the edges quickly. Spread with warm jam. Roll by taking the edge of the paper at one end between the thumb and fingers and turn the edge of the sponge over. Then pull the paper firmly away from the body and the sponge should roll up under it. A firm, light pressure is needed to make it roll neatly.

762. Butterfly Cakes. Cooking time 10–15 minutes

Temperature 375° F. (190° C.) Mark 5.

Quantities for 24 cakes:

Make Sponge, No. 756 or 761, and bake in small greased patty-tins in a moderately hot oven. Cool and cut a circle out of the top of each. Fill with a little jam and whipped or butter cream, cut each top slice in half and replace in the cream to look like wings. Dust with icing sugar.

763. Meringues. *Method 1.* Cooking time 2 hours or more
Temperature 250–275° F. (120–140° C.) Mark $\frac{1}{4}$–$\frac{1}{2}$.

Quantities for 18 Meringues:

2 egg whites
4 oz. caster or granulated
  sugar ($\frac{1}{2}$ c.) or use half
  and half

Vanilla essence

Measures level. Beat the egg whites until they are stiff and look dry and rocky. Add half the sugar and beat again until the mixture is very stiff and will stand up in peaks. Fold in the rest of the sugar and flavouring. Force from a tube or put spoonfuls on a greased tray and bake in a slow oven, until quite dry. Serve separately, or join in pairs with cream.

764. Meringues. *Method 2.* Cooking time 1 hour or more
Temperature 250–275° F. (120–140° C.) Mark $\frac{1}{4}$–$\frac{1}{2}$.

Quantities for 18 Meringues:

1 egg white
3 Tbs. hot water

6 oz. granulated sugar
($\frac{3}{4}$ c.)

Measures level. Put all the ingredients in a basin and beat over a pan of boiling water until the mixture is thick and will keep its shape. Put in small spoonfuls on a greased tray and bake in a slow oven.

765. Meringue for Puddings and Pies

Make according to No. 763, using 3–4 oz. (6–8 Tbs.) granulated sugar. Pile on the pudding or pie and bake in a moderately slow oven 350° F. (180° C.) Mark 4, for about 15–20 minutes, until lightly browned.

766. Pavlova Cake (to use as a cake or cold sweet).

Cooking time 1–1½ hours

Temperature 250° F. (120° C.) Mark ¼.

Quantities for an 8-inch (20 cm.) tin:

3 egg whites
Pinch of salt
6 oz. caster sugar (¾ c.)
1 tsp. cornflour

1 tsp. vinegar
½ tsp. vanilla
Fresh or bottled fruit
Cream

Measures level. Line the tin with non-stick paper. Beat the egg whites and salt until stiff. Beat in half the sugar. Mix the cornflour with the rest and fold in gently. Add the essence and vinegar and mix. Spread in the tin and bake slowly until firm on the outside but still soft inside. Turn upside down on a large dish and leave to cool. It will shrink a little during cooling. Arrange the fruit on top (cake still upside-down) and serve with cream in a jug or decorate with whipped cream.

767. Cornflake Meringues. Cooking time 45 minutes

Temperature 350° F. (180° C.) Mark 3.

Quantities for 16 meringues:

2 egg whites
Pinch of salt
2½ oz. chopped walnuts
　(½ c.)

1 doz. glacé cherries,
　chopped
2 oz. cornflakes (2 c.)
4 oz. sugar (½ c.)

Measures level. Beat the egg whites and salt until stiff. Fold in the other ingredients and place in spoonfuls on well-greased trays. Bake until pale brown and firm, but be careful not to brown them too much, or the flavour will be spoiled.

768. Lemon Meringue Nests. Cooking time 1 hour
Temperature 275° F. (140° C.) Mark 1.

Quantities for 6–8 nests:

Make Meringue mixture, No. 763. Put in rounds on non-stick paper on a greased baking-tray or on rice paper. Hollow out the centres and rough up the sides with a fork to make nests. Bake until firm. Place on a large dish or individual plates. Fill the centres with Lemon Curd, No. 694, and serve with a purée of strawberries, or Chocolate Sauce, No. 99.

STEAMED PUDDINGS

769. How to Steam a Pudding

1. Grease the basin and have it big enough to be only three-quarters full.

2. The best cover for the top is greased paper or aluminium foil. The wrapping-papers from margarine are

suitable for small basins. The paper should be a little larger than the top of the basin, and can be made to stay on without tying by twisting the overhanging paper under the rim of the basin.

3. The pudding may then either be cooked in the top half of a steamer, in which case it is essential to keep plenty of water boiling below to provide steam; or it may be cooked in a saucepan with water coming half-way up the sides of the basin and kept boiling gently. If you do need to add water during cooking, be sure to have it boiling, but this should not be required for a pudding taking about 2 hours.

4. If you are in a hurry, a pudding mixture can be cooked in small individual moulds, when the cooking time will be about half that required for the large basin. Puddings cooked this way look very attractive for serving on special occasions.

5. To turn a pudding out of the basin run a knife round the edge. Put the warm serving-plate over the top and quickly turn the basin over. Lift it up, and the pudding should be on the plate.

770. Steamed Jam or Marmalade Pudding. Cooking time 1½–2 hours

Quantities for 3–4 helpings:

2 oz. margarine or other fat (50 g.)
2 oz. sugar (¼ c.)
1 egg
4 oz. S.R. flour (¾ c.)
Pinch of salt

About ¼ pt. milk (½ c.)
Lemon essence or grated rind
3–4 Tbs. jam or marmalade

Measures level. Mix to a soft cake consistency by the Creaming Method, No. 732, or the Rubbing in Method, No. 731. Put the jam or marmalade at the bottom of a greased pudding-basin, add the mixture, cover and steam as in No. 769. Serve with Custard Sauce, No. 105, or Lemon Sauce, No. 102.

771. Steamed Chocolate Pudding

Use Recipe No. 770, omitting the jam and adding 2 level Tbs. cocoa with the flour. Flavour with vanilla essence. Steam for 1½–2 hours as in No. 769, and serve with Chocolate Sauce, No. 99.

772. Steamed Fruit Pudding

Use Recipe No. 770, omitting the jam and adding 2 oz. ($\frac{1}{3}$ c.) of any dried fruit, chopped, and $\frac{1}{2}$ level tsp. mixed spice. Steam for $1\frac{1}{2}$–2 hours according to No. 769, and serve with Custard Sauce, No. 105, or Cinnamon Sauce, No. 98, or Lemon Sauce, No. 102.

773. Steamed Ginger Pudding

Use Recipe No. 770, omitting the jam and 1 oz. (2 Tbs.) of sugar. Add 1 level tsp. ground ginger to the flour and 1 level Tbs. syrup with the milk. Steam according to No. 769 for $1\frac{1}{2}$–2 hours and serve with Syrup Sauce, No. 107.

774. Carrot Plum Pudding. Cooking time 3–4 hours

Quantities for 4 helpings:

1 c. raw grated carrot	1 tsp. bicarbonate of soda
1 c. raw grated potato	1 tsp. salt
4 oz. sugar ($\frac{1}{2}$ c.)	1 tsp. nutmeg
4 oz. plain flour ($\frac{3}{4}$ c.)	1 tsp. cinnamon
$\frac{3}{4}$ lb. mixed dried fruit	3 oz. melted fat (6 Tbs.)
(2 c.)	

Measures level. Mix all the ingredients together with the melted fat. Steam according to No. 769 in a 2-pt. (1 l.) basin for 3–4 hours. Serve with Lemon Sauce, No. 102.

775. Christmas Pudding

Quantities for $1\frac{1}{2}$–2 pt. (1 l.) basin:

2 oz. plain flour ($\frac{1}{2}$ c.)	1 lb. mixed dried fruit
$\frac{1}{2}$ tsp. grated nutmeg	(some peel) (500 g.)
$\frac{1}{4}$ tsp. cinnamon	2 oz. breadcrumbs (1 c.)
1 tsp. mixed spice	2 eggs

$\frac{1}{4}$ tsp. salt

4 oz. suet ($\frac{3}{4}$ c.)

4 oz. sugar ($\frac{1}{2}$ c.)

2–4 Tbs. brandy or other spirit

Measures level. Sift the dry ingredients together and add all the other ingredients, mixing thoroughly to a fairly soft mixture. Steam 4 hours the first time, and then 2–3 hours before using. To store put a fresh piece of paper on top and cover with a cloth. Store in a cool, dry place.

Steamed Suet Puddings. See Nos. 801–805.

BISCUITS

776. General Information

Biscuits may be mixed by any of the cake methods, Nos. 729–32. The consistency required depends on the way the biscuits are to be shaped. If they are to be rolled out and stamped in shapes, the dough should be very stiff. Some biscuit recipes, especially if mixed by the creaming method, are a little soft for rolling. Rather than knead in extra flour put the mixture in a very cold place for a while to harden up.

A mixture which is to be put through a biscuit forcer should be fairly soft, or the forcing will be difficult and the biscuits will break as they come out of the tube.

A quick and easy method of shaping is to roll small portions of the dough between the palms of the hands, floured well. Then press flat. If this is done with the bottom of a cut-glass tumbler the biscuits will have pretty patterns on top.

Biscuits should be made all the same size and thickness, or they will bake unevenly. They should be cooked slowly to make them crisp. Most are baked until they turn pale brown, but not necessarily until crisp. The richer mixtures always harden during cooling, and may be left to cool on the trays. Then lift off on to a wire cake-rack, using a fish-slice or palette knife, and leave until quite cold before storing in airtight tins.

777. Almond Biscuits. Cooking time 20–25 minutes

Temperature 350° F. (180° C.) Mark 4.

Quantities for 24 biscuits:

4 oz. margarine (125 g.)   6 oz. plain flour (1¼ c.)
4 oz. sugar (½ c.)   ¼ tsp. salt
½ egg   1 tsp. baking powder
½ tsp. almond essence   12 blanched almonds

Measures level. Mix by the Creaming Method, No. 732. Flour the hands and roll the mixture in small balls. Press half an almond on each and bake in a moderate oven until pale brown and crisp.

778. Chocolate Biscuits. Cooking time 15–20 minutes

Temperature 350° F. (180° C.) Mark 4.

Quantities for 24 double biscuits:

4 oz. margarine (125 g.)   ¼ tsp. salt
4 oz. sugar (½ c.)   1 tsp. baking powder
1 egg   2 Tbs. cocoa
½ tsp. vanilla   ¼ tsp. bicarbonate of soda
8 oz. plain flour (1½ c.)

Measures level. These are improved by using the special soft flour, see No. 721. Mix by the Creaming Method, No. 732. Force into fingers and bake in a moderate oven until crisp. When cold join together in pairs with vanilla-flavoured Butter Icing, No. 677.

N.B. If this mixture is left to stand in a cold place until firm it may be rolled and cut in the usual way.

779. Gingernuts. Cooking time 15–20 minutes

Temperature 350° F. (180° C.) Mark 4.

Quantities for 18 biscuits:

2 oz. dripping or cooking
    fat (50 g.)
2 oz. syrup (2 Tbs.)
4 oz. S.R. flour ($\frac{3}{4}$ c.)
$\frac{1}{4}$ tsp. salt

2 tsp. ground ginger
$\frac{1}{2}$ tsp. cinnamon
$\frac{1}{2}$ tsp. mixed spice
$\frac{1}{2}$ tsp. bicarbonate of soda

Measures level. Mix by the Melting Method, No. 730, to make a stiff consistency. Roll in small balls, and leave room on the tray for spreading a little. Bake in a moderate oven until brown. They will still be slightly soft, but become crisp on cooling.

780. Honey-nut Cookies. Cooking time 20 minutes

Temperature 350° F. (180° C.) Mark 4.

Quantities for 24 biscuits:

1 oz. chocolate (25 g.)
2 oz. margarine (50 g.)
2 eggs, beaten well
4 oz. honey (4 Tbs.)

4 oz. sugar ($\frac{1}{2}$ c.)
4 oz. plain flour ($\frac{3}{4}$ c.)
2 oz. chopped nuts ($\frac{1}{2}$ c.)
$\frac{1}{2}$ tsp. vanilla essence

Measures level. Melt the chocolate and margarine together. Add the rest of the ingredients and mix well. Drop in small spoonfuls on a greased tray and bake in a moderately slow oven. These cookies are still soft when they come out of the oven, but will become crisp on cooling.

781. Lemon Finger Biscuits. Cooking time 15–20 minutes

Temperature 350° F. (180° C.) Mark 4.

Quantities for 48 biscuits:

4 oz. margarine (125 g.)	1 tsp. baking powder
4 oz. caster sugar (½ c.)	¼ tsp. salt
1 egg	Grated rind of 1 lemon
8 oz. plain flour (1½ c.)	

Measures level. Mix by the Creaming Method, No. 732. Force into fingers through a biscuit forcer, or leave to stand for a little and then roll out thinly and cut into fingers. Bake in a moderate oven until a very pale gold, and crisp. The flavour is spoilt if they are allowed to brown.

782. Nutties. Cooking time ½–¾ hour

Temperature 350° F. (180° C.) Mark 4.

Quantities for a tin 10 × 6 (25 × 15 cm.) inches:

4 oz. margarine (125 g.)	½ tsp. salt
1 Tbs. syrup	½ tsp. vanilla
4 oz. brown sugar (¾ c.)	2 oz. chopped walnuts
7 oz. rolled oats (2 c.)	(½ c.)

Measures level. Mix by the Melting Method, No. 730. Spread in a flat baking-tin and cook in a moderately slow oven. Leave to cool in the tin and cut in fingers when almost cold.

783. Anzac Nutties. Cooking time about 20 minutes

Temperature 350° F. (180° C.) Mark 4.

Quantities for 24 Nutties:

4 oz. granulated sugar (½ c.)	1 oz. chopped nuts (¼ c.)
2 oz. whole-meal flour (½ c.)	2 oz. desiccated coconut (½ c.)
	1 Tbs. golden syrup

2 oz. plain white flour
  ($\frac{1}{2}$ c.)
Pinch of salt

2 oz. butter (50 g.)
$\frac{1}{2}$ tsp. bicarbonate of soda
1 Tbs. hot water

Measures level. Mix sugar, flours, salt, nuts, and coconut in a basin. Melt the syrup and butter together, but do not boil. Dissolve the soda in the hot water and mix all the ingredients together. Roll into balls or put in small rounds, with room to spread, on a greased tray. Bake in a moderate oven for about 20 minutes. They will become crisp on cooling, and it is advisable to cool them on the trays.

784. Shortbread. Cooking time $\frac{3}{4}$ hour

Temperature 325° F. (160° C.) Mark 3.

Quantities for two 6-inch (15 cm.) rounds:

4 oz. butter (125 g.)
2 oz. caster sugar ($\frac{1}{4}$ c.)

8 oz. plain flour ($1\frac{1}{2}$ c.)
Pinch of salt

Measures level. Mix by the Creaming Method, No. 732. Press into rounds. Prick well, bake until pale brown, and cut in pieces while warm. Or roll out $\frac{1}{4}$ inch ($\frac{1}{2}$ cm.) thick, cut into biscuits, and bake about 25–30 minutes.

785. Langues de Chat. Cooking time 20–30 minutes

Temperature 350° F. (180° C.) Mark 4.

Quantities for 2 dozen biscuits:

4 oz. margarine (125 g.)
4 oz. caster sugar ($\frac{1}{2}$ c.)
4 oz. plain flour ($\frac{3}{4}$ c.)
1 oz. cornflour (3 Tbs.)

Vanilla essence
3 egg whites
Pinch of salt

Measures level. Cream the margarine and sugar until very thick and light. Add the essence and fold in the stiffly-beaten egg whites. Sift the flour, cornflour, and salt together and stir into the creamed mixture. Pipe on to well-greased trays in small finger-shapes using a $\frac{3}{8}$–$\frac{1}{2}$-inch (1 cm.) plain

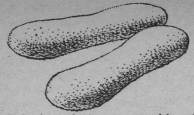

forcing tube. Bake in a slow oven, watching them well, as they burn readily. They should be only slightly coloured when cooked.

786. Almond Macaroons. Cooking time 30–40 minutes

Temperature 350° F. (180° C.) Mark 4.

Quantities for 18 macaroons:

2 egg whites	8 oz. caster sugar (1 c.)
Pinch of salt	1 Tbs. ground rice or fine
6 oz. ground almonds	semolina
(1¼ c.)	18 blanched almonds

Measures level. Beat the egg whites and salt until stiff. Fold in the almonds, sugar, and rice-flour. Put in rounds on rice-paper or heavily greased baking-trays. Place an almond on each. Bake in a slow oven. The easiest way of shaping the macaroons is to roll the mixture in balls in the palms of the hands and then flatten with a knife.

787. Chocolate Crispies. Cooking time 10 minutes

Temperature 375° F. (190° C.) Mark 5.

Quantities for 2 dozen cakes:

6 oz. plain chocolate	3½ c. cornflakes
(175 g.)	
½ pt. sweetened condensed	
milk (1 c.)	

Measures level. Melt the chocolate over hot water. Add the milk and cook for 5 minutes or until the mixture thickens. Cool and add the cornflakes, mixing thoroughly. Place in spoonfuls on a greased tray and bake for 10 minutes.

788. Afghans. Cooking time 20 minutes

Temperature 350° F. (180° C.) Mark 4.

Quantities for 2 dozen cakes:

7 oz. melted butter or margarine (200 g.)
6 oz. plain flour (1¼ c.)
3 oz. sugar (6 Tbs.)
2 oz. cornflakes (2 c.)

1 oz. cocoa (3 Tbs.)
¼ tsp. salt
Vanilla essence
1 doz. shelled walnuts
Chocolate Icing, No. 675

Measures level. Mix all the ingredients together and put in small spoonfuls on an ungreased tray. Bake until firm. When cold drop a blob of icing on top of each and press on half a walnut.

789. Date Bars. Cooking time ½ hour

Temperature 375° F. (190° C.) Mark 5.

Quantities for 16 fingers:

⅔ c. sweetened condensed milk
2 oz. plain flour (½ c.)
½ tsp. baking powder
Pinch of salt

3 oz. stoned, chopped dates (½ c.)
¼ c. minced nuts
½ tsp. vanilla essence

Measures level. Mix all the ingredients together and spread in a greased tin about 9 × 6 inches (22 × 15 cm.). Cut into fingers while still hot.

790. Coconut Macaroons. Cooking time 25–30 minutes

Temperature 350° F. (180° C.) Mark 4.

Quantities for 18 macaroons:

3 egg whites
Pinch of salt
2 tsp. flour
8 oz. sugar (1 c.)

Vanilla essence
8 oz. desiccated coconut
   (2 c.)

Measures level. Beat the egg whites and salt until stiff. Add the flour and sugar and warm in a saucepan until well blended. Add vanilla to taste and the coconut. Put in small heaps on greased trays and bake until pale brown.

791. Melting Moments or Viennese Pastry. Cooking time 10–15 minutes

Temperature 350° F. (180° C.) Mark 4.

Quantities for 12 completed cakes:

4 oz. butter or margarine
   (125 g.)
2 oz. cornflour (6 Tbs.)
1 tsp. baking powder

1 oz. icing sugar ($\frac{1}{4}$ c.)
2 oz. plain flour (6 Tbs.)
Vanilla essence
Butter Icing, No. 677

Measures level. Mix by the Creaming Method, No. 732. Put in a forcing bag and force into 24 small rosettes on a baking-tray. Bake until very pale brown. Cool and join in pairs with a little butter icing.

SCONES AND TEA BREADS

792. Plain Scones or Tea Bread. Cooking time 10–12 minutes

Temperature 450–475° F. (230–250° C.) Mark 7–8.

8 oz. S.R. flour ($1\frac{1}{2}$ c.)
1 tsp. salt
1–2 oz. margarine
   (25–50 g.)

About $\frac{1}{4}$ pt. milk ($\frac{1}{2}$ c.)

Measures level.

1. Sift the flour and salt together.

2. Rub the fat into the flour, using the tips of the fingers, and rub until it is well mixed in. For sweet scones add 1 oz. sugar (2 Tbs.).

3. Add the liquid quickly, putting most of it in at once. Use a knife for mixing, and toss the mixture lightly. Sour milk or cream may be used for mixing in place of fresh milk. Add enough to make a soft dough, see No. 726.

4. Do not knead, but pat the mixture or roll lightly on a floured board to about ½ inch (1 cm.) thick. Very thick scones are not nearly so nice to eat as the thinner, crusty ones.

5. The mixture may be shaped in a round and then cut in triangles, or may be cut in rounds with a plain biscuit-cutter. To obtain a smooth brown top brush over with a little milk or beaten egg.

6. Bake in a hot oven for 10–12 minutes, depending on the size. Alternatively, the mixture may be baked in a greased loaf-pan, cut in slices, and used in place of bread. Bake at 425° F. (220° C.) Mark 7, for ½–¾ hour.

N.B. All scones are nicer if eaten while still warm.

793. Cheese Scones

Make according to No. 792, adding 2 oz. grated cheese (50 g.) after the fat has been rubbed in.

794. Date Scones

Make according to No. 792, and roll the dough to ¼ inch (6 mm.) thick. Spread one half with 3–4 oz. chopped dates (½ c.). Fold over the other half and cut into 8 or 10 squares.

795. Fruit Scones

Add 1 oz. sugar (2 Tbs.) to No. 792 and 1–2 oz. dried fruit (2–4 Tbs.) after the fat has been rubbed in.

796. Fruit Rolls

Make according to No. 792, and roll out to a rectangle about ¼ inch (6 mm.) thick. Cream 1½ oz. margarine (3 Tbs.) with a few drops of lemon essence and spread over the dough. Sprinkle with 2 oz. dried fruit (⅓ c.), ½ tsp. cinnamon, and 1½ oz. (3 Tbs.) sugar. Brush the edges with a little water and roll the dough up tightly with floured hands. Cut into slices ¾ inch (2 cm.) thick and place cut side up on a greased baking-tin. Bake in a hot oven for 20 minutes 450° F. (230° C.) Mark 8.

797. Girdle Scones

Make as No. 792, and roll out ¼ inch (½ cm.) thick. Cut in triangles and place on a fairly hot girdle. Bake steadily until risen and light brown underneath. Turn and bake on the other side until cooked in the centre, about 10–15 minutes in all.

798. American Doughnuts

Quantities for 18–24 doughnuts:

8 oz. S.R. flour (1½ c.)	1 egg
½ tsp. salt	1 oz. margarine (25 g.)
¼ tsp. grated nutmeg or mace	2 oz. sugar (¼ c.)
	Milk to mix about 2–3 Tbs.

Measures level. Mix by the scone method, No. 792, but make the dough a little stiffer, as the doughnuts crack if too soft. Roll out to ⅓–½ inch (1 cm.) thick and cut in rounds, taking out the centres with a smaller cutter, to give a ring. Fry in deep fat, see No. 149, for 5–8 minutes, turning once to brown evenly. Serve with Syrup Sauce, No. 107.

799. Date and Nut Loaf. Cooking time 1 hour

Temperature 375° F. (190° C.) Mark 5.

Quantities for 1 lb. (½ kg.) loaf:

6 oz. chopped dates (1 c.)	½ tsp. salt
½ tsp. bicarbonate of soda	4 oz. S.R. flour (¾ c.)
¼ pt. boiling water (½ c.)	2 oz. plain flour (½ c.)
1 egg	2 oz. chopped walnuts
2 oz. brown sugar (¼ c.)	(¼ c.)

Measures level. Put dates and soda in a basin and pour over the hot water. Leave to cool. Mix dry ingredients together with the beaten egg and date mixture, with additional water to make a soft consistency. Bake in a greased tin until firm in the middle. Keep at least a day before cutting in thin slices and spreading with butter or margarine.

800. Sultana and Nut Loaf. Cooking time 45 minutes

Temperature 400° F. (200° C.) Mark 6.

Quantities for a 1 lb. (½ kg.) loaf:

4 oz. plain flour (¾ c.)	2 oz. chopped walnuts (½ c.)
4 oz. S.R. flour (¾ c.)	2 oz. sultanas (⅓ c.)
½ tsp. salt	1 egg
3 oz. fine brown sugar (½ c.)	About ¼ pt. milk (½ c.)

Measures level. Grease the loaf tin. Sift the flours and salt into a bowl and add the sugar, nuts and fruit. Beat the egg and add it with enough milk to make a stiff cake consistency (see No. 726). Turn into the tin and spread the top level. Bake until firm in the centre. Turn out on a rack. When cold store in a polythene bag and leave 24 hours before cutting.

PASTRY

801. Suet Pastry

Suet pastry is used for steamed puddings, savoury puddings such as steak-and-kidney, roly-poly pudding, and dumplings.

1. Allow 3 oz. suet ($\frac{1}{2}$ c.) to 8 oz. flour ($1\frac{1}{2}$ c.). Use packet suet or see No. 141.

2. Sift the flour with 1 level tsp. salt and 2 level tsp. baking powder for each 8 oz. ($1\frac{1}{2}$ c.) plain flour, or use self-raising flour.

3. Add the suet and mix well. Then mix in enough water to make a soft dough, using a knife for mixing and adding the water as quickly as possible.

4. Roll and use as required.

802. To Line a Basin with Suet Pastry

1. Cut off a quarter of the pastry and keep it for the lid.

2. Roll the rest into a circle $\frac{1}{4}$–$\frac{1}{2}$ inch (1 cm.) thick and lift it gently into the basin. Press to fit the sides and bottom and have a little overhanging the top. 8 oz. ($1\frac{1}{2}$ c.) flour makes enough to line a $1\frac{1}{2}$–2 pt. basin (1 l.).

3. Roll the small piece into a circle the size of the top of the basin. Put in the filling, which should come to the top.

4. Damp the edges of the pastry and put on the lid. Press the edges together to make a tight seal.

5. Cover with greased paper or aluminium foil and steam in the usual way, see No. 769. Puddings of this kind generally take at least 2 hours, and 3–4 hours for a meat pudding. They may be turned out of the basin, but are often served in it with the basin wrapped in a cloth, or use a heat-resisting glass basin. They may also be cooked in small individual moulds, when the cooking time will be about half that for a large one.

803. Fruit Pudding (suitable for apples, plums, damsons, blackberries, rhubarb, elderberries)

Quantities for 4 helpings:

Suet Pastry, No. 801,   1–2 lb. fruit ($\frac{1}{2}$–1 kg.)
    using 8 oz. flour ($1\frac{1}{2}$ c.)   3–4 oz. sugar (6–8 Tbs.)

Prepare the pastry and line the basin as in No. 802. Steam for 2 hours. Serve with custard or cream.

804. Steak-and-Kidney Pudding

Quantities for 4 helpings:

Suet Pastry, No. 801,   Pinch of pepper
    using 8 oz. flour ($1\frac{1}{2}$ c.)   2 sheep's kidneys, or $\frac{1}{2}$ lb.
1 lb. stewing steak (500 g.)   ox kidney (250 g.)
3 Tbs. flour   2 onions, sliced
1 tsp. salt   Water or stock

Measures level. Cut the meat in cubes and roll it in the flour, salt, and pepper, mixed. Cut the kidney in small pieces. Line the basin as in No. 802, and put the meat, kidney, and onions in layers. Add water or stock to come half-way up the meat. Cover with the pastry and steam for $2\frac{1}{2}$–3 hours. Long cooking improves this pudding, and even 4 hours may be given.

805. Jam or Marmalade Layer Pudding

Quantities for 4 helpings:

Suet pastry, No. 801,   Cream or custard
    using 8 oz. flour ($1\frac{1}{2}$ c.)
8 oz. jam or marmalade
    (250 g.)

Grease a 1-pint ($\frac{1}{2}$ litre) basin. Divide the pastry into four pieces. Roll one to fit the bottom of the basin and spread with some of the jam. Roll the other pieces, spreading each with jam and finishing with a lid of pastry. Cover the basin with foil and steam for 2 hours. Serve with cream or custard.

806. Dumplings

Shape half the suet-pudding mixture, No. 801, into small balls and drop into boiling stock or water. Put the lid on the pan and boil for 15–20 minutes. The lid should not be lifted during cooking, or the dumplings will be heavy.

807. Short Pastry

1. 4 oz. fat (125 g.) to 8 oz. flour (1½ c.) makes the best short pastry; plain flour should be used. Self-raising flour makes a light, soft crust, especially when less fat is used, but will not give a crisp short crust.

2. Weigh or measure the ingredients carefully and sift the flour and salt together, allowing ½–1 level tsp. salt to 8 oz. flour (1½ c.).

3. Lard or a good cooking fat makes the shortest pastry. Butter gives the best flavour. A mixture of half lard or cooking fat and half butter or margarine is the best for general purposes. Cut the fat in small pieces and rub into the flour, using the tips of the fingers only. Rub until the mixture looks like fine breadcrumbs. Most electric mixing machines can be used for rubbing or cutting fat into flour. Very soft cooking fats and margarines do not need to be rubbed in and can be added to the flour and mixed in with the water.

4. Use a knife for mixing, and mix to a stiff dough with cold water (2–3 Tbs.). Too much water and too soft a pastry means that it will be tough and hard when baked. Do not knead the pastry, as this also tends to make it tough.

5. Flour the pastry board very lightly and roll the pastry

with light, quick rolls. When scraps of pastry have to be re-rolled pile them one on top of the other and roll lightly.

6. It is always a good plan to leave the pastry to stand in a cool place for ¼–½ hour before baking, as this helps to reduce any toughness due to over-handling. Standing before baking also helps to reduce the shrinkage, which sometimes spoils the shape of a tart or pie.

7. Bake in a hot oven; a low temperature makes the pastry hard. Temperature 400° F. (200° C.) Mark 6.

808. Quickly Made Flaky Pastry

1. The same sort of fat is suitable as for short pastry, but allow 6 oz. fat (175 g.) to 8 oz. flour (1½ c.), and plain flour must be used. It is important to keep everything as cold as possible, and not to handle the pastry more than is absolutely necessary.

2. Sift the flour with 1 tsp. salt to each 8 oz. (1½ c.). Cut the fat, using two knives like scissor blades in the basin. Cut until the fat is in pieces the size of a pea.

3. Use a knife, and mix with cold water to a stiff dough.

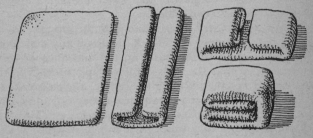

4. Roll to an oblong about ¼ inch (6 mm.) thick and keep the sides and ends as straight as possible.

5. Fold the pastry by bringing the sides to the middle, then the top and bottom edges to the middle, fold in half and press the edges together with a rolling-pin.

6. Turn the pastry so that the unbroken edges are on

your right-hand side. Roll out and use as required. It improves the pastry to put it in a cold place to 'rest' between rollings and again before baking. Rest for 15–20 minutes.

7. This pastry needs a hotter oven than short pastry, but not too hot. Slow cooking prevents rising and lets the fat run out, while having the oven too hot also prevents rising. Temperature 425–450° F. (220–230° C.) Mark 7–8.

809. Rough Puff Pastry

This is used chiefly for Vol-au-Vent, patties, jam puffs, and other sweet pastry. It should consist of many fine layers of pastry which rise very high when baked. To achieve this, the pastry needs many rollings and foldings, but is not difficult to make if you have a really cold place to put it in between rollings.

1. Allow 8 oz. margarine or butter (250 g.) to 8 oz. plain flour (1½ c.) and ½ level tsp. salt. The fat should be cold and firm.

2. Sift the flour and salt into a basin and cut the fat in ½-inch (1 cm.) cubes. Add to the flour.

3. Mix to a stiff dough with cold water to which a squeeze of lemon juice has been added.

4. Flour the pastry board and roll the dough to an oblong about ½ inch (1 cm.) thick. Brush off any loose flour and fold one-third of the paste on top and another third underneath, so that the ends come on opposite sides. The edges should not be folded to the centre, as this breaks up the layers. Give the pastry a half turn, roll again, and fold as before. Put in a cold place for 20 minutes to rest. Then roll and fold a further four times with two more rests, always brushing off loose flour before folding.

5. Roll and cut, allowing another rest before baking. For good patties and Vol-au-Vent use only the first cuttings, and the trimmings for custard slices, tarts, and other sweet pastries.

810. To Shape Patties or Jam Puffs (using frozen or fresh puff pastry)

If the pastry is lifted up off the board after rolling and before cutting, it helps to retain a better shape, as the lifting allows air to get underneath and relaxes any stretching the pastry has had.

Roll the pastry $\frac{1}{8}$ inch (3 mm.) thick and cut it in rounds with a 3-inch (8 cm.) cutter. Remove the centres from half of these with a $1\frac{1}{2}$-inch (4 cm.) cutter. It is advisable to

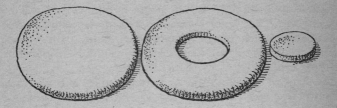

turn the pastry upside down after cutting, as this makes it rise a better shape. Moisten the plain halves and place the ring evenly on top. Place on a moistened baking-tray. Prick the centres and allow to rest in a cold place for 20 minutes. Bake in a hot oven, 450–475° F. (230–250° C.) Mark 8–9. Too slow an oven prevents rising and allows the fat to run out, while too hot an oven causes the tarts to brown before they have risen.

A Vol-au-Vent is a large patty, and is generally filled with a savoury filling of cooked chicken or shell-fish mixed with a well-flavoured sauce, see Nos. 294 and 300.

Before filling patties, remove any doughy pastry from the centre.

811. Sweet Pastry or Biscuit Crust (for fruit and jam tarts)

Temperature 400° F. (200° C.) Mark 6.

Quantities for two 8-inch (20-cm.) tarts:

3 oz. margarine (75 g.)	8 oz. S.R. flour (1½ c.)
2 oz. caster sugar (¼ c.)	Pinch of salt
1 egg	

Measures level. Mix by the Rubbing in Method, No. 731. Knead to work in loose flour. If possible avoid adding water. Bake in a cooler oven than for other pastry, as the sugar makes it inclined to catch.

812. Making a Flan

Special metal rings are sold for making flans, or you can use a sandwich tin. The advantage of the ring is that it can more easily be removed from the flan after cooking. Either short or sweet pastry is generally used for flans. 4 oz. flour (¾ c.) makes enough for an 8-inch (20-cm.) flan.

1. Roll the pastry into a circle ⅛–¼ inch (3–6 mm.) thick and about 2 inches (5 cm.) bigger than the ring.

2. Place the flan-ring on a baking-tray and ease the pastry into it without stretching. Press it down well to fit the bottom and sides.

3. Roll over the top with the rolling-pin to cut off surplus pastry. The edge may be left plain or fluted with a knife or fork.

4. If the flan is to be baked without a filling (i.e. 'blind'), line the bottom with a piece of foil, removing it before adding the filling. Bake in a hot oven 400° F. (200° C.) Mark 6, for 15–20 minutes for an empty shell, 30–40 minutes for a filled shell.

5. Lift off the baking-tray and remove the ring.

813. Making an Open Tart

These are used in the same way as flan-cases, but the tart is generally served in the dish, which should be suitable for sending to the table. Heat-resisting glass is useful for this purpose.

1. Roll the pastry to $\frac{1}{8}$ inch (3 mm.) thick and 3–4 inches (8–10 cm.) wider than the plate. Fold it in half to lift it into the plate without stretching. Open out and press to fit the plate.

2. Trim the edges with a sharp knife, leaving $1\frac{1}{2}$ inches (4 cm.) of pastry hanging over.

3. Fold the overhanging piece underneath to make a double edge level with the edge of the plate. Then bend the double edge upright. Pinch into flutes by using the first finger of one hand to make the dents and the thumb and first finger of the other hand to pinch the dents to a point.

4. Bake as for flan, No. 812.

814. Making a Lattice Top

This is used for decorating an open tart baked with the filling in.

1. Line the plate as in No. 813, but trim the pastry level with the edge of the plate. Then put in the filling.

2. Cut strips of pastry the width of the plate and $\frac{1}{4}$–$\frac{1}{2}$ inch ($\frac{1}{2}$–1 cm.) wide. Brush the edge of the tart with water and lay the strips over the filling in criss-cross fashion, pressing the ends well into the pastry edge. The strips may be twisted into a spiral first.

3. Cut a strip of pastry $\frac{1}{4}$ inch (6 mm.) wide and long enough to go right round the edge of the plate. Brush the edge and press the strip over the lattice ends. Press the edges together with a fork. Bake as for No. 812.

815. Continental Flan

This is made with Flaky Pastry, No. 808, or Puff Pastry, No. 809, and is filled after baking. It is similar to a large Vol-au-Vent, see No. 810.

1. Roll the pastry to about ¼ inch (6 mm.) thick and cut it into a large circle, with a big plate as a guide.

2. Then cut another circle the same size, but cut out the centre with a second plate, 1–1½ inches (2–3 cm.) smaller, as a guide. This gives you a circle and a ring.

3. Turn the circle upside down and put it on a baking-tray. Damp the edges and press the ring on carefully and evenly. Prick the bottom well to prevent rising, and brush the edge with beaten egg. As with all rich pastry, it is advisable to let the flan stand before baking. Bake in a very hot oven 450° F. (230° C.) Mark 8, for about 20 minutes. Cool and then place on a serving dish and add the filling.

816. Uncooked Biscuit Flan

Quantities for a 7-in. (18-cm.) flan:

2 oz. butter or margarine (50 g.)	4 oz. crushed digestive or ginger biscuits (125 g.)
½ Tbs. honey or syrup	

Measures level. Heat the fat and honey together until just melted. Add the crushed biscuits (quickest way of crushing is in the blender). When using digestive biscuits a little cinnamon adds to the flavour. When thoroughly blended, press the mixture into a flan ring placed on a serving plate, or into a pie plate. Leave in a cold place until set.

Suitable fillings are Fruit Flan, No. 822; Butterscotch Tart, No. 819; Chiffon Pie Filling, No. 818; or fill the case with fresh strawberries or raspberries mixed with whipped cream or Cream Chantilly, No. 163.

817. Uncooked Cornflake Flan

Quantities for a 7-in. (18-cm.) flan:

2 oz. soft butter or
 margarine (50 g.)
1 Tbs. syrup

2 tsp. sugar
1½ oz. cornflakes (1½ c.) or
 ½ c. cornflake crumbs

Measures level. Crush the cornflakes or put them in the blender. Mix the butter or margarine, syrup and sugar, and stir in the crumbs, combining thoroughly. Press the mixture into a pie plate and leave in a cool place to set. Fill in the same way as the Uncooked Biscuit Flan, No. 816.

818. Chiffon Pie Filling

Quantities for a 7-in. (18-cm.) uncooked flan, Nos. 816–17:

½ Tbs. gelatine
2 Tbs. cold water
¼ c. lemon juice
½ tsp. grated lemon rind

4 oz. sugar (½ c.)
2 eggs
Whipped cream (optional)

Measures level. Mix the gelatine and cold water together and put it in a small pan with the lemon juice, rind, half the sugar and the egg yolks. Stir and cook over a gentle heat until it thickens. Beat the egg whites until stiff and beat in the rest of the sugar. Fold in the lemon mixture and pile in the flan case. Leave to set, and store in the refrigerator. Serve the whipped cream as a garnish, or hand separately.

819. Butterscotch Tart. Cooking time 20–30 minutes

Quantities for an 8-inch (20-cm.) tart:

Short or Flaky Pastry,
 No. 807 or 808, using
 4 oz. flour (¾ c.)
1 oz. butter or margarine
 (25 g.)

4 oz. brown sugar (¾ c.)
½ pt. hot milk (1 c.)
2½ Tbs. cornflour
Pinch of salt
½ tsp. vanilla

Measures level. Make the pastry-case as described in Nos. 812 or 813, and bake without any filling. Heat the fat and sugar, and when the sugar is melted add it to the hot milk and stir until it dissolves. Mix the cornflour and salt to a paste with a little cold milk. Add the hot milk mixture, return to the pan, and stir until it boils. Cook for 5 minutes and add the vanilla. Pour into the cooked pastry-case and serve hot or cold. This may be made into a Butterscotch Meringue tart by adding the yolks of one or two eggs to the filling and making Meringue, No. 765, with the whites. Pile on top of the filling, and bake.

820. Custard Tart. Cooking time 40–45 minutes

Temperature 400° F. (200° C.) Mark 6.

Quantities for an 8-inch (20-cm.) tart:

Short pastry, No. 807, using 4 oz. flour (¾ c.)	½ pt. hot milk
	Vanilla
2 eggs	Grated nutmeg
1 Tbs. sugar	

Measures level. Line the flan ring or pie plate with the pastry. Prick the bottom and line with foil. Bake blind until the pastry is almost firm, about 20 minutes. Remove the foil. Mix egg and sugar and add the milk and vanilla. Pour into the pastry case and sprinkle with nutmeg. Bake until the custard is set, about 20–25 minutes. Serve hot or cold. The mixture can also be used for small tarts, adding the filling to raw pastry cases. Bake about 20 minutes.

821. Lemon Meringue Pie. Cooking time 20 minutes

Quantities for an 8-inch (20-cm.) tart:

Short or Flaky Pastry, No. 807 or 808, using 4 oz. flour (¾ c.)	½ pt. water (1 c.)
	2 eggs
	1 oz. margarine (25 g.)

2½ Tbs. cornflour   3–4 oz. sugar (6–8 Tbs.)
Rind and juice of 1 lemon

Measures level. Bake the pastry-case without a filling, as in
Nos. 812 or 813. Mix the cornflour to a smooth paste with
a little of the water. Boil the rest of the water with the grated
lemon rind. Pour on to the cornflour, mix well, return to
the pan, and boil for 5 minutes. Add the egg yolks and cook
for a few minutes without boiling. Add the sugar, lemon
juice, and margarine, and mix well. Pour into the cooked
case. Make the egg whites into a meringue for the top of the
tart as in No. 765.

822. Fruit Flan

Use Short Pastry, No. 807, or Sweet Pastry, No. 811. The
pastry case may be made as in Nos. 812–13, and is baked
without filling.

Stewed or Canned Fruit Filling. Stew fruit carefully to keep
a good shape. Drain stewed or canned fruit and arrange it in
the flan. Take ½ pt. (1 c.) of the juice and either thicken with
1 level tablespoon arrowroot or potato fécule, and pour over
the fruit while hot; or melt 1 tablespoon gelatine in the hot
juice, allow to cool to begin thickening and then spoon over
the fruit.

Fresh Fruit. Arrange in the flan. Either cover with a packet
jelly of the same flavour, cooled until it begins to thicken
and then spooned over; or melt ¼ pound (125 g.) of jam of
the same flavour with 1 tablespoon water, strain if necessary,
cool a little, and spoon over the fruit.

823. Open Apple Tart or Flan. Cooking time ½ hour

Quantities for an 8-inch (20-cm.) tart:

Short Pastry, No. 807, or   3 oz. sugar (6 Tbs.)
   Flaky, No. 808, using   1 Tbs. chopped peel or a
   4 oz. flour (¾ c.)   little grated lemon rind

1 lb. apples (500 g.)   2 or 3 Tbs. currants
1 oz. margarine (25 g.)   ¼ tsp. ground cinnamon

Measures level. Line the dish with pastry as for No. 813 or make Continental Flan, No. 815. Bake blind. Peel the apples and cut them in eighths. Put in a pan with the other ingredients and cook very gently until tender but not broken. Arrange the apple in the flan and pour over the juice. Serve cold with cream.

824. Plum Flan. Cooking time ½ hour

Temperature 425° F. (220° C.) Mark 6.

Quantities for an 8-inch (20-cm.) flan:

Short Pastry, No. 807,   2 oz. cottage cheese (50 g.),
    using 4 oz. flour (¾ c.)   optional
1 lb. plums (500 g.)
2–3 oz. demerara sugar
    (4–6 Tbs.)

Measures level. Line a flan ring or sandwich tin with the pastry as in Nos. 812 or 813. Cut the plums in quarters or thick slices, removing the stones. Arrange in the pastry and sprinkle the sugar over and the cheese on top of that. Bake for ½ hour or until the plums and pastry are cooked. Serve hot or cold.

825. Small Jam Tarts

Roll Short Pastry, No. 807, ⅛-inch (3 mm.) thick. Cut in rounds with a plain or a fluted cutter a little larger than the patty-tins. Turn the pastry upside down and press into the tins. Put a little jam in each and cover the top of the jam with a thin layer of cold water. This prevents the jam from drying out during cooking. Bake in a hot oven 425° F. (220° C.) Mark 6, for 10–15 minutes.

826. Fairy Tarts

Make as for Jam Tarts, No. 825, using Sweet Pastry, No. 811. Bake the cases without filling, and then fill with jam, lemon curd, crushed fresh fruit, or Fruit Purée, No. 602, and decorate with Whipped Cream.

827. Curd Cheese Cakes. Cooking time $\frac{1}{2}$–$\frac{3}{4}$ hour

Temperature 425° F. (220° C.) Mark 7.

Quantities for a 7–8-inch (18–20-cm.) tart:

Short Pastry, No. 807, using 4 oz. flour ($\frac{3}{4}$ c.)	2 oz. sugar (4 Tbs.)
	1 egg
$\frac{1}{2}$ lb. cottage cheese (250 g.)	Rind $\frac{1}{2}$ lemon
1 oz. melted butter (25 g.)	Grated nutmeg
1 oz. currants (2 Tbs.)	

Measures level. Roll the pastry and line the flan ring or sandwich tin as in Nos. 812 or 813. Mix the cheese, melted butter, currants, and sugar in a basin. Add the beaten egg and the lemon rind. Pour into the pastry case and sprinkle grated nutmeg on top. Bake in a hot oven for 30–45 minutes. Alternatively, the mixture may be made into small tarts and baked for about 20 minutes. Serve hot or cold.

828. Treacle Tart. Cooking time 20 minutes

Temperature 425° F. (220° C.) Mark 7.

Quantities for a 7-inch (18-cm.) tart:

Short Pastry, No. 807, using 4 oz. flour ($\frac{3}{4}$ c.)	6 oz. treacle or syrup (6 Tbs.)
3 oz. breadcrumbs ($1\frac{1}{2}$ c.)	

Measures level. Roll the pastry to fit a flan ring or pie-plate. Cover the bottom with syrup and add the breadcrumbs. Leave to stand for $\frac{1}{2}$ hour before baking. Any remaining pastry may be cut in strips to make a lattice top. Serve hot or cold.

829. Cranberry Pie. Cooking time 25 minutes

Temperature 450° F. (230° C.) Mark 8.

Quantities for an 8-inch (20-cm.) pie:

4 oz. flour made into Short Pastry, No. 807	8 oz. sugar (1 c.) 2 Tbs. flour
8 oz. cranberries (250 g.)	¼ pt. water (½ c.)

Measures level. Roll the pastry and cut to line a deep tin or plate. Mix the other ingredients and boil gently for 10 minutes. Cool. Put in the pastry-case and put strips of pastry across to make a lattice and a double rim round the edge to cover the ends, see No. 814. Bake in a hot oven. Serve with cream or custard.

830. Louise Cakes. Cooking time 20 minutes

Temperature 400° F. (200° C.) Mark 6.

Quantities for 2 dozen cakes:

5 oz. plain flour (1 c.)	2 eggs
½ tsp. baking powder	Raspberry jam
Pinch of salt	*Filling*
1 oz. sugar (2 Tbs.)	4 oz. sugar (½ c.)

2 oz. margarine
  (50 g.)
	2 oz. desiccated coconut
	  (½ c.)

Measures level. Sift the flour, baking powder, and salt. Add the 1 oz. sugar and rub in the margarine. Mix to a stiff dough with the egg yolks, slightly beaten. Roll out and cut in rounds to line small patty tins. Beat the egg whites until stiff and fold in the sugar and coconut. Put a small spoonful of jam in the bottom of each pastry-case and two-thirds fill with the coconut mixture. Bake until a pale brown.

831. Kolac. Cooking time 35–40 minutes

Temperature 375° F. (190° C.) Mark 5.

Quantities for a tin 12 × 9 inches (30 × 22 cm.):

8 oz. wholemeal flour
  (1½ c.)
½ tsp. baking powder
¼ tsp. salt
4 oz. butter (125 g.)
3 oz. fine brown sugar
  (½ c.)

1 egg
2 apples and 2 bananas
OR 1 lb. red plums (500 g.)
2 oz. cottage cheese (50 g.)
Brown sugar
½ oz. butter (1 Tbs.)

Measures level. Mix the flour, baking powder, and salt, and rub in the butter. Add the fine brown sugar. Mix to a soft dough with the beaten egg. Knead lightly and roll to fit the greased tin. A Swiss roll tin is ideal. Peel and chop the apples and bananas or stone and chop the plums. Cover the pastry with the fruit and sprinkle the cottage cheese over the top. Cover this with a generous layer of soft brown sugar and dot with the ½ oz. butter. Bake in a moderate oven and, when cool, cut in squares.

832. Macaroon Tartlets. Cooking time 20 minutes

Temperature 425° F. (220° C.) Mark 7.

Quantities for 18 tartlets:

6 oz. flour (1¼ c.) made
  into Flaky Pastry, No.
  808
Apricot jam
2 egg whites

2 oz. ground almonds
  (½ c.)
4 oz. caster sugar (½ c.)
Almond essence

Measures level. Roll the pastry ⅛ inch (3 mm.) thick and cut into rounds to line small patty-tins. Put ½ tsp. of jam in the bottom of each. Beat the egg whites with a pinch of salt. When stiff, fold in the almonds and sugar and add a few

drops of almond essence. Put a little in each tart and bake in
a hot oven until firm and pale brown.

833. Kipper Flan. Cooking time 50 minutes

Temperature 400° F. (200° C.) Mark 6 for pastry; 375° F.
(190° C.) Mark 5 for filling.

Quantities for an 8-inch (20-cm.) flan:

Short pastry, No. 807, using 4 oz. flour (¾ c.)	4 oz. stoned black olives (125 g.)
2 filleted kippers, chopped	2 eggs
1 small onion, chopped	4 Tbs. milk
½ oz. butter (1 Tbs.)	Pepper

Measures level. Roll the pastry and line the flan. Bake blind.
Melt the butter in a small pan and cook the onion slowly
until it is soft but not brown. Put kipper, onions and olives in
the cooked flan case. Beat the eggs to break up, add the milk
and pepper to taste. Pour over the fish and bake for 30
minutes or until set. Suitable for hors-d'œuvre or for a main
dish with salad.

834. Salmon Flan. Cooking time 30 minutes

Temperature 400° F. (200° C.) Mark 6.

Quantities for an 8-inch (20-cm.) flan:

Short pastry, No. 807, using 4 oz. flour (¾ c.)	¼ c. chopped green peppers
8 oz. canned salmon (250 g.)	½ oz. flour (1½ Tbs.)
¼ pt. canned, sliced mushrooms (½ c.)	¼ tsp. salt
1 oz. butter (25 g.)	1 Tbs. chopped red pimento
1 stick chopped celery	Pinch of garlic salt
	Sliced red pimento

Measures level. Roll the pastry, line the flan and bake blind.
While it is cooking make the filling. Drain the salmon and

mushrooms, retaining the liquids. Melt the butter and stew the celery and green pepper in it until they are tender. Mix in the flour and salt. Make the mushroom and salmon liquids up to $\frac{1}{4}$ pt. ($\frac{1}{2}$ c.) with milk. Add to the pan and stir until it boils, boil for a few minutes. Add the salmon, mushrooms, chopped red pimento and garlic salt. Heat thoroughly and pour into the pastry case. Serve hot or cold, garnished with slices of red pimento.

835. Making a Double Crust Tart (using short or sweet pastry)

N.B. 8 oz. flour ($1\frac{1}{2}$ c.) makes enough pastry for an 8–9-inch (20–23 cm.) tart. They are always nicer if the pastry is kept fairly thin.

These may be made in sandwich tins, enamel plates, or plates of heat-resisting glass.

1. Roll a piece of pastry into a circle $\frac{1}{8}$ inch (3 mm.) thick and 1–2 inches (2–5 cm.) wider than the dish. Fold in half and lift into the dish, then open it out and press gently into the dish without stretching. Trim off the overhanging pastry level with the edge of the dish.

2. Add the filling, having enough to come level with the top of the plate, or above, for a fruit that shrinks a lot during cooking.

3. Roll another piece of pastry 2 inches larger than the plate.

4. Moisten the edge of the under-piece and lift the top on, easing and not stretching. Fold the overhanging pastry under the lower crust and press the edges well together. This makes a good seal to prevent juices from boiling out. Flute the edge as described in No. 813 or scallop, as in No. 841.

5. Cut a hole in the centre of the tart to allow steam to escape. Brush the top with milk or beaten egg and bake in a hot oven 425° F. (220° C.) Mark 6, for $\frac{1}{2}$–$\frac{3}{4}$ hour, depending on the kind of filling used.

836. Double Apple Tart

Make as No. 835, using for the filling of an 8-inch (20-cm.) tart, 1 lb. (500 g.) sliced cooking apples, 4–6 oz. sugar ($\frac{1}{2}$–$\frac{3}{4}$ c.), $\frac{1}{4}$ tsp. nutmeg or cinnamon, $\frac{1}{4}$ level tsp. salt, 2 tsp. lemon juice, 1 tsp. grated lemon rind.

837. Double Berry Tart (suitable for black currants, cherries, gooseberries, blackberries, elderberries, raspberries, loganberries)

Make as No. 835, and for an 8-inch (20-cm.) tart allow $1\frac{1}{2}$ lb. (750 g.) fruit, 4 oz. sugar ($\frac{1}{2}$ c.), and 2 level Tbs. flour to sprinkle over. The flour thickens the juice.

838. Bacon and Egg Tart. Cooking time 30–40 minutes

Temperature 425° F. (220° C.) Mark 6.

Quantities for an 8-inch (20-cm.) tart:

Short Pastry, No. 807, using 6 oz. flour ($1\frac{1}{4}$ c.)	1 sliced tomato
4 rashers of bacon	4 eggs
1 oz. sliced mushrooms (25 g.)	1 Tbs. chopped parsley
	$\frac{1}{2}$ tsp. mixed herbs
	Salt and pepper

Measures level. Make according to No. 835, spreading the bacon, mushrooms and tomato on the bottom of the pastry and pouring over the eggs and seasoning. Serve hot or cold.

839. Small Double Crust Tarts

Roll the pastry, short or flaky, to $\frac{1}{8}$ inch (3 mm.) thick and cut in rounds. Make the tarts in patty-tins. Use a cutter a little bigger than the tin. Line the tins and put in the filling, which may be the same as in Nos. 836–8. Cover with pastry and press the edges together. Cut a slit in the top. Bake in a hot oven 425° F. (220° C.) Mark 6, for 20–30 minutes, depending on the size. If meat-filling is used it should be stewed first.

840. Mincemeat for Tarts

8 oz. raisins (250 g.)
8 oz. apples (250 g.)
8 oz. currants (250 g.)
2 oz. almonds (50 g.)
2 oz. crystallized cherries (50 g.)
Grated rind and juice 1 lemon

8 oz. prepared suet (250 g.)
8 oz. sugar (1 c.)
6 oz. candied peel (150 g.)
1 small nutmeg, grated
½ tsp. salt
2–3 Tbs. brandy or rum

Measures level. Mince the dried fruit and apples. Mix all the ingredients well and store in covered jars. To make the tarts use Short Pastry, No. 807, or Flaky Pastry, No. 808, and bake in patty-tins (see No. 839) or on a baking sheet.

841. Quick Method of Covering a Pie (suitable for short pastry)

1. Fill the pie-dish well, using a pie-funnel or inverted egg-cup to hold the pastry up if the contents of the pie are likely to shrink a lot during cooking.

2. Roll the pastry to ⅛–¼ inch (3–6 mm.) thick and about 2 inches wider all round than the dish. Place the pastry over the rolling-pin and lift it gently on to the pie without stretching. Trim off all round leaving ½ inch (1 cm.) over-hanging.

3. Turn the overhanging piece under to make it level with the edge. Damp the edge of the pie-dish and press the pastry down.

4. Decorate by slashing the edge of the pastry hori-zontally with a sharp knife. Then scallop by pressing with the thumb and cutting with a knife.

5. Cut a slit in the top of the pie to let out steam. Brush with egg or milk and bake in a hot oven 425° F. (220° C.) Mark 6, for ½ hour or longer, according to the kind of pie.

842. Standard Method of Covering a Pie (suitable for all pastry)

1. Fill the pie-dish as for the Quick Method, No. 841.
2. Roll the pastry ⅛–¼ inch (3–6 mm.) thick and about 1 inch (2 cm.) wider than the top of the dish.
3. Cut a strip of pastry the width and length of the rim of the dish. Damp the edge of the dish and then put the strip of pastry round. Damp it on top.
4. Place the large piece of pastry over the rolling-pin and lift it gently on top of the pie, taking care not to stretch it. Press down the edge.
5. Trim off any surplus and slash and decorate the edge. Finish in the same way as for the Quick Method, No. 841.

843. Fruit Pies

Use Short or Flaky Pastry, No. 807 or 808, made with 8 oz. (1½ c.) flour. Allow 2 lb. (1 kg.) of fruit for a 2-pt. (1 l.) size pie-dish, 4 oz. sugar (½ c.), and ¼ pt. (½ c.) or less of water. Juicy fruit needs very little water. Stand the pie on a baking-tray to cook, as this will catch the juice if it boils over. Cook for ½–¾ hour at 425° F. (220° C.) Mark 6.

844. Steak-and-Kidney Pie. Cooking time 2 hours

Quantities for 6–8 helpings:

2 lb. stewing steak (1 kg.)	1 Tbs. flour
8 oz. kidney (250 g.)	½ tsp. pepper
1 tsp. salt	Hot water

Measures level. Cut the meat in small pieces and chop the kidney. Roll in the flour and seasoning and pack in the pie-dish. Add water to come three-quarters of the way up the meat and cover with Short or Flaky Pastry, No. 807 or 808, using 8 oz. flour ($1\frac{1}{2}$ c.).

Bake in a hot oven 450° F. (230° C.) or Mark 8, for about 15 minutes, and then reduce the heat to moderate 300–325° F. (160° C.) Mark 1, for the rest of the 2 hours.

845. Veal-and-Ham Pie. Cooking time 2 hours

Quantities for 4 helpings:

$1\frac{1}{2}$ lb. fillet veal (750 g.)	1 tsp. grated lemon rind
6 oz. bacon (150 g.)	1 tsp. salt
1 hard-boiled egg	Pinch of pepper
1 tsp. chopped parsley	$\frac{1}{4}$ pt. stock or water ($\frac{1}{2}$ c.)

Measures level. Make and bake in the same way as No. 844, chopping the egg and bacon and mixing it with the meat.

846. Rabbit Pie. Cooking time $1\frac{1}{2}$–2 hours

Quantities for 4–6 helpings:

1 rabbit	Rabbit stock
$\frac{3}{4}$ lb. bacon or pickled pork (750 g.)	1 tsp. salt
	Pinch of pepper
Forcemeat balls, see No. 135	Flaky Pastry, No. 808

Measures level. Boil the rabbit trimmings and giblets to make stock. Divide the rabbit in joints. Dice the bacon or pork. Pack the meat into a pie-dish with the forcemeat balls. Add salt and pepper and stock to fill the dish three-quarters full. Cover with the pastry and bake in a hot oven 450° F. (230° C.) Mark 8, for about 15 minutes and then reduce the heat to moderate 300–325° F. (150–160° C.) Mark 1, for the rest of the cooking time. Serve hot or cold.

847. Apple Dumplings

Roll Short or Flaky Pastry, No. 807 or 808, into squares $\frac{1}{4}$ inch (6 mm.) thick and large enough to cover the apples. Peel and core the apples, and fill the centres with brown

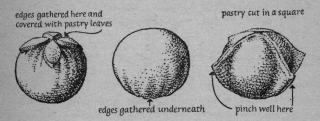

edges gathered here and covered with pastry leaves

pastry cut in a square

edges gathered underneath

pinch well here

sugar, a knob of margarine, and a pinch of grated nutmeg. Stand in the middle of the pastry squares, damp the edges of the pastry, and fold in one of the shapes shown above. Place them on a baking-tray and bake in a hot oven 425° F. (220° C.) Mark 6, for 30 minutes or until the apples are tender and the pastry cooked. Test the apples by pushing a fine skewer into one of them.

848. Sausage Rolls

For $\frac{1}{2}$ lb. (250 g.) sausage meat make 4 oz. ($\frac{3}{4}$ c.) flour into Short or Flaky Pastry, No. 807 or 808. Roll out $\frac{1}{4}$ inch (6 mm.) thick and cut in 8 oblongs, about 3 × 4 inches (8 × 10 cm.). Divide the meat into 8 sausage-shaped pieces, place on the pastry, and fold over. Slash the edges as for pie No. 841, and cut three diagonal slits in the top of each. Brush with milk or egg and bake in a hot oven 450° F. (230° C.) Mark 8, for 25–30 minutes.

849. Cornish Pasties. Cooking time 30–40 minutes

Temperature 425° F. (220° C.) Mark 6.

Quantities for 4 pasties:

Short Pastry, No. 807,   1 small onion, chopped
    using 8 oz. flour (1½ c.)   1 tsp. salt
8 oz. raw minced beef   Pinch of pepper
    (250 g.)
4 oz. diced raw potato
    (1 medium)

Measures level. Mix the filling ingredients. Divide the pastry into four and roll each to ⅛ inch (3 mm.) thick. Place a quarter of the filling on each, damp the edges, and fold over. Slash the edges as for pie No. 841, cut a small hole in the top, and brush with egg or milk. Bake in a hot oven.

850. Fish Pasties. Cooking time 30 minutes

Temperature 450° F. (230° C.) Mark 8.

Quantities for 4 pasties:

Short Pastry, No. 807,   1 small onion, chopped
    using 8 oz. (1½ c.) flour, 1 rasher bacon, chopped
    or Flaky Pastry, No. 808   1 tsp. salt
8 oz. white fish or shell-fish Pinch of pepper
    (250 g.)
4 oz. raw potato, diced
    (1 medium)

Measures level. Remove any bone or skin from the fish and cut it into small cubes. Mix with the other ingredients. Roll into four rounds, and finish as for Cornish Pasties, No. 849.

851. Baked Jam Roll

Use Short or Flaky Pastry, No. 807 or 808. Roll the pastry to a rectangle ⅛ inch (3 mm.) thick or less. Spread with a thin layer of jam to within ½ inch (1 cm.) of the edges. Fold over the edges to hold the jam, brush with milk or water, and roll up like a Swiss roll. Place on a baking-tray. Cook in a hot oven 425° F. (220° C.) Mark 6, for 30–45 minutes, according to the size.

Alternative fillings are:

Lemon curd instead of jam.
Jam, chopped apples, sultanas, and mixed spice.
Honey, chopped nuts, and mixed spice.

852. Vanilla Squares or Custard Slices

Cut flaky or puff pastry in strips 4 inches (10 cm.) wide and about ⅛ inch (3 mm.) thick. Prick well and bake in a hot oven 450° F. (230° C.) Mark 8, for about 10 minutes. Sandwich together with Confectioner's Custard, No. 692, and ice the top with Water Icing, No. 674. Sprinkle with chopped nuts. Cut in squares or fingers with a sharp knife, held upright and pulled through carefully.

853. Cake of a Thousand Leaves (*Mille-feuilles*)

Puff Pastry, No. 809, or use frozen
½ pt. Confectioner's Custard, No. 692 (1 c.)
½ pt. thick apple purée, sweetened (1 c.)
Grated rind ½ lemon

Lemon Water Icing, No. 674
2 Tbs. chopped walnuts or almonds
Crystallized fruit
Whipped Cream

Measures level. Cut the pastry into 6 equal pieces and roll each one very thinly. Cut into rounds using an 8-inch (20 cm.) sandwich tin as a guide. It helps to keep the pastry in shape if it is rolled and baked on greaseproof paper. Prick well and chill for 15–20 minutes before baking in a hot oven 450° F. (230° C.) Mark 8, for 8–10 minutes. Cool on the paper. Add the lemon rind to the apple. Sandwich the pastry in layers, using the custard and apple alternately. Ice the top with the water icing and decorate with nuts and fruit. Ice the sides with the cream or pipe it on with an icing bag and rosette tube. Cut in wedges and serve as a cake or cold sweet.

854. Cream Crisps or Palmiers. Cooking time 5–10 minutes

Temperature 450° F. (230° C.) Mark 8.

Puff Pastry, No. 809,   Caster sugar
  or use frozen

Roll the pastry on a board sprinkled with caster sugar instead of flour. Roll to a rectangle. Fold the sides to the centre and then the folded sides to the centre again. Cut

sides to centre   sides to centre   cut here
first time   second time

downwards into slices about $\frac{1}{2}$ inch (1 cm.) thick. Put on a greased tray, cut side up, allowing room for spreading. Sprinkle with sugar and bake to a pale brown. If liked, join together with whipped cream.

855. Eccles Cakes. Cooking time 15–20 minutes

Temperature 450° F. (230° C.) Mark 8.

Quantities for 18 cakes:

8 oz. flour made into
  Flaky Pastry, No. 808
½ oz. melted butter or
  margarine (1 Tbs.)
4 oz. brown sugar (½ c.)

4 oz. currants (⅔ c.)
½ tsp. cinnamon
¼ tsp. nutmeg
Grated rind 1 lemon
1 oz. chopped peel (2 Tbs.)

Measures level. Roll the pastry ⅛ inch (3 mm.) thick and cut in rounds with a 4-inch (10 cm.) cutter. Mix all the other ingredients together. Put 2–3 tsp. on each round. Brush the edges with water and press them together to form a ball. Turn over and roll the top until the fruit begins to show through. Cut 3 gashes on top with a sharp knife. Bake until lightly browned.

856. Choux Pastry (for cream puffs and éclairs)

Quantities for 18 small:

1 oz. margarine (25 g.)
¼ pt. water (½ c.)
Pinch of salt

2 oz. plain flour (6 Tbs.)
2 eggs

Measures level.

1. Put the first three ingredients in a pan and bring to the boil.

2. Then add all the flour at once and mix well. Cook for a few minutes over a gentle heat until the mixture leaves the side of the pan.

3. Allow to cool a little. Beat in the eggs one at a time and continue beating until the mixture is smooth and shiny. Very thorough beating is essential for good results, and it is hard work, as the mixture is fairly stiff. Beating takes about 10 minutes.

4. Bake on greased trays, in spoonfuls for puffs and finger lengths for éclairs. A forcing-tube helps to give even shapes and sizes. Bake in a hot oven 450° F. (230° C.) Mark 8, for 10–15 minutes and then reduce the heat to moderate 375° F. (190° C.) Mark 5, for at least another 20–25 minutes. Allow to cook for 30 minutes before opening the oven door. The buns should be quite dry in the centre, or they will become flabby on cooling. Leave plenty of room for them to rise.

5. When cold, split and fill with whipped cream, Confectioner's Custard, No. 692, or Butter Cream, No. 696. The tops of éclairs are iced with Chocolate Glacé Icing, No. 675, or Coffee Glacé Icing, No. 676.

857. Profiteroles with Chocolate Sauce

Quantities for 6 helpings:

Choux Pastry, No. 856   Chocolate Sauce, No. 99
Whipped cream or
    Butter Cream, No. 696,
    or Confectioner's
    Custard, No. 692

Make the choux pastry into 24 small cream puffs, baking about 30 minutes. Fill with the cream or custard and pile on a serving dish. Pour over the hot sauce and serve at once.

BATTERS

858. General Method for Mixing Batters

1. Sift the dry ingredients into a basin and make a well in the centre. Put the eggs in the well with half the liquid.

2. Start mixing from the centre, gradually working in all the flour from the sides.

3. Thin batters, like pancakes and Yorkshire pudding, need very thorough beating to mix in plenty of air, but

thick batters containing baking powder should be beaten only enough to make a smooth mixture. Too much beating makes them tough. Add the rest of the liquid.

4. Cook as described for the various kinds of batters.

Blender Method. Put eggs, flour and milk in the blender goblet in that order, and mix for one minute.

859. Pancakes. Cooking time 1–2 minutes each

Quantities for 8 pancakes:

4 oz. flour (¾ c.)	About ½ pt. milk (1 c.)
½ tsp. salt	Fat for frying
1 egg	

Measures level.

1. Mix according to the general method for batters given in No. 858, making a thin batter. The correct consistency is important, as, if the batter is too thin, the pancakes will stick, and if too thick, they will be heavy.

2. Heat a little fat in a small saucepan. Pour some into a clean, smooth frying-pan, using one 6–7 inches (15 cm.) across. Turn the frying-pan well, to make sure it is evenly coated with fat, and then pour off any surplus into the small saucepan. When the pan is hot, but not smoking, pour in a little of the batter from a jug, tilting the pan to make it flow over evenly.

3. Cook for a minute or two until brown underneath, shaking the pan to keep the pancake loosened. Keep the edges free with a knife. When it is cooked on one side toss or turn with a broad palette knife or fish-slice and finish cooking. Turn out on to a piece of paper sprinkled with sugar, and sprinkle the pancake with lemon juice. Roll up and keep hot until all are cooked. Sprinkle with more sugar and serve with slices of lemon. Grease the pan as before, and continue until all the batter is used.

860. Jam Pancakes

Make in the same way as No. 859, spreading warm jam on each one before rolling up. Marmalade is very good on pancakes, and a little grated orange or lemon rind may be added to the batter before cooking.

861. Stuffed Savoury Pancakes

Quantities for 8 pancakes:

Pancake batter, No. 859
4 oz. cooked minced
   meat or game ($\frac{1}{2}$ c.)
1 onion, chopped

1 oz. fat (25 g.)
2 Tbs. bottled sauce
Salt and pepper to taste

Measures level. Make the pancakes and put them in a pile one above the other to keep hot. Then spread each one with the filling which is made by frying the onion in the fat and then adding the other ingredients. Season well. Roll up, place in a baking-dish, and cook in a moderate oven 400° F. (200° C.) Mark 6, until they are crisp on top, or cover them with $\frac{1}{2}$ pt. (1 c.) of Tomato Sauce, No. 89, or Mushroom Sauce, No. 82, or Brown Sauce, No. 73, or Cheese Sauce, No. 75, and cook for about 20 minutes or until well heated.

862. Yorkshire Pudding

Quantities for 4–6 helpings:

Make the same batter as for Pancakes, No. 859. Heat some dripping in a shallow pan 8 × 10 inches (20 × 25 cm.), and when it is very hot pour in the batter and cook in a very hot oven 475° F. (250° C.) Mark 9, for about 10 minutes, and then reduce the heat to 425° F. (220° C.) Mark 7, for another 30 minutes, or until the batter is cooked. It should be well risen, brown, and hollow inside, without any soggy, uncooked layers. These are generally due to insufficient cooking.

BATTER PUDDING, which is more solid, is made by using double the amount of flour.

TOAD-IN-THE-HOLE is made like Yorkshire Pudding, but 1 lb. (500 g.) skinned sausages is heated in the fat for 5 minutes before adding the batter.

MEAT IN BATTER is made in the same way, but using 1 lb. (500 g.) small chops, or steak cut in pieces.

863. Individual Yorkshire Puddings or Popovers

These are made in exactly the same way as the larger one, but are baked in small, deep patty-tins or pudding-moulds. In the U.S.A. they are eaten hot with butter and jam in place of scones. Baking time is 10 minutes at the high temperature and 20–30 minutes at a lower heat, as with Yorkshire Pudding, No. 862.

864. Apple Batter

Add 1 oz. (2 Tbs.) sugar to the Batter recipe, No. 859, and pour it into the hot pan. Cover with 2 or 3 sliced apples and sprinkle on a little cinnamon or nutmeg. Bake in the same way as No. 862. Cut in squares and serve hot.

865. Fritter Batter. Cooking time 10–15 minutes

4 oz. S.R. flour ($\frac{3}{4}$ c.)	$\frac{1}{4}$ pt. milk, approx. ($\frac{1}{2}$ c.)
1 tsp. salt	Flavouring, see Nos.
$\frac{1}{4}$ tsp. pepper (savoury only)	866–70
	Fat for frying
1 egg	

Measures level. Mix to a thick batter according to No. 858 for general batters. Add the flavouring and fry spoonfuls in hot fat until brown on both sides or fry in deep fat.

866. Bacon Fritters

Add 3 oz. chopped bacon ($\frac{1}{2}$ c.) to Fritter Batter, No. 865. Serve with Tomato Sauce, No. 89, or Brown Sauce, No. 73.

867. Meat or Fish Fritters

Add 3 oz. minced cooked meat ($\frac{1}{2}$ c.) or flaked cooked or canned fish to Fritter Batter, No. 865. Serve with Tomato Sauce, No. 89, or Brown Sauce, No. 73, or Cheese Sauce, No. 75.

868. Dried Fruit Fritters

Add 2 oz. dried fruit (4 Tbs.) to Fritter Batter, No. 865. When cooked sprinkle with caster sugar and cinnamon mixed, and then with lemon juice or serve with Lemon Sauce, No. 102, or Jam Sauce, No. 101.

869. Cheese Fritters

Add 2–3 oz. grated cheese (50–75 g.) to Fritter Batter, No. 865. Serve with Tomato Sauce, No. 89.

870. Apple Fritters

Peel and core 4 medium-sized cooking apples and cut them across in $\frac{1}{3}$-inch (8 mm.) slices. Make Fritter Batter, No. 865. Take each apple-ring on the point of a skewer and dip it into the batter, coat well, lift out, and drop into the hot fat, deep or shallow. Fry until golden brown all over. Serve with caster sugar and lemon juice sprinkled over.

871. Drop Scones, Pikelets, Girdle Cakes, or Scotch Pancakes. Cooking time 3–4 minutes each batch

Quantities for 24 small cakes:

4 oz. S.R. flour ($\frac{3}{4}$ c.)	$\frac{1}{2}$ oz. melted margarine
$\frac{1}{4}$ tsp. salt	(1 Tbs.)
2 eggs	$\frac{1}{8}$–$\frac{1}{4}$ pt. milk ($\frac{1}{4}$–$\frac{1}{2}$ c.)
1 oz. sugar (2 Tbs.)	

Measures level. Mix to a thick batter according to the general method, No. 858, adding the sugar with the flour and the margarine at the end. These are baked either on a girdle, heavy frying-pan, or solid electric hot-plate. Heat until the girdle feels hot when the hand is held just above it, or until drops of cold water will dance about. Grease slightly with lard or cooking fat, using a twist of paper. Drop the mixture from the tip of a tablespoon, when it should flow into a perfect circle. Cook until bubbles begin to appear on the top but do not break. Turn and cook the other side. The girdle should be hot enough to brown both sides by the time the mixture is cooked through. If too hot they will brown before the inside is done, and if too slow they will be heavy and of poor appearance. Serve with butter and jam, syrup, or honey. As they are cooked put them on a cake-rack. The practice of putting them in a towel is apt to make them damp and soggy.

N.B. Very light pancakes may be made by beating the eggs and sugar until thick and light and then mixing in the other ingredients.

872. Girdle Pancakes

Add about half as much milk again to Recipe No. 871, and make in large, thin cakes similar in size to a pancake. Then serve in any of the ways mentioned for pancakes, see Nos. 859–61, or pile the cakes one on top of the other with a little butter or margarine in between each. Cut in wedges and serve with Syrup Sauce, No. 107. They may also be piled in the same way with jam in between.

CHAPTER 19
Bread and Sandwiches

873. Food Value

Eating bread is one of the better ways of getting necessary calories. This is because bread is also a good source of protein, calcium, iron and some B vitamins (thiamine and niacin).

There are small differences in nutritive value between wholemeal and white or brown bread (see No. 611), but these are of little significance in a good mixed diet. Fancy breads and buns sometimes contain dried milk, eggs, fruit and sugar, while others have added protein or reduced starch. Unless a person is on a strictly controlled diet, personal taste is the best guide for choosing bread.

Sandwiches can make nourishing and satisfying meals, even better than many a hot meal. Whether this will be the case depends on the choice of filling and the amount. Protein-rich foods such as cheese, eggs, meat and fish are the best fillings and to make a balanced meal there should be some vegetables such as tomato, watercress etc. with it, or some fresh fruit to follow.

874. Keeping Bread Fresh

Wrapped bread should be stored in its wrapping, preferably in a bread bin. Unwrapped bread keeps well for several days in a polythene bag but will eventually develop mould. Keeping the bread in a refrigerator delays the onset of mould but does not prevent staling. Bread keeps well for a month or more in the freezer and can be quickly thawed in a warm oven or more slowly at room temperature. Slices can be toasted while frozen.

If a bread bin is used for storing bread it should be cleaned out regularly and stale pieces of bread used for breadcrumbs. If you are unlucky enough to have bread go mouldy scald out the container with boiling water to destroy mould spores. Then dry thoroughly before using it again.

875. Toast

Better toast is made with bread one or two days old than with new bread. If you like toast soft in the middle, use thick-cut sliced bread and toast quickly near a fierce heat. If crisper toast is preferred, use thin-cut and turn several times during toasting so that it dries as it toasts.

Melba toast is made by drying thin slices of stale bread. Dry in a very slow oven until they are crisp and brown. When cool they may be stored in an airtight tin and will keep well.

Very stale bread may be used for toasting if it is first dipped in a little water, then toasted slowly, and buttered while hot.

876. Preparing Breadcrumbs

FRESH CRUMBS. When a recipe specifies fresh crumbs it generally means crumbs made from bread one or two days old. The crusts are removed and kept for making brown crumbs.

The quickest way of preparing breadcrumbs is to use an electric blender. Failing that, use a small mouli-grater. An ordinary grater can be used but will not give such fine, even crumbs as the other two. Fresh crumbs will keep for several days in a covered container in a refrigerator or cold larder and keep almost indefinitely in a deep freezer.

DRIED CRUMBS. These are made by drying bread until crisp. Then crush it with a rolling-pin, put it through a fine mincer, or in an electric blender. Sieve to remove any coarse crumbs. Store in a covered tin. White crumbs are made by drying the crumb of the bread and drying it so slowly that it does not colour. They are used for coating food to be fried. Brown crumbs are made by drying crusts and crumb until golden brown.

'Raspings' may be either these brown crumbs or finely grated crust from a stale loaf.

Dried crumbs may be used in most recipes in place of fresh crumbs, but only half the amount is needed. Additional liquid must be used for mixing, as dried crumbs soak up more than fresh crumbs.

BUTTERED CRUMBS. Melt 1 oz. butter or margarine and add 2 c. fresh breadcrumbs. Stir until well mixed. This is used for the top of sweet and savoury dishes which are to be browned in the oven or under the grill, and is very much nicer than using ordinary breadcrumbs dotted with fat.

877. Queen of Puddings. Cooking time 1 hour

Temperature 350° F. (180° C.) Mark 4–5.

Quantities for 4–6 helpings:

3 oz. breadcrumbs (1½ c.)   ½ tsp. vanilla essence or
2 Tbs. sugar   a pinch of spice
½ oz. margarine (1 Tbs.)   ¼ tsp. salt
1 pt. hot milk (2 c.)   2–3 Tbs. softened red jam
2 eggs

Measures level. Put the breadcrumbs, sugar and margarine in a bowl and pour on the hot milk. Leave to soak for a few minutes. Separate the egg yolks and whites; beat the yolks and add to the milk mixture. Add flavouring and salt. Pour into a greased 2-pint (1 l.) pie-dish or baking dish and cook until set, about 45 minutes. Remove from the oven and allow to stand for a few minutes. Meanwhile beat the egg whites and make a meringue with 2–4 Tbs. sugar, according to taste. Soften the jam by warming or adding a little hot water. Spread jam on top of pudding and cover with meringue. Bake until the meringue is lightly coloured, 15–20 minutes. Serve hot or cold.

878. Banana Pudding

Make in the same way as No. 877, but add a mashed banana to the bread mixture. Mashed banana may also be mixed with the jam to spread on top, or cover the top with sliced banana and omit the jam.

879. Butterscotch Pudding

Use the same recipe as No. 877, but with 4 oz. brown sugar ($\frac{1}{2}$ c.) instead of the white sugar, and heat it with the margarine until the sugar melts. Dissolve this in the hot milk before proceeding in the usual way.

880. Chocolate Pudding

Use Recipe No. 877, adding an extra tablespoon of sugar and 4 level Tbs. cocoa to the breadcrumbs.

881. Coconut Pudding

Use Recipe No. 877, adding $\frac{1}{2}$ c. desiccated coconut to the crumbs.

882. Orange or Lemon Pudding

Use Recipe No. 877, adding the grated rind of one orange or lemon. Leave out the vanilla or spice and use marmalade instead of jam.

883. Brown Betty. Cooking time $\frac{3}{4}$–1 hour

Temperature 375° F. (190° C.) Mark 5.

Quantities for 4–6 helpings:

1 oz. margarine (25 g.)
2 c. fresh breadcrumbs
1$\frac{1}{2}$–2 lb. sliced apple
  ($\frac{3}{4}$–1 kg.)
2 oz. brown or white
  sugar (4 Tbs.)

$\frac{1}{4}$ tsp. grated nutmeg
Rind and juice of $\frac{1}{2}$ lemon
$\frac{1}{4}$ pt. hot water ($\frac{1}{2}$ c.)

Measures level. Melt the margarine, add the crumbs, and mix well. Put alternate layers of crumbs and apples in the dish, sprinkling each layer with sugar, nutmeg, and lemon rind, finishing with crumbs. Pour over the water and lemon juice and bake in a moderate oven until the apples are cooked and the pudding brown on top. Serve with custard or cream.

884. Swedish Apple Cake. Cooking time $\frac{1}{2}$ hour

Temperature 375° F. (190° C.) Mark 5.

Quantities for a 7–8 inch (20 cm.) sandwich tin:

1$\frac{1}{2}$ lb. apples (750 g.) .
4 oz. sugar ($\frac{1}{2}$ c.)
4 oz. breadcrumbs (2 c.)
$\frac{1}{2}$ oz. margarine (1 Tbs.)

$\frac{1}{2}$ oz. grated chocolate
  (3 Tbs.)
Custard Sauce, No. 105

Measures level. Peel, core, and slice the apples and stew to a pulp with 2 oz. (4 Tbs.) sugar but no water. Heat the margarine in a frying-pan. Add the breadcrumbs and rest of the sugar and cook until crisp, stirring frequently. Grease the tin and put in a layer of crumbs, then a layer of the apple, and repeat these, finishing with crumbs. Bake in a moderate oven for $\frac{1}{2}$ hour and leave to cool. Turn out on a large dish and sprinkle the chocolate on top. Cut in wedges to serve. Hand the sauce separately.

885. Making Sandwiches

1. The butter or margarine should be soft, so that it will spread easily. You will find a suggestion for making it go further in No. 140.

2. For picnic sandwiches use thick-sliced bread; for dainty ones use thin-cut. Crusts may be removed or left on, according to taste.

3. To keep sandwiches fresh wrap them in foil or in polythene, keeping each kind separate.

4. Fillings should be moist enough to spread easily, but not so moist as to make the bread soggy if the sandwiches have to stand.

886. Rolled Sandwiches

Use brown or white bread which must be new. The filling may be a spread, or a piece of asparagus with a little mayonnaise, or a few shrimps held together with mayonnaise. Spread the bread with softened butter, trim off the crusts, add the filling and roll up. Pack close together so that they keep one another in shape. Chill to set the butter and filling and keep them in shape.

887. Open Sandwiches

These consist of a single layer of bread with the filling on top. They may be made very small for parties or made from whole slices of bread with a lot of filling on top and served for lunch or supper. This sort is very popular in Denmark, and all kinds of breads are used there for the base – white bread, rye or black bread, hard breads, and so on. It is a very useful idea when you have small amounts of food to use up, as two or three different kinds of these sandwiches are enough for a meal. They can be decorated to look very attractive. The small party kind should be as dainty and decorative as possible. They are best served on large flat meat-dishes, platters, or small trays.

888. Fried Sandwiches

This is a good way of using up stale sandwiches, or you can make them specially for the purpose, and in that case there is no need to spread them with butter or margarine. Fry the sandwiches in a little hot fat until brown on both sides.

889. Toasted Sandwiches

These are merely ordinary sandwiches toasted brown on both sides. An alternative method is to toast a thick slice of bread, split it, and then add the filling.

890. Savoury Fillings

EGG AND GHERKIN. Mix 2 chopped hard-boiled eggs with 2 chopped gherkins and moisten with salad dressing.

FISH. Mix any cooked, flaked fish with salad dressing.

COTTAGE CHEESE. Mix with chopped chives or pickles.

SCRAMBLED EGG. Fry a little chopped bacon or onion in the fat before cooking the eggs in the usual way. Use cold.

WATERCRESS. Chopped and mixed with salad dressing.

SALMON. Mix flaked, canned salmon with chopped gherkins or fresh cucumber and salad dressing.

APPLE AND CELERY. Mix equal quantities of chopped celery and apple and moisten with salad dressing. Chopped walnuts may be added.

MEAT AND CHUTNEY. Mince any cooked or canned meat and moisten with chutney.

GRATED CHEESE and chopped watercress, spinach, apple, or celery moistened with dressing.

GRATED CHEESE and chopped nuts.

COTTAGE CHEESE and sliced radishes.

COTTAGE CHEESE and raw grated carrot.

EGG AND SAUCE. Mix 2 chopped hard-boiled eggs with 1 Tbs. tomato sauce, 1 tsp. Worcestershire sauce, 1 Tbs. chopped parsley, and season with salt and pepper.

CHEESE AND ONION. Grated cheese mixed to a paste with onion-juice and hot water (grate onion to provide the juice).

MUSHROOM. Mix chopped mushrooms into a white sauce and cook until tender.

LIVER AND HAM. Mince together 4 oz. (125 g.) cooked liver, 4 oz. cooked ham. Season well with salt and pepper and add 2 Tbs. chopped capers or gherkins.

LOBSTER. Finely chopped, cooked lobster moistened with salad dressing and seasoned well with salt, pepper, and lemon juice.

891. Sweet Fillings

BANANA. Mash well and add a little lemon juice.

PEANUT BUTTER AND HONEY. ½ c. honey warmed and mixed with 1 Tbs. peanut butter.

PEANUT BUTTER AND APPLE. Mix peanut butter with raw grated apple.

MINT AND RAISIN. Mince equal quantities of mint and raisins and add a little hot water to make a spreading consistency.

DATE. Chop the dates and heat them with a little water until they make a smooth paste. Flavour with lemon juice or spice. A few chopped nuts may be added.

892. Suggestions for Open Sandwiches (large type)

CHEESE. Cover the buttered bread with a thin slice of any kind of cheese. Decorate with gherkins.

MEAT. Place a thin slice of any kind of meat on the bread. Decorate with pickles.

SCRAMBLED EGG. Mix cold scrambled egg with a little chopped fried onion and place in a curled lettuce leaf on the bread.

SARDINE. Place 2 or 3 sardines on the bread and decorate with radishes or watercress.

SAUSAGE. Split a cold cooked sausage and spread with mustard. Place on the bread with a row of cucumber slices down one side and tomato slices down the other.

SMOKED FISH. Mix flaked, smoked fish with enough Parsley Sauce, No. 87, or Tartare Sauce, No. 117, to moisten. Decorate with parsley.

Smoked salmon and eel are cut in thin slices and placed on the bread.

SHRIMPS. Arrange in rows on the bread and decorate with lemon and parsley.

SCRAMBLED EGG AND SHRIMPS. Spread scrambled egg on the bread (egg hot or cold) and decorate with shrimps.

FRIED FILLET OF PLAICE garnished with tomato, cucumber, and lemon.

COLD HAM AND SCRAMBLED EGG.

SLICED COLD TONGUE with asparagus and mayonnaise.

CORNED BEEF with horse-radish sauce.

SALAMI SAUSAGE with scrambled egg and chives.

SCRAMBLED EGG and tomato.

TOMATO and fried onions.

HARD-BOILED EGG slices with pickles.

COLD HAM slices with vegetable salad mixed with mayonnaise.

COLD ROAST PORK and beetroot or pickled cucumber.

PICKLED HERRING and potato salad.

YEAST MIXTURES

893. How to Handle Yeast

Using yeast is not difficult, provided you remember it is a living plant which can be killed by wrong treatment and that when it is dead it will not work to lighten the dough.

Yeast needs food and warmth to make it grow. Its food is sugar and flour. As it grows it produces bubbles of a gas called carbon dioxide, and this gas makes the dough light. The same gas is produced by the chemicals used to make baking powder, see No. 725.

The warmth yeast likes is just below blood heat, or 80–83° F. (30° C.). If the dough is heated above 95° F. (35° C.) the yeast dies, and if below 77° F. (25° C.) it goes to sleep and does not produce any gas. Cooks who are used to handling yeast doughs can tell the correct temperature by the feel. Beginners will find it a help to use a thermometer, pushing the bulb into the dough. Any thermometer that registers up to 100° F. (40° C.) will do.

The best places to put the dough to keep it warm are on the rack over the stove, in the warming cupboard, or airing cupboard. If none of these is suitable the basin with the dough in it may be stood over a pan of hot water; but be careful not to have the water too hot. The dough should be covered with a clean tea-towel or polythene during rising.

When the mixture goes in the oven the yeast is killed and no more gas is produced. For this reason it is important to be sure that all yeast mixtures have risen thoroughly, or been 'proved', before baking, otherwise they will be close and heavy. On the other hand, over-rising or proving can so stretch and weaken the dough that it cannot hold up, and collapses in the oven, again giving a heavy result.

With most yeast mixtures the dough should be allowed to double its size during rising, whether it is just allowed one rising before baking, or whether it is kneaded after one rising and then put to rise again before baking.

Remember, too, that only plain flour is suitable for making yeast mixtures, and special strong bread flours are the best to use.

Most yeast-doughs are kneaded, though some rich ones containing eggs are beaten hard instead. Kneading is working the dough lightly with the knuckles, folding it over and over as you knead. Use only just enough flour to prevent it from sticking to the board.

Kneading or beating mixes the yeast and the gas it produces evenly through the dough, and makes the mixture elastic.

894. Quick Bread. Cooking time ¾–1 hour

Temperature 450° F. (230° C.) Mark 7, then 375° F. (190° C.) Mark 5.

Quantities for two 1-lb. (½ kg.) loaves:

1 lb. plain flour, wholemeal or white (3¼ c.)	2 tsp. sugar
2 tsp. salt	½ pt. tepid water (1 c.) or milk and water
½ oz. fresh yeast (10 g.) or 2 tsp. dried	1 oz. melted fat (25 g.)

Measures level. Sift the flour, salt, and sugar and put in a warm place. Crumble the yeast into the tepid water. Make a well in the centre of the flour and pour in the water and the fat. Mix to a dough and knead well for 10 minutes. Divide in two and shape into loaves either to bake in greased loaf-pans or as cottage loaves on a greased baking-tray. Stand in a warm place with a clean tea-towel over the top. When it has doubled its size bake in a hot oven for 15 minutes, and then reduce the heat to moderate for a further ½–¾ hour. If the loaf sounds hollow when tapped on the bottom, it is done. Cool on a rack.

895. Vienna Bread. Cooking time 20 minutes

Temperature 375° F. (190° C.) Mark 5.

Quantities for 2 loaves:

1 lb. plain flour (3¼ c.)	1 egg
2 tsp. salt	1–2 oz. melted butter or margarine (25–50 g.)
½ oz. yeast (10 g.)	¼–½ pt. milk (½–1 c.)
2 tsp. sugar	

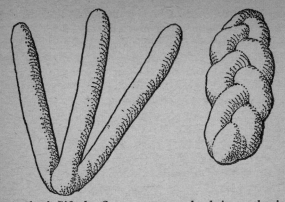

Measures level. Sift the flour, sugar, and salt into a basin and put in a warm place. Crumble the yeast into half the lukewarm milk. Add the beaten egg and the fat, melted but not hot. Mix to a sticky dough, adding more milk if needed. Beat hard for 10 minutes and leave to rise in a warm place until double its bulk. Cover with a clean cloth. Knead well and divide in half. Divide each piece in three and roll into a long sausage about 1 inch (2 cm.) thick. Plait the pieces, securing the ends firmly together. Put on greased trays, and leave to rise until double in bulk. Bake for about 20 minutes or until firm. Tap the bottom of one, and if it sounds hollow it is cooked. Cool on a rack.

896. Swedish Pastry. Cooking time 20 minutes

Temperature 425° F. (220° C.) Mark 7.

Quantities for 1 dozen buns:

8 oz. plain flour (1½ c.)
1½ Tbs. sugar
1 egg
1 oz. yeast (25 g.)
Milk to mix
5 oz. butter or margarine
　(125 g.)

Apple purée or
　Confectioner's Custard,
　No. 692
1 egg white

Measures level. Sift the flour into a basin and add the sugar. Make a well in the centre and add the egg, crumbled yeast and enough milk to make a stiff dough. Knead well. Roll to a rectangle about 1½ inches (4 cm.) thick. Put the butter or margarine on in small dabs. Fold in three and then in three again, like a napkin. Roll and repeat the rolling and folding three times. Leave in a cold place for 1 hour to become firm. Roll out ½ inch (1 cm.) thick, and cut in 4-inch (10 cm.) squares. Put a teaspoonful of apple or custard  in the centre of each. Fold the corners to the centre like an envelope and press well together. Put in a warm place to rise to double the bulk, about 1 hour. Brush with slightly beaten egg white and bake until light brown. When cold ice with Water Icing, No. 674, or serve plain.

897. Rum Babas. Cooking time 20 minutes

Temperature 425° F. (220° C.) Mark 7.

Quantities for 6–8 small babas:

½ oz. yeast (10 g.)
1 tsp. sugar
6 Tbs. warm milk
2 oz. butter or margarine
   (50 g.)
2 oz. sugar (¼ c.)
2 eggs
6 oz. plain flour (1¼ c.)

¼ tsp. salt
4 oz. dried fruit (currants, peel, and raisins, ⅔ c.)

Syrup
4 oz. sugar (½ c.)
4 Tbs. water
2 Tbs. rum

Measures level. Mix the sugar with the warm milk and crumble in the yeast. Sprinkle the top with a little flour. Cover with a cloth and put in a warm place to begin rising. Leave for 15–20 minutes. Use the other ingredients except the fruit to make a cake mixture by the Creaming Method, No. 732. Add the yeast mixture and beat hard for 5 minutes. Add the fruit and half fill small greased moulds. Leave to rise to the tops. Bake until they feel springy when pressed in the centre. Turn out carefully, pour over the warm syrup, allowing it to soak in. To make the syrup, boil the sugar and water for 5–10 minutes and then add the rum. Serve hot or cold. Cold ones may be decorated with whipped cream flavoured with rum.

898. Bath Buns. Cooking time 20 minutes

Temperature 425° F. (220° C.) Mark 7.

Quantities for 1 dozen buns:

8 oz. flour (1½ c.)	3 oz. sugar (6 Tbs.)
1 tsp. salt	2 oz. sultanas (⅓ c.)
3 oz. lard (75 g.)	1½ oz. chopped peel
½ oz. yeast (10 g.)	(3 Tbs.)
1 tsp. sugar	Little egg for brushing
1 egg	Coarse sugar
¼ pt. milk (½ c.)	

Measures level. Sift the flour, 1 tsp. sugar, and salt into a basin and rub in the lard. Crumble the yeast into the liquid and add to the flour with the beaten egg. Beat well, cover, and leave to rise until double the bulk. Beat in the rest of the sugar and the fruit. Put on a greased tray in small heaps. Leave to rise until double the size. Brush with egg and sprinkle with coarse sugar. Bake until they are brown and springy in the centre.

899. Hot Cross Buns. Cooking time 20 minutes

Temperature 425° F. (220° C.) Mark 7.

Quantities for 12–16 buns:

½ oz. yeast (10 g.)	2 oz. sugar (¼ c.)
1 tsp. sugar	1 tsp. spice

½ pt. warm milk (1 c.)   2 oz. sultanas (¼ c.)
1 lb. plain flour (3¼ c.)   *Glaze*
1 tsp. salt   2 Tbs. sugar
1 oz. lard (25 g.)   2 Tbs. water

Measures level. Add the sugar to the milk and crumble in the yeast. Sprinkle a little flour on top, cover, and put in a warm place for about 15 minutes to begin rising. Sift the rest of the flour into a warm bowl, with the salt. Rub in the lard. Add the sugar, fruit, and spice, and then the yeast mixture. If necessary add more milk to make a soft dough. Knead well. Cover and leave to rise until double in bulk. Knead lightly, shape into buns, and place on greased trays. Cut a cross on the top of each with a sharp knife and leave to rise until double the size. Bake until they sound hollow when tapped on the bottom. While still hot brush with the glaze made by mixing the sugar and water and bringing it to the boil. Use while hot.

CHAPTER 20

Beverages

900. Food Value

Tea and coffee are stimulants which have a little food value added when served with milk and sugar.

Cocoa is a milder stimulant, and also provides some calories and some iron. Its value is very much increased when it is made with a large amount of milk.

Milk and egg beverages are very nourishing, and are ideal for invalids and children, as they are rich in nutrients.

Fruit drinks are most valuable as thirst quenchers, but may provide vitamins if they are freshly made from fresh or canned fruit juices.

Alcoholic beverages are stimulants. In small amounts they stimulate the flow of digestive juices and help to digest a meal, but in large amounts have the opposite effect.

TEA

901. Making Tea

1. Always keep tea in a covered container, for if allowed to lie about in an open packet it loses flavour.

2. Use water freshly drawn from the cold tap, and make the tea as soon as it boils.

3. Just before the water boils scald the teapot with some of the water. Throw this away.

4. Put in the tea, allowing two or more level teaspoons for each half-pint ($\frac{1}{4}$ l.) of tea required.

5. When the water boils, take the teapot to the kettle and pour on the boiling water. Allow to stand for 3–8 minutes before using. A tea with fine leaves needs less time to brew than one with coarse leaves. Stir well before pouring.

6. Tea is usually served with a little cold milk or cream and sugar to taste, but some people prefer it without milk and with a slice of lemon or orange in it. Tea without milk should be weaker.

COFFEE

902. General Information

1. Always keep coffee in an airtight container, as the flavour is volatile and the coffee quickly loses flavour if left in an open packet or tin. Freshly roasted and ground coffee gives the best flavour, and the ideal is to have a small home coffee-grinder and grind the beans yourself as you want them. You can then buy small amounts of freshly roasted beans and store them in a covered jar.

2. Allow 2–4 level Tbs. coffee for each $\frac{1}{2}$ pt. of water (1 c.) being used. This will give you 3 small coffee-cups full. The mistake most people make is in using too little coffee.

3. A better flavour is obtained if glass, earthenware, or stainless steel is used for the coffee-brewer.

4. It is important to keep all equipment clean. Scald all utensils as soon as they have been used, and dry and air them well before putting them away.

5. Coffee may be served black, or with milk or cream. Many people serve a mixture of half coffee and half milk. In this case the coffee should be made twice as strong as usual. (The milk should not be allowed to boil, only scalded.) Coffee-lovers prefer to use a little cold top milk, evaporated milk, or cream in black coffee, about the same amount as you would use for tea.

903. Some Different Methods of Making Coffee

There are many different ways of making coffee of varying quality, the difference being mainly one of strength, but also of flavour, and clarity of the finished product.

The method using the simplest apparatus is the jug method, see No. 904, but it is also the one requiring the most attention and handling during making. With black coffee made this way, it is necessary to heat the coffee cups to offset the cooling process which starts during straining into the coffee jug. When hot milk is added for white coffee, there is no need to heat the cups. This is the best way to serve coffee made by the jug method.

For good black coffee it is better to use a coffee-making machine of some kind. For really strong, yet economical coffee, a household Expresso is one of the best. The Cona vacuum-type glass coffee-maker makes excellent coffee and can be obtained with a portable electric base so that coffee can be made at table, or it can be used on the cooker, or over a spirit lamp. There are many types of coffee-makers using the filter principle and they, too, make excellent coffee, though some of them are quite complicated to use.

When you buy a coffee-maker of any kind, make sure you get a copy of the instructions for using it correctly.

904. Using a Jug

Coarsely ground coffee is the best for this method, as the finer grinds tend to make a muddy and bitter brew. Measure the coffee into the jug (2–4 Tbs. to $\frac{1}{2}$ pt. or 1 c.). Pour on the boiling water. Stir and stand in a warm place or in a pan of boiling water for 5–8 minutes. Strain through muslin into the heated coffee-pot and serve.

905. Iced Coffee

Sweeten the coffee to taste and chill. Serve with top milk or cream or ice-cream. An alternative method is to add coffee essence to chilled milk and flavour with a few drops of vanilla essence.

COCOA

906. Making Cocoa

For each half-pint (1 c.) allow 2 level tsp. cocoa, one of sugar, and a pinch of salt. The liquid may be all milk or half milk and half water. Mix the cocoa, sugar, and salt to a smooth paste with some of the cold liquid. Boil the rest and pour on to the cocoa. Return to the pan and boil for 1–2 minutes to cook the cocoa and improve the flavour. At this stage the cocoa may be beaten with a small egg-whisk to make it frothy and a few drops of vanilla added. If dried milk is being used, the powder may be mixed dry with the cocoa and sugar.

SOFT DRINKS

907. Lemonade

Quantities for 4–6 glasses:

4 lemons

4 oz. sugar ($\frac{1}{2}$ c.)

2 pt. boiling water (4 c.)

Measures level. Peel the lemons thinly and put the rind in a jug with the sugar. Pour over the boiling water and stir until the sugar dissolves. Leave until cold. Strain and add the lemon juice. Serve with ice.

908. Grape Juice Lemonade

Quantities for 8 or more glasses:

8 Tbs. lemon juice

1 pt. water (2 c.)

1 pt. grape juice (2 c.)

4 oz. caster sugar
($\frac{1}{2}$ c.) or to taste

Ice cubes

Measures level. Mix all the ingredients together, stirring to dissolve the sugar. This can be chilled and then diluted to taste with ice-water or, after mixing, serve it with ice cubes.

This is also very good when mixed with sweetened fresh grapefruit juice.

909. Ginger Ale Lemonade

Quantities for 3 glasses:

⅔ c. lemon juice
1 c. canned or fresh
    orange juice

2 oz. sugar (4 Tbs.)
2 bottles ginger ale

Mix the fruit-juice and sugar and chill. Just before serving add the ginger ale and serve with crushed ice.

910. Fruit Punch

Quantities for 25 glasses:

2 lb. sugar (4 c.)
2 qt. water (8 c.)
12 oranges
6 lemons
4 sliced bananas
8 oz. small green grapes
    (250 g.)

8 oz. stoned cherries
    (250 g.)
1 qt. ginger ale (4 c.)
1 pt. cold, clear tea (2 c.)
2 qt. soda-water (8 c.)

Boil the sugar and water together for 10 minutes. Add 6 oranges peeled and cut in thin slices, removing as much white pith as possible. Add the strained juice of the rest of the oranges and the lemons. Add the bananas, grapes, and cherries. Chill thoroughly. Add the ginger ale, tea, and soda-water. Just before serving add cubes of ice.

911. Orangeade

Quantities for 4–6 glasses:

3 small oranges
2 Tbs. sugar

2 pt. boiling water (4 c.)

Make in the same way as Lemonade, No. 907, using the orange rind grated.

912. Orange Julep

Quantities for 8–10 glasses:

1 pt. unsweetened canned
    orange juice (2 c.)
¼ pt. lime juice cordial
    (½ c.)
2 oz. caster sugar (4 Tbs.)

2 Tbs. chopped mint
Soda water
Mint and orange slices to
    garnish

Measures level. Mix the orange juice, lime cordial and sugar
and stir to dissolve. Add the chopped mint and chill for an
hour. Strain and dilute half and half, or to taste, with soda
water. Ice cubes are an optional extra. Decorate with a sprig
of fresh mint and a slice of fresh orange.

913. Tomato-juice Cocktail

Quantities for 4–6 glasses:

½ pt. tomato juice (1 c.)
1 Tbs. vinegar
1 Tbs. lemon juice
2 tsp. sugar
¼ bay leaf

1 tsp. grated or finely-
    chopped onion
¼ tsp. celery salt
½ tsp. Worcester sauce

Measures level. Mix all the ingredients together and leave to
stand for 15 minutes. Strain through muslin or a fine
strainer and chill. Serve in small glasses.

914. Rhubarb Sherbet

1 lb. rhubarb (500 g.)
4 oz. raisins or figs,
    chopped (¾ c.)

3 pt. water (6 c.)
Canned orange-juice or
    orange or lemon squash

Measures level. Wash and cut up the rhubarb and put in a
pan with the dried fruit and water. Cover and boil gently

for ½ hour. Strain through muslin and cool. Add the orange-juice or squash to taste and serve with ice.

EGG AND MILK BEVERAGES

915. Malted Milk

½ pt. milk (1 c.)   1 Tbs. malt extract

Heat the milk and stir in the malt extract. Serve hot.

916. Milk Drinks (for children who do not like plain milk)

½ pt. milk (1 c.)   Colouring
2 tsp. sugar
Flavouring essence or fruit
  syrup

Mix well. Fruit syrups, or vanilla, are the best to use. Serve cold.

917. Milk Posset

½ pt. milk (1 c.)   ½–1 Tbs. syrup or honey

Heat the milk and stir in the syrup or honey. Serve hot.

918. Hawaiian Egg Nog

Quantities for 1 glass:

1 egg   Pinch of nutmeg
Pinch of salt
¼ pt. canned pineapple
  juice (½ c.)

Separate the white and yolk. Beat the yolk well and mix in the cold juice. Stir in the stiffly beaten white and salt and pour into a deep glass. Sprinkle with nutmeg.

919. Egg Nog

1 fresh egg
1–2 tsp. sugar
½ pt. hot or cold milk
  (1 c.)

Few grains salt
Vanilla essence to taste

Beat the egg and sugar very thoroughly and then pour on the milk. Flavour to taste adding a little grated nutmeg if liked, and 2 Tbs. sherry or other wine.

ALCOHOLIC BEVERAGES

920. Cherry Gin

1 lb. Morello cherries
  (500 g.)
½ lb. caster sugar (1 c.)

12 almonds
1 bottle gin (about 1¼ pt.)

Put the fruit in screw-top jars in layers with the sugar. Screw down and shake occasionally for 3 days. Add the blanched almonds and the gin and leave for at least 3 months before decanting. Stone the cherries and add them to fruit salad.

921. Sloe Gin

1 c. sloes
6 oz. sugar (¾ c.)

3 drops almond essence
¾ pt. gin (1½ c.)

Wash the sloes and prick them with a darning-needle. Put them in an empty gin-bottle. Add the sugar and almond essence. Pour in the gin and cork well. Leave for at least 3 months before decanting. Stone the sloes and use them in fruit salad.

922. Jamaican Long Drink

Put 2–3 Tbs. rum in each tumbler. Fill up with ginger ale, cider, or fruit squash and soda-water. Add a lump of ice.

923. Vermouth Long Drink

About a quarter fill tumblers with French or Italian Vermouth. Fill up with iced water or soda-water and add a slice of lemon and a sprig of mint. Add a lump of ice.

924. Martini

Mix half gin and half French or Italian Vermouth.

925. Grog

Put a slice of lemon in a small tumbler with 1 tsp. of sugar. Put in a spoon to absorb the heat and prevent the glass from cracking and then three-quarters fill with boiling water. Stir and add 2 Tbs. of rum and serve at once.

926. Rum Cocktail

$\frac{1}{3}$ rum $\frac{1}{3}$ orange squash
$\frac{1}{3}$ cider

Mix well.

927. Claret Cup

2 tsp. mixed spice $\frac{1}{2}$ pt. water (1 c.)
1 bottle claret   Rind of $\frac{1}{2}$ lemon
1 oz. sugar (2 Tbs.)

Measures level. Mix all except the lemon and stir until the sugar dissolves. Peel the lemon rind very thinly and add to the cup. Chill before serving.

928. Hock Cup

1 oz. sugar (2 Tbs.)   1 small glass sherry
$\frac{1}{4}$ pt. boiling water ($\frac{1}{2}$ c.)   1 bottle hock or Chablis
Rind of $\frac{1}{2}$ lemon

Measures level. Peel the lemon rind thinly and put it in a jug with the sugar and water. Allow to infuse for 15 minutes. Add the sherry, ½ pint cold water (1 c.), and the hock or Chablis. Stand for 30 minutes and then chill before serving.

CHAPTER 21

Ice-cream and Frozen Puddings

929. Food Value

The food value varies with the ingredients. Ice-cream is usually made with fat, oil or cream and milk, sugar, perhaps egg, as well as flavouring and sometimes fruit. All ices are a source of calories and will usually contribute a small amount of protein, minerals and vitamins as well.

Ice-cream made under hygienic conditions is an excellent food, but, if made and handled under dirty conditions, can be a cause of food poisoning.

930. General Information

Many people do not think it is worth while making their own ice-cream, preferring to use the commercial product or a ready-mix. While these are very good and can be varied by different methods of service with sauces, fruit, cake and pies, it is pleasant to have a change and make your own sometimes. Ices are very easy to make and can be stored in the ice-making compartment of the refrigerator for a day or so, longer in the freezer. Most ices are improved by quick freezing, and it is usual to turn the control to the coldest number. An ice-cream should take 2–3 hours to freeze, and the richer the mixture, the colder the refrigerator should be. Freezing a plain mixture too fast and too hard can make it coarse and full of ice crystals. To avoid freezing too hard, turn the control back from quick freezing before the ice is frozen in the centre. Beating and stirring help to make a smooth ice-cream. Some mixtures are beaten well before freezing, others are beaten or stirred during freezing.

A high fat content, such as is given by the use of cream, helps to make a smooth ice-cream. Cream made in a cream machine is suitable, and evaporated milk may be used, but does not give quite such a smooth texture as the other two. Half cream and half evaporated milk is a good alternative.

931. Evaporated Milk in Place of Cream

Use less of the evaporated milk than you would of cream, $\frac{1}{2}$–$\frac{2}{3}$ the amount. Chill the milk in the refrigerator or cold larder. Whip in the same way as for cream. Evaporated milk increases the amount of protein in the ice-cream and decreases the amount of fat.

932. Chocolate Ice-cream

Quantities for 6–8 helpings:

2 oz. plain chocolate (50 g.)	1 oz. sifted icing sugar ($\frac{1}{4}$ c.)
$\frac{1}{4}$ pt. evaporated milk ($\frac{1}{2}$ c.)	$\frac{1}{2}$ tsp. vanilla
$\frac{1}{4}$ pt. whipping cream ($\frac{1}{2}$ c.)	1 egg white

Measures level. Melt the chocolate over hot water and add 2 Tbs. evaporated milk. Stir and warm until well blended. Whip the rest of the milk until thick and light and beat in the chocolate mixture. Rinse the beaters and whip the cream. Add the sugar and vanilla and combine with the chocolate mixture. Rinse beaters and whip the egg white stiff. Fold this into the other mixture. Put in freezing trays and freeze without stirring.

933. Mocha Ice-cream

Use recipe No. 932 and add 1 Tbs. soluble coffee to the warm chocolate and evaporated milk mixture.

934. Vanilla Mousse

Quantities for 4–6 helpings:

½ pt. cream, whipped   ½ tsp. vanilla
  (1 c.)   1 egg white
1 oz. sifted icing sugar
  (¼ c.)

Measures level. Add the sugar and vanilla to the cream. Fold in the egg white beaten stiffly, with a pinch of salt. Pour in the freezing-trays and freeze without stirring. Serve plain or as a basis for sundaes.

935. Peppermint Ice-cream

Make as No. 934, flavouring with peppermint essence and colouring pale green. Serve with Chocolate Sauce, No. 99.

936. Fruit Mousse (using cream or evaporated milk)

Quantities for 4–6 helpings:

1 tsp. gelatine   3–4 oz. sugar (6–8 Tbs.)
1 Tbs. cold water   1 c. cream or ⅔ c.
½ pt. Fruit Purée, No.   evaporated milk
  602 (1 c.)

Measures level. Soak the gelatine in the water for 5 minutes and then heat over hot water to dissolve it. Add to the fruit and sugar. Leave until cold. Then beat well and fold in the whipped cream or milk. Pour into the trays and freeze without stirring. The best fruits to use are raspberry, loganberry, strawberry, damsons, apricots, peaches, pineapple, and rhubarb.

937. Coffee Ice-cream

Quantities for 6–8 helpings:

¼ pt. evaporated milk (½ c.)   ¼ pt. whipping cream (½ c.)
1 Tbs. soluble coffee   1 Tbs. rum (optional)
1 oz. icing sugar (¼ c.)

Measures level. Mix the coffee and sugar with a little of the milk until dissolved. Whip the rest of the milk and the cream separately. Combine and add the coffee mixture. Blend well and add the rum. Pour into freezing trays and freeze without stirring.

938. Orange Parfait

Quantities for 4 or more helpings:

¼ pt. orange juice (½ c.)   3 egg yolks
4 oz. caster sugar (½ c.)   ¼ pt. whipping cream
Pinch salt   (½ c.)

Measures level. Heat the orange juice, sugar and salt in the top of a double boiler or in a basin over a pan of boiling water. Stir until the sugar dissolves and then add the egg yolks beaten until thick and lemon-coloured. Continue beating over hot water until the mixture thickens. Remove from the heat and stand the pan or basin containing the mixture in a bowl of cold water. Whisk as it cools. Whip the cream until light but not stiff, and fold it into the cold orange mixture. Pour into freezing trays and freeze without stirring.

939. Meringue Glacé

Join two meringues together with vanilla ice or chocolate ice. Serve with chopped fresh fruit.

940. Chocolate Ice-cream Cake

Sandwich two slices of sponge cake with a portion of vanilla ice-cream. Pour chocolate sauce over and sprinkle with chopped nuts.

941. Cherry Coupe

Put vanilla ice-cream at the bottom of glasses and cover with a layer of cold stewed cherries. Decorate with cream or mock cream, coloured pink with sieved raspberry jam.

942. Raspberry Sorbet. Cooking time 5 minutes

Quantities for 4 helpings:

4 oz. sugar (½ c.)   ¼ pt. raspberry purée
½ pt. water (1 c.)   (½ c.)
1 tsp. gelatine   1 egg white
1 Tbs. lemon juice

Measures level. Mix sugar and water in a small pan, stir until boiling and boil 5 minutes. Remove from the heat. Add the gelatine and stir until dissolved. Cool.

Fresh or thawed frozen raspberries can be used to make the purée. Add purée and lemon juice to the cooled syrup. Pour into a tray and freeze to a mush. Beat the egg white stiff. Put the frozen ice in a bowl and beat smooth. Fold in the egg white. Finish freezing. It should be softish when served and will keep several days in the ice compartment of a refrigerator.

943. Lemon Sorbet. Cooking time 5 minutes

Quantities for 4–6 helpings:

3 strips yellow lemon rind   1 tsp. gelatine
½ pt. water (1 c.)   ¼ pt. lemon juice (½ c.)

3 oz. sugar (6 Tbs.)   1 egg white, beaten
2 Tbs. golden syrup or
  honey

Measures level. Heat lemon rind and water until boiling.
Strain, add the sugar to the water and boil for 5 minutes.
Add the syrup or honey and gelatine and stir until dissolved.
Cool. Add the lemon juice and pour into freezing trays.
Freeze to a mush. Beat the egg white until stiff. Remove
the frozen mixture to a bowl and beat smooth Fold in the
egg, return to the trays and freeze. This should be softish
when served and will keep several days in the ice compartment of a refrigerator.

944. Mocha Refrigerator Cake. Chilling time 12 hours

Quantities for 4 helpings:

4 oz. butter or margarine   4 sponge cakes or half
  (125 g.)   Recipe Nos. 756–7
2 oz. caster sugar ($\frac{1}{4}$ c.)   Whipped cream
3 egg yolks   3 Tbs. chopped almonds
1 Tbs. soluble coffee in
  4 Tbs. water

Measures level. Cream the butter and sugar until very white
and light. Beat in the egg yolks and coffee. Slice the sponge
thinly, and put the sponge and coffee mixture in layers in
a 6-inch (15 cm.) cake-tin or soufflé-dish, beginning and
ending with cake. Cover and put in the refrigerator for 12
hours. Turn out of the mould and ice with whipped cream
and sprinkle with the nuts. Cut in wedges and serve as a
cake or cold sweet.

945. Lemon Refrigerator Cake. Chilling time 12–24 hours

Quantities for 8 helpings:

4 oz. butter or margarine (125 g.)
6 oz. caster sugar ($\frac{3}{4}$ c.)
3 eggs
Rind and juice 1 lemon

6–8 small sponge cakes
Whipped cream, or
    Chocolate Sauce, No. 99

Measures level. Cream the butter and sugar until very white and light. Beat in the egg-yolks, the grated rind, and juice of the lemon. Fold in the stiffly-beaten egg whites. Split the sponge cakes into 2 or 3 layers, and line an oblong tin or pie-dish with some of them. Fill with alternate layers of sponge and lemon mixture, finishing with sponge. Cover and chill for 12–24 hours. Turn out and cut in slices. Serve with cream or hot chocolate sauce.

CHAPTER 22

Hors-d'œuvre and Savouries

946. Food Value

Hors-d'œuvre are meant to be appetizers at the beginning of a meal and their nutritional value is comparatively unimportant. They should be well seasoned, colourful and attractively served in small portions.

Today, savouries are most commonly served as party food chiefly at buffet parties, but are still sometimes included in dinner menus. In either case they should be small, attractive to look at, and well flavoured. For a buffet party they should be easy to pick up in the fingers.

947. General Information

Although in the home it is not practical to serve the restaurant type of hors-d'œuvre of a dozen or more different foods, yet a small one of four or five dishes is easily prepared, and is a useful and pleasant beginning to a meal. Hors-d'œuvre are generally served in place of soup, and if you have no suitable small dishes for serving the foods separately, a selection can be arranged attractively on individual plates ready for each person.

Only small amounts of each kind of food should be served, and they should be well seasoned. The range of suitable foods is almost unlimited, but the following are a few suggestions using foods which are generally available.

948. Anchovies

Anchovy fillets are sold ready for use, and may be served as they are with a little chopped parsley sprinkled over, or used to decorate potato or cauliflower salad, or served on a bed of shredded lettuce.

949. Asparagus Tips

Cooked or canned asparagus is served with French Dressing, No. 118.

950. Beans (butter or haricot)

Use canned beans, or boiled as described in No. 550, drained and served cold with Vinaigrette Sauce, No. 119.

951. Beetroot

This is boiled in the usual way and served cold. It may be sliced and dressed with salt, pepper, and vinegar or made into the following pickle. Cut 2 medium-sized beetroot into dice and mix with 2 Tbs. grated horse-radish and 6 peppercorns. Cover with cold vinegar and store in jars for 2 or 3 weeks before using.

952. Bloaters

Soak the fish in equal parts of milk and water for 2 hours. Remove the heads, and skin and fillet the fish. Cut in thin strips and serve raw.

953. Cauliflower

Boil the cauliflower in small sprigs, as in No. 464. Allow to cool, and dress with French Dressing, No. 118, or Mayonnaise, No. 113. Sprinkle with chopped parsley or decorate with anchovy fillets.

954. Celery

Cut it in slices and serve raw with French Dressing, No. 118;
or boil it as in No. 427, drain and serve cold with dressing,
or chop raw celery and mix with sliced cooked beetroot
and serve with French dressing.

Cucumber. See Cucumber Salad, No. 561.

Curried Salad. See No. 577.

955. Eel (smoked)

Cut in thin slices and serve without cooking. Sprinkle with
lemon juice or vinegar and freshly ground pepper.

956. Eggs (hard-boiled)

Cut in halves and mask with Mayonnaise, No. 113, or stuff
as in No. 188.

Fish Mousse. See No. 286.

957. French Beans

Slice and boil in a little water, as in No. 427. Serve cold
with French Dressing, No. 118.

958. Herrings (salt)

Soak 2 salt herrings or bloaters in cold water for 12 hours.
Drain and fillet, cutting the fillets in $\frac{1}{2}$-inch (1 cm.) strips,
diagonally. Put in a shallow dish and sprinkle with 2 Tbs.
chopped onion, a pinch of pepper, and 1 Tbs. brown sugar.
Pour over 3–4 Tbs. vinegar or enough to cover and allow to
stand 5–6 hours before serving.

959. Kipper Pâté. Cooking time 5–10 minutes

Quantities for 4 or more helpings:

¾ lb. kippers (375 g.) or 6 oz. fillets (175 g.)	½ tsp. anchovy essence
4 oz. butter or margarine (125 g.)	Pepper
	Lemon juice

Grill the kippers or put them in a large jug, pour boiling water over them, cover and stand in a warm place for 5–10 minutes. Drain the fish and allow to become cold. Remove bones and skin. Warm the butter to soften but not melt. Add it to the kippers with anchovy and seasoning. Rub the mixture through a sieve or mix in the blender to make smooth. Put in a dish and chill. Serve with thin toast.

960. Leeks

Cut in half and boil in a little water, as in No. 484. Drain well and serve cold with Vinaigrette Sauce, No. 119.

961. Canned Mussels or Oysters

Serve with vinegar or lemon and chopped parsley.

Potato Salad. See No. 565.

962. Prawns and Shrimps

Shell as described in No. 307, and serve very cold, decorated with parsley and lemon.

963. Radishes

Wash well and cut off the roots. Trim the tops but retain about 2 inches (5 cm.) of the leaves to hold them by. If put in a small dish with iced water they keep crisp during service.

964. Red Cabbage

Serve pickled red cabbage sprinkled with grated horse-radish.

965. Sardines

Serve whole, decorated with parsley and lemon.

966. Smoked Salmon

Serve in very thin slices with lemon and cayenne pepper.

967. Tomato Salad

Slice tomatoes thinly and serve with French Dressing, No. 118. Sprinkle with chopped parsley or fresh tarragon.

968. Hard-boiled Egg Salad

3 hard-boiled eggs	2 Tbs. olive oil
$\frac{1}{2}$ tsp. salt	1 Tbs. chopped spring
Pinch of pepper	onions
1 Tbs. wine vinegar	

Measures level. Cut the eggs in half and remove the yolks. Mash them in a small bowl with the salt and pepper. Work in the vinegar and oil and beat well. Add the chopped whites and the onions and pile in a glass dish. Decorate with parsley.

969. Fish Cocktail

Quantities for 4–6 helpings:

$\frac{1}{4}$ pt. tomato ketchup ($\frac{1}{2}$ c.)	$\frac{1}{4}$ pt. thick cream ($\frac{1}{2}$ c.)
1 tsp. Worcestershire sauce	About $\frac{1}{2}$ pt. flaked cooked fish or shell-fish (1 c.)

1 Tbs. horse-radish sauce
½ Tbs. lemon-juice
¼ tsp. dry mustard

4–6 lettuce leaves
Chopped parsley or other
  herbs

Measures level. Mix all ingredients except the fish and lettuce. When well blended add the fish and mix gently. Arrange the shredded lettuce in deep individual glasses or bowls and place the fish mixture on top. Decorate with chopped parsley or other herbs.

970. Shrimp and Orange Cocktail

Quantities for 4 helpings:

2 large oranges
4 oz. shelled shrimps
  (125 g.)
1 Tbs. chopped cucumber
  or gherkin

Mayonnaise, No. 113
Shredded lettuce

Peel the oranges and remove all pith, pips and membrane. Mix the pulp with the shrimps and cucumber and enough mayonnaise to moisten. Put some lettuce in the bottom of 4 large glasses, add the fish mixture and chill.

971. Liver Pâté or Terrine. Cooking time 1 hour

Temperature 350° F. (180° C.) Mark 4.

Quantities for 4–5 helpings:

8 oz. calf or lamb's
  liver (250 g.)
6 oz. fat bacon pieces
  (150 g.)
Pepper

¼ tsp. ground mace or
  nutmeg
4 oz. thinly sliced streaky
  bacon (125 g.)

Measures level. Remove rind from the bacon and mince fat bacon and liver together twice. If a very fine pâté is required, put the liver and bacon through an electric blender or a sieve. Add pepper to taste and the mace or nutmeg. Mix very thoroughly. Line a small cake or loaf tin with the streaky bacon and pack in the liver mixture. Cover with greased paper or aluminium foil and bake in a moderate oven for 1 hour. Leave in the tin to cool. Turn out and slice.

972. Potato and Egg Salad

8 oz. potatoes (250 g.)
2 eggs, hard-boiled
½ tsp. salt
Pinch of pepper

1 Tbs. wine vinegar
2 Tbs. olive oil
1 Tbs. chopped onion
2 Tbs. chopped gherkins

Measures level. New potatoes or waxy old ones are the best. Scrub and boil them in their jackets. Peel and cool. Shell the eggs and separate the whites and yolks. Mash the yolks in a basin and add the salt and pepper, vinegar, and oil. Beat well and add the onion and gherkins. Slice the potatoes or cut in small cubes. Add the chopped whites and pour over the dressing. Mix well.

973. Tomatoes and Sweet Peppers

8 oz. tomatoes (250 g.)
2 canned or cooked sweet peppers
1 small onion, chopped
½ tsp. salt

Pinch of pepper
½ Tbs. wine vinegar
1 Tbs. olive oil
1 Tbs. chopped parsley

Measures level. Slice the tomatoes. Remove the seeds, peel, and slice the peppers. Put in a dish with the onion. Mix the seasoning, vinegar, and oil and pour over. Sprinkle with chopped parsley.

974. Tongue or Beef Salad

Cut cold, cooked tongue or beef in very thin, small slices. Pour over French Dressing, No. 118, and sprinkle with chopped parsley.

Tongue Salad. See No. 579.

975. Sardine Butter

Mash the sardines, including the skin and bone. Beat in an equal weight of softened margarine or butter. Beat until quite smooth, seasoning highly with salt and pepper. Press into a small glass dish and serve very cold with thin, crisp toast.

976. Cold Sausage (Mortadella, salami, etc.)

Remove any skin and cut in very thin slices. Arrange in a shallow dish and decorate with parsley or radishes.

977. Olives (black, purple, or green)

Drain from the pickling liquid and serve in a small glass dish.

978. Smoked Sprats

Serve with lemon juice and brown bread-and-butter.

Soused Herrings. See No. 256.

979. Celery and Blue Cheese Mayonnaise

1 Tbs. Blue cheese	Black pepper
$\frac{1}{2}$ Tbs. cream	1 c. chopped celery
$\frac{1}{4}$ pt. Mayonnaise, No. 113 ($\frac{1}{2}$ c.)	

Measures level. Mash the cheese and cream together until very smooth. Add the mayonnaise, and season highly with pepper. Mix with the chopped celery.

980. Sweet Pickled Cherries

4 lb. Morello cherries (2 kg.)	3-inch (8 cm.) stick of cinnamon
1 pt. vinegar (2 c.)	4 pieces of root ginger
2 lb. brown or white sugar (1 kg.)	6 cloves

Measures level. Stone the cherries or slit the skins to allow the syrup to penetrate. Boil the other ingredients for 10 minutes with the lid on the pan. Remove the spices and add the cherries. Simmer for 5 minutes. Drain from the liquid and pack loosely into warm jars. Boil the liquid until syrupy and pour over the cherries. Seal down while hot and keep for a few weeks before using. They will keep at least 12 months, and improve with keeping.

981. Marinaded Trout

Use small trout about the size of herrings. Clean and remove the fins, but leave the heads on. Poach as described in No. 237, using $\frac{1}{3}$ vinegar and $\frac{2}{3}$ water. Allow to cool in the liquid. Drain and serve with a little of the liquid. Garnish with slices of lemon.

982. Marinade of Cold Fish

Quantities for 4–5 helpings:

1 lb. cold boiled or fried fish (500 g.)	1 slice lemon
$\frac{1}{2}$ pt. wine vinegar and water mixed (1 c.)	1–2 bay leaves
3 Tbs. salad oil	4 cloves
Few slices of onion	8 peppercorns
	Salt and pepper

Divide the fish into convenient pieces for serving. If fried fish is used it is nicer if coated in milk and flour than in batter. Arrange the fish in a wide, shallow dish. Mix the remaining ingredients and pour over the fish. Leave to marinade for 1–2 hours, turning occasionally. Arrange the fish on a serving dish. Strain the liquor and serve as a sauce.

983. Melon

Serve slices of ice-cold melon, and hand separately some caster sugar or ground ginger, or both.

984. Pickled Eggs

1 doz. eggs	1 Tbs. whole allspice
1 qt. vinegar (4 c.)	4 pieces whole root ginger
2 tsp. black peppercorns	

Hard-boil the eggs and shell them. Boil the other ingredients together for ½ hour. Add the eggs and boil gently for 10 minutes. Put the eggs in a jar and pour the vinegar and spices over. Cover and store in a cool place. They will be ready for use in 4 days, but will keep several weeks.

SAVOURIES

985. Cheese Straws. Cooking time 5–7 minutes

Temperature 450° F. (230° C.) Mark 8.

2 oz. plain flour (6 Tbs.)	3 oz. grated cheese (75 g.)
Pinch of salt	1 egg yolk
Few grains cayenne pepper	
2 oz. butter or margarine (50 g.)	

Measures level. Sift the flour and seasonings together and rub in the fat. Add the cheese, using some Parmesan.

Mix to a stiff dough with the egg yolk, adding a little cold water if it is needed. Roll out to about ⅛ inch (3 mm.) and cut in very narrow strips. Cut some rounds with a 2-inch (5 cm.) cutter and stamp out the centres with a 1½–1¾-inch (4 cm.) cutter, to give rings. Place on baking-trays and cook in a hot oven, watching them carefully, as they burn very easily. To serve, put bundles of the straws through the rings. Serve hot.

986. Cheese Bonbons. Cooking time 10 minutes

Temperature 450° F. (230° C.) Mark 8.

Quantities for 2 dozen:

Flaky Pastry, No. 808, using 4 oz. flour (¾ c.)	½ tsp. salt
½ c. cottage cheese	Few grains cayenne pepper
2 Tbs. bottled tomato sauce	24 walnut halves

Measures level. Roll the pastry about ⅛ inch (3 mm.) thick and cut in rounds with a 1-inch (2 cm.) cutter. Bake in a hot oven until lightly browned. Mash the cheese and mix to a smooth paste with the other ingredients. Put a little on top of each round of pastry and press a walnut half on top.

987. Angels on Horseback

Trim the rind from thin slices of streaky bacon. Wrap an oyster or mussel (fresh or canned) in each slice of bacon, and secure with a tooth-pick or thread several on a skewer. Grill or bake in a hot oven until the bacon is crisp. Serve on rounds of toast with Tomato Sauce, No. 89, or serve plain.

988. Soft Roe and Mushroom Canapés

Dip soft roes in seasoned flour and fry them for a few minutes in a little butter or margarine. Fry some chopped mushrooms separately. Prepare some small rounds of hot buttered toast. Place one soft roe on each with chopped mushrooms on top. Serve at once.

989. Sardine Rolls. Cooking time 15–20 minutes

Allow 1 sardine per roll.

4 oz. flour (¾ c.) made into Flaky Pastry, No. 808, will make 12 rolls.

Roll the pastry to ⅛ inch (3 mm.) and cut in strips the width of the sardines. Sprinkle the fish with lemon juice or grated cheese or curry powder and roll each in pastry in the same way as for sausage rolls. Brush with egg and bake until brown. Serve hot.

990. Toasted Prunes in Bacon

10 large prunes   10 rashers streaky bacon

Soak the prunes in cold water until soft. Remove the stones. Roll each prune in a strip of bacon and thread the rolls on skewers or fasten with tooth-picks. Grill or bake in a hot oven until the bacon is crisp. Serve hot.

991. Egg Creams. Cooking time 5–8 minutes

Temperature 450° F. (230° C.) Mark 8.

4 oz. flour (¾ c.) máde into Flaky Pastry, No. 808	1 Tbs. grated Parmesan cheese
4 olives	2 Tbs. thick cream
2 hard-boiled eggs	Salt, pepper, and mustard to taste

Measures level. Roll the pastry ⅛ inch (3 mm.) thick and cut in very small rounds with a fluted cutter. Prick well with a fork, and bake in a hot oven until light brown. Chop the olives finely and rub the eggs through a sieve. Mix all the ingredients together and season highly. When the pastry is cold sandwich together with the filling.

992. Cheese and Anchovy Toast

2–3 slices toast	1 tsp. vinegar
½ c. grated cheese	Few drops anchovy essence
½ tsp. dry mustard	

Measures level. Mix all the ingredients to a smooth paste and spread on the hot toast. Cut in fingers and serve hot.

993. Cheese Biscuits with Anchovy

Cheese Straw recipe, No. 985	1 Tbs. chopped parsley
	Anchovy essence to taste
2 hard-boiled eggs	Few grains of cayenne
1 oz. butter or margarine (25 g.)	pepper

Measures level. Cut the cheese-straw mixture into small biscuits with a fluted cutter and bake in the usual way. Sieve or mash the eggs with the other ingredients, seasoning to taste. Sandwich the biscuits together in pairs with the mixture. Heat in the oven before serving.

994. Cheese Puffs. Cooking time 20–25 minutes

Temperature 450° F. (230° C.) Mark 8.

4 oz. flour (¾ c.) made into Flaky Pastry, No. 808, or Puff Pastry, No. 809	2 oz. grated Parmesan cheese (50 g.)
1 egg white	Pinch of salt
	Pinch of cayenne pepper

Measures level. Roll the pastry ⅛ inch (3 mm.) and cut in small rounds. Brush with stiffly-beaten egg white and sprinkle three-quarters of the number with cheese and seasoning. Put these together in pairs and top with a plain one, so that each puff consists of three layers of pastry. Bake in a hot oven until lightly brown and cooked through. Serve hot.

995. Salted Almonds

Blanch the almonds by pouring on boiling water. Leave for a few minutes, and then plunge in cold water. Squeeze gently to remove the skins. Dry on a clean cloth. Fry golden brown in butter or oil, turning frequently; or bake in a moderate oven with butter, turning frequently. Drain on absorbent paper and sprinkle with salt and cayenne pepper while they are still hot. Serve cold.

CHAPTER 23

Planning and Preparing Meals

996. General Information

Our bodies cannot get the materials to keep them in good working order from anywhere except the food eaten. Thus by a wise choice of diet we have the power to influence our state of health.

One of the most noticeable and widespread misuses of this power is seen in the large numbers of children and adults who are over-weight, and in the degenerative diseases that so often follow untreated obesity.

Today we have a very wide choice of food in the shops and the majority of people have enough money to indulge their personal tastes; but a lot of what you fancy does not necessarily do you good, whether it is 'gourmet' food or 'nosh'. This is where some knowledge of the science of nutrition can help to avoid serious mistakes in meal planning.

But in meal planning the nutritive value of the food is not the only thing to be considered. Other important factors are palatability, digestibility, cost, and the time and labour required to prepare the meals.

NUTRITIVE VALUE

I have already given brief notes on the nutritive value of individual foods in each chapter under the heading Food Value.

Food is made up of complex chemical substances called nutrients. These are:

PROTEIN, the most important nutrient in the structure of the body, important to everyone, but most of all to the growing body of the foetus, infant, child and adolescent. Protein is found in cheese, milk, eggs, meat, fish, peas, beans, cereals and nuts.

MINERALS are also important in the structure of the body. Calcium and phosphorus help to give strength to bones and teeth. Other minerals have different roles, such as the iron in blood, the fluorine in tooth enamel, the iodine in the thyroid gland, and others too numerous to list here. Calcium is found particularly in milk, cheese, fish, green vegetables, and bread; phosphorus is present in most foods; iron-rich foods are liver, heart, kidney, beef, eggs, green vegetables, bread, cocoa, chocolate, and dried fruit. The most important source of fluorine is drinking water; iodized salt and salt-water fish are the most reliable sources of iodine.

VITAMINS are substances present in very small amounts in foods but they play a vital role in regulating all body processes, including growth in children. A diet which includes the protein-rich foods and butter or margarine, green vegetables and fresh fruit will provide most of the necessary vitamins. It might, however, be lacking in vitamin D which is why cod-liver oil or vitamin tablets are prescribed for expectant mothers and babies.

FATS include solid fats and oils. These are a concentrated source of energy, measured as calories. Some fats, such as butter and margarine, cod-liver oil, and halibut-liver oil, also contain vitamins A and D and for this reason are the most valuable ones in the group.

CARBOHYDRATES are the starches and sugars, important as a cheap and popular source of calories. They include sugar of all kinds, cereals, bread and flour (and things made with flour), and potatoes. The best sources of carbohydrate to eat are the foods which contain other nutrients as well. Chief among these are bread and potatoes, which between them contribute some of all the other nutrients except vitamins A and D, which can be got by spreading the bread with butter or margarine. No sugary foods have the same all-round good nutritive value as bread and potatoes.

By looking back over this list of nutrients it will be clear that a good diet will include: cheese, milk, eggs, meat, fish, peas, beans, green vegetables, fresh fruit, bread, potatoes, butter or margarine, drinking water containing fluorine, iodized salt, and cod-liver oil or alternative for the vulnerable groups such as expectant mothers and young children.

The most practical household method I have found for planning meals which include the necessary foods is given in the following Menu Planning Guide. If you follow this as closely as possible you will be including all the foods needed to keep the family in good health. It is suitable for adults and all except very small children, who have their own special requirements.

MENU PLANNING GUIDE

Foods to include for each person every day.

Food	Amount	Modifications
Milk	1 pt. ($\frac{1}{2}$ l.) for adults. $1\frac{1}{2}$–2 pt. (1 l.) for children, expectant and nursing mothers, and adolescents. This includes milk used in cooking.	Canned or dried milk for cooking.
Eggs	3–5 a week, preferably one a day, including those used in cooking.	When eggs are too expensive be sure to use milk liberally, and plenty of the foods containing iron.
Meat or fish or cheese	1 or more helpings a day. 2 oz. (50 g.) cheese replaces an average 4-oz. (125 g.) portion of meat or 5 oz. (150 g.) of fish. Serve liver, heart or kidney once a week.	Use a little of one of these mixed with dried peas, beans, lentils, or milk, or eggs.

Food	Amount	Modifications
Potatoes	Once or twice a day.	
Vegetables	One or more servings daily. At least one green, and salads often.	The cheaper vegetables such as cabbage, swedes, and carrots are amongst the most valuable.
Fruit	One or more servings daily, including fresh, bottled, dried, and juices. One should be rich in vitamin C, see No. 580.	When fruit is scarce or expensive increase the quantities of vegetables and potatoes served.
Cereals, bread, cakes, pastry	To satisfy the appetite. Serve as much variety as possible.	People doing hard work, and active children need most of these. People who eat more than they need get fat.
Butter or margarine	1 oz. (25 g.) a day.	Fats which do not contain vitamins A and D are not an adequate substitute.
Cod-liver oil or its equivalent	According to directions on the bottle.	For older children and adults serve oily fish regularly.

N.B. The number and kind of meals taken is a matter of habit and personal preference. The important thing is to include all the essential foods each day.

PALATABILITY

This covers the serving of attractive-looking food, good flavouring and cooking, and combining foods which go well together.

Combining foods which go well together is learnt by experience, and is very largely a matter of personal taste and habit. The sort of meal most English people enjoy, for example, is very different from that a Chinese family would choose. The important thing is that the meal should contain the foods needed for health, be eaten with pleasure, and easily digested.

With many recipes I have given suggestions for ways of serving the dishes, such as the sort of sauce or vegetable to choose. I think beginners will find this helpful as a guide.

DIGESTIBILITY

To most people this means a lack of discomfort after a meal. A good meal-plan does not include two foods which are difficult to digest. Chief among these are fried foods, pastry, cream, and any dish containing a lot of fat or oil, fatty meat, shell-fish, twice-cooked or re-heated food, and sometimes cheese.

Most people can take cheese as the main course, while if served as an extra at the end of an already adequate meal, it would cause indigestion. It is more easily digested if served grated, and this is the best way for children. If cheese is cooked it should be done lightly and not allowed to become tough or stringy.

Very sweet food causes digestive upsets. Children should not be allowed unlimited sweets between meals. They are best at the end of a meal, when they just add to the satisfied feeling without doing harm.

Fried foods are responsible for more indigestion than any others. This is because a fatty coating prevents the digestive juices from getting to the food properly, and it stays in the stomach too long, causing a feeling of discomfort. Another reason is that fat is often allowed to smoke and burn during frying, when it produces a substance very irritating to the stomach and intestines. If you are studying your digestion, figure, and complexion you should cut fried foods down to the minimum.

COST

Unfortunately an inexpensive diet generally contains too much sugar and too many buns and cereal foods, because these are cheap and filling. By using the cheaper foods from each group in the Menu Planning Guide it is possible to have a balanced diet which is still inexpensive.

It is important to try to have the full amounts of milk and vegetables. The cheapest vegetables, potatoes, cabbage, and carrots, and the cheapest fish, herrings, are the most valuable nutritionally. Lentils or dried peas or beans served with some egg, milk or cheese are an excellent meat substitute in food value and can be made very tasty. Eggs are usually cheaper than meat, taking 2 eggs as equal to 4 oz. meat, in food value.

TIME AND LABOUR SAVING

For the busy woman the written menu plan is the best way out. A few minutes spent once a week working out the meals for each day will make shopping and catering much easier. Most people find it best to plan from Saturday to Saturday or Friday to Friday. The fact that you probably have to alter the plan as you go along does not make it any less useful. You will be able to make out a list of non-perishable foods needed for the week and buy them all at once, leaving only the perishables to get every day. You will find, too, that if you have a plan you can often do some preparation for the next meal or for next day while cooking the current one. A plan leaves your mind free for other things, instead of the eternal worry of what to get for the next meal. The busier you are, the more valuable you will find this method of catering.

997. Preparing Meals (for the beginner)

One of the most difficult things for a beginner is to organize the preparation and cooking of a meal so as to have everything ready on time.

The quickest way to learn this is to do a little planning on paper first. Write down the dishes with the rough time each will take to cook, according to the recipe. Then write down the time you must be ready to start cooking each one. Be sure to start preparing the ingredients well before hand, so that you are ready to begin the actual cooking on time.

After doing this a few times it will become almost automatic, and you will be able to do the planning in your head; but I always go back to this method for special occasions, such as cooking for a party. There is nothing like a little careful planning beforehand to see you through without worry and fuss.

When you are very new to cooking it is always a good plan to have one course cold – e.g. the pudding, which can be prepared in advance. Then you will be able to give all your attention to the main dish. If you are attempting a new or complicated recipe, make the rest of the meal simple.

998. Recipes Suitable for Lunch, High Tea, or Supper

Whatever the third meal of the day may be called, it does present a problem to many housewives. Far too often the solution is bread, buns, cake, and tea, which is not the ideal for most people. If possible, serve a protein-rich food of some kind – e.g. fish, cheese, or milk – and a vegetable or salad.

Below is a list of suggestions for recipes which would be suitable for the main dish of this meal.

CHEESE DISHES. Cheese Pudding, No. 176; Macaroni Cheese, No. 620; Cheese Fondue, No. 175; Chutneyed Cheese, No. 174; Welsh Rarebit, Nos. 171–2; Cheese

Cakes, No. 153; Cheese Tart, No. 173; Quiche Lorraine, No. 178.

EGG DISHES. Any in Chapter 10.

SOUPS. Substantial ones, such as Fish Chowder, No. 58; Mussel Soup, No. 54 or 59; Chestnut Soup, No. 55; Cream Soups, No. 46; Lentil Soup, No. 41.

FISH. Fish Roes, Nos. 317–19; Sardines on Toast, No. 288; Salmon Loaf, No. 285; Fish au Gratin, No. 249; Fish Pie, No. 248; Fish Cakes, No. 152; or any other fish recipe.

VEGETABLE DISHES. Vegetables au Gratin, No. 432; Vegetable Stew, No. 436; Broad Beans and Bacon, No. 446; Beans Béarnaise, No. 448; Cabbage and Bacon, No. 457; Stuffed Cabbage Leaves, No. 458; Chicory with Cheese and Ham, No. 471; Onion Toast, No. 497; French Peas, No. 502; Stuffed Sweet Peppers, No. 507; Baked Stuffed Potatoes, No. 513; Potatoes with Cheese, No. 521; Potato Ragoût, No. 522; Stuffed Tomatoes, No. 541; Salads, Nos. 557–579.

MISCELLANEOUS. Corned Beef Hash, No. 422(2); Open Sandwiches, No. 892; Toasted Sandwiches, No. 889; Risotto, No. 615; Meat Cakes or Rissoles, No. 151; Spaghetti and Meat Sauce, No. 623.

999. Recipes Suitable for a Buffet Party

BEVERAGES. Wine Cups, Nos. 927–8; Fruit Punch, No. 910; Lemonade, Nos. 907–9; Tomato-juice Cocktail, No. 913; Jamaican Long Drink, No. 922; Vermouth Long Drink, No. 923; Rhubarb Sherbet, No. 914; Iced Coffee, No. 905.

SAVOURY DISHES. Toasted Sandwiches, No. 889; Vol-au-Vent, No. 810; Welsh Rarebit, Nos. 171–2; Lobster Patties, No. 300; Stuffed Eggs, No. 188; Crab Patties, No. 294; Filled Cheese Scones, No. 793 (using sandwich fillings); Chutneyed Cheese, No. 174; Open Sandwiches, No. 892; Hors-d'œuvre, Nos. 946–84; Swedish Meat Balls, No. 413; Salted Almonds, No. 995; Savouries, Nos. 985–95.

SWEETS. Apple and Orange Salad, No. 586; Fruit Fool, No. 603 (in sundae glasses); Ice-creams, Nos. 932–43; Crème de Menthe Jelly, No. 705; Refrigerator Cakes, Nos. 944–5; Chocolate Mousse, No. 230; Zabaglione, No. 229; Pavlova Cake, No. 766; Fresh Fruit Salad, Nos. 584–8; Bavarois, No. 710; Charlotte Russe, No. 713; Chiffon Pie, No. 818.

CAKES. Butterfly Cakes, No. 762; Lemon Layer Cake, No. 743; Meringues, No. 763; Orange Cake, No. 738; Langues de Chat, No. 785 (to go with ices and fruit salad); Almond Macaroons, No. 786; Chocolate Layer Cake, No. 751.

PASTRY. Continental Flan, No. 815; Fruit Band, No. 758; Éclairs, No. 856; Jam Puffs, No. 810; Custard Slices, No. 852; Fairy Tarts, No. 826; Cream Crisps, No. 854; Cake of a Thousand Leaves, No. 853.

1000. Recipes Suitable for a Children's Party

BEVERAGES. Rhubarb Sherbet, No. 914; Lemonade, Nos. 907–9; Orangeade, No. 911; Fruit Punch, No. 910.

SAVOURIES. Plain Sandwiches, Nos. 890–91; Open Sandwiches, No. 892; Toasted Sandwiches, No. 889; Filled Cheese Scones, No. 793 (using sandwich fillings); Watercress, Radishes, Crisp Celery.

JELLIES AND COLD PUDDINGS. Fruit Salad, Nos. 584–8; Fruit Fool, No. 603; Ice-creams, Nos. 932–43; Milk Jelly Squares, No. 707; Cream Whip, No. 708; Orange Mousse, No. 709.

CAKES. Butterfly Cakes, No. 762; Layer Cakes, Nos. 741–4; Meringues, No. 763; Louise Cakes, No. 830; Chocolate Crispies, No. 787; Chocolate Layer Cake, No. 751; Butter Sponge, No. 756; Sponge Roll, No. 761; Chocolate Biscuits, No. 778; American Doughnuts, No. 798; Madeleines, No. 749.

PASTRY. Sausage Rolls, No. 848; Jam Puffs, No. 810;

Custard Slices, No. 852; Fairy Tarts, No. 826; Éclairs, No. 856; Cream Puffs, Nos. 856–7.

SWEETS. Toffee Apples, No. 665; Crumb Fudge, No. 669; Coconut Ice, No. 670; Turkish Delight, No. 672.

1001. Suggestions for Using Up Leftovers

VEGETABLE TRIMMINGS. Vegetable Stock, No. 33; Mushroom Stock, No. 35.

VEGETABLES. Potato Cakes, Nos. 150–53; Vegetables au Gratin, No. 432; Macedoine of Vegetables, No. 437; Brussels Sprouts Salad, No. 559; Cauliflower Mayonnaise, No. 560; Potato Salad, No. 565; Russian Salad, No. 566; Hors-d'œuvre, Nos. 948–76; Potato and Egg Salad, No. 972; Creole Potato Salad, No. 576

FISH. Trimmings for Fish Stock, No. 34, and Fish Chowder, No. 58.

Cooked Fish in: Fish Cakes, No. 152; Fish Pie, No. 248; Fish au Gratin, No. 249; Fish Fritters, No. 867; Fish Sandwiches, Nos. 890 and 892; Salmon Mayonnaise, No. 570; Kedgeree, No. 616.

BACON TRIMMINGS AND RINDS. For flavouring Vegetable Stock, No. 33, and Bone Stock, No. 31, and for Lentil Soup, No. 41, Tomato Soup, No. 56, Tomato Sauce, No. 89.

STALE BREAD. Forcemeats, Nos. 126–35; Melba Toast, No. 875; Dried Crumbs, No. 876; Buttered Crumbs, No. 876; Brown Betty, No. 883; Queen of Puddings, No. 877; Bread Puddings, Nos. 878–82.

SOUR MILK. For mixing scones, cakes, and puddings and for Cottage Cheese, No. 160.

EGG WHITES. Meringues, No. 763; Langues de Chat, No. 785; Almond Macaroons, No. 786; Vanilla Mousse, No. 934; Pavlova Cake, No. 766; Cheese Puffs, No. 994; Cornflake Meringues, No. 767; Macaroon Tartlets, No. 832; Coconut Macaroons, No. 790; White Mountain Icing, No. 689.

EGG-YOLKS. For brushing pastry and scones before baking; Scrambled Egg, Nos. 195–200 (adding 1 Tbs. of water to each egg yolk. 2 yolks equal 1 egg); Custards, Nos. 217–21 (2 yolks equal 1 egg); Zabaglione, No. 229; Cheese Straws, No. 985.

MEAT. Re-heating, No. 393; Cold Meat Hash, No. 420; Shepherd's Pie, No. 421; Corned Beef Hash, No. 422; Fricassée of Veal, No. 423; or Poultry; Plain, Open, and Toasted Sandwiches, Nos. 886–92; Chicken Blanquette, No. 342; Creamed Rabbit, No. 343; Tongue or Beef Salad, No. 974.

FRUIT. Fruit Fool, No. 603; Fruit Soufflé, No. 604.

BOILED RICE. Re-heated and Fried, No. 614; Kedgeree, No. 616.

COLD COFFEE. Iced Coffee, No. 905.

1002. Cooking for Invalids

An invalid's diet naturally depends on what the doctor recommends. In some illnesses the patient will be on a special diet, and these suggestions are not intended to cover such cases. They are meant for the invalid whose doctor has prescribed a 'light' diet. In planning this sort of meal the following points need to be considered.

1. Be very careful to serve foods as attractively as possible, because the appetite generally needs tempting. Small portions look better than large ones. It is much better for the patient to ask for a second helping than to risk taking away his appetite by the sight of too much food on the plate. As far as possible use small, individual dishes, as this helps to make the food look more tempting; for example, set jellies in small moulds or cups. Coloured china, too, helps to make the tray more attractive.

2. Most invalids need building up. Illness is generally accompanied by wasting of muscle and body-tissue, and this has to be replaced by the nutrients in food. The best foods for building up are milk and eggs, and these should

always have a prominent place in invalid cookery. The eggs should always be lightly cooked so that they are easy to digest, for example, coddled, see No. 183, or poached or lightly scrambled.

3. Other good foods for building up are fish, chicken, rabbit, cheese, and meat. They, too, should be served in their most easily digested form. Cheese should always be finely grated and, if cooked in a sauce, add the cheese after the sauce has finished cooking, and do not allow it to boil again. Fish should be steamed or poached and meat should be minced, grilled, stewed, or roast.

4. Avoid all indigestible foods, but particularly pastry, any fried foods, highly flavoured and seasoned foods, pickles, spices, new bread, hot scones, hot buttered toast. (Toast should be thin and crisp and buttered cold.)

5. All invalids need food rich in vitamin C. This vitamin helps them to get well, and especially to heal wounds and broken bones. Blackcurrant syrup, rosehip syrup, orange-juice, tomato-juice, and green vegetables cooked quickly in very little water, see No. 427, all provide a good supply of vitamin C. If the patient is allowed raw fruit and salads, use these as often as possible.

6. Clear soups and aspic jellies have very little building-up value, but they do stimulate the appetite, and are useful to serve before the main, and more nourishing, course. Soups containing milk are very good for invalids, and sweet jellies are much more valuable foods if they have milk or eggs added.

7. The following recipes are suitable for most people on a light diet.

SOUPS. Cream Soup, No. 46; Consommé, Nos. 62–5.

BEVERAGES. Lemonade, Nos. 907–9; Orangeade, No. 911; Egg Nog, No. 919; Milk Posset, No. 917; Malted Milk, No. 915.

EGG DISHES. Coddled Egg, No. 183; Steamed Egg, No. 194; Poached Egg, No. 189; Scrambled Egg, No. 195; Baked Custard, No. 217.

FISH AND MEAT. Boiled Fish, No. 237, with Parsley Sauce, No. 87; Steamed Fish, No. 246, with Parsley Sauce, No. 87; Creamed Soft Roes, No. 318; Boiled Chicken or Rabbit, No. 336; Creamed Chicken or Rabbit, No. 343; Brains, No. 335–9.

VEGETABLES. Green Vegetables, No. 427; Mashed Potato, No. 511; Creamed Spinach, No. 533.

PUDDINGS. Fruit Purée, No. 602; Fruit Fool, No. 603; Sago Cream, No. 625; Creamed Semolina, No. 636; Cornflour Mould, No. 645; Cornflour Desserts, No. 652; Lemon Jelly, No. 703; Milk Jelly, No. 706; Cream Whip, No. 708; Junket, No. 165; Queen of Puddings, No. 877.

CAKES. Butter Sponge, No. 756; Sponge Roll, No. 761; Victoria Sandwich, No. 742.

BREAD. Melba Toast, No. 875.

1003. Feeding the Overweight

The chief cause of putting on weight is thought to be eating more food, especially starches and sugars, than the body requires for the energy it expends. Individual needs vary a great deal, which is why, on the same diet, one will stay thin while the other puts on weight.

Weight can be reduced by dieting if the necessary will-power is exercised. The only danger is that an ill-chosen diet may reduce the weight but at the same time disastrously affect the person's health.

The simplest and safest way of dieting is to follow the Menu Planning Guide at the beginning of this chapter, but cut down the amounts of potatoes, cereals, bread. All cakes, pastry, and sweets should be excluded from the reducing diet. Instead of puddings serve raw fruit and/or a piece of cheese. Use a non-sugar sweetener for drinks.

Index

Numbers refer to paragraphs

Abbreviations used   6
Afghans   788
Alcoholic beverages   920–28
Almond
  Biscuits   777
  and Honey filling   697
  Macaroon   786
  Paste   685
  Salted   995
Aluminium utensils   27
Anchovy
  Canned   289
  Hors-d'œuvre   948
  Sauce   72
  Toast and Cheese   992
  Toast and Egg   191
Angels on Horseback   987
Anzac Nutties   783
Apple
  Baked   597
  Batter   864
  Brown Betty   883
  Cake, Swedish   884
  and Celery Sandwich   890
  Cinnamon   605
  Compote   589
  Crisp   606
  Crumble   606
  Dumplings   847
  Flan   822–3
  Fool   603
  Fritters   870
  Meringue, baked   598
  and Orange Salad   586
  and Peanut Butter Sand-
    wich   891

Pie   843
  Preparing   581
  and Prune Stuffing   132
  Pudding, steamed   803
  Sauce   108
  Soufflé   604
  Stuffed, stewed   590
  Tart, double   836
  Tart, open   823
  Toffee   665
Apricots
  Compote   589
  Dried   592–4
  Flan   822
  Fool   603
  Pie   843
  Preparing   581
  Soufflé   604
Arrowroot
  Desserts   652–7
  for Cakes   721
  Moulds   645–51
  Source of   612
Artichokes
  Globe   439
  Jerusalem   440
  Soup   38
  Soup, Cream   52
Asparagus
  Preparing and using   441
  Rolls   886
  Tips   949
Aspic Jelly
  Glaze   717
  with Stock   716
  without Stock   716

Aubergine 476
Au gratin 12

Babas, Rum 897
Bacon
  Baked 399
  Boiled 337–9
  and Egg Tart 838
  Fried 383
  Fritters 866
  Grilled 375
  Omelet 202
  and Scrambled Egg 199
Baking
  Effects of incorrect 734
  General 12
  Trays and tins 24
Balm 442
Banana
  Bread Pudding 878
  and Chocolate Creams 608
  Meringue 643
  Preparation and use 581
  and Prunes, baked 599
  Sandwich 891
Barley
  for Cakes 721
  Uses of 612
Basil 443
Basting 12
Basting Sauces 122
Bath Buns 898
Batter
  Apple 864
  Coating 865
  Fritter 865
  General method 858
  Meat in 862
  Pancake 859
  Pudding 862
  Thick and Thin 726
  Toad-in-the-hole 862
  Value as food 719
  Yorkshire 862
Bavarois 710

Bay leaf 397
Bean
  and Apple Salad 557
  Béarnaise 448
  Broad 445
  Broad, and Bacon 446
  Dried, à la Bretonne 551
  Dried, Italian 552
  French 447
  French, Hors-d'œuvre 957
  for Hors-d'œuvre, Dried 950
  Runner 447
Beating 12
  Eggs 181
Béchamel Sauce 90
Beef
  Boiled 336–9
  Boiled, with Horse-radish
    Sauce 341
  Braised 404
  Curry 350
  Cuts to use 325
  Goulash 349
  Minced 407–17
  Pot Roast 403, 405
  Roast 390–92
  Rolls 357
  Salad 974
  Stew 345–65
Beef Steak
  with Beer 352
  Fried 379
  Fried with Onions 380
  Grilled 367–9
  -and-Kidney Pie 844
  -and-Kidney Pudding 804
  Marinaded 369
  Spiced 365
  Stewed with Olives 356
Beetroot
  Harvard 450
  Hors-d'œuvre 951
  and Mint Salad 558
  Preparation and use 449
Beverages 900–928

Bilberries 581
Birthday Cake 752
Biscuit Crust 811
Biscuits
  Afghans 788
  Almond 777
  Almond Macaroons 786
  Anzac Nutties 783
  Chocolate 778
  Chocolate Crispies 787
  Date Bars 789
  General information 776
  Gingernuts 779
  Honey-nut Cookies 780
  Langues de Chat 785
  Lemon Finger 781
  Nutties 782
  Shortbread 784
Biscuit Flan, uncooked 816
Black Radishes 525
Blackberries
  Compote 589
  Dessert 657
  Double Tart 837
  Flan 822
  Fool 603
  Preparation and use 581
  Soufflé 604
  Steamed pudding 803
Blackcock
  Quantities to allow 322
  Roast 390–92
Blanching 12
Blending 12
Blending method for sauces 95
Bloaters
  Grilled 258
  Hors-d'œuvre 952
Blueberries 581
Boiling 12
Bone Stock 31
Bortsch 61
Bouquet garni 12
Boysenberries 581

Brains
  Amount required 322
  Boiled 335–9
  Preparing 331
  Ways of cooking 329
Braising 404
Brawn 718
Bread
  Crumbs 876
  Keeping 874
  Quick 894
  Sauce 121
  for Stuffings 127
  Tea 792–800
  Toast 875
  Vienna 895
Bream 234
Brill 234
Broccoli 451
Brown Betty 883
Brown Butter Sauce 111
Brown Sauce 73
Brush with egg or milk 12
Brussels Sprouts
  Lyonnaise 453
  Preparation and use 452
  Salad 559
Buffet party, recipes for 999
Buns
  Bath 898
  Hot Cross 899
Butter
  Cream 691
  Cream Filling 696
  Cumberland Rum 125
  Icing 677
  Parsley 123
  Sardine 975
  for Spreading 140
  Watercress 124
Butterscotch
  Bread Pudding 879
  Dessert 653
  Sauce 96
  Tart 819

Cabbage
and Bacon	457
Fried	455
Preparation and use	454–9
Red	459
Red, Hors-d'œuvre	964
Sour–Sweet	456
Stuffed leaves	458

Cakes
Almond Fruit	753
Assorted Iced	759
Basic mixes	735, 741, 748
Birthday	752
Butterfly	762
Cherry	736
Chocolate Layer	751
Christmas	752
Coffee	744
Creaming method	732
Dundee	754
Fairy	746
Fats for	141
Fillings	692–7
Fruit, plain	737
General information	719–28
Gingerbread	755
Girdle	871
Kolac	831
Lemon	738, 743
Louise	830
Madeleines	749
Melting method	730
Melting Moments	791
Meringues	763–5
Methods of mixing	729–33
One-stage method	729
Orange	738
Pavlova	766
Queen	745
Rock	739
Rubbing in method	731
Six Spice	750
Sponge method	733
Sponges	756–61
of a Thousand Leaves	853

Cakes
Tins and trays	24
Truffles	760
Upside-down	747
Victoria Sandwich	742

Caper Sauce	74
Capsicums	506–7

Caramel
Crème	219
Dessert	654
Milk Pudding, baked	639
Mould	219
Sauce	97

Carbonnades Flamandes, Les	352
Carp	234

Carrots
and Peas	503
Plum Pudding	774
Purée	462
Recipes	460–63
Soup, Cream	51
and Sprouts	463
Vichy	461

Carving	323

Casseroles
Kinds	12, 25

Cauliflower
and Bacon Sauce	465
Hors-d'œuvre	953
Lyonnaise	466
Mayonnaise	560
Milanaise	467
Recipes	464–7

Celeriac	469

Celery
and Apple Sandwich	890
Hors-d'œuvre	954
Preparation and use	468
and Blue Cheese	979
Soup	47

Cereals
Breakfast	632
Methods and recipes	611–57
Topping	633

Chard, Swiss   530
Charlotte Russe   713
Cheese
    and Anchovy Toast   992
    Biscuits with Anchovy   993
    Blue and Celery   979
    Bonbons   986
    Cake, Curd   827
    Cakes, potato   153
    Chutneyed   174
    Cottage   160
    Fondue   175
    Fritters   869
    General information   170
    Macaroni   620
    Omelet   203
    Pudding   176
    Puffs   994
    Quiche Lorraine   178
    Rarebit   171–2
    Sandwich   890, 892
    Sauce   75
    Scones   793
    and Scrambled Eggs   196
    Soufflé   222
    Spread, potted   177
    Straws   985
    Tart   173
Cherry
    Cake   736
    Compote   589
    Coupe   941
    Flan   822
    Gin   920
    Pie   843
    Preparing   581
    Sweet Pickled   980
    Tart   835
Chervil   473
Chestnut
    Soup   55
    Stuffing   129
Chicken
    Amount required   322
    Blanquette   342

Chicken
    Boiling, to roast   398
    Braised   404
    Casserole   360
    Choosing and cooking   330
    Fricassée   423
    Fried with Almonds   424
    Grilled   370
    Paprika   361
    Pot roasted   406
    Preparing   332
    Roast   390–92
    Sauté   387
Chicory
    with Cheese and Ham   471
    Preparation and use   470
Chiffon Pie Filling   818
Children's party recipes   1000
China utensils   27
Chinese Gooseberries   581
Chives   472
Chocolate
    Biscuits   778
    Bread Pudding   880
    Butter Icing   678
    Crispies   787
    Fudge   668–9
    Glacé Icing   675
    Ice-cream   932
    Ice-cream Cake   940
    Junket   166
    Layer Cake   751
    Milk Pudding   638
    Mould   647
    Mould with Raisins   648
    Mousse   230
    Orange Icing   680
    Peppermint Dessert   655
    Pudding, steamed   771
    Sauce   99
    Soufflé   225
Chowder, Fish   58
Chutney
    Cheese   174
    and Meat Sandwich   890

Cider Jelly 714
Cinnamon
  Drops 667
  Sauce 98
Claret Cup 927
Coat 12
Coating for frying 144–7
Cockles 234
Cocktail, Rum 926
Cocoa Making 906
Coconut Bread Pudding 881
  Ice 670
  Macaroons 790
Cod
  Boiled 239
  Roe, fried 319
  Ways of cooking 234
Coffee
  Butter Icing 681
  Cake 744
  Filling 693
  Glacé Icing 676
  Ice-cream 937
  Iced 905
  Junket 167
  Making 902–5
  Mould 220, 649
Coley 234
Conger Eel 234
Consistency 12, 726
Consommé 62–5
Cooking fats 141–2
Corn Salad 474
Corn, Sweet 486–7
Corned Beef
  Hash 422
  Rissoles 151
Cornflake Flan, uncooked 817
Cornflake Meringues 767
Cornflour
  for Cakes 721
  Moulds 645–51
Cornish Pasties 849
Courgettes 544–7

Crab
  Canned 279
  Choice and use 291
  Dressed 292
  Hot Buttered 295
  Patties 294
  Salad 293
Cranberry
  Dessert 657
  Fool 603
  Pie 829
  Preparation 581
  Sauce 109
Crawfish, canned 279
Cream, to 12
Cream
  Butter 691
  Chantilly 163
  Crisps 854
  from Evaporated Milk 161
  General notes 161
  Machine 162
  Puffs 856–7
  Reconstituted 162
  of Vegetable Soup 46
  for Whipping 161
  Whip, jelly 708
Creaming method 732
Crème de Menthe Jelly 705
Crème de Menthe Sweets 672
Crème Pâtissière 692
Creole Potato Salad 576
Croûtons 12
Cucumber
  Preparation 475
  Salad 561
Currant
  Dessert 657
  Fool 603
  Preparation 581
  Soufflé 604
Curry
  Egg 184
  Fish 250
  Meat 350

Curry
Salad   577
Sauce   76
and Scrambled Egg   197
Custard
Baked   217–21
Caramel   218–19
Confectioner's   692
Sauce   105
Slices   852
Tart   820
Cut and fold   12

Dab   234
Damson
Compote   589
Dessert   657
Flan   822
Fool   603
Mould   650
Pie   843
Preparing and using   581
Pudding, steamed   803
Soufflé   604
Date
Bars   789
Butterscotch Pudding   627
and Nut Loaf   799
Sandwiches   891
Scones   794
Desserts   652–7
Dice   12
Dissolve   12
Dot   12
Doughnuts, American   798
Dredge   12
Dripping   12
Clarified   139
for Cakes and Pastry   141
Dry ingredients   12
Dublin Bay Prawn   314
Ducks and Ducklings
Amount required   322
Choosing and cooking   330

Ducks and Ducklings
Preparing   332
Roasting   390–92
Dumplings   806
Dundee Cake   754

Ears, Pig's
Amount to allow   322
Boiled   335–9
to Prepare   331
Earthenware utensils   27
Eccles Cakes   855
Éclairs   856
Eels
Boiled   240
Fried   264
Smoked   955
Suggestions for cooking   234
Eggplant   476
Eggs
and Bacon Tart   838
Boiled   182–7
with Brown Butter   215
Cheesed   196
en Cocotte   194
Coddled   183
Creams   991
and Crumb Coating   146
Curried   184
Custards   216–21
Fricassée   187
Fried   214
General information   179–80
for Hors-d'œuvre   956
Lyonnaise   185
Mornay   190
Nog   918–19
Omelets   201–213
Pickled   984
Poached   189–93
Poached, in Aspic   193
Portuguese   198
Salad   568
Salad Hors-d'œuvre   968, 972
Sandwiches   890, 892

Eggs
  Sauce 77
  Scotch 186
  Scrambled 195–200
  Steamed 194
  Stuffed 188
Elderberries
  Dessert 657
  Fool 603
  Preparation and use 581
  Soufflé 604
  Steamed pudding 803
  Tart 835, 837
Enamel utensils 27
Endive 477
Espagnole Sauce 93

Fats and frying 136–49
Feet
  Amount to allow 322
  Boiled 335–9
  Preparing 331
  Ways of cooking 329
Fennel
  Sauce 78
  Uses of 478
Figs 581
Fillet 12
Fish
  à la Bretonne 277
  au Gratin 249
  Baked 270–77
  Boiled 237–50
  Cakes 152
  Canned 278–89
  Chowder 58
  Cleaning 236
  Cocktail 969–70
  Curried 250
  Doré 263
  en Papillote 274
  Filleting 236
  Fillets with Lemon Sauce 251
  Fried 263–9
  Fritters 867

Fish
  Frozen 235
  General information 232–3
  Grilled 257–62
    Basting Sauce for 122
  Hungarian 255
  Kedgeree 616
  Marinade 982
  Mousse 286
  Pasties 850
  Pie 248
  Preparing 236
  Roes 317–19, 988
  Sandwiches 890, 892
  Scaling 236
  Shell 290–316
  Skinning 236
  Smoked Hotpot 273
  Soufflé 223
  Soused 256
  Steamed 246
  Stewed 254–6
  Stock 34
  Stuffing 130
  Suggestions for Cooking 234
Flan
  Apple 822–3
  Biscuit, uncooked 816
  Cheese 173
  Continental 815
  Cornflake, uncooked 817
  Kipper 833
  to Make 812
  Plum 824
  Salmon 834
Flavouring
  for Cakes 724
  General 14
Flounders 234
Flour for cakes 721
Forcemeat 126–35
Fowl
  Boiled 335–9
  Choosing and cooking 330
  Roast 390–92, 398

French cooking terms 13
French Dressing 118
French Mustard 112
Fritters 865–70
Frozen
  Fish 235
  Fruit 583
  Meat 331
  Poultry 333
  Vegetables 429
Fruit
  Band 758
  for Cakes 723
  in Casserole 595
  Compote 589, 594
  Dessert 652, 657
  Flan 822
  Food value 580
  Fool 603
  Fritters 868, 870
  Moulds 645, 650
  Mousse 936
  Pie 843
  Preparation of 581
  Pudding, steamed 803
  Purée or Pulp 602
  Punch 910
  Salad 584–8
  Sauce 100
  Scones 795
  Soufflé 604
  Sponge 740
  Stewed 589–95
  Stewed, Dried 593–4
  Tarts 835–7
Frying
  General information 136–49
  Fish 263–9
  Meat 378–89
  Pans 22
Fudge
  Chocolate 668
  Crumb 669
  Icing 688

Game
  Braised 404
  Choosing 330
  Pot Roasting 403
  Preparing 332, 334
  Roast 390–92
Gammon, baked 399
Garlic 479
Garnish 12, 16
Gaspacho 60
Gelatine 698–718
Genoese Sponge 757
Gherkins 480
Giblets 332
Gin, sloe 921
  cherry 920
Ginger
  Ale Lemonade 909
  and Pear Salad 585
  Pudding, steamed 773
Gingerbread 755
Gingernuts 779
Girdle
  Cakes 871
  Pancakes 872
  Scones 797
Glass utensils 27
Glaze
  with Aspic Jelly 717
  General 12
  Sugar 661
Glucose 659
Golden Jelly 712
Goose
  Amount required 322
  Roast 390–92
Gooseberries
  Chinese 581
  Compote 589
  Flan 822
  Fool 603
  Pie 843
  Preparation and use 581
  Tart 835
Goulash 349

Granadilla	581	Hares		
Grapefruit	581	Jugged	351	
Grilled	607	Preparing	334	
Grape Juice Lemonade	908	Roast	390–92	
Grapes	581	Hash		
Grate	12	Corned Beef	422	
Gravy	79	Red Flannel	422	
Gray Mullet	234	Hawaiian Egg Nog	918	
Greengages		Heads		
Compote	589	Amount required	322	
Flan	822	Boiled	335–9	
Fool	603	to Prepare	331	
Pie	843	Ways of cooking	329	
Preparation and use	581	Hearts		
Tart	835	Amount required	322	
Grilling		Braised	404	
Basting Sauces for	122	to Prepare	331	
Fish	257–62	Ways of cooking	329	
General	12	Herb Omelet	204	
Meat	366–77	Herbs	442–539	
Grog	925	Herrings		
Grouse		Canned	280–81	
Amount required	322	Fried	265	
Choosing	330	Salad	562	
Roast	390–92	Salt	958	
Guinea-fowl		Soused	256	
Amount required	322	Steamed	247	
Choosing and cooking	330	Suggestions for cooking	234	
Roast	390–92	Swedish, baked	276	
Gumbo	494	High tea, recipes for	998	
Gurnet	234	Hock Cup	928	
		Hollandaise Sauce	94	
Haddock		Honey		
Finnan, boiled	241	and Almond Filling	697	
Finnan, grilled	259	Nut Cookies	780	
Fresh, boiled	242	Sandwiches	891	
Suggestions for cooking	234	Sauce	107	
Hake	234	Uses	659	
Halibut	234	Hors-d'œuvre	946–84	
Ham, boiled	335–9	Horse-radish		
Hard Sauce	125	Sauce	80	
Hares		Uses	481	
Amount required	322	Hot Cross Buns	899	
Choosing and cooking	330	Hungarian Fish Stew	255	

Ice-creams
Cherry Coupe 941
Chocolate 932
Chocolate Ice Cake 940
Coffee 937
Fruit Mousse 936
General information 929–31
Meringue Glacé 939
Mocha 933
Orange Parfait 938
Peppermint 935
Vanilla Mousse 934
Icings
Butter 677–84
Chocolate Glacé 675
Coffee Glacé 676
General information 673
Glacé 674
Milk Chocolate 690
Royal 686
Water 674
White Mountain 689
Invalid cookery 1002

Jam
Junket 169
Pancakes 860
Pudding, steamed 770, 805
Puffs 810
Roll, baked 851
Sauce 101
Tarts 825
Use of 659
Jamaican Long Drink 922
Jellies 698–718
John Dory 234
Junkets 165–9

Kale 482
Kebabs 377
Kedgeree 616
Kidneys
Amount to allow 322
Fried 383
Grilled 373–4

Kidneys
Omelet 205
to Prepare 331
Ragoût 355
Ways of cooking 329
Kipper
Grilled 260
Flan 833
Pâté 959
Kitchen equipment 17–18
Knead 12
Knives, Kitchen 23
Kohl Rabi 483
Kolac 831

Ladies' Fingers 494
Lamb
Amount to allow 322
Baked with Rosemary 401
Boiled 335–40
Boiled Breast 340
Braised 404
Casserole 363
Chops, fried 382
Chops with Cucumber 371
Cutlets, fried 381
Cuts to use 326
Goulash 349
Grilled 370
Pot Roast 403
Roast 390–92
Roast, stuffed 396
Shashlik 372
Spanish Cutlets 364
Langoustine 314
Langues de Chat 785
Lard for cakes and pastry 141
Leek
for Hors-d'œuvre 960
Preparation and use 484
Soup 40
Leftovers, using up 1001
Lemon
Biscuits 781
Bread Pudding 882

Lemon
Butter Icing   682
Butter Stuffing   128
Curd   694
Delicious Pudding   610
Jelly   703
Layer Cake   743
Meringue Nests   768
Meringue Pie   821
Meringue Pudding   644
Preparation and use   581
Refrigerator Cake   945
Sago   626
Sauce   102
Soufflé   226
Snow   704
Sorbet   943
Sugar   663
Lemonade   907–9
Lentils
Preparation and use   550
Soup   41
Lettuce
Preparation and use   485
Salad   563
Light diet   1002
Ling   234
Liqueur Icing   683
Liver
Amount to allow   322
Braised   404
Fried   383
Grilled   373
Minced   408–10
and Onions   388
Pâté   971
Pilaf   618
to Prepare   331
Provençale   354
Ways of cooking   329
Lobsters
au Gratin   299
Cold   297
Mayonnaise   298
Patties   300

Lobsters
to Prepare   296
Salad   298
Sauce   81
Loganberries   581
Louise Cakes   830
Lunch, recipes for   998

Macaroni   619–21
Cheese   620–21
Macaroons, Almond   786
Coconut   790
Tartlets   832
Mackerel
Boiled   243
Suggestions for using   234
Madeleines   749
Maize   486–7
Mangetout   505
Margarine   141
Marinade   12, 369
Marjoram   488
Marmalade
Pudding, steamed   770, 805
Sauce   101
Marrow   544–7
Marshmallow Icing   687
Marshmallows   671
Martini   924
Marzipan   685
Mayonnaise   113
Meal planning and prepar-
ing   996–1003
Measures   1–5
Meat
Balls   413–15
in Batter   862
Boiled   335–41
Braised   404
Brown stew   347
Cakes   151
Canned   419
Carving   323
Casseroles   345–65
Choosing   324–30

Meat
  Cooked, re-heating   393
  Curry   350
  Fricassée   423
  Fried   378–89
  Fritters   867
  Frozen   331
  General information   321
  Goulash   349
  Grilled   366–77
  Hash   420
  to Keep   324
  Loaf   416
  Minced   407–18
  Pot Roasting   403, 405
  Preparing   331
  Quantities to allow   322
  Rissoles   151
  Roast   390–92
  Sandwiches   890, 892
  Shape   417
  Stewed   345–65
Melba Sauce   110
Melons   581, 983
Melon and Plum Salad   587
Melting Moments   791
Meringue Glacé   939
Meringues   763–5
Milk
  Beverages   915–19
  Chocolate Icing   690
  General information   154–60
  Jellies   706–7
  Malted   915
  Posset   917
  Puddings, baked   637–9
  Topping   164
Mille-feuilles   853
Mincemeat   840
Minestrone   37
Mint
  and Potato Soup   43
  and Raisin Sandwich   891
  Sauce   120

Mint
  Stuffing   131
  to Use   489
Mixing   12
Mocha
  Butter Icing   679
  Dessert   656
  Refrigerator Cake   944
Moulds, Cereal   640–51
Moussaka   418
Mousse
  Chocolate   230
  Fish   286
  Orange   709
  Vanilla   934
Mullet   234
Mushrooms
  Mousseline   491
  Omelet   206
  Sauce   82
  Soup   57
  Stock   35
  to use   490
Mussels
  Angels on Horseback   987
  Canned   282
  to Choose   301
  for Hors-d'œuvre   961
  Marinières   304
  to Prepare   301
  Sauce   83
  Served cold   302
  Served hot   303
  Soup, canned   54
  Soup, fresh   59
Mustard
  and Cress   492
  French   112
  Sauce   84
Mutton
  Boiled   335–9
  Braised   404
  Casserole   363
  Curry   350
  Cuts to use   326

Mutton
  Pot Roasting   403
  Roast   390–92

Nasturtiums   493
Nectarines
  Compote   589
  Flan   822
  Pie   843
  Preparation and use   581
Noodles, boiled   619
  and Cultured Cream   622
Norwegian Trifle   715
Nut and Honey Cookies   780
Nutmeg Sauce   98
Nuts   580, 582
Nutties   782

Oatmeal
  for Cakes   721
  Porridge   629
Oats
  Porridge   630
  Swiss, Breakfast   631
  Uses   612
Offal   329
Oil
  for Cakes and Pastry   141
  for Frying   142
Okra   494
Olives   977
Omelet à la Crème   210
Omelet, Swedish   213
Omelets   201–13
Onion
  Omelet   207
  Preparation and use   495
  and Sage Stuffing   133
  Sauce   85
  Sauce, Sour–sweet   88
  Soup   42
  Spring   536
  Sugared   496
  Toast   497
  Welsh   536

Orange
  and Apple Salad   586
  Baked Custard   221
  Bread Pudding   882
  Butter Icing   682
  Cake   738
  Caramel   609
  Filling   695
  Jelly   703
  Julep   912
  Mousse   709
  Parfait   938
  Preparation and use   581
  and Rhubarb Compote   596
  Salad   564, 586
  Sauce   103
  Snow   704
  Sugar   663
Orangeade   911
Ortolans
  Amount required   322
  Roast   390–92
Oven placing for baking   728
Overweight, Feeding the   1003
Ox-tail
  Amount required   322
  Stewed   353
  Ways of cooking   329
Oysters
  au Naturel   306
  Canned   282
  to choose and open   305
  Sauce   83
  Soup   54
  Soup, Mock   39

Pancakes   859–61
  Girdle   872
  Scotch   871
Pans, choosing   21
Paprika Sauce   86
Parboiling   12
Parsley
  Butter   123
  Sauce   87

Parsley
  Uses   498
Parsnips   499–500
Partridge
  Amount required   322
  Roast   390–92
Passionfruit   581
Pasteurizing   155
Pastry
  Apple Dumplings   847
  Apple Tart, double   836
  Apple Tart, open   823
  Bacon and Egg Tart   838
  Berry Tart, double   837
  Biscuit   811
  Butterscotch Tart   819
  Chiffon Pie   818
  Choux   856
  Continental Flan   815
  Cornish Pasties   849
  Cranberry Pie   829
  Cream Crisps   854
  Custard Slices   852
  Custard Tart   820
  Eccles Cakes   855
  Fairy Tarts   826
  Fish Pasties   850
  Flaky   808
  Flan, Fruit   822
  Flan, shaping   812
  Fruit Pie   843
  Jam Puffs   810
  Jam Roll, baked   851
  Jam Tarts   825
  Kipper Flan   833
  Lemon Meringue Pie   821
  Lining a basin   802
  Macaroon Tartlets   832
  Mince Tarts   840
  Palmiers   854
  Patties   810
  Pie, covering   841–2
  Plum Flan   824
  Puff   809
  Rabbit Pie   846

Pastry
  Salmon Flan   834
  Sausage Rolls   848
  Short   807
  Steak-and-Kidney Pie   844
  Suet   801
  Sweet   811
  Swedish   896
  Tart, double crust   835
  Tart, lattice top   814
  Tart, open   813
  Tart, small double   839
  Treacle Tart   828
  Uncooked   816–17
  Vanilla Squares   852
  Veal-and-Ham Pie   845
Pâté
  Kipper   959
  Liver   971
Patties
  Crab   294
  Lobster   300
  to Shape   810
Pavlova Cake   766
Peaches
  Compote   589
  Condé   642
  Flan   822
  Pie   843
  Preparation and use   581
Peanut Butter Sandwiches   891
Pears
  Armandine   591
  Baked   600
  Compote   589
  Condé   642
  Flan   822
  and Ginger Salad   585
  Preparation and use   581
Peas
  and Carrots   503
  Dried   550
  Edible-podded   505
  French method   502
  Preparation and use   501–4

Peas
  Soup 49
  Spanish 504
  Sugar 505
Pease Pudding 553
Peppermint Ice-cream 935
Peppers, Sweet 506–7
Perch
  to Scale 236
  Suggestions for cooking 234
Pheasant
  Amount required 322
  Roast 390–92
Pie-dishes 25
Pies 841–6
Pigeon
  Amount required 322
  Choosing 330
  Jugged 351
Pike 234
Pikelets 871
Pilaf, Liver 618
Pilchards
  Canned 280–81
  Fresh 234
Pineapples 581
Pink Foam 231
Plaice 234
  with Cream and Grapes 253
  Mornay 252
  Suggestions for Cooking 234
Plover
  Amount required 322
  Roast 390–92
Plums
  Compote 589
  Flan 824
  Fool 603
  and Melon Salad 587
  Pie 843
  Preparation and use 581
  Pudding, steamed 803
  Soufflé 604
Poaching 12
Pomegranates 581

Popovers 863
Pork
  Braised 404
  Casserole 358
  Chops, fried 382
  Cutlets à la Charcutière 389
  Cuts, to use 327
  Grilled 370
  Minced 413–17
  Pot Roast 403
  Rissoles 411
  Roast 390–92
  Roast, with Orange Sauce 400
  Roast, savory 397
  Roast, stuffed 395
  Salt, boiled 337–9
  Stew 358
Porridge 628–30
Pot Roasting 403, 405
Potato
  Baked 512–13
  Boiled 509
  Browned 510
  Cakes 150–53
  Cakes with Egg 192
  with Cheese 521
  Chip 515
  Crisps 516
  Duchess 518
  Flour 612
  Mashed 511
  New 520
  Paprika 523
  Parisian 519
  Preparation 508
  Ragoût 522
  Roast 514
  Salad 565, 576
  Soup 43–4
  Starch 612
  Straws 517
Poultry
  Boiled 335–9
  Choosing and cooking 330
  Fricassée 423

Poultry
  Frozen 333
  to Prepare 332
Prawns
  Canned 283
  Curried 308
  Dublin Bay 314
  Hors-d'œuvre 310
  to Prepare 307
  Salad 309
Pressure cookers 28
Profiteroles with Chocolate
  Sauce 857
Prune
  and Apple Stuffing 132
  and Bacon 990
  Fool 603
  Jelly 711
  Soufflé 604
Ptarmigan
  Amount required 322
  Roast 390–92
Puddings
  Batter 862–5
  Bread 877–84
  Cereal Milk 625–56
  Custards 217–21
  Doughnuts, American 798
  Fats for 141
  Fritters 865–70
  Frozen 944–5
  Fruit 583–610
  Fruit Sponge 740
  Fruit, steamed 772
  Ices 932–43
  Jellies 703–15
  Junkets 165–9
  Omelets 208–9
  Pancakes 859–60
  Pastry. See 'Pastry'
  Upside-down 747
Puddings, steamed
  Carrot Plum 774
  Chocolate 771
  Christmas 775

Pudding, steamed
  Fruit 772, 803
  Ginger 773
  How to steam 769
  Jam 770, 805
  Marmalade 770, 805
  Rhubarb 803
  Steak-and-Kidney 804
Pulses 12
Pumpkin 524
Purée
  Fruit 602
  General 12

Quail
  Amount required 322
  Roast 390–92
Queen of Puddings 877
Quiche Lorraine 178
Quince, preparation and use 581
Quince, Stewed 589

Rabbit
  Amount required 322
  Boiled 335–9
  Choosing and cooking 330
  Creamed 343
  Curry 350
  Jugged 351
  Pie 846
  to Prepare 334
  Roast 390–92
  Stew or casserole 347
Radishes
  Black 525
  for Hors-d'œuvre 963
  Preparation and use 525
Raisin
  and Chocolate Mould 648
  and Mint Sandwich 891
Raising agents 725
Rarebit 171–2
Raspberry
  Flan 822
  Fool 603

Raspberry
  Mould 650
  Preparation and use 581
  Sorbet 942
  Tart 837
Raspings 876
Recipes, how to use 1–7
Red Flannel Hash 422
Red Mullet 234
Refrigerator Cakes 944–5
Rendering fat 138
Rhubarb
  Baked Spiced 601
  Compote 589
  Flan 822
  Fool 603
  Mould 650
  and Orange Compote 596
  Preparation and use 581
  Sherbet 914
  Soufflé 604
  Steamed pudding 803
Rice
  Baked pudding 637–9
  Boiling 613
  Fried 614
  Ground, for cakes 721
  Ground, moulds 645–51
  Ground, pudding 634–6
  Kedgeree 616
  Lemon Meringue 644
  Mould 640–42
  Raisin 617
  Re-heating 614
Risotto 615
Rissoles
  Minced Meat 409–12
  Potato 150–53
Roasting
  General information 390–92
  Pans 24
Rock Salmon 234
Roe Canapés, Soft 988
Roes 317–19
Rosemary with Chicken 406

Rosemary with Lamb 401
Rôtisserie 390
Roux method for sauces 69
Royal Icing 686
Rubbing in method 731
Rum
  Babas 897
  Butter, Cumberland 125
  Cocktail 926
  Omelet 209
Rye, uses 612

Sage
  and Onion Stuffing 133
  Uses 526
Sago
  Moulds 640–41
  Puddings 625–7
Salads 554–79
  Asparagus 574
  Bean and Apple 557
  Beef 974
  Beetroot and Mint 558
  Brussels Sprouts 559
  Carrot and Apple 572
  Cauliflower 560
  Celery and Cheese 573
  Crab 293
  Cucumber 561
  Curried 577
  Dressings 113–19
  Ham Roll 575
  Herring 562
  Lettuce 563
  Lobster 298
  Orange 564
  Potato 565, 576
  Prawn 309
  Russian 566
  Salmon 570
  Shrimp and Egg 578
  Spring 567
  Stuffed Egg 568
  Swiss 571
  Tomato and Sweet Pepper 973

Salads
　Tongue　　　　　　　579, 974
　Waldorf　　　　　　　　569
Salmon
　Boiled　　　　　　　　244
　Canned　　　　　　　284–6
　Flan　　　　　　　　　834
　Grilled　　　　　　　　261
　Loaf　　　　　　　　　285
　Mayonnaise　　　　　　570
　Mousse　　　　　　　　286
　Open Sandwich　　　　892
　Rock　　　　　　　　　234
　Sandwich　　　　　　　890
　Smoked　　　　　　892, 966
Salsify　　　　　　　　　527
Sandwiches　　　　　　885–92
Sardines
　Butter　　　　　　　　975
　Canned　　　　　　　287–8
　with Cheese Sauce　　　288
　for Hors-d'œuvre　　　965
　Rolls　　　　　　　　989
　Sandwiches　　　　　　892
Saucepans　　　　　　　21
Sauces　　　　　　　　69–125
Sausages
　Amount required　　　322
　Fried　　　　　　　　383
　Grilled　　　　　　　376
　and Paprika Potatoes　523
　Rolls　　　　　　　　848
　Sandwich　　　　　　892
　Smoked　　　　　　　523
　Suggestions for cooking　329
　Toad-in-the-hole　　　862
Sauté, to　　　　　　　148
Savory　　　　　　　　528
Savouries　　　　　　985–95
Savoys　　　　　　　　454
Scald　　　　　　　　12, 155
Scales　　　　　　　　　4
Scallops　　　　　　　311–13
Scampi, Scampo, Scampolo　314

Scones
　Cheese　　　　　　　793
　Date　　　　　　　　794
　Drop　　　　　　　　871
　Fruit　　　　　　　　795
　Fruit Rolls　　　　　　796
　Girdle　　　　　　　797
　Plain　　　　　　　　792
Seakale　　　　　　　　529
Seakale Beet　　　　　　530
Sear　　　　　　　　　12
Seasoned Flour　　　　　12
Seasonings　　　　　　12, 14
Semolina
　for Cakes　　　　　　721
　Moulds　　　　　　645–51
　Puddings　　　　　634–6
Serving and Garnishing　15, 16
Shallots　　　　　　　531
Shell-fish　　　　　　290–316
Shepherd's Pie　　　　　421
Sherry Sauce　　　　　104
Shopping suggestions　　8–10
Shortbread　　　　　　784
Shrimps
　and Egg Salad　　　　578
　for Hors-d'œuvre　　　962
　and Orange Cocktail　　970
　Potted　　　　　　　316
　Preparation and use　315–16
　Sauce　　　　　　　81
Sift　　　　　　　　　12
Silver Beet　　　　　　530
Simmer　　　　　　　12
Skate
　Boiled　　　　　　　245
　Suggestions for using　234
Skewer　　　　　　　12
Sloe Gin　　　　　　　921
Smelts, fried　　　　　266
Snipe
　Amount required　　　322
　Roast　　　　　　390–92
Soft Drinks　　　　　907–14

Sole 234
  with Cream 253
  Meunière with Orange 267
  Mornay 252
Sorbet, Lemon 943
Sorbet, Raspberry 942
Soufflé Omelet 211
Soufflés 222–8
Soups 36–65
Sour–Sweet Onion Sauce 88
Sousing 256
Soya flour 721
Spaghetti 619, 623
Spaghetti and Meat Sauce 623
Spanish Cutlets 364
Spanish Omelet 212
Spice
  Cake 750
  Icing 684
  Steak 365
Spinach
  au Gratin 535
  Creamed 533
  Cream Soup 50
  with Poached Eggs 534
  Preparation and use 532–5
Spit-roasting 390
Sponges 756–62
Sprats
  Grilled 262
  Smoked 978
  Suggestions for using 234
Squash 524
Steel Utensils 27
Stew
  Fish 254–5
  Meat 345–65
Stock 31–5
Strawberry
  Flan 822
  in Orange Juice 588
  Preparation and use 581
  Soufflé 228
Stuffings 126–35
Suet 141

Sugar
  for Cakes 722
  coloured 662
  and Sweets 658–72
Sultana and Nut Loaf 800
Supper, recipes for 998
Suprême Sauce 92
Swede
  Cream Soup 53
  Preparation and use 537
Swedish Apple Cake 884
  Herrings, baked 276
  Omelet 213
  Pastry 896
Sweetbreads
  Amount required 322
  to Prepare 331
  Ways of cooking 329
Sweets 664–72
Swiss Breakfast Dish 631
Swiss Chard 530
Syrup
  Sauce 107
  Uses 659

Tail, Ox-
  to Prepare 331
  Stewed 353
  Ways of using 329
Tapioca
  Baked, Pudding 637–9
  Boiling 624
  Cream 625
  Date Butterscotch 627
  Lemon 626
  Moulds 640–41
  Source 612
Tarragon 538
Tartare Sauce 117
Tarts 813–30, 835–40
Tea, to make 901
Tea Breads 792–800
Teal
  Amount required 322
  Roast 390–92

Temperatures
  General   11
  Frying   148–9
  Sugar   660
Tepid   12
Terrine   971
Thyme   539
Tin Utensils   27
Tins, to prepare   727
Toad-in-the-hole   862
Toast   875
Toffee
  Apples   665
  Marzipan   666
  Plain   664
Tomato
  Cream Soup   48
  Juice Cocktail   913
  and Marrow   545
  Preparation and use   540
  Salad   967
  Sauce   89
  Soup   56
  Stuffed   541
  and Sweet Pepper   973
Tongues
  Amount required   322
  Boiled   335–9
  to Prepare   331
  Salad   579, 974
  Ways of cooking   329
Tournedos Vert Pré   368
Trays, baking   24
Treacle   659
Treacle Tart   828
Tripe
  Amount required   322
  Casserole   348
  to Prepare   331
  Ways of cooking   329
Trout   234
  Marinaded   981
Tuna   284–5
Turbot   234

Turkey
  Amount required   322
  Choosing and cooking   330
  Preparation   332
  Roast   390–92
  Stuffing   134
Turkish Delight   672
Turnip, ragoût   543
Turnips   542

Utensils
  Care of   27
  Choice of   17–26

Vanilla
  Mousse   934
  Soufflé   225
  Squares   852
Veal
  Blanquette   362
  Braised   404
  Breast, boiled   340
  Chops, fried   382
  Cuts to use   328
  Escalopes   384–6
  Forcemeat   135
  Fricassée   423
  Galantine   344
  Goulash   349
  Grilled   370
  and Ham Pie   845
  Jellied   718
  Minced   408–17
  Mould   718
  Olives   359
  Pot Roast   403
  Roast   390–92
  Roast with Orange Sauce   400
  Roast, stuffed   394
Vegetable Marrow   544–7
Vegetables
  au Gratin   432
  Baked in casserole   434
  Boiling   427
  Canned   430

Vegetables
  Choosing and keeping 426
  Dehydrated 431
  Dried, boiling 550
  Frozen 429
  General methods 427–38
  Jardinière 438
  Macedoine 437
  Pressure cooking 428
  Recipes 427–579
  Roast 435
  Sauce for 71
  Soups 35–57, 61
  Stewed in fat 433
  Stew or Ragoût 436
  Stock 33
Velouté Sauce 91
Venison
  Jugged 351
  Roast 390–92
  Stew 347, 351
  Suggestions for cooking 330
Vermicelli 619
Vermouth Long Drink 923
Vichyssoise Soup 45
Vienna Bread 895
Viennese Pastry 791
Vinaigrette Sauce 119
Vol-au-Vent 810

Watercress
  Butter 124
  and Potato Soup 44
  Preparation and use 548
  Sandwiches 890
  Stuffing 131
Weigh, How to 4
Weights and Measures 1–5
Wheat 612
Whipping 12
Whitebait, fried 268
White Mountain Icing 689
White Sauce 69, 90
White Stew 347
Whiting 234
  à la Bercy 275
  Fried 269
Widgeon, roast 390–92
Wiener Schnitzel 386
Woodcock, roast 390–92
Wooden Utensils 27

Yams 549
Yeast, use of 893–9
Yogurt 160
Yogurt Salad Dressing 116
Yorkshire Pudding 862–3

Zabaglione 229

Another Penguin Handbook by Bee Nilson

COOKING FOR SPECIAL DIETS

This is the first book written entirely with the problems of a special diet in mind. The sections begin with short explanations of such diseases as diabetes, anaemia, ulcers, heart diseases, and obesity, followed by the reasons for prescribing fat-free, low protein, liquid, or other restricted diet and a description of the diet itself. A general meal pattern, suggestions for eating out, ideas for packed lunches, and a set of fourteen dinner and fourteen lunch or supper menus round off the discussion of each variety of disease and diet. The recipes for these menus are given in the second half of the book, together with the names and addresses of manufacturers of special products.

Cooking for Special Diets will be of direct interest to the families of patients released from hospital, in cases where the housewife is expected to turn a prescribed diet into palatable meals. All the recipes given here by Bee Nilson have been tested by herself as well as by student dieticians in college.